# CHILD ABUSE

## A COMMUNITY CONCERN

# CHILD ABUSE
## A COMMUNITY CONCERN

Edited by
### KIM OATES

*Royal Alexandra Hospital for Children*
*Sydney*

BRUNNER/MAZEL, *Publishers* • New York

**Library of Congress Cataloging in Publication Data**
Main entry under title:

Child abuse.

Reprint. Originally published: London ; Boston :
Butterworths, c1982.
Includes bibliographies and index.
1. Child abuse—Addresses, essays, lectures.
2. Child abuse—Prevention—Addresses, essays,
lectures. I. Oates, Kim.
HV713.C3814   1984       362.7'044       84-16968
ISBN 0-87630-378-5

*Published by*
BRUNNER/MAZEL, INC.
19 Union Square West
New York, New York 10003

# Preface

Although child abuse was virtually unheard of 25 years ago, today there is a wide literature and a considerable number of books on the topic. Why produce another book? This book is firstly an attempt to place child abuse in a broad perspective, as a problem concerning the whole community. The contributors come from many disciplines: psychology, anthropology, law, medicine, nursing, social work, psychiatry, journalism and sociology, emphasizing just how widely child abuse affects a community.

All of the authors have had considerable experience in the child abuse field and have established expert reputations in their own areas. They come from England, Canada, the United States, Europe and Australia. The substantial Australian component is the second reason for producing a book whose aim is to be suitable for an international readership, but which reflects a proportion of the work on child abuse that is being done in Australia.

A preface is a suitable place to thank people. My past and present colleagues from the Royal Alexandra Hospital for Children and from the International Society for the Prevention of Child Abuse and Neglect, while too numerous to name, all deserve thanks for their insights and the way they have influenced and supported my own work in this field. The contributors to this book deserve special thanks for their enthusiasm for the project and their readiness to assist in it. John Rowe from Butterworths has given helpful advice and encouragement. Lorraine Nitsos and Helen Georgiou have helped in the typing while Val Muir, who has typed and retyped more material on child abuse than she cares to remember, deserves special thanks. My greatest debt is to my own parents, to Robyn, my wife, and to my children who are all amazingly tolerant and who together have taught me more about parenting than any other source.

A note should be made about the use of the pronouns "she" and "he". Where the text refers to children, the convention of using the pronoun "he" in a general sense, has been followed. Where the authors refer to their respective professions, the choice of gender has been left up to them.

Working with abused children and their families can be frustrating, often leading to job dissatisfaction and high staff turnover. It is hoped that this volume will in some small measure help to broaden the perspective of those who work in the area and that they will be encouraged, by looking back at how much has been achieved in the last 25 years, to then look forward to what could be achieved if the community can be made aware of its responsibility to children. It is our responsibility to see that this awareness comes about.

KIM OATES
ROYAL ALEXANDRA HOSPITAL FOR CHILDREN
MAY 1982

# Contents

# Contributors

**Robert G Adler,** MB, BS, FRACP, FRANZCP, is a senior lecturer in child psychiatry in the Faculty of Medicine at the University of Newcastle. His training in child psychiatry was undertaken at the Royal Alexandra Hospital for Children and his interests have included the prediction of problems in the parent-infant relationship and child abuse and the role of the child psychiatrist in child abuse case conferences.

**Jane Brazier,** BA, Dip Soc Work(University of Western Australia), Executive Officer, Montrose Child Protection and Family Crisis Service, Burwood, New South Wales. Jane Brazier previously worked with the Department for Community Welfare in Perth working with abusive families. She is currently responsible for the operational aspects and the programme development of the Montrose Child Protection and Family Crisis Service. Her interests in the field of child protection lie in both clinical work and in policy development.

**Sarah P Briggs** is an active member of the Samaritans organization. She has worked as a research assistant at the National Society for the Prevention of Cruelty to Children (NSPCC) and is currently pursuing a career in nursing.

**Nigel Cantwell** holds an MA in Economics from Cambridge University and a Diploma in Applied Social Studies from Nottingham University, England. He has been working in Child Welfare internationally since 1974 and is now Secretary General of the Geneva-based Defence for Children international movement. He is principally concerned with promoting solidarity for and application of the rights of the child through linking international efforts with initiatives at national and local levels.

**Jan Carter,** M Sc Sociology(London), BA, Dip Soc Stud(Melbourne), is a social worker, social researcher and writer. She was formerly the Principal Investigator for the National Day Care Project (1974-79) at the National Institute for Social Work Research Unit, London. She was a keynote speaker at the First and Second Australian Conferences on Child Abuse and Neglect.

**Raymond L Castle,** CQSW, Child Abuse Consultant to the NSPCC in London, directs the work of the Society's Consultation and Information Service. Prior to this he was the Head of the

Battered Child Research Department which later became the
NSPCC's National Advisory Centre. He was involved in much of the
early research into child abuse in the United Kingdom and is also
an Executive Member of the International Society for Prevention of
Child Abuse and Neglect and on the Executive Council of Defence
for Children. He acts as professional consultant to the National Co-
ordinating Committee of Self-Help Groups for Parents Under Stress.

**Alison Davis,** RGN, RHN, RCHN, DCHN, NCN(NSW), has
worked at the Montrose Child Protection and Family Crisis Service
since 1978. She has developed the role of a community paediatric
nurse at that Unit. This work includes the clinical assessment of
children in residence at the Unit, matters related to Children's Court
hearings and having responsibility for education in child protection
for hospital Schools of Nursing and Community Health Centres.

**Anne Deveson** is a journalist and film maker. She has been a
member of the New South Wales Antidiscrimination Board and a
Commissioner with the Royal Commission on Human Relationships. In 1978 she wrote a book on the Commission's findings called
*Australians at Risk.* Her films have mainly been concerned with
social issues and include award winning films on child abuse,
handicapped children and refugees. She has twice won gold citations
in the United Nations Media Peace Prize. She is on the Board of the
South Australian Film Corporation and a Council Member of the
Australian Film and Television School and the Family Planning
Association of South Australia. She is currently working on a series
of six television documentaries for the Australian Broadcasting
Commission on Women in the Eighties.

**Robyn Dolby,** Ph D, MAPS, Research Fellow in Psychology at the
Child Development Unit of Foundation 41, The Women's Hospital,
Crown Street, Sydney.

**Brian English,** BA Hons, MAPS, Research Psychologist at the
Child Development Unit Foundation 41, The Women's Hospital,
Crown Street, Sydney.

Robyn Dolby and Brian English are involved in research
concerned with the study of infant development, particularly infants
born at risk. In this context they are especially concerned with
promoting optimal parent-infant interaction, or more simply helping
parents and infants to enjoy each other more. This includes trying
to learn more about infant behavioural organization, understanding
what impact this has on parenting and helping parents to adjust to
their infant's individual behaviour.

**Lindsey Fletcher,** B Soc Stud, is a psychiatric social worker. During the time that she worked in the Institute of Child Health at the Royal Alexandra Hospital for Children she was a member and consultant for the hospital's child abuse team. She is currently working part-time in private practice as an analytical psychotherapist.

**Henry Giaretto,** BA, MA, Ph D, founded the Child Sexual Abuse Treatment Programme (CSATP) of Santa Clara County and its associated self-help group, Parents United and Daughters and Sons United. For over nine years the CSATP has provided professional and self-help treatment for more than 2500 children and their families. He is also the principal developer and Executive Director of the CSATP training project which has resulted in the establishment of 45 new centres based on this model.

**Dorothy E Ginn,** Director of the Child Abuse Prevention Service, Randwick Community Centre, Randwick, New South Wales. Dorothy Ginn is a nurse by background and in 1973 formed "Prevention" which later became the Child Abuse Prevention Service. She has presented papers on the work of this service at national and international meetings.

**Louise Gyler,** B Soc Stud(Sydney), is a social worker, working in the Department of Child and Family Psychiatry at the Royal Alexandra Hospital for Children. Her main interest is in child and adult psychotherapy. She has previously worked at the Royal Alexandra Hospital for Children attached to the Child Development Unit in full-time child abuse work.

**Anne Harris Cohn** is the Executive Director of the National Committee for Prevention of Child Abuse, Chicago, Illinois. She holds a BA in Sociology, MA in Medical Sociology and MPH and DPH qualifications in Health Administration and Planning. As a 1979-80 White House Fellow she served as a Special Assistant to the Secretary of the Department of Health and Human Services. She also helped in the preparation of the Department's National Plan for Co-ordination of Child Abuse Activities and the Department's Consumer Affairs Plan. As associate and member of the Board of Directors of Berkeley Planning Associates, Dr Cohn designed and directed the first National Evaluation Study of Child Abuse and Neglect Treatment programmes. She has lectured and published widely on this and related research. She is currently a public member of the Federal Advisory Board on Child Abuse and Neglect.

**John H Kennell,** MD, Professor of Paediatrics, Case Western Reserve University School of Medicine, Rainbow Babies and

Children's Hospital, Cleveland, Ohio. Doctor Kennell is a paediatrician interested in maternal-infant bonding who has written extensively on this topic. Both Doctors Klaus and Kennell were in the forefront of the movement which has led to an increased understanding of the importance of the early bond between mother and child and which has led to major improvements in this area in obstetric hospitals throughout the world.

**Marshall Klaus,** BS, MD, Professor of Paediatrics, Case Western Reserve University School of Medicine, Rainbow Babies and Children's Hospital, Cleveland, Ohio. Doctor Klaus is a paediatrician with a major interest in neonatology who has become increasingly interested in maternal-infant bonding. He has written extensively on this subject and is active in research in this area.

**Jill E Korbin,** Ph D, Assistant Professor of Anthropology, Case Western Reserve University, Cleveland, Ohio. Jill Korbin received her Ph D in Anthropology from the University of California, Los Angeles in 1978 and trained as a scholar-in-residence at the National Center for the Prevention and Treatment of Child Abuse and Neglect in Denver, Colorado in 1978. She is an associate editor for *Child Abuse and Neglect: The International Journal* and is on the Executive Board of the International Society for the Prevention and Treatment of Child Abuse and Neglect. She has published several papers on culture and child abuse and has recently published a book, *Child Abuse and Neglect: Cross-Cultural Perspectives,* published by the University of California Press.

**Ian C Lewis,** MD, FRCP, FRACP, DPH, DCH, Professor of Child Health, Department of Child Health, Faculty of Medicine, University of Tasmania. Ian Lewis is a paediatrician to the Royal Hobart Hospital, Tasmania and the paediatric representative on the State Child Protection Assessment Board. He has had a longstanding interest in child abuse work as well as in community child health, medical education and nutrition. He is on the Editorial Board of *Child Abuse and Neglect: The International Journal.*

**Anthony Lipson,** MB, BS, FRACP, Paediatrician, Department of Medicine, Royal Alexandra Hospital for Children. Doctor Lipson's main interests involve genetics and the effect of various drugs and substances on the foetus. He is actively involved in the management of babies and children with malformations, congenital limb deficiency, cystic fibrosis and phenylketonuria. He is also a Research Associate at the Children's Medical Research Foundation.

**Sally Longstaffe,** MD, Assistant Professor of Paediatrics (Ambulatory Section), University of Manitoba, Winnipeg Children's Hospital. Doctor Longstaffe specializes in ambulatory medicine and child development. She has acquired particular skills in dealing with the medical and social problems of Indian children, is active in the community as an advocate of children's rights and is an active participant on the Winnipeg Child Abuse Team.

**Kenneth N McRae**, MD, Professor of Paediatrics at the University of Manitoba and Director of the Child Development Clinic at Winnipeg Children's Hospital. Doctor McRae is a paediatrician who specializes in child development and heads a multidisciplinary group of professionals at his Child Development Clinic which focuses on developmental and behavioural problems of the pre-school child. He is actively involved in community work, particularly school education, the legal system and the welfare system. He was instrumental in starting the Winnipeg Children's Hospital Child Abuse Team in 1967.

**Harold Martin**, MD, has worked in a child development centre at the University Colorado Medical School since 1966. His research and clinical work with abused children coincided with his interest in developmentally handicapped children and started in the late 1960's. In addition to training in paediatrics and child development, he has trained at the Denver Psychoanalytic Institute. He has been associated with the National Center in Denver in the past. His research and writings have focused on the child who is mistreated with special interest in the neurodevelopmental-psychological consequences of these patterns of parenting. He was one of the first clinicians to study the development of abused children and has been at the forefront of this field.

**Ann Murray**, Ph D, MAPA, Research Fellow in Psychology at the Boys Town Institute for Communication Disorders in Children, Omaha, Nebraska, United States. Ann Murray is involved in research concerning the study of infant development, particularly infants born at risk. She is especially concerned with promoting optimal parent-infant interaction, which includes learning more about infant behavioural organization, understanding what impact this has on parenting and helping parents to adjust to their infant's individual behaviour.

**Kim Oates**, MD, BS, MHP, FRACMA, MRCP(UK), FRACP, DCH(RCP&S). Kim Oates is a paediatrician with a particular interest in child development, mental handicap and child abuse. He practises at the Royal Alexandra Hospital for Children in Sydney where he is Director of Medical Services. He was formerly Head of the Department of Medicine and Head of the Child Development Unit at this Hospital. He is Chairman of the Hospital's Child Abuse Advisory Panel, is a member of the Executive Council of Defence for Children and is on the Executive Council of the International Society for the Prevention of Child Abuse and Neglect.

**Susan O'Connor,** MD, Assistant Professor of Paediatrics, Vanderbilt University Medical School and Assistant Chief of Paediatrics, Nashville General Hospital, Nashville, Tennessee. Susan O'Connor is a general paediatrician working in academic medicine and is interested in infant behaviour, mother infant relationships and child abuse. Her current research is on the causes and prevention of child maltreatment.

**Jan Shier,** BA Applied Science (Soc Work), WAIT, Senior Executive Officer, Montrose Child Life Protection and Family Crisis Service, Burwood, New South Wales. Jan Shier is a social work graduate from the Western Australian Institute of Technology. She has previously worked with the Department for Community Welfare in Western Australia and currently is responsible for the overall operation of the Montrose Child and Family Crisis Service.

**Earl Siegel,** MD, MPH, is the Professor of Maternal and Child Health and Clinical Professor of Paediatrics at the School of Public Health and School of Medicine, University of North Carolina at Chapel Hill, the United States. He is a Board certified paediatrician who writes from a background in private practice and a career in academic maternal and child health and paediatrics. His current interests and publications include the epidemiology of pregnancy outcome, regional perinatal care and strategies for promoting parent-infant relationships.

**Peter M Vietze,** Ph D, is the Head of the Mental Retardation Research Center's programme of the National Institute of Child Health and Human Development in Bethesda, Maryland. He has worked on several studies of early experience and child development and is currently conducting research on early parent-infant interaction and motivational development in normal infants and in infants with Down's syndrome.

**Richard A H White,** LLB, Solicitor. Richard White's practice involves family and child care legal work both in private practice and local government. Since 1978 he has been doing a government funded research project examining social work and legal aspects of the rights of parents whose children enter care without a court order. He is involved in teaching, consulting and writing on the legal aspects of child care and is co-editor of a book *Wards of Court* published by Butterworths in 1979. He is a member of the International Society on Family Law and on the Executive Committee of the British Association for the Study and Prevention of Child Abuse and Neglect.

# Chapter 1

# Child Abuse — A Community Concern

R Kim Oates

The world's best known puppet show, which had its origins in Italy in the mid-seventeenth century[1], tells how Judy gives Mr Punch her baby to mind. At first Mr Punch rocks the baby on his knee. The baby begins to cry. Mr Punch responds by rocking the baby harder and then violently, but the crying persists. In an uncontrollable rage at the baby, Punch hits it and throws it out of the window to its death. Many generations of adults and children alike have enjoyed the violence and aggression portrayed in this "children's" puppet show. But even before this time child abuse had been an accepted feature of society. Infanticide had been an accepted method of family planning in many cultures[2] and weak, premature or deformed infants were also likely to be disposed of. At times children were killed or injured for superstitious reasons. It was believed that slain infants would benefit the sterile woman, cure disease and confer health, vigour and youthfulness. To ensure durability of important buildings, children were sometimes buried under the foundations.[3]

Shakespeare was aware of the infanticidal impulse when he had Lady Macbeth say:

> I have given suck and know,
> How tender 'tis to love the babe that milks me;
> I would while it was smiling in my face
> Have pluck'd my nipple from his boneless gums,
> And dashed the brains out . . .
>
> (*Macbeth*, Act 1, Scene VII)

The mid-eighteenth century saw the industrial revolution begin in England. Children from poor families provided industry with a cheap workforce. Children from five years of age worked in factories for up to 14 hours a day, seven days a week and often suffered additional cruel treatment during this time. In an attempt to prevent this the English parliament passed the Factory Act in the early 1800's. However this Act applied only to poor children who had been separated from their parents. It did not apply to young children

1

who were still living with their own parents. This enabled parents, who were entitled to their child's earnings, to put their children out to work in factories, often under the circumstances which prevailed before the passage of the Factory Act.

Although illegal, there were many cases of infanticide in England as late as the nineteenth century. Eighty per cent of illegitimate children put out to nurse in London in the nineteenth century died. It was discovered that this was often because many nurses who took the children would kill them and continue to collect the nursing fees. A newborn child could be insured for about £1 under a "Burial Club" insurance policy. If the child died the insurance premium gave a profit between £3 and £5.[4] This led to many children being killed by their parents or given to a third party and killed to collect the insurance.

In 1860, about one hundred years before the classic paper from Henry Kempe's team[5], Ambrose Tardieu published a medico-legal study of 32 children who had been battered to death.[2] His description presented clearly all the features which eventually came to be recognized as the battered child syndrome.

Sexual abuse has only become recognized as a problem in recent years, some time after the recognition of child physical abuse.[6] However it too, has a long history. In the mid-nineteenth century, Ambrose Tardieu reported 60 cases of sex offences to children[7] and in 1839 a Police Commissary in Paris devoted one chapter of his annual report to the sexual abuse of children.[8] However little was done in France or in England to prevent these problems. In England child prostitution was common, particularly because of the widespread belief that intercourse with a child would cure venereal disease. Child prostitutes frequented the streets of London often under the guise of flower sellers.

Incest, although taboo in most societies has been practised for centuries. Because it occurred in secret, the incidence is difficult to ascertain. Rosenfeld, in a study of 530 female college students found that 8·5 per cent had experienced sexual activity with a family member.[9]

Although child physical and sexual abuse have been features of society for centuries, public awareness of the problem is only a recent event and follows the pioneering work of Kempe and others for physical abuse in the 1960's[5] and sexual abuse in the 1970's.[6]

The last 20 years has seen wide public acceptance that the problems exist, an extensive literature, wide media publicity and some (although many would say inadequate) public funding devoted towards the provision of services for abused children and their families.

In 1976 the International Society for the Prevention of Child Abuse and Neglect was formed. Groups looking at abuse of children in specific situations, such as Parents and Teachers Against Violence in Education, have been formed and in 1979 the International Year of the Child, Defence for Children, an international movement, whose activities are described in Chapter 24, was formed.

There has been very little written about emotional abuse. This is far more difficult to define, the scars are less obvious and it is probably more common than the combined total of child physical and sexual abuse.

Attitudes in the community to child abuse have changed. They have swung from the position where the community did not want to know that child abuse existed through to attitudes of outrage that events such as these should occur and on to a wider acceptance of the scope of the problem, its complexity and the need for understanding of the problem with the provision of treatment for the parents and the children. All three attitudes can still be found in the community, but with increased education and discussion, it is hoped that the third attitude will predominate.

Whether child abuse is a community responsibility or not needs to be considered. Some would see it as a family problem to be dealt with by medical and social work personnel. However a good case can be made for child abuse also being considered as a community problem influencing as it does the subsequent development of the next generation and having important implications for the community. These implications include the cost to the community of treatment programmes, the cost in terms of inadequate functioning of families where there has been a background of child abuse and the problems this causes the community's next generation when adults with a background of child abuse are at risk for repeating this in their own children.

Indeed it could be argued that child abuse is not a medical and social problem at all but that it is a problem of society as a whole. From the medical and social work viewpoint child abuse is often considered to be a result of family maladjustments and failings of particular family members. This is in contrast with Gil's view.[10,11] He considers that the common medical and social work assumption is false and that the fundamental problem is within a social structure which condones poverty and condones physical force in rearing children. These two views are complementary to each other. While recognizing the need for major changes in society's values and attitudes to children it is important not to lose sight of the valuable role played by the professional working with individual families. There is no doubt that overcrowding and poverty are stress factors which may trigger child abuse, particularly in a family with the risk factors known to be associated with the syndrome.[12] However we also need to remember that the majority of families living in adverse social circumstance do not abuse their children. Gil's contention that violence and force in child-rearing are an integral part of our society is reinforced when we recall that this theme is common in children's stories and nursery rhymes, such as this favourite which first appeared in 1797[1]:

> There was an old woman who lived in a shoe,
> She had so many children she didn't know what to do;
> She gave them some broth without any bread;
> She whipped them all soundly and put them to bed.

One needs to ask whether child abuse is something that is "common and normal" or "rare and abnormal".[13] There is certainly evidence that child abuse is very common. Gelles in 1978 showed that out of 46 million children in the United States aged between 3 and 17 years and living with their parents, between one and 1·9 million in the year of his survey were bitten, kicked or punched by their parents.[14] This survey was based on a true cross-section of American families. Gelles makes the disturbing comment that the parents may have admitted to these acts because they felt they were *acceptable* ways of bringing up children. Graham has shown that in a survey of normal mothers interviewed one month after the birth of their children, 61 per cent admitted that there had been times when they felt angry with their babies and 81 per cent felt that the experience of having a young baby to cope with had made them more sympathetic to baby batterers.[15] Frude and Goss surveyed 111 mothers in Wales with children aged between one and four years and found that 26 per cent had punished their children in ways that they believed to be wrong; 57 per cent admitted that at least on one occasion they had lost their tempers completely and hit the child really hard, while 40 per cent had entertained the fear that they might one day lose their tempers and seriously damage the child.[16] Even though child abuse is a common problem, these findings indicate that, considering the frequency with which mothers seem to become very angry with their babies, and the fact that this emotional reaction is often quite intense, the strategies of most people for self control are effective.

It is sometimes difficult to draw the line between acceptable punishment and physical abuse. The well-known study of the Newsons in Nottingham showed that 62 per cent of children at one year, and 97 per cent of children at four years were subject to physical modes of correction and that in 8 per cent of these children physical correction occurred daily.[17]

This information is complicated by the fact that some children may be more at risk of abuse than others. At times certain factors and behaviours in the child may trigger an abusive incident in a parent who already has the potential for child abuse.[18,19] Added to this is the fact that abused children may be difficult children. George and Maine showed, in a study of abused children in special day care centres in San Francisco, that abused toddlers physically assaulted their peers more than twice as often as control children did this. The abused children were also much more likely to assault their care givers.[20]

Other factors that need to be considered are the stresses of modern society and the problems of alcoholism and drug addiction. It has been shown, in a nationally representative sample of 1146 United States parents, that stressful events have a direct correlation with the incidence of child abuse. The greater the number of stressful events occurring in the year covered by the survey, the higher the incidence of child abuse. Parents who experienced the least stress had the lowest rate of child abuse.[21] A study of the adequacy of child care in families with alcohol or opiate addicted parents showed that in 41 per cent of these families abuse and/or neglect of a child occurred.[22]

Clearly the environment in which the child is brought up is an important factor in determining whether abuse will occur. An extreme example has been described by Margaret Mead in her study of different types of child-rearing in two New Guinea tribes.[23] She found the Arapesh to be extremely kind to children. They quickly responded to all the needs of their infants and small children and shared their care amongst many extended family members. Members of this tribe turn with confidence to other tribal members from an early age. They are peaceful, somewhat passive people. In the Mundugumor tribe, infants are treated in ways which repeatedly stimulate frustration and rage. Suckling babies would be pulled from the breast and not allowed to start nursing again until thoroughly enraged. In childhood the children are encouraged to express anger and violence freely in their daily interactions with others. The adults of this tribe tended to be angry and violent.

However, the explanation that attitudes of the community are a major factor in perpetuating disturbed behaviour, particularly in child rearing, into the next generation is too simple. Children are on the whole resilient. There are numerous examples of children from adverse social situations who have come to be community leaders or who have made major contributions to the arts science, politics and social welfare. The great majority of people from poor environments and a background of poverty do not end up by being violent or having criminal behaviour. Similarly, being brought up in a middle class suburb with a good education does not confer protection against becoming involved in crime, violence and child abuse. The reasons for these individual differences are poorly understood. Probably it is the basic relation between the child and parent that is the most important factor in determining the child's ability to become a good parent. Steele has found that a history of having been significantly deprived or neglected, with or without child abuse, in their own earliest years is the factor that stands out in maltreating parents more than any other factor such as socio-economic status, living conditions, race, religion, education, psychiatric state, cultural milieu or family structure.[24]

What should be the attitude of the community to child abuse? Should it be indignation that children could be injured, neglected or sexually misused by their parents? Should there be a community outcry that this is a crime which should be punished? The public indignation that accompanies sensational stories of child abuse published in the media is common. This public concern often falls short of the elected representatives of the public making a commitment to provide substantial funds to provide preventative and supportive services for child abuse. Should the community be taking Gil's attitude[10] that child abuse is a symptom of some of the problems in society, and that there is a community responsibility to make radical changes in the structure of society with the aim of preventing or significantly reducing the problem? The community attitude could be that children do not belong solely to their parents but are members of the community and one of the communities' most valuable resources. Perhaps more to the point is the fact that children belong first to themselves and that every child as specified in the United Nations Declaration of the Rights of the Child should "... be given opportunities and facilities, by law and by any other means to enable him to develop physically, mentally, morally, spiritually and socially in a healthy and normal manner ...".[25]

The complexity of the problem of child abuse is confounded by the fact that many cases fall into a grey area where it is difficult to be sure of the situation.

*Jane, aged two years presented to the Casualty Department of a city hospital.* Jane was dirty and unkempt, one of three children of a mother whose husband had recently deserted her. She had a black eye and swelling of the cheek on the same side. Her mother could not give a satisfactory explanation of what happened. The medical staff were in no doubt that this was a case of child abuse. However, within 20 minutes a neighbour arrived at the hospital with the explanation. Jane had wandered into her yard and accidentally got in the way of a cricket bat being swung by the ten-year-old child of that family. The ten-year-old had been too distressed and anxious to tell his mother immediately what had happened and Jane had wandered back to her own home where her mother noticed the injury and took her straight to hospital.

*Michael aged 13 months presented with fractured ribs.* The explanation was that Michael had been in his baby basket on the back seat of the family car, when the father, who was driving had to brake suddenly to avoid an accident. Michael was projected forward onto the floor of the car (the carry basket had not been harnessed) and some heavy items from the rear parcel shelf had landed on top of him. However there were several factors in the family's presentation, behaviour and background which made the medical and social work staff particularly suspicious that this was not the correct explanation.

In both of these instances, rather than concentrating on trying to make a positive diagnosis, it would be more appropriate to look at the problems uncovered in the families, to take steps to relieve some of these and to provide some realistic supportive services to the families. The aim would be to prevent child abuse incidents from occurring in the future. This would be particularly relevant if assessment of the families suggested that the potential for abuse was present. If one simply looks at the physical injuries, the problem in the family may be missed altogether. Physical injuries often depend on the circumstances at the time of the act of violence. For example a child may be pushed roughly to the ground by his father. He first lands against a soft armchair and then falls to the carpet. No injury is sustained. Exactly the same amount of force and aggression could be used where a different child is pushed but in falling hits his head on a protruding cupboard, sustaining a fractured skull and then falls to the cement floor sustaining further head injury. One of these cases will present to a medical service and is likely to be diagnosed as child abuse. The other will not present at all. It is the *act* of violence on the part of the parent which is the constant feature rather than the visible injury.

If the community is to be concerned with child abuse and interested enough to provide major services in this area, there needs to be knowledge about what happens to battered children. The best documented studies are those of Martin and they are depressing indeed.[26] A follow-up of 50 abused children showed that 66 per cent had an impaired capacity to enjoy life, 52 per cent had low self-esteem and psychiatric symptoms occurred in 62 per cent. Thirty five per cent of the children had IQs below 85 as compared to the expected finding of 15 per cent of the normal population.[27] Follow-up studies of children with non-organic failure to thrive due to parental neglect, which have been shown to correlate with child abuse[28], are equally depressing. These are described in Chapter 11 of this volume.

In trying to assess what can be done in the community to prevent child abuse there has been a strong move for instruction in parenting to be taught in the high school curriculum. In theory this is an ideal place as there is a captive population of adolescents and future parents. However it is doubtful if a theoretical knowledge at this stage would be of much use. People learn when they are motivated to learn and when they have a practical need to learn. It would seem more appropriate for parenting information to be provided during pregnancy but even more importantly for parenting courses to be held in the first few months after the child is born. The very practical difficulties of being an exhausted parent, feeling insecure about washing a baby, the difficulties of coping with constant screaming, the feelings of inadequacy and frustration that occur when food is refused, to quote just a few of the problems faced by most parents, are brought sharply into focus at this period. This is the time when practical help in child-rearing could be most effectively provided. If child-rearing and parenting information is to be given to adolescents in high school this should be done at a very practical level with experience in caring for small children provided in child care centres so that adolescent males as well as females can learn some of the practical problems associated with caring for infants and young children.

If increased community resources are put towards coping with the problem of child abuse, decisions need to be made about the most appropriate sort of people to work in this area. Obviously the medical profession becomes involved in this area because the doctor is often the first person to whom the injured child is presented. Many doctors are reluctant to make decisions in child abuse work which will affect the lives of children and families. This is in contrast to other aspects of their professional work where they are regularly making major decisions which will affect the lives of their patients. Perhaps the reluctance to do this in the field of child abuse is because of a lack of confidence in the avenues available for management of the child abuse problems. It is a misconception that all medical practitioners should be expert in child abuse. This is just as unreasonable as the expectation that all medical practitioners should be expert in all other complicated medical problems such as the management of malignant disease or the provision of cardiac surgery. While it is unreasonable to expect that all medical practitioners should be expert in the field of child abuse, it *is* reasonable to expect that they should be aware of the problem, to recognize or suspect it when it presents and to refer these families to colleagues and other agencies which are expert in the field.

There is no doubt that people with adequate training in understanding the problems of families and the problems of society are needed in child abuse work. However this is not all that is needed. The successful counsellor should have qualities which are independent of his theoretical beliefs and techniques. These are qualities of empathy, a genuine care for the child and a concern for the family and the ability of conveying these feelings in down-to-earth terms. At the same time, child abuse workers should not become so emotionally involved in the problems of these families that they cease to be effective. It is important to retain a sense of proportion, to be realistic and to realize that often there is no perfect solution and that it is the least detrimental alternative that may have to be taken. Workers in the child abuse field need to be able to co-ordinate their activities and work co-operatively with other agencies. Sadly, an accepted feature of many welfare and health services is that poor co-ordination is widespread. There should be no need to point out that in child abuse work the consequences of poor co-ordination and poor communication can be serious for the child.[29]

Probably the greatest problem in working with abusive families is the lack of continuity. This is why individual case work with families needs to be supplemented by simultaneously integrating the family into community support systems so that even if there is a loss of contact for valid reasons with the individual case worker, the family is still linked with supportive community facilities.[13]

Hand in hand with the provision of adequate personnel to work in the area should be the education of persons in positions of authority including magistrates, judges, senior police officers and politicians. It is only when the decision makers in the community have a good understanding of the problem of child abuse and an understanding of the available techniques for prevention and protection that adequate community resources will be channelled to this area. Even when child abuse is accepted as a community problem and responsibility, and the community increases its response to the problem in some of the ways that have been outlined, there are still other areas which need to be considered. The vast area of emotional abuse of children is poorly understood and difficult to document. Problems of child abuse in institutions need to be considered. This includes problems in schools, detention centres and institutions for the mentally handicapped.[30,31] The level of care provided in many institutions for the mentally handicapped is of a standard which would not be tolerated in a normal family. While the community may prefer not to know about these problems it is nonetheless part of the caring community's responsibility.

There are also some socially acceptable but more subtle forms of child abuse which, while peripheral to the real problem of child abuse, do reflect some of our communities' less laudable attitudes to children. These include activities which produce unrealistic expectations for children. An example is the average child of academically bright parents who is expected to perform in school work in a way which is far beyond his intellectual abilities and is then made to feel inadequate as a result of his inability to live up to his parents' high expectations. Many parents have unrealistic expectations for their children in competitive sports. One wonders if it is sometimes the parents who are competing against one another via their children's sporting activities. One sees children subjected to long hours of training, often forced upon them by their parents, and then subjected to abuse rather than praise from the sidelines. An even more subtle form of abuse is the commercial exploitation of children, particularly by television advertising which exhorts children, who do not yet have the ability to discriminate and look critically at salesmanship, to buy or encourage their parents to buy a particular product. These are but some of the more subtle problems faced by children growing up in the community. They draw attention to the ways in which children can be exploited to meet their parents' own needs or to meet commercial needs.

The international community also has a responsibility to become involved in some areas of child abuse care and prevention. The ways that exploitation of children can be fought on an international level as described in Chapter 24 need to be considered. With many communities becoming multiracial the task of understanding child-rearing techniques in different societies and a tolerance for different attitudes has to be addressed. This is discussed by Jill Korbin in Chapter 23.

Child abuse is a community concern. There are a vast variety of ways that the community can respond to this problem. These include prenatal and neonatal services, traditional medical and social work care, media awareness, community-based support groups and appropriate legal resources. These and other responses are described in the following chapters. It is hoped that an increased community concern and awareness will lead to an increased community responsibility towards the provision of appropriate services for abused children and their families.

# Notes

1 I Opie and P Opie, *The Oxford Dictionary of Nursery Rhymes* (Oxford University Press, London, 1951) p 355

2 D Bakan, *Slaughter of the Innocents: A Study of the Battered Child Phenomenon* (Jossey-Boss, San Francisco, 1971)

3 S X Radbill, "A History of Child Abuse and Infanticide" in R E Helfer and C H Kempe (eds) *The Battered Child* (University of Chicago Press, Chicago, 1968)

4 B G Fraser, "The Child and his Parents: a Delicate Balance of Rights" in H P Martin (ed) *The Abused Child* (Ballinger, Cambridge, Massachusetts, 1976)

5 C H Kempe, F N Silverman, B F Steele, P W Droegemueller and H K Silver, "The Battered-Child Syndrome" (1962) *JAMA* **181**:17

6 C H Kempe, "Sexual Abuse: Another Hidden Pediatric Problem (1978) *Pediatrics* **62**:382

7 S X Radbill, "Children in a World of Violence" in C H Kempe and R E Helfer (eds) *The Battered Child,* 3rd ed (University of Chicago Press, Chicago, 1980)

8 J B Beraud, *Les Filles Publiques de Paris* (Paris, 1839)

9 A A Rosenfeld, "Endogamous Incest" (1979) *Am J Dis Child* **133**:406

10 D G Gil, *Violence Against Children* (Harvard University Press, Cambridge, Massachusetts, 1973)

11 R J Gelles, "Child Abuse as Psychopathology: a Sociological Critique and Reformulation" (1973) *Am J Orthopsychiat* **43**:611

12 R K Oates, A A Davis, M G Ryan and L F Stewart, "Risk Factors Associated with Child Abuse" (1979) *Child Abuse and Neglect* **3**:547

13 J A Carter, "Controversies in Child Abuse" in *Proceedings of Second Australasian Conference on Child Abuse* (Brisbane, 1981)

14 R J Gelles, "Violence Towards Children in the United States" (1978) *Am J Orthopsychiat* **48**:580

15 H Graham, "Mothers' Accounts of Anger and Aggression towards their Babies" in N Frude (ed) *Psychological Approaches to Child Abuse* (Batsford Academic, London, 1980)

16 N Frude and A Goss, "Maternal Anger and the Young Child" in N Frude (ed) *Psychological Approaches to Child Abuse* (Batsford Academic, London, 1980)

17 J Newson and E Newson, *Patterns of Infant Care in an Urban Community* (Penguin, London, 1965)

18 W N Friedrich and J A Boriskin, "The Role of the Child in Child Abuse: A Review of the Literature" *Am J Orthopsychiat* **46(4)**:580

19 H P Martin, "Which Children Get Abused: High Risk Factors in the Child" in H P Martin (ed) *The Abused Child* (Ballinger, Cambridge, Massachusetts, 1976)

20 C George and M Main, "Social Interactions of Young Abused Children: Approach, Avoidance and Aggression" (1979) *Child Development* **50**:306

21 M A Strauss and S K Steinmetz, *Behind Closed Doors: Violence in the American Family* (Doubleday, New York, 1980)

22 R Black and J Mayer, "An investigation of the relationship between substance abuse and child abuse and neglect". Final Report to the National Center on Child Abuse and Neglect (US Dept Health, Education and Welfare, 1979)

23   M Mead, *Male and Female* (Penguin Books, London, 1950)

24   B F Steele, "Violence within the Family" in R E Helfer and C H Kempe (eds) *Child Abuse and Neglect — the Family and the Community* (Ballinger, Cambridge, Massachusetts, 1976)

25   *Declaration of the Rights of the Child* (United Nations General Assembly Resolution 1386 (XIV), 1959)

26   H P Martin, "Personality of Abused Children" in H P Martin (ed) *The Abused Child* (Ballinger, Cambridge, Massachusetts, 1976)

27   H P Martin, "Learning and Intelligence" in H P Martin (ed) *The Abused Child* (Ballinger, Cambridge, Massachusetts, 1976)

28   R K Oates and I W Hufton (1977), "The Spectrum of Failure to Thrive and Child Abuse" (1977) *Child Abuse and Neglect* 1:119

29   J W Polier, "Professional Abuse of Children, Responsibility for the Delivery of Services" (1975) *Am J Orthopsychiat* 45:3

30   S M Fiaber, "Life in a Children's Detention Centre: Strategies for Survival" (1972) *Am J Orthopsychiat* 42:3

31   C Duncan, "They Beat Children Don't They?" (1973) *J Child Psychol* 2:3

# Chapter 2

# The Behaviour of Battered Children — An Aid to Diagnosis and Management

Kenneth N McRae and Sally E Longstaffe

Awareness of the damaging influences of environment on the development of children received a major impetus in 1952 with John Bowlby's World Health Organization presentation on Maternal Deprivation and Mental Health.[1] Though modified and redefined in later years, the impact of this concept was sharply felt by professionals involved in the care of children. Ten years later a second major landmark was Henry Kempe's paper on "The Battered Child Syndrome".[2] This paper focused on the physical abuse of children, primarily by their parents, a concept that had previously been largely unappreciated clinically other than its radiographic recognition 16 years earlier.

The current bibliography on child abuse is vast. In recent years researchers have flooded the literature with new information detailing the physical and emotional methods used to destroy children, along with recommendations for treatment and prevention. The primary thrust has been towards clarification of the psychodynamics of the syndrome, with definitions as to the medical, social, and legal actions necessary to protect the child and reunite the family as a viable unit. Legislation brought forward throughout North America emphasized more than ever before, the child's right to grow and develop to his potential.

The identification of the abused child has primarily rested on the medical evidence of trauma: bruises, fractures and brain injuries, supported by the social history, usually one of deprivation, whereby the parents were themselves deprived or abused in childhood. The objective of this chapter is to focus on the behaviour and development of the child at the time of abuse, and to present patterns of behaviour and development that are often associated with abuse. Clinical awareness of such behaviour can help in supporting the diagnosis when the medical evidence is unsure, and bring to the fore the children who are vulnerable to future physical assault, some of which might be lethal.

Early descriptions by Kempe, Helfer and others included the typical behaviour of battered infants detailing their immobility and passivity.[3,4] Typically, abused children in the first year of life were seen as passive, crying minimally but hopelessly during treatment, and seemingly to expect no comfort from those about them. In time, as awareness of the complexity of the syndrome increased, with a greater understanding of the variations in types of abuse and the dynamics of parental pathology, the different behavioural presentations of the children emerged.

Though physical abuse is common to all the children under discussion, the children are exposed to a whole spectrum of environmental influences, primarily parental, which include emotional deprivation, understimulation, neglect, or rejection along with intermittent periods of positive nurturing.

It is our experience that children exposed to physical maltreatment will *present differently* depending on the degree to which the above factors are involved. These factors are, we feel, distinct, and not interchangeable, and when coupled with the developmental stage of the child, his innate strengths and personality differences, allow recognizable clinical and behaviour patterns.

We will present a number of clinical patterns which we recognize and group them into a workable classification which we have developed following observation of 50 children treated at the Children's Hospital of Winnipeg over an 18 month period (1978-80). The primary usefulness of such a classification is to allow a more comprehensive view of the child and his needs and thus aid in planning for the future whether the child returns to his home or not.

Before outlining the classification, it is necessary to define several concepts applicable in clinical descriptions.

ENVIRONMENTAL DEPRIVATION

The early model of the phenomenon as presented by Bowlby was the developmental failure of the child as a result of institutionalization.[1] Subsequently, it became apparent that institutional experiences were not only depriving the child of nurturing care but also stimulation, so that the emerging clinical picture represented a composite of both factors, the result of bonding failure, and the result of understimulation. We recognize the difference in our definitions, individualizing them as: (a) Maternal Deprivation, and (b) Understimulation, existing separately or together.

**Maternal Deprivation**

Implied in the term maternal deprivation, is an absence of consistent "mothering" with subsequent failure for the child of a bonding experience. The child does not have the opportunity to develop trust and the associated emotional ties with a consistent person, because of rapidly changing adult figures in his environment or their physical or psychological absence.

This phenomenon is part of the older institutional pattern, but currently is possible if the child rapidly moves through the foster home or hospital circuit or is in an inadequate home.

### Understimulation

This term refers to a paucity of experiences offered to the child in terms of being handled, talked with and cuddled with an overall diminution of sounds and visual stimuli.

The meagreness of the baby's experiences interferes with the attainment of expected milestones in all areas of development and are recognized clinically. In the older child understimulation may continue in the absence of toys, books and meaningful language interplay with those around him. Though frequently coupled with bonding failure, understimulation can produce its effects in spite of possible bonding success.

### NEGLECT

This term implies an avoidance of parental responsibilities with an absence of the surveillance necessary for the child's physical and emotional welfare. Failure to provide nutritional input, immunization procedures along with other health needs, safeguards from physical danger, all emphasize physical neglect. Failure in surveillance of the child's emotional life allowing his or her exposure to verbal abuse, or sexual indulgence, can be equally destructive.

### REJECTION

This is seen as a harmful form of deviant parenting with a negative thrust toward the child who becomes an object of dislike or even repulsion by the parent who may or may not have had a background of deprivation as a child. The infant's first year experiences are relevant historically, with frequent parental complaints about the intolerability of the baby's messiness, demands, and irritability. Bonding failure becomes obvious on careful review of these early events. The child subsequently proceeds to provocative, irritable, aggressive behaviour in vain attempts to reach his mother, attempts which generally alienate her further. Abuse becomes a distinct possibility if maternal pathology is appropriate.

### EMOTIONAL ABUSE

The term emotional abuse in this chapter is used to encompass deprivation, neglect, rejection and verbal abuse, all the negative experiences other than frank physical abuse, affecting the child's emotional and psychological development.

## OUR POPULATION — METHODS OF STUDY

Fifty children treated for physical abuse at the Children's Hospital of Winnipeg over an 18 month period were studied. The children ranged in age from the first year of life to age 11; 30 of the 50 being 2 years of age or less. The injuries consisted mainly of multiple bruises in 21 children, fractures in 9 children and burns in 7 children, with the rest having a variety of other injuries (Figure I).

**FIGURE I**

TYPES OF INJURIES IN FIFTY ABUSED CHILDREN AT CHILDREN'S
HOSPITAL, WINNIPEG — 1978-80

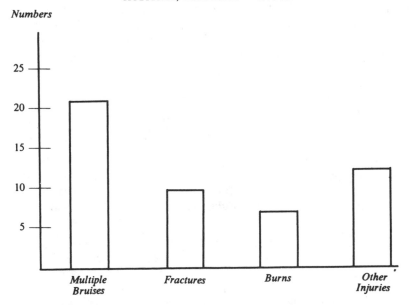

The length of hospitalization varied with the severity of injuries and the relative period required for complete investigation and development of an immediate plan of therapy. The diagnosis of child abuse was accomplished by team assessment, with the medical, social work, and police components all contributing. Information on each child's immediate and later behavioural characteristics was collated on the study form (Figure II).

Observations of behaviour were made:

(a) By Child Development specialists, nursing staff, hospital play therapists, and abuse team social workers during the child's hospital stay.

## FIGURE II

### FAMILY PEDIGREE

Name _____

Address_____

Hospital _____

Doctor _____

Past Abuse Information_____
_____

(1) Development CA_____

    Developmental Level: Motor_____

                    Adaptive _____

                    Language _____

                    Social_____

(2) Behaviour Reaction in Hospital: Major Affect _____

    Passivity _____ Withdrawal _____

    Silence, Immobility_____ Excessive Compliance_____

    Anxiety & Irritability_____ Acting out Behaviour_____

    Indiscriminate Behaviour _____ School Problems _____

    "Precocious" Behaviour _____ Low Self Esteem_____

    Impaired Ability for Enjoyment ____ Activity Rate _____

    Hypervigilance to Dangerous Circumstances _____

    Mechanism for Coping with Own Needs? Reaches Out _____

    Impulsivity _____

(3) Change in Behaviour while in Hospital (period in hospital) _____
_____
_____

(4) Child Relating: to examiner _____
_____

              to parents _____
_____

(5) Observations of Parenting on the Ward (visits, child-mother interaction) ____
_____
_____
_____

(6) Pre-Hospitalization Behaviour (according to mother)_____
_____

(7) Follow-Up Exam _____

    Comments_____

(b) By foster parents and child protection workers if already involved in the initial two weeks after the abusive episode.

(c) By hospital staff of parent-child interaction during hospital visits.

(d) By formal behavioural evaluations.

(e) By parent interviews when possible regarding their child's behaviour prior to and around the time of the abusive episode. Specific behavioural characteristics of the child were studied including the estimated major affect while in hospital, activity rate and capacity for enjoyment in play activities, mechanisms for coping with frightening circumstances, changes in behaviour while in hospital, and varied ways of relating to hospital staff and parents during visits.

## CLASSIFICATION OF BEHAVIOUR

Our analysis suggested five major categories of behaviour (Table I).

**Behaviour Seen as the Child's Attempt to Cope with a Hostile Environment — A Direct Result of the Abuse**

Local experience has tended to confirm the available world literature on abused children with clinically recognizable states as the child attempts to cope with a threatening environment. The child may become particularly oriented to danger with a high anxiety level, visual and auditory hyperalertness, and unusually compliant behaviour that suggests past conditioning to danger from punitive, inconsistent measures. Children of this description in our cohort resemble strikingly those described by Malone who detailed the influences of external danger in the lives of children from disorganized families.[7] He described four interrelated characteristics of such children that we were able to observe:

(i) Danger orientation with distrust of guardians.

(ii) Visual and auditory hyperalertness, the children repeatedly scanning those about them.

(iii) Use of avoidance and denial.

(iv) Overmature ego function with compliant coping behaviour and social skills beyond their age. The pre-school-aged boy or girl who is capable of sitting motionless for long periods when requested, who performs household tasks and errands beyond that expected for his or her age, and who doesn't seek comfort from parents when injured in play, is classic.

Fourteen participants in our series demonstrated behavioural pictures which were distinct reflections of their attempts to cope with

## TABLE I

### CLASSIFICATION OF CLINICAL TYPES OF BEHAVIOUR SEEN IN ASSOCIATION WITH PHYSICAL ABUSE

---

I    BEHAVIOUR SEEN AS THE CHILD'S ATTEMPT TO COPE WITH A HOSTILE ENVIRONMENT DIRECT RESULT OF THE ABUSE

(a) **Infancy:** passive, whiney behaviour with developmental lags; may be failure to thrive associated with the injuries (classic "battered baby").[5]

(b) **Older Child:** overcompliant behaviour; characterized by fear, with acute awareness of dangers in the environment.[6]

---

II   BEHAVIOUR PRIMARILY RELATED TO EMOTIONAL ABUSE IN ASSOCIATION WITH PHYSICAL ASSAULT

(a) Behaviour secondary to maternal deprivation (bonding failure).

   (i) **Infancy:** Indiscriminate behaviour with absence of stranger anxiety.[1]

   (ii) **Older Child:** Behaviour characterized by hyperactivity, decreased impulse control, indiscriminate behaviour, and excess eating.[6]

(b) Behaviour secondary to aggressive parent-child conflict.

   (i) Aggressive reaction patterns in response to parent rejection beginning in the first year of life.[3]

   (ii) Aggressive reaction patterns in response to aggressive parental disciplinary measures, onset in second year.[5]

---

III  BEHAVIOUR AND DEVELOPMENT SEEN AS NORMAL IN SPITE OF PHYSICAL ASSAULT

Evidence of some positive nurturing plus environmental stress factors. Circumstances included.

(a) Family Stress.[3]

(b) "En passant" neglectful injury.[4]

(c) Abuse from one of multiple caretakers.[7]

(d) Adequate parenting from the non-abusing parent.[1]

---

IV   BEHAVIOUR COLOURED BY MASSIVE NATURE OF INJURIES.[3]

---

V    MIXTURE OF THE ABOVE BEHAVIOURS.[2]

---

their environment. This group (28 per cent), comprised the largest category of children. Eight older children showed evidence of overcompliant, fear-ridden, behaviour with heightened awareness of danger to themselves from those about. Six infants fell into the category of "battered baby" as described previously with passive irritable behaviour and frequently associated physical features of failure to thrive. Motor development delay was generally present, as well as a disinterest in toys. Preoccupation with oral intake was sometimes present even at this early stage.

### Behaviour Related Primarily to Emotional Abuse in Association with Physical Assault

*Behaviour Secondary to Maternal Deprivation — (Bonding Failure)*

Clinically, this picture can be recognized as early as the latter half of the first year of life (at a time when normal stranger anxiety with preference for the baby's mother appears) with indiscriminate behaviour toward an adult which may continue on through early childhood, changing only if the child is offered bonding opportunities. Subsequently, coupled with this characteristic are growing difficulties in developing personality organization manifesting as increased activity rate, poor impulse control, and preoccupation with oral intake.

The signs of such deprivation in older children have been reported by Goldfarb[5], Glasser[6] and Lewis[8]. There is a consistency in the clinical picture that bears resemblance to an "organic state" because of the hyperactivity and decreased impulse control. The excessive eating and indiscriminate behaviour stand out as being distinct.

In spite of the consistency of bonding failure, the child can achieve reasonable developmental landmarks if stimulation in motor and language areas has been present. As a result, cognitive successes as measured by early developmental tests and standard psychological tests, may make the child appear intellectually normal.

Nine children (18 per cent) in our population presented a behavioural picture suggestive of serious maternal deprivation, one in infancy, and eight in older children. These children demonstrated behaviour which was distinctly abnormal with indiscriminate social responses beginning as early as the latter part of the first year of life with the classic increasing behavioural difficulties already described.

*Behaviour Secondary to Aggressive Parent-Child Conflict*

*Aggressive reaction patterns to parental rejection beginning in the first year of life.* Three children (6 per cent) in our series were recognized as having been abused as part of a picture of intense maternal rejection beginning in the early months of life. The behavioural picture here was not quite as consistent as other clinical presentations of behaviour, depending on the degree of indiscriminant behaviour seen. The "wildly" overactive destructive and intensely provocative pre-school child whose behaviour settles rapidly, perhaps within days, when separated from his rejecting parent and given quiet controls in hospitals, or in a foster home, is characteristic.

The history of the first year reveals maternal antagonistic attitude towards the child in association with unacceptable sleeping, eating, spitting behaviours on the child's part. This was apparent even when the mother had shown some skills in parenting other children. In this particular type of conflict, the child specifically contributes to the abuse by his "personality", resulting in a failure of bonding and rejection by the mother.

*Aggressive reaction patterns to aggressive and inconsistent parental disciplinary measures (onset — second year).* Six children (12 per cent), in our series were found to have been abused as a result of disciplinary efforts which parents deemed appropriate, but by current Canadian societal standards were physically excessive and damaging. The parent-child relationships during the first year of life as determined retrospectively, were often of a reasonable nature, the difficulties arising during later stages of the child's development where the normal determination and struggle for independence of the second and third year of life were inappropriately interpreted by parents as being abnormal, threatening, with warnings of future delinquency if not contained by physical discipline. Their normal negative behaviour thus invited aggressive counter-measures by the parents, ending in abuse.

### Normal Behaviour

It has long been our experience that many physically abused children may present a reasonably normal picture developmentally. Evidence of parental bonding, normal intellect, normal activity rate and impulse control, stranger reserve, and the ability to relate in an age appropriate way to their peers, suggests a background that must have included some positive nurturing experiences although intermittent. The spectrum of normal behaviour included evidence of hospitalization anxiety, which is a well recognized and an expected phenomenon in children, varying in manifestation and intensity depending on the emotional strength of the child, his previous experiences, and age. Children may demonstrate a large variety of behaviours during and after the hospitalization including anxiety, sleep disturbances, food refusal, and temporary developmental regression, that are seen in all children without abusing experience.

The relative normality of the child's development suggests an exposure to some reasonable parental care at some time in his life, a fact of importance for future planning. This second largest group included 13 of 50 (26 per cent) children. The children's behaviour was determined to be as expected considering their abrupt removal from familiar persons and surroundings in a hospital environment, and the recent occurrence of injuries.

### Circumstances Associated with Abuse and Normal Development

*Family Stress* was a concomitant of some abusive episodes where the child's behaviour was deemed normal and where nurturing under other circumstances was historically and sometimes by previous observation found to be relatively intact. Financial, medical and marital problems, were examples of stress, not primarily child focused, but which tipped the balance causing the parents to abuse.

*"En Passant" Injuries* included a specific type of neglectful accidental injury, the incident occurring under unusual circumstances where alcohol abuse or family aggression had resulted in a child being "in the way of some flying object" or otherwise injured because of the circumstances. Nurturing at other times was sometimes satisfactory. This type of injury in our experience occurs more frequently, although not exclusively, in Native Canadian children, and is seen as being generally on the lower end of a scale of potential future physical risk to the child. Four children experienced abuse in this context.

*Multiple Caretakers.* This situation somewhat resembled that just described in its tendency to a lesser degree of underlying pathology. Though the child had experienced physical abuse, there was evidence that he had received some nurturing from other than the adult abuser in the past. Occasionally a babysitter was involved as the abuser. Evidence of neglect was a frequent concomitant. There were two children in this category.

*Adequate Parenting from the Non-abusing Parent.* The child in this one case had received sufficient parenting of a normal nature to present a normal picture in spite of physical aggression from the other parent.

### Behaviour Coloured by the Massive Nature of the Injuries

In three instances (6 per cent), the children had such massive injuries that initial behaviour patterns could not be observed in a formal way. Two of the children had severe head injuries requiring intensive life supports, and one infant had severe dehydration and shock secondary to lack of any intake over several days.

## Mixture of the Behaviours

In two cases (4 per cent), there appeared to be a variety of operative factors. Behaviour of the child attempting to cope with a hostile environment was coloured by associated evidence of severe deprivation as well.

## THE BEHAVIOURAL CLASSIFICATION AS AN AID TO EARLY MANAGEMENT

Our experience with the child victim suggests the importance of his special behavioural characteristics as a reflection of the family's pathology. The features peculiar to each individual child, along with the physical abuse need to be a factor in understanding the degree of pathology to which he or she has been subjected and thus become an aid in planning appropriate management.

Although a complete overview of approaches to early management and disposition is beyond the scope of this chapter, some broad categorization is possible. It is clear that provision of a place of safety for the victim is only one early objective, and that therapeutic approaches to concomitant emotional deficits must be of equal consideration.

The abused child's behavioural characteristics can serve as important indicators as to:

(1) The degree of emotional damage, and hence a measurement of the nurturing capacities within the family. This is an important determinant affecting the decision as to whether the child can ever successfully be replaced in the natural home.

(2) The type of immediate handling necessary to support and manage the child's behaviour as he moves into a fostering situation, or back into his own home.

(3) A baseline by which the child's developmental and behavioural progress can be measured, whatever the child's early disposition.

Children whose behaviour and development are found to be reasonable at the time of abuse, might be expected to have a better prognosis providing that contributing causative stresses and neglectful behaviour can be ameliorated, and positive nurturing influences are continued and supported as the family stresses are alleviated.

The remainder of the children who present developmental and behavioural abnormalities secondary to their past experiences obviously require special supports and planning in order to maximize chances for full recovery.

It is stressed that a goal ending with the prevention of physical abuse alone must be considered unsuccessful if emotional abuse as already defined continues.

Recognizing the importance of factors such as the constitutional differences between children, and the duration and intensity of abnormal nurturing, the remaining groups of children can be inferred to have poorer future prognoses without vigorous inter-vention.

The over-compliant child whose major psychological energies are focused on survival in a hostile environment is in urgent need of intervention, which in the older pre-school or school age child of this type, often requires permanent removal from previous influences. The classic battered baby within the first year of life who displays behaviour of this type, will frequently experience a dramatic spurt of physical and developmental progress over weeks when hospitalized or otherwise placed in more appropriate surroundings. Successful replacement of the infant with the natural family depends on the extent of change possible with simultaneously focused family interventions.

With the group of emotionally deprived children (with or without major behavioural conflicts), provision of a place of safety where physical assault will not recur must be associated with an opportunity for the child to develop a long-term relationship with a giving parent-surrogate, with appropriate handling of secondary behaviour problems.

Whether this can be accomplished with the natural parent depends on parental insight, potential for change, and support systems. If these cannot be assured, long-term placement is indicated.

The physically abused child who is also emotionally rejected is also in need of immediate and radical intervention with permanent removal often indicated unless major attitudinal changes on the parents' part are possible and can be demonstrated. Keeping a child in limbo, awaiting parental healing, is not a solution always in the child's best interests. Long-term planning is essential, with a focus primarily on the children.

Further prospective studies are greatly needed regarding outcome in the long-term when related to treatment approaches. Current efforts often achieve the prevention of further battering, but less often succeed in modifying other and equally devastating effects on the total child.

# Notes

1   J Bowlby, *Maternal Care and Mental Health,* Monograph 2 (World Health Organization, Geneva, 1952)

2   C H Kempe, F N Silverman, B F Steele, et al, "The Battered Child Syndrome" *JAMA* 181:14 (1962)

3   R E Helfer and C H Kempe (eds), *The Battered Child* (University of Chicago Press, Chicago, 1968)

4   R Goldston, "Observations on Children Who Have Been Physically Abused and Their Parents" (1965), *Am J Psychiatry* 122:440

5   W Goldfarb, "Infant Rearing and Problem Behaviour" (1943) *Am J Orhopsychiat* 13:249

6   K Glasser and L Eisenberg, "Maternal Deprivation" (1956) *Pediatrics* 18:628

7   C A Malone, "Safety First: Comments on the Influence of External Danger in the Lives of Children of Disorganized Families" (1966) *Am J Orthopsychiat* 36:6

8   H Lewis, *Deprived Children* (Oxford University Press, London, 1954)

# Chapter 3

---

# The Hospital Child Abuse Team

R Kim Oates, Louise Gyler and Robert Adler

The management of child abuse is a team problem. Child abuse teams don't just happen. A team of individuals who work in parallel without mutual trust and respect for each other and without close co-operation is a team in name only. Considerable effort has to go into creating a child abuse team where the members can work comfortably with each other. This can be done by first selecting team members because of their skills and interest in child abuse. However, real team work will only come from the team members working closely together on cases. Within a hospital setting the team leader is usually the paediatrician. The paediatrician needs to learn to be comfortable in working with other professionals and to respect their skills and abilities. The paediatrician should not expect to be able to perform all the functions required in caring for the abused child but often assumes the role of co-ordinator.

## THE ROLE OF THE PAEDIATRICIAN

## R Kim Oates

The paediatrician needs to first be an expert in making the diagnosis of child abuse, including neglect and sexual abuse. Some paediatricians are uncomfortable in dealing with this sort of problem. If so it is appropriate to seek consultation with an expert colleague in this field just as one would seek a consultation if dealing with a complicated renal or cardiac problem where assistance was required.

The paediatrician who becomes concerned with child abuse should be involved in the assessment and management of the child and family from the time of presentation rather than delegating too much of this responsibility to junior members of the hospital clinical staff. He should be on-call as child abuse cases, like other emergencies, do not occur only during the accepted working week. Many cases present at unusual hours and the paediatrician should be prepared to see cases at the time they present. This is often a critical time for the family and one when effective groundwork can be done.

## The Diagnosis

The diagnostic features of the abused child have been well described.[12] In particular concern should be expressed about injuries in young children, delay between the injury occurring and the parents presenting the child for help, bruising in areas not normally bruised in play situations and most important of all, injuries which are inconsistent with the history that has been given. The paediatrician needs to be aware that because of the natural tendency not to want to make the diagnosis of child abuse, if one thinks of child abuse as being a possible diagnosis one is usually right. Cases of neglect are usually obvious from the history and physical examination of the child. Of particular value is the child's weight compared with that of the normal population.

In sexual abuse there is often little to find on physical examination and the history is particularly important. Children who give detailed information about sexual encounters should be believed. It is most unusual for this sort of history to be fabricated.

If the child is old enough a history should always be taken from the child as well as from the parents, although many children are reluctant to implicate their parents.

> Four children aged three to seven years were brought to the hospital by their mother. Each child had a black eye. The mother could not give a satisfactory explanation for the lesions. When the children were spoken to alone and separately each child promptly volunteered that the injury had occurred when they "fell out of a window". They were quite anxious that their mother should not be implicated for causing the injury.

It is particularly important in cases of sexual abuse for the history to be taken in privacy and for the physical examination to be done sensitively and with care.

Appropriate investigations should be done to assist in the diagnosis. These include a skeletal survey in children under two years to look for old fractures at different stages of healing. Although coagulation studies rarely give helpful information it is important to do them as, should the case come to court and the parents claim the child has a bruising tendency, the coagulation studies will usually be able to refute this claim. It is helpful to take photographs both in colour and black and white. In cases of sexual abuse specimens for semen analysis should be collected and blood taken from the child for evidence of venereal infection. If there is *any* suspicion of venereal infection the child should be promptly treated with antibiotics. Most Child Abuse Centres now contain sexual assault kits providing instructions about the necessary collection of specimens. A pelvic examination of young children is usually not necessary. The vaginal orifice can be clearly inspected with the child in the knee-chest position when the labia are gently separated. If there is any evidence of physical damage the pelvic examination should be performed under general anaesthetic.

After taking the history and examining the child it is important to be honest with the parents. There is a natural tendency, particularly in severe cases of abuse to feel angry with the parents. This must be resisted, the whole aim of the treatment being to assess the family with a view to helping them to prevent further episodes of child abuse. This is usually the common point where parents can be met. It is important to inform the parents of the concern held about the nature of the child's injuries. When a notification about the child abuse has to be made to a Government authority it is essential that the paediatrician tell the parents that this notification is to be made. Nothing is calculated to destroy trust more than the sudden and unexpected appearance on the parents' doorstep of a Welfare Officer.

It is often appropriate at the initial interview to introduce the social worker to the family and to conduct the interview jointly with the social worker. This is a stressful time for the parents and not a particularly comfortable time for the paediatrician and social worker. Usually the one common area the team has with the parents at this stage is that of concern for the child's welfare and the desire that similar injuries should not occur in future. It is surprising how often parents accept this approach. It is sometimes difficult to be sure in the early stages of the assessment whether one is actually dealing with a case of abuse and neglect. If the assessment reveals many of the risk factors known to be associated with abusive families one can be confident that, whether the particular injury is a case of direct abuse or not, the child is in an "at risk" situation and assessment of the family and provision of services to support the family in parenting is indicated. All of the information required to make the assessment is usually not obtained at the first interview and several interviews over the ensuing days are required. For this reason it is usually wisest to admit the child to hospital for medical care and observation and to allow the opportunity to continue the assessment of the family and formulate a management plan.

An important duty of the paediatrician is to carefully document details of the history taken and to document details of all injuries. An essential part of the assessment is to also assess the child's developmental level and make an assessment of his behaviour and emotional state. This is important in formulating the continuing management programme for the child. As it is well-known that other children in the family may be "at risk" for physical abuse[3] an opportunity should be taken to examine the other siblings.

The paediatrician must take care not to confuse his responsibility to the family with his responsibility to the child. He should be aware of a natural tendency to not want to become involved in the case and also of the temptation that sometimes occurs to empathize so closely with the parents that the child's needs are overlooked. While being able to have some sympathy with and understanding for the parents' problems, it is important to be able to look carefully at the needs and rights of the child. This includes the provision of a treatment programme made specifically for the child's needs. This is particularly important in view of the follow-up studies which show developmental delay in these children.[4,5] Because of the responsibilities involved in caring for children and families with this problem and the difficulties in reaching decisions it is important to be able to share these concerns with other members of the child abuse team.

### The Paediatrician's Role in the Team

The paediatrician must work in close co-operation with the other team members. It is important to establish a comfortable working relationship with the social worker who will be involved in much of the day-to-day assessment of the family. It is natural in a team for anger and frustration to be felt. The paediatrician should try to help other team members and other people involved in the hospital such as nursing staff on the child's ward to contain this anger or to express it constructively. As well as supporting other team members from time to time, the paediatrician should be able to look to the other team members for personal support. Many teams find it helpful to have an advisor not directly involved with the family with whom they can discuss the problems of the case as well as their own feelings about it. The psychiatrist can fulfil an important role in this regard.

The case conference is an important part of team management. The paediatrician is often responsible for calling and chairing the case conference although other team members may take this role. We have found that the most appropriate person to chair a case conference is a psychiatrist acting as advisor to the team but not directly involved in the management of the child. There is considerable value in having somebody sufficiently distant from the case to be able to take an objective view. Child abuse is an area which arouses all sorts of emotions and professionals should not assume that they will be immune from the problem of their emotional response getting in the way of their objectivity.

## Going to Court

Medical practitioners are notoriously reluctant to attend court. The paediatrician in the child abuse team should be prepared to go to court and should develop some expertise at presenting medical evidence clearly and concisely. Court attendance in child abuse cases should not be delegated to the most junior member of the hospital medical staff who has seen the child. In presenting evidence in court it is important to confine information to the facts and to be confident in one's medical judgement. A prepared statement, with prior approval of the magistrate can usually be referred to. A court hearing can often be used quite successfully to help a child and family.

*Doug presented to the hospital with a fractured skull and multiple bruising at nine months of age.* Assessments clearly showed that this was a case of child abuse and that the young family were going through considerable marital difficulties at that time. An early court hearing was held and a decision made for Doug to be placed in the foster care of his paternal grandmother. Regular case work by the social worker with the natural mother, an infant stimulation programme for Doug, who was well behind in early milestones, and regular medical follow-up were instituted. After 12 months Doug was returned to the care of his mother. Social work and medical support has continued and 18 months after being returned to the family Doug is developing normally and his mother is exhibiting mature coping abilities.

*Andrew at 16 months presented with multiple bruising.* Evaluation of the family found several major risk factors and it was apparent that this was a case of physical abuse. Further assessment of the family showed major disturbances. The child abuse team was reluctant to use the court on this occasion, partly due to unfamiliarity with the court system. The child remained with his parents while attempts were made to help the family. Problems in the family were patched up over the next three years but with little success. No specific treatment programme for the child was made. After four years the situation deteriorated to such an extent that the child was removed from the family. However by this stage he was severely emotionally disturbed, quite unsuitable for fostering and is requiring prolonged psychiatric care.

These two contrasting cases illustrate the need for a management programme to be made from the outset, the importance of combining this with a specific programme for the child's needs and the way in which legal proceedings may be able to assist in helping to implement the programme.

## Follow-up

The paediatrician has a key role in providing regular follow-up of the child. Regular medical follow-up is usually acceptable to the family. Attendance at the medical clinic is often an opportunity for the social worker to see the family at the same time. Follow-up should include a careful examination of the child on each occasion and also assessment of the siblings. The child's general development should be reviewed and any health problems in the child and family should be attended to. It has been shown there is a higher incidence of physical ill health in the parents[5] and siblings[6] of these children and this is one practical area where medical help can be provided. Medical follow-up also gives an opportunity to provide anticipatory guidance for the parents and provide general health and safety education. There is a subtle tendency not to become involved in the follow-up of these children. It is important to make an effort to ensure that the families keep their medical appointments and to send a new appointment or to arrange for a visit from a community nurse if they fail to attend. Regular medical follow-up, in co-operation with other members of the team, provides both surveillance of the child and support and guidance for the family.

## Teaching

The paediatrician has an important role in teaching about child abuse both within his own profession, amongst other professional groups and in the community. He should be involved in training others in the assessment and management of child abuse and also be prepared to speak up within the community for the rights of children. This may involve addressing public functions, being prepared to lecture to a wide variety of groups, providing literature for those interested in learning more about child abuse and approaching politicians and other government authorities for improving resources, facilities and personnel for these children and their families.

Many paediatricians working in this area see a need to have other interests besides child abuse. Working in this field is time consuming, often frustrating and although there are rewards in seeing some families do well, these rewards come slowly and are often countered by disappointments with other families. For these reasons many paediatricians believe it is important to be involved in other aspects of child care, perhaps quite removed from the child abuse field where, by gaining a different degree of professional satisfaction, one can be refreshed enough to continue as paediatrician to the child abuse team on a long-term basis.

## THE ROLE OF THE SOCIAL WORKER

### Louise Gyler

Social work practice is essentially concerned with individuals, their families and the nature and quality of their interactions with their social environment. Undoubtedly it is well suited to make a central contribution to the issue of child abuse, a complex social and family issue. There are a number of interesting and sometimes controversial papers that examine the social worker role in child abuse cases.[7,8,9,10] Davoren wrote in 1968 that the role of the social worker was the "role of curing". She did expand that the only "cure" possible might be the removal of the child from the home.[7] I think very few social workers today would be optimistic enough to think in terms of "cure", for most look beyond the abusive behaviour of parents, to the patterns of disturbed family relationships and parenting problems. There is also an increased awareness that work with parents is at times not sufficient to have a therapeutic impact upon the abused child's impaired development and damaged capacity for relationships.[11] With these shifts in thinking, it is apparent that there are no easily generalizable solutions forthcoming either on a broad social level or an individual clinical level. For social workers working in this area the complexities and uncertainties are unavoidable.

I do not think it possible, nor helpful to delineate too tightly the social worker's role in the child abuse team, as the social worker's broadly defined practice allows for a flexibility and fluidity. In turn, the social work role is also influenced by numerous idiosyncratic and situational factors, including the personality and orientation of the worker, and the agency's needs and values. However, in a hospital setting, where the primary interests and priorities are medical, it is important for the social worker to keep the medically oriented team aware that other factors are involved in patient care. Hence, the social worker not only needs a good understanding of the needs and problems of families, but also she needs to demonstrate practically the effectiveness and limitations of her understanding and knowledge. In the multidisciplinary child abuse team, constant clarification of roles is required. Otherwise, role confusion, competitiveness and devaluation can interfere with team relationships and the quality of the service as described in Chapter 21. For this reason, I plan to discuss one particular aspect of the social worker's clinical involvement with families, the use of the assessment: the assessment of the parents, the family's functioning and the environmental stresses. It is not appropriate to consider here the developmental and emotional assessment of the child. It is vital to understand a particular child's capacity to cope in his home environment. However, most social workers in this country, do not have adequate training to assess children. This is the task of other team members: the paediatrician, the occupational therapist and child psychiatrist or psychologist.

Before proceeding to explore the role of assessment, I wish to consider generally some functions of the child abuse team. I think there are two central functions related to the needs of families and staff. Firstly abusive families often have broad ranging problems, requiring help which extends beyond the expertise of any one discipline or professional group.[12] The problems and needs of abusive families are similar to that of other families in need of help. However, the legal implication of child abuse work is a major difference, not only for families but also for staff. When an abused child is seen at a hospital, staff are not only confronted with their feelings about an injured child, but also with the need to make some significant decisions, for example about whether to admit the child, when to discharge the child home, and when to recommend court proceedings. These issues can arouse anxiety in staff. A supportive multidisciplinary setting is necessary to contain these anxieties so as to enable all staff to provide the necessary help for families. For a team to fulfil these needs well, some structure is essential. For example, regular team meetings which review and evaluate the work of the team, case conferences and the development of good liaison networks with statutory agencies, all facilitate team functioning. It is important that the social worker actively promotes the development of satisfactory, reliable structures. Otherwise, as Trowell stated in describing unsatisfactory structures: "workers are so busy maintaining structures to avoid being overwhelmed by anxiety that there is little time or energy for tasks which the institution ostensibly exists to perform."[13]

It is well recognized that abusive families often require long-term help extending over years.[12] The reality for the hospital-based social worker is that she often has a relatively brief contact with many families. This poses the hospital social worker with a difficult challenge of developing a feasible and effective contribution that will facilitate the link between the families and community workers, who may have statutory responsibilities to provide further help. However, when parents present their child at a hospital, they are on some levels seeking help even if not a direct request for help, with their abusive behaviour or parenting problems. It is for the family often a time of crisis of special stress, when anxiety is likely to be heightened and feelings more accessible. As Salzberger-Wittenberg wrote: "The same condition provides an optimum point for therapeutic intervention, for it is when anxieties are 'hot' (or the client 'cold' with anxiety) that he needs help most and the case worker has greatest chance of being therapeutic by making herself available to the client's mental pain."[14] Therefore the hospital social worker is afforded an opportunity to intervene at a crucial time for the family.

During the child's admission, the primary goal of the social worker's intervention is to make an assessment. The assessment is understanding the nature of the family problems, and more specifically the child's need for protection. The social worker attempts to engage the non-destructive and caring aspects of the parents in looking to make their family safe. The implications of the assessment raise issues and conflicts about parental and children's rights. They also give rise to questions about the use of authority and offering help. Misjudgements and mistakes seem inevitable, particularly when the anxiety aroused by child abuse work can lead to hasty and ill-conceived reactions by workers. It seems to me once a child is physically safe in a hospital, the process of making an assessment and sharing the implications of it with the team can provide a space for reflection and discussion. With careful consideration, an appropriate response may be formulated.

In a hospital setting, the social worker can lose sight of the fact that her concerns and feelings about a family do not necessarily correspond with those of the medical staff, who are primarily concerned with the severity of the child's medical condition. In the ambience of life and death medical emergencies, it is easy for the social worker to find herself parallelling her priorities with those of the medical staff. For example, the social worker can overlook the clinical reality that the physical symptom of abuse does not necessarily indicate the degree of family disturbance. Sometimes small children with "just a bruise" live in very damaging home environments. Another pitfall can be the temptation to make decisions about a particular family on the basis of criteria describing the characteristics of abusive parents and abused children. While such descriptive and predictive data may be useful in defining populations "at risk", the application of it to practice has major shortcomings. It invites staff to accept "the fact" and does not encourage them to look beyond to understand the *context* of "the fact". I recall one well-intentioned doctor who could not grasp the possibility that a baby with slight facial bruising may have been non-accidentally injured, as his mother was adamant that her baby had been much wanted. Indeed, this baby had been much wanted by the mother "to fill the big black empty hole inside of me". This baby was wanted to protect the mother against her own feelings of emptiness and despair and to meet her needs for love and companionship. When the baby failed to fulfil her mother's unrealistic expectations, the mother felt angry, hurt and disillusioned with her baby.

Various attempts have been made to explain and define the nature and characteristics of abusive families.[15,16,17] Most have been found incomplete in explaining individual family variations. In practice, there seems no substitute for a comprehensive assessment; though often initially provisional and tentative. Central to making an assessment is some understanding of the family dynamics, the degree to which the child is at risk, particularly some insight into what the child represents to the parents, the capacity to use help and some consideration of ongoing resources available. The assessment can take from a few interviews over a few days to several weeks depending on the family and circumstances surrounding the child's admission. This type of assessment often requires more structuring of the interview setting than many social workers often use for other families. For example, parents are best not seen in busy wards. Sometimes in the early stages of the assessment, some parents find it difficult to tolerate more than brief interviews. Sometimes the family is unable for a time to keep appointments with the social worker, or on occasions even visit their child in hospital, so great are their fears and anxieties. The social worker may need to work with the family's fear about attending the hospital in their own home. This may facilitate the parents visiting their child. Other parents may fail arranged appointment times but attend at other times angrily demanding to be seen. In attempting to assess such a family, the social worker needs to respond flexibly, but equally, it is not helpful to the family to feel they can manipulate and control the social worker.

It is through the assessment process that the social worker is able to focus on the fact that each child and family is unique and individual and thereby sustain the team's involvement to help a particular family. Of course this goal is not unique to the social worker and is hopefully shared by all team members. However, because of the social worker's understanding of the family, she is frequently in the best position to give this goal a practical dimension. The social worker can clarify the implications of the assessment for the team. The understanding of a family's capacity to use help and more specifically to use potentially helpful persons is crucial. It enables the formulation of specific recommendations for particular families. There are a number of ways of helping abusive families. These range from the provision of broadly based environmental containment by utilizing neighbourhood support such as baby health centres and schools, to offering psychotherapeutic relationships.

When the assessment is inadequate or non-existent there is a tendency for the team to take precipitous actions or alternatively, to minimize the family's difficulties. Generally, the team is restricted to a limited range of management options. There is a danger in making decisions on the basis of stereotypic descriptions and recommending rather mechanistically "support" for all families by a community worker. On these occasions, there is often a failure to give sufficient recognition to the clinical observation that individuals require sufficiently good ego strengths to perceive, understand and integrate the more positive aspects of a therapeutic relationship. This implication is not considered carefully enough in the context that some abusive parents have quite severe personality and relationship difficulties, which greatly impair their ability to enter into and sustain any kind of lasting relationships. Many families require quite skilled, supervised casework or family work. It is my impression that it is best for both the parents and the child to offer some meaningful help from the onset. Otherwise, situations that are perhaps all too common can readily develop where the focus becomes one of merely monitoring the family's situation and waiting for the next catastrophe to occur when more appropriate action may be taken. These situations are no doubt unavoidable in child abuse work. It seems a careful assessment in the early stages while the child is still in hospital, to some extent mitigates against this.

I have argued the importance and value of social work assessment role in a total management programme but I would like to look at some difficulties in sustaining this role. These problems are centred mainly around the impact of the parent's behaviour on the social worker. The anxiety aroused in staff when caring for the abused child and his family has been well recognized in the literature. If it is not understood and contained it can result in denial of the problem and/or punitive attacks on the parents.[15] The effects of these feelings can take more subtle form, for example the "who done it" investigative approach to families described by Alexander.[9] But, we need to be mindful that it is not only our feelings that can create problems, but also the expectations of the families and that "there were always some who seemed unable to accept one as friendly and helpful, and repulsed all attempts at sympathy and understanding. There is no better way of appreciating the strength of the compulsion such clients are under to recreate the present in the image of the past than to observe the determination with which they insist that one must play some role of their choosing, whether it be teacher, judge or policeman."[18] Some families' guilt can make them very hostile and rejecting of the social worker, making her feel helpless and impotent, so that it becomes very arduous to sustain a commitment to look beyond the family's defensiveness. At other times, for example when a child dies from injuries inflicted by his parents, it is hard too for the social worker and the team to believe in the value of an assessment when confronted with feelings about such irreparable damage. However, it is precisely at these times an assessment is vital if the social worker is to be of help to the family during the subsequent events.

Child abuse presents social workers with painful personal and professional issues. It seems so much of the social worker's professional identity is associated with the way she is perceived as being caring, understanding and helpful. It is often difficult for the social worker to carry through with actions which are likely to provoke further the parents' anger and hostility. The social worker may intellectually acknowledge the necessity of these actions not only to protect the child but also the parents from the consequences of their violent, destructive behaviour. Emotionally, it is still stressful, particularly when in Australia the authority and control elements of social work are usually not well integrated into practice. Good case consultation, apart from, for example case conferences, is vital to enable the social worker to follow through with such tasks as facing parents with painful decisions and helping the parents bear them. If workers are not supported with the inevitable uncertainties, conflicts and frustrations of this work, they are often at risk of turning away from direct work with families and giving excessive attention to structure and administrative procedures in the hope of finding a solution to their dilemma.

## THE CHILD PSYCHIATRIST AND CHILD ABUSE
## Robert Adler

Child psychiatry, like most other child health disciplines, denied that child abuse existed as a serious problem until recently. In the past 20 years, however child psychiatrists have been involved in assessing abused children and their parents and in contributing in various other ways to child abuse programmes. The role of the child psychiatrist in any programme is determined by two key factors: firstly, the basic skills which he can bring to bear; secondly, the specific needs of and other resources available to the particular programme which determine to some extent the role of the child psychiatrist within it.

The model of the mental health consultaton[19] will be used to consider the role of the child psychiatrist in the light of the author's experience as the child psychiatric consultant to the child abuse programme, first of a major metropolitan paediatric teaching hospital and, subsequently, to a regional programme in a large urban centre in New South Wales. This approach assumes that child psychiatrists are a rare and expensive commodity who will almost invariably act as consultants rather than primary care-givers.

The key questions in any mental health consultation are "Who is the client?" and "What is the purpose of the consultation?"

## Client Centred Case Consultation

In this instance, the consultant is asked to assess the client, the child and his parents, and to make recommendations about treatment. The child psychiatrist, with his knowledge of the psychosocial development of the child, as well as an understanding of family dynamics, is in a unique position to offer consultation in selected cases. The major purpose of the child psychiatrist's involvement is to ensure that the child's needs remain paramount, despite the neediness of his parents. The experienced consultant should be able to advise the consultee in terms familiar to the latter, rather than in jargon comprehensible only to fellow child psychiatrists.

### Case Illustration

The smaller of twins was admitted to hospital for the fourth time for investigation of failure to thrive. She was below the third percentile for height and weight and physical investigations had failed to establish a cause. Consultation was sought and a family assessment carried out. The focus of the consultation was the family's isolation from their usual supports and the impact of early separation from the baby. The parents were encouraged to ventilate their feelings, to be involved in the care of their daughter in hospital and referral was made to a local "mother of twins" group through the baby health centre.

## Consultee Centred Case Consultation

The primary goal in this situation is to increase the consultee's expertise in dealing with similar patients. Therefore, the consultant will only rarely see the patients himself and then only after careful discussion of the indications and contraindications for direct assessment. Given that work in the area of child abuse gives rise to powerful emotions on the part of the workers[20] one vital function of the child psychiatrist or similarly trained consultant is to help the primary workers to contain their anxiety. In this way, workers can be helped to avoid collusion with the parents (denying abuse has taken place) or identification with the child, leading to a punitive attack on the parents.

*Case Illustration*

In the case described above, considerable time was spent with the ward nursing staff discussing the importance of their helping the mother to care for her own baby, rather than undermining her by demonstrating their competence. Also, ward discussions allowed the staff to ventilate their feelings of rejection towards the mother. This enabled the staff to understand and accept her more readily.

## Programme Centred Administrative Consultation

The client here is no longer the abusive family, but rather the child abuse programme and its workers. Fletcher and Adler[20] have underlined the risk of abusive feelings experienced by the family enveloping the workers as well. The outcome of this situation is likely to be the development of divisions among workers with a search for scapegoats who can be held responsible for therapeutic failures. The consultant's understanding of group dynamics, expecially as they apply to child abuse programmes, is essential to the fulfilment of this function. While the consultant need not be a child psychiatrist, he or a psychiatric social worker are the ones most likely to have the necessary skills.

*Case Illustration*

The author was asked to take over as chairman of a Suspected Child Abuse and Neglect (SCAN) programme from the local paediatrician. A lack of resources combined with insufficient understanding of the group's dynamics had led to the previous chairman becoming the scapegoat for the group's problems. These problems were at least in part a function of the group attempting to perform too many incompatible tasks, as will be described below.

## Consultee Centred Administrative Consultation

Such a consultation is usually initiated by someone responsible for the organization of a programme who is concerned about the way it is running. The requirement here is for an outside consultant who is more objective by virtue of not being embroiled in the feelings of workers in the programme itself. The primary focus of the consultation is not the programme, but rather the consultee's expertise as in the consultee centred case consultation. Clearly, it is not necessary for this consultant to be a child psychiatrist.

*Case Illustration*

In the situation described above, the establishment of a new child protection centre in the area led to the revision and renaming of the SCAN group. The previous group's functions were divided among an advisory group under the author's chairmanship; a small panel of consultants, available for case conferences; and a supervision group aimed at supporting workers involved directly with abusive families.

The roles outlined above cannot always be kept as distinct as suggested. Furthermore, one person could not possibly fulfil all of these functions simultaneously, and indeed, some are mutually exclusive. Therefore, the child psychiatrist's contribution needs to be decided on the basis of his personal skills and the needs and other resources available to the programme. The first two types of mental health consultation are clearly the domain of the child psychiatrist where one is available. The last two may be offered by a child psychiatrist, but could equally well be done by another professional with training and expertise in group dynamics and the running of a child abuse programme.

## Notes

1   C H Kempe, F N Silverman, B F Steele, W Droegemueller and H K Silver, "The Battered Child Syndrome" (1962) *JAMA* **181**:17

2   J T Weston, "The Pathology of Child Abuse" in R E Helfer and C H Kempe (eds) *The Battered Child,* 2nd ed (University of Chicago Press, Chicago, 1974)

3   A E Skinner and R C Castle, *Seventy-eight Battered Children: A Retrospective Study* (NSPCC, London, 1969)

4   H P Martin and P Beezley, "Behavioural Observations of Abused Children" (1977) *Devl Med Child Neurol* **19**:373

5   M A Lynch, "Ill Health and Child Abuse" (1975) *Lancet* **1**:317

6   R K Oates, A A Davis and M G Ryan, "Predictive Factors for Child Abuse" (1980) *Aust Paediat J* **17**:239

7   E Davoren, "The Role of the Social Worker" in R E Helfer and C H Kempe (eds) *The Battered Child* (University of Chicago Press, Chicago, 1968)

8   J Stroud, "The Social Worker's Role" in A W Franklin (Ed) *Concerning Child Abuse* (Churchill Livingstone, Edinburgh, 1975)

9   H Alexander, "The Social Worker and the Family" in C H Kempe and R E Helfer (eds) *Helping the Battered Child and his Family* (University of Chicago Press, Chicago, 1972)

10  J Chapman, "Social Work Intervention in Cases of Child Abuse" in A W Franklin (ed) *The Challenge of Child Abuse* (Academic Press, London, 1977)

11  M Lynch, "Annotation: The Prognosis of Child Abuse" (1978) *J Child Psychiat* **19**:175

12  J Roberts, "There's more to Child Abuse than Spotting Bruises" (1978) *Community Care* June 28

13  J Trowell, "Child Abuse: The Role of a Consultant Psychiatrist in a Specialist Institution" (1981) *Child Abuse and Neglect* **5**:23

14  I Salzberger-Wittenberg, *Psychoanalytic Insights and Relationships — A Kleinian Approach* (Routledge and Kegan Paul, London, 1970) p 142

15   B F Steele, *Working with Abusive Parents from a Psychiatric Point of View* (US Dept Health, Education and Welfare, 1975)

16   D G Gill, *Violence against Children* (Harvard University Press, Cambridge, Massachusetts, 1970)

17   D Lagerberg, "Child Abuse: A Literature Review" (1978) *Acta Paediat Scand* **67**:683

18   E E Irvine, "The Function and Use of Relationship between Client and Psychiatric Social Worker" (1952) *Br J Psychiat Social Work* **6**:23

19   G Caplan, "Types of Mental Health Consultation" (1963) *Am J Orthopsychiat* **33**:470

20   L Fletcher and R G Adler, "Prevention of Abuse by the Child Abuse Team: The Consultant's Responsibility?" in E J Anthony and C Chiland (eds) *The Child and His Family* Vol 6 (J Wiley and Sons, New York, 1980)

## Chapter 4

# Contamination of the Foetal Environment — A Form of Prenatal Abuse

Anthony Lipson

In our society standards of nutrition and obstetric care and the virtual elimination of infectious disease and gastroenteritis as significant causes of mortality has resulted in a situation where up to 20 per cent of all still-births and infant deaths can be associated with severe birth defect. In addition there is a large number of children in the community with disorders of growth and brain development which are thought to have their origins in prenatal development.

For the purposes of this chapter prenatal abuse is discussed in the broad context of how exposure of the foetus to drugs, alcohol and other toxic substances may damage foetal development. However I do intend to confine myself to scientifically proven causes of foetal wastage, birth defects and disorders of growth and development in babies and children. So many times one is confronted with an assumed connecton of a drug or substance to an adverse effect of the foetus. These claims are often exposed to vigorous publicity in newspapers and journals. However when a valid scientific study then refutes or is unable to confirm the initial claims, these results do not receive the same measure of publicity that heralded the initial report. I will confine myself to agents which have a valid and scientific basis for a claim that they can abuse the foetus or agents worth mentioning for their lack of an effect. The reader is directed to the excellent review articles for in-depth analysis of individual agents.[1,2,3,4]

The effect of any agent on the foetus depends not only on obvious variables such as dose and route of administration but also on the time in gestation that the insult occurred, the length of time that it continued, on the genetic makeup of the mother, father and the foetus, in addition to interaction with other agents.

For instance the effect of a teratogen in the first weeks of pregnancy can result in major or minor birth defects. The later stages of foetal development are relatively resistant to abuse. Once an organ is formed an agent cannot then be applied and cause it to develop abnormally. The most notable and important exception is the central nervous system whose later development make it susceptible to *functional* defects such as mental retardation, cerebral palsy and deafness in the second and third trimester.

## PRESCRIBED DRUGS

There is no doubt that the Thalidomide catastrophy has heightened the awareness of the community to the effects of drugs on the foetus. Many drugs have been implicated as the cause of birth defects but only cancer therapeutic agents, anticoagulants, anticonvulsants and Thalidomide itself have been shown conclusively to cause an increased incidence of defects in *human* offspring. There are excellent reviews on this area.[1,2,3,4]

## ALCOHOL

Despite references in Greek mythology, the Bible and literature that alcohol could be dangerous to the foetus it was only since Lemoine, from France in 1968[5] and Jones and Smith from the United States in 1973[6] described their studies that it has been accepted that alcohol can have an adverse effect on the foetus. These children are born with a variety of major and minor malformations including congenital heart disease, cleft palate, mental retardation and cerebral palsy. They are small at birth, grow relatively poorly[7] and have a peculiar facial appearance due to relatively small facial bones, nose and eyes. The incidence of severely affected babies is said to be about two per 1000 live births. The incidence of moderately or mildly affected babies is not known. The difficulties in retrospectively ascertaining the amount of alcohol actually consumed during a pregnancy are great particularly when intake is usually underestimated and even denied. Some studies based on interviews during and after pregnancy have indicated that three standard drinks per day constitute a significant risk to the foetus.[8,9] Acute intoxications or binges particularly early in pregnancy may be important in outcome.[10] Inherent differences in metabolism and tolerance despite prior experience with alcohol, could identify an at-risk group of women who are particularly sensitive to the detrimental effects of alcohol.

Alcohol abuse is commonly associated with abuse of other drugs such as barbituates, narcotics and smoking. Although alcohol consumption by itself is associated with the foetal alcohol syndrome the additive or potentiating effects of other drugs may be important.

## NARCOTICS[1,3,4]

These drugs have generally been assumed not to cause birth defects in humans and in general animal studies have confirmed this. The effect on growth and development appears to be general smallness in both weight and length at birth but as the typical withdrawal symptoms abate at four to six months an acceleration in the growth pattern occurs with catch-up growth. Long-term follow-up of psychomotor development in these babies is still not available but preliminary reports indicate it is normal albeit "near the lower limit".[11]

## LSD AND MARIJUANA

There have been several claims incriminating LSD as a cause of birth defects. The view of the reported cases and animal studies has, however indicated that there is no reason to believe that LSD alone has adverse effects on the foetus.[12] Marijuana has no substantive effect on the human foetus and animal studies in general have been negative.

## SMOKING

Smoking alone does not appear to cause birth defects. However there is a direct relationship between the weight of the newborn child and the number of cigarettes smoked.[13] Studies on postnatal development and brain function are variable and therefore controversial with reading, maths and cognitive skills questioned.[14,15,16]

## INFECTION

Infection with the Rubella virus, particularly in the first trimester is associated with an increase in birth defects such as congenital heart disease and cleft palate, mental deficiency, cataracts and deafness.[1,3] Immunization against Rubella is thought to prevent these effects. Congenital syphilis has been known for many years to cause developmental defects and mental retardation if not treated in the neonatal period.

Cytomegalovirus, herpes virus and toxoplasma infections during the first and second trimesters in a mother will cause central nervous system damage (mental defect, microcephaly) in her offspring.[1,3]

## HEAT

An increase in core temperature of the mother can cause birth defects, physical and mental retardation and miscarriage.[17] Of interest is not only reported cases after infection but those associated with sauna baths.[18] High environmental temperatures do not increase core temperature because of the body's efficient cooling mechanisms from sweating or dilation of the skin blood vessels. However vigorous exercise coupled with a high environmental temperature can cause the core temperature of above 38°C for longer than 24 hours appears to be necessary to produce significant effects on the human foetus.[18]

## VITAMIN DEFICIENCY

In western society specific vitamin deficiency is extremely rare. Some birth defects have been associated with folic acid deficiency. This is a controversial area which seems to revolve around the definition of folate deficiency during pregnancy.[19]

Multi-vitamin supplements have been found in a pilot study[10] to reduce the incidence of neural tube defects in at risk pregnancies. Whether this constitutes a direct effect or correction of a deficiency remains to be elucidated.

## VITAMIN EXCESS

Excess amounts of vitamin A and D have been shown in many animal studies and some human case reports to cause birth defects, foetal wastage and adverse effects on growth and development.[3,4]

## METABOLIC DISEASES

### Phenylketonuria

Offspring of mothers with Phenylketonuria show mental retardation, increased incidence of birth defects such as congenital heart disease and cleft palate, are small-for-dates at birth and have poor growth thereafter.[21] Mothers with classic Phenylketonuria are most at risk of abnormal offspring, though some studies indicate that hyperphenylalanaemia can increase the risk to the foetus.[22] This condition can be treated, and the adverse effects on the foetus obviated by a low phenylalanine diet started prior to conception.[22]

### Diabetes

The offspring of mothers with insulin dependent diabetes have an increased risk of birth defects. The presence of retinopathy or vascular kidney disease could increase this incidence. The quality of control of the diabetes in the first trimester appears to have a close relationship to the incidence of malformation.[23] Good control of insulin dependent diabetes at conception and pregnancy is now thought to be essential to reduce morbidity.[24]

## IRRADIATION[1,4]

That radiation can cause birth defects is well accepted in animal experimentation. However it appears that from both animal studies and the extensive studies of survivors of Hiroshima and Nagasaki that relatively massive doses are needed before an effect is seen on the foetus. No increased malformation rate was observed in mothers who were exposed in the first trimester to the atomic bomb.[25] The major effect appears to be in those who are exposed between the 10th and the 18th week where small heads, mental retardation and to a certain extent intra-uterine growth retardation was recorded. The irradiation received by these women was massive compared with any standard X-ray procedure performed with modern equipment in the human. Therapeutic pelvic radiation for malignancy inevitably involves massive doses and has been associated with brain and eye malformation in addition to spontaneous abortion. The lowest dosages associated with significant effects vary from 10-150 Rads with the real damage occurring with hundreds of Rads. The dose from a single abdominal film is 1 Rad. Radiation exposure is an emotional issue with political overtones. It is however probably safe to have standard X-ray exposure during pregnancy.[26] The risk of cancer in offspring of mothers exposed to X-rays during pregnancy once thought to be increased[27] is now indeterminate due to lower dosage levels. Children exposed in utero to the radiation from the atomic bomb do not show an increased malignancy rate.[28]

## CONCLUSION

A significant number of women are unaware that they are pregnant in the first 60 days of pregnancy when agents can cause miscarriage and major and minor birth defects. Any progress aimed at reducing the effect of these agents by reduction or avoidance during pregnancy must not neglect this most critical period. Recognition that combinations of agents can have an additive effect on the foetus is important in any individual assessment. The present state of the art should recognize that in 30-50 per cent of all mental and physical defects no specific cause can be identified.

Many of the factors which damage the foetus cannot be prevented. However, excess alchohol, narcotic addiction and even heavy smoking during pregnancy are more clearly areas where the foetus may be damaged by the direct action of the mother, even though this would usually be unintentional. Education and publicity, while providing only a partial answer is one area that should be explored to reduce this form of foetal abuse.

# Notes

1   T H Shepherd, "Teratogenicity of Therapeutic Agents" (1979) *Current Problems in Paediatrics* **10** No 2

2   J D Scrimageour, *Towards the Prevention of Foetal Malformation* (Edinburgh University Press, 1979)

3   J G Wilson and E. Clarke Fraser, *Handbook of Teratology* Vol 1 (Plenum Press, New York, 1977)

4   G F Chernoff and K L Jones, "Teratogens and the Unborn Baby" (1981) *Paediatric Annals* **10**:210

5   P Lemoine, H Harousseau and J P Berteyrn, "Les Enfants de Parents Alcooliques" (1968) *Ouest Medical* **25**:476

6   K L Jones, D W Smith, C N Ulleland and A P Streissgath, "Pattern of Malformation in Offspring of Alcoholic Mothers" (1973) *Lancet* **1**:781

7   S J Clarren and D W Smith, "The Foetal Alcohol Syndrome" (1978) *N Engl J Med* **298**:1063

8   J W Hanson, A P Streissguth and D W Smith, "The Effects of Moderate Alcohol Consumption during Pregnancy on Foetal Growth and Morphogenesis" (1978) *J Paediatrics* **92**:457

9   R E Little, "Moderate Alcohol Use during Pregnancy and Decreased Birth Weight" (1957) *Am J Public Health* **67**:1154

10  W S Webster, D A Walsh, A H Lipson and S E McEwen, "Teratogenesis after Acute Alcohol Exposure in Mice" (1980) *Neurobehavioural Toxicology* **2**.227

11  I J Chesnoff, R Hetcher and W J Burns, "Early Growth Patterns of Methadone Addicted Infants" (1980) *Am J Dis Child* **134**:1049

12  J M Aase, N Laestahdius and D W Smith, "Children of Mothers who took LSD in Pregnancy" (1970) *Lancet* **2**:100

13  T H Merritt, "Smoking Mothers Affect Little Lives" (1981) *Am J Dis Child* **135**:507

14  J B Hardy and D D Mellitts, "Does Maternal Smoking during Pregnancy Have a Long-term Effect on the Child? (1972) *Lancet* **2**:1332

15  R Davie, N Butler and H Goldstein, *From Birth to Seven — the Second Report of the National Child Development Study* (Longman, London, 1972)

16  H G Dunn, A K McBurney, S Ingram and C M Hunter, "Maternal Cigarette Smoking during Pregnancy and the Child's Subsequent Development" (1977) *Can J Public Health* **68**:43

17  D W Smith, S K Clarren and M A Harvey, "Hyperthermia as a Possible Teratogenic Agent" (1978) *J Pediatrocs* **92**:878

18  H Pleet, J M Grahame and D W Smith, "CNS and Facial Defect Associated with Maternal Hyperthermia at 4-14 Weeks Gestation" (1981) *Pediatrics* **67**:785

19  E D Hibbard and R W Smithells, "Folic acid Metabolism and Human Embryopathy" (1965) *Lancet* **1**:1254

20  R W Smithells and S Shepperd, "Possible Prevention of Neural Tube Defects by Preconceptual Vitamin Supplementation" (1980) *Lancet* **1**:339

21  A H Lipson, J S Yu, M O'Halloran and R D Williams, "Alcohol and Phenylketonuria" (1981) *Lancet* **1**:717

22  R R Larke and A H Levy (1981), "Maternal Phenylketonuria and Hyperphenylalanaemia" (1980) *N Engl J Med* **281**:1202

23   E Miller, J W Hare, J P Cloherty and P J Dunn, "Elevated Maternal
     Haemoglobin A1c in early Pregnancy and Major Congenital Anomalies in
     Infants of Diabetic Mothers" (1981) *N Engl J Med* **304**:1331

24   N Freinkel, "Pregnant Thoughts About Diabetes" (1981) *N Engl J Med*
     **304**:1357

25   G Plummer, "Anomalies Occurring in Children Exposed In Utero to the Atomic
     Bomb in Hiroshima" (1952) *Pediatrics* **10**:687

26   H M Swartz and B A Reichling, "Hazards of Radiation Exposure for Pregnant
     Women" (1978) *JAMA* **239**:1907

27   J F Bithell and A M Stewart, "Pre-natal Irradiation and Childhood Malig-
     nancy" (1975) *Br J Cancer* **31**:271

28   H Kato, "Mortality in Children Exposed to the Atomic Bomb In Utero" (1971)
     *Am J Epidemiology* **93**:435

# Chapter 5

# The Maternity Unit —The Beginnings of Attachment

Robert Adler

"Begin at the beginning", the King said gravely, "and go on till you come to the end: then stop".

> Lewis Carroll,
> *Alice's Adventures in Wonderland*

The discovery of antisepsis by Semmelweiss in the late nineteenth century was a major step in the reduction of maternal obstetric mortality. It also represented the beginning of modern, scientific, hospital obstetrics which, ironically, has probably done more to hamper the normal development of a relationship between the mother and her newborn than any other single event in the history of mankind. It is only in the last twenty years that the trend towards "sterile" hospital obstetrics has begun to reverse. The popularity of this move towards more family oriented obstetrics with greater paternal involvement and the appearance of alternatives to traditional hospital labour ward delivery speaks for itself. Many factors have contributed to this change in attitude, including: the insistence of the women's movement that women should have a greater say in the delivery of their babies; the trend towards the demystification of medicine; the work of Bowlby[1] and others in drawing attention to the importance of "attachment" between mother and infant for later development; the widely acclaimed technique of delivery advocated by Leboyer[2] and the recognition of the serious consequences of "failure of bonding" such as non-organic failure to thrive and child abuse.[3] Attachment or bonding as it is more popularly known runs the risk of becoming the slogan of the eighties. The risk of such a fad is that bonding is seen as an end in itself rather than a small part of an ongoing process which begins before birth and continues long after. Such zeal readily turns to disillusionment if unrealistic expectations are not realized.

49

The process of maternal-infant bonding in the maternity unit and its bearing on child abuse will be considered in the light of these remarks.

If bonding is the process by which a parent or parents develop a relationship with their baby then clearly we should listen to the advice of the wise king and "begin at the beginning".

## PREGNANCY

When a woman learns she is pregnant, there are many factors which determine her feelings about the pregnancy. These include the quality of her relationship with the baby's father, her own experiences as a young child and her present relationship with her own mother, her previous experiences of pregnancy, her current social and economic circumstances and the circumstances surrounding this pregnancy. In most instances these factors also lead to a degree of ambivalence about the pregnancy. But if negative feelings outweigh positive over a period of time, then the opportunity may lead to a decision to terminate a pregnancy, to surrender a baby for adoption or to sufficient resolution of the negative feelings to allow the pregnancy to continue.

As the pregnancy continues these feelings will be modified to some extent by events during pregnancy such as her own physical well-being, any illnesses which might jeopardize the baby's well-being, other life stresses such as changes in the relationships outlined above or bereavements. Thus long before "movements" begin the mother will have strong feelings about the baby. With the appearance of movements and the associated physical changes the pregnancy is often described by the mother as becoming more "real". For the first time qualities of the foetus make themselves felt in the form of varying activity levels. The determinants, maternal or foetal, of these activity levels, remain unclear. It has been suggested that maternal anxiety may have some effect, or that intra-uterine activity levels are the earliest expression of infantile temperament.[4] In either case movements will effect the mother's feelings about her baby, her expectations and her sense of "fit" with it.

The importance of the feelings which develop during pregnancy are best seen in the event of miscarriage or stillbirth. In both cases there is a period of mourning which varies in duration. Frequently mothers are encouraged to deny this mourning by advice to get pregnant again as soon as possible, rather than allowing the sadness over one loss to be resolved before embarking on a further pregnancy.

## DELIVERY

A pregnant woman is often described as being "expectant". Delivery is the culmination of this period of expectation and as such represents a developmental crisis in the life of the family. As with any crisis there is the potential for change: for the better, with the development of new coping skills; or for the worse, with resort to more pathological ways of coping. The outcome of this crisis will be determined by many factors including those already listed, as well as the mother's premorbid personality, the experience of delivery and the baby itself.

Current obstetric practice can be broadly categorized into four types:

(1)   High technology obstetrics where the technology is essential for the safety of mother and baby.

(2)   High technology obstetrics for its own sake, which includes the use of routine induction, analgesic medication and foetal monitoring.

(3)   Low technology obstetrics where this is safe for mother and baby.

(4)   Low technology obstetrics which is simply hazardous.

In recent years there has been a move, endorsed to greater or lesser degree by the medical and nursing professions, from the second to the third type of practice. Much of this move has been based on current fashion and relatively little exposed to critical research. A recent editorial in a leading medical journal[5] described Leboyer's book *Birth Without Violence*[2] as "an appealing work of art that celebrates the joy of normal birth and protests against unnecessary violence during delivery". The same editorial goes on to point out that scientific oversimplification should not be used as a justification for not providing pregnant women with ample support and opportunity for contact with their babies and families. The writer is commenting on a randomized clinical trial of Leboyer delivery[6] which concluded that when compared to a gentle but conventional delivery at which husbands were present and early postpartum contact was encouraged, only two significant differences between the groups were found. Eight months later the Leboyer group were more likely to say that the event had influenced their child's behaviour and the Leboyer group also had shorter active labours. This study at least raises some questions about Leboyer's ambitious claim that children born by his method grow up "free without conflict".[2]

In another study the outcome for mothers and babies in an alternative birth centre was compared to that of conventional delivery.[7] The groups were not randomized and the author comments on the different approach to pregnancy of the two groups. The outcomes were generally better for the babies in the alternative birth centre group. Of particular interest is the complete absence of child abuse in this group, compared to a 2·4 per cent incidence in the conventional group. This difference in child abuse may be partly explained by the differences in attitude to pregnancy of the groups and also the 3 per cent incidence of congenital anomalies among the conventional group, compared with 0·6 per cent in the study group. However, the alternative birth group did have a higher incidence of meconium aspiration and readmission and the mothers in this group had a higher incidence of postpartum complications, mainly infections.

However, if there is little research to support some of the "gimmicks" of delivery which are currently fashionable there is equally little research to support the use of high technology in routine obstetrics. Indeed studies such as those cited above suggest that the outcome of low technology obstetrics may be as good or better than that of high technology among carefully selected patients. With whom should the onus of proof reside? Should the advocates of high technology be required to demonstrate an improved outcome through the use of their technical advances? Should the advocates of low technology have to show an improved outcome or is the lack of a worse outcome sufficient evidence to support their claims? These are essential questions when one is considering how much freedom of choice to give parents and whether obstetricians and midwives are prepared to step down from their roles as "directors" of delivery and assume the less glamorous roles of "co-stars" with the family.[8] Garbarino points out that changes in institutionalized practices such as obstetrics frequently are hampered by inertia and prejudice amongst doctors, nurses and hospital administrators.[8]

## EARLY CONTACT

Having successfully delivered the baby, what of early contact? Many ethological studies in animals have demonstrated the critical place of early contact between mother and infant in a variety of species.[9] Contact during this critical or sensitive period is essential for normal development and in some species, for survival. However, there is clearly variation between species in the nature and timing of this period. The evidence for a similar period in humans is much less clear. Prior to the last 20 years the newborn was often seen by scientists as a passive recipient of care whose senses to events around him were relatively dull. In keeping with this view was the classical psychoanalytic position that early affectional bonds depended upon the infant's oral needs being satisfied. More recently a great deal of evidence to the contrary has been forthcoming. It is now clear that the healthy newborn who is *not* sedated by obstetric analgesics is both alert and receptive to a large range of sensory stimuli; visual, auditory, olfactory and tactile.[10]

The recognition of this phase together with the pioneering work of Klaus and Kennell[3] has drawn attention to the importance of skin contact between mother and infant immediately after birth in the development of a good relationship. In these studies mothers were allowed to spend an hour with their infants immediately after the birth and to spend an additional five hours each day for the first three days of the puerperium. The outcome for the two groups was significantly different on a number of parameters. The extended contact group spent more time fondling their babies and holding them in the "en-face" position. At 12 months extended contact mothers spent more time soothing their babies during a physical examination. At two years and five years the early contact group showed evidence of more advanced speech development.[3]

However, the significance of some of these differences is as yet unclear. Further evidence for the importance of early contact is drawn from the problems facing the premature infant who has to be cared for in a humidicrib.[3] Until recently fear of infection, at times unfounded, has been used to keep parents out of premature nurseries. The most dramatic consequence of this practice was the increased incidence of child abuse among these infants.[11] In addition, the clinical experience of paediatricians and child psychiatrists such as this author confirm the sense of alienation reported by many of these mothers with words such as: "It was like I didn't have a baby" and "When I got him home I was scared to touch him." Much significance has been attached to the visiting patterns of mothers in this situation.[3,12] While maternal visiting may well be an important indicator of the mother's interest and involvement with her baby, it is equally important that institutional determinants of this behaviour should not be ignored. Hospitals may overtly or covertly discourage mothers from visiting their infants. An awareness of even the premature baby's ability to respond to sensory stimulation has led to the provision of early stimulation in many intensive care nurseries. The short-term benefits in terms of cognitive development and alertness of these stimulated babies is clear.[3] It is also clear that many mothers involved in such programmes feel more confident with and less "cut off" from their babies when they are eventually discharged from hospital. However, the long-term effects of such programmes are much less clear. This is discussed in Chapter 8.

Although recent interest has centred on the question of early contact immediately after birth, a debate of much longer standing has focused on the question of "rooming-in". Rooming-in is of course not new. In fact it is only with the advent of hospital obstetrics that any alternative was available. As with "early contact" there has been relatively little research which critically examines the benefits or otherwise of rooming-in. One possible problem of research in this area has been the selection of inappropriate outcome criteria. Attempts to demonstrate that rooming-in or early contact have lifelong consequences for personality development and babies growing up "free without conflict" are far too ambitious and therefore doomed to failure. These studies are critically reviewed in Chapter 7. Such research is a reflection of the "one shot" attitude to bonding, rather than an attitude which sees the maternity hospital and early contact as just one step in the development of a relationship. Rutter, in a recent review, points out that "claims concerning a sensitive period for maternal attachment rather outrun the empirical evidence".[13] It may be more appropriate and sufficient to demonstrate that these practices lead to parents feeling more confident with their babies at the time they are discharged from hospital. Such evidence could then be used as part of an education campaign aimed at encouraging parents to seek, and hospitals to provide, opportunities for greater contact whenever possible. Rutter even raises the possibility that the ill effects of early separation may be as much a function of hospitals denying mothers' contact as of a lack of skin to skin contact.[13]

The available research would seem to support the notion that in humans there is a period during which maternal-infant contact helps to promote a good relationship. This is in keeping with the concept of "primary maternal preoccupation" which Winnicott described as an illness were it not for the fact of the pregnancy. Winnicott says the following of this phase of maternal development:

It gradually develops and becomes a state of heightened sensitivity during, and especially towards the end of, the pregnancy. It lasts for a few weeks after the birth of the child. It is not easily remembered by mothers once they have recovered from it.

I would go further and say that the memory mothers have of this state tends to become repressed.[14]

Although most of the data advocating early contact was not available when Winnicott wrote this, it may be that early contact is an important variable in promoting this maternal state. This stage of heightened sensitivity may help the mother to identify or feel "in tune" with her child. However, the *absence* of such early contact does not mean that a good relationship cannot be established. Winnicott acknowledges that the adoptive mother "who can be ill in the sense of primary maternal preoccupation" can also make a successful adaptation. It is clear from the successful outcome of many premature and adopted infants that a significant proportion of infants and parents are able to adapt. However, both premature and adopted groups have been shown to have an increased risk of subsequent difficulties in many developmental areas.[15,16,17] Many factors including genetic and physical variables in the infant, as well as a range of maternal and environmental variables may be significant in determining this relatively poor outcome. The real challenge for those interested in the development of satisfactory maternal-infant relationship may be the identification of vulnerable mothers and babies so that therapeutic efforts can be concentrated on this group.

With this approach, interference by the experts can remain minimal with those able to look after themselves. It does not matter from a scientific standpoint whether parents choose to be delivered by the Leboyer or any other method provided these are compatible with safe obstetrics for mother and infant. The mere fact that the "customers" (patients) see these techniques as desirable and the "salesmen" (the health professionals) can safely provide them is sufficient justification for their use. This also recognizes that many of these practices are determined by a wide range of sociocultural fashions and will undoubtedly change with time. The role of the health professionals is to remain sufficiently open-minded to be able to critically examine such fashions, only rejecting those which are unsafe.

**"And go on till you come to the end: then stop."**

With the current preoccupation with bonding and early contact there is a danger that parents and professionals will see this as an end in itself. Thus if all has gone according to plan they can sit back complacently feeling nothing more needs to be done. If, on the other hand, all has not gone as planned there is a danger of parents in particular feeling that all is lost.

The maternity unit is clearly only the beginning, or rather the climax of the first phase of the attachment process. The relationship between the child and his parents continues to evolve over many years effected by many constitutional and environmental variables. Therefore, despite the King's advice, an end is difficult to define.

# Notes

1  J Bowlby, *Attachment and Loss* Vol I (Basic Books, New York, 1969)

2  F Leboyer, *Birth Without Violence* (Knopf, New York, 1976)

3  M H Klaus and J H Kennell (eds), *Maternal-Infant Bonding* (C V Mosby Co, Saint Louis 1976)

4  A Thomas and S Chess, *Temperament and Development* (Brunner and Mazel, New York, 1977)

5  R S Duff, "Care in Childbirth and Beyond" (Editorial) *N Engl J Med* **302**:685-6

6  N Nelson, M Erkin, S Saigel et al, "A Randomized Clinical Trial of the Leboyer Approach to Childbirth" (1980) *N Engl J Med* **302**:655-61

7  R C Goodlin, "Low-risk Obstetric Care for Low-risk Mothers" (1980) *Lancet* **1**:1017-9

8  J Garbarino, "Changing Hospital Childbirth Practices" (1980) *Am J Orthopsychiat* **50**:588-97

9  M Trause, M H Klaus and J H Kennell, "Maternal Behaviour in Mammals" in M K Klaus and J H Kennell (eds) *Maternal-Infant Bonding* (C V Mosby Co, Saint Louis, 1976) pp 38-98

10  R N Ende and J Robinson, "The First Two Months: Recent Research in Developmental Psychobiology and the Changing View of the Newborn" in J H Noshpitz (ed-in-chief) *Basic Handbook of Child Psychiatry* Vol 1 (Basic Books, New York, 1979)

11  R S Hunter, N Kilstrom, E N Draybill, et al, "Antecedents of Child Abuse and Neglect in Premature Infants: A Prospective Study in a Newborn Intensive Care Unit" (1978) *Pediatrics* **61**:629-35

12  K Minde, S Trehub, C Carter et al, "Mother-Child Relationships in the Premature Nursery: An Observational Study" (1978) *Pediatrics* **61**:373-9

13  M Rutter, "Separation Experiences: A New Look at an Old Topic" (1979) *J Pediatrics* **95**:147-54

14  D W Winnicott, "Primary Maternal Pre-occupation" in Winnicott D W, *Through Pediatrics to Psycho-Analysis* (Basic Books, New York, 1975) pp 300-305

15  A M McWhinnie, *Adopted Children — How They Grow Up* (Routledge and Kegan Paul, London, 1967)

16  J Seglow, M K Pringle and P Wedge, *Growing Up Adopted* (National Foundation of Educational Research, Great Britain, 1972)

17  B Tizard and J Rees, "A Comparison of the Effects of Adoption, Restoration to the Natural Mother and Continued Institutionalization on the Cognitive Development of Four Year Old Children" (1974) *Child Dev* **45**:92

Chapter 6

# Hospital Practices that Strengthen Parent-Infant Attachment

Robyn Dolby, Brian English and Ann Murray

Child abuse represents, in extreme form, the breakdown of the parent-child relationship. It is anticipated that early efforts to help strengthen that relationship will also tend to reduce the likelihood of child abuse occurring. In this chapter we examine some ways in which hospital procedures can facilitate the beginning parent-infant bond. It is our belief that parents' long-term commitment to their child is best served through pride in parenting, and in the development of a mutually rewarding parent-infant relationship. Hospital procedures can affect how confident parents feel in their parenting role and influence how they get to know and respond to their new baby. The approaches suggested build upon both parent and infant strengths, in recognition of the important role of the infant as well as the parent in the attachment process.

## HOSPITAL PROCEDURES AND THEIR INFLUENCE ON PARENTS' CONFIDENCE IN THE PARENTING ROLE

**Hospital evaluation which results in parents feeling important to their baby will be a powerful force for parents' earlier and more sensitive attachment.**

### Preparation for Parenthood Classes

Birth represents the first step into parenthood. Preparation for childbirth classes aim to help mothers and fathers participate more autonomously in this experience so that birth is met with a sense of achievement. Doering and Entwisle found that the more preparation a woman had for childbirth, the more aware she was at delivery and that awareness was strongly associated with positive reactions to the birth and baby.[1] These authors suggest that the mothers' positive feelings can be attributed to the rewards of their active achievement.

Background variables like the mothers' education or motivation for a natural childbirth or the level of difficulty of their labour did not relate to these positive reactions. Mothers who responded more positively to their infants continued to have a more satisfying mother-child relationship in the immediate postpartum period, as shown by their preference for rooming-in rather than nursery care and a more successful breast-feeding relationship.

Lumley and Astbury caution that preparation classes must be accurate, in particular emphasizing the individual differences in labour and delivery, in order to be supportive for parents.[2] A recent survey of Australian women found that mothers attending childbirth classes were more knowledgeable about labour and delivery but were less positive in their adjustment to birth, when interviewed in the week after delivery.[3] Their actual experience of childbirth, particularly in relation to pain, did not match their expectations, so that many mothers judged themselves as not coping and felt unsuccessful. The more preparation classes can be tailored to the individual mother the better; so too with labour and delivery and postnatal care.

### Support During Labour and Delivery

Newton and Newton report that mothers who received more reassurance and personal care from attendants during labour and delivery were more pleased at first sight of their babies.[4] Following these clinical observations Klaus and Kennell designed a well controlled study to investigate the impact of human companionship on labour and delivery.[5] The study was conducted in Guatemala where women usually labour alone. The introduction of a supportive lay woman (doula) during labour of healthy primigravidous women was associated with both major perinatal and psychological benefits. Labour was shortened and mothers were more attentive and responsive to their infants in the first hour after delivery in the support group. Unexpectedly, the likelihood of development of certain complications requiring intervention (like arrests of labour and foetal distress) was lower for mothers who had had a supportive companion. Initial assignment of mothers to the support or control groups was at random, but it was necessary to admit 103 control compared to 33 support mothers to obtain 20 in each group with uncomplicated labours and normal deliveries. Klaus and Kennell suggest that the supportive companion reduced maternal anxiety. Perhaps similar or greater benefits could be expected when a family member or friend remains with the mother through labour and delivery and values her efforts.

*Early Contact and Rooming-in*

Practices like provision of immediate postpartum contact and rooming-in can communicate to the parent that they are the most important person to their infant. This positive evaluation is a good start for helping parents adjust to the responsibilities of parenthood. Seashore studied mothers who had delivered infants prematurely.[6] Half the mothers had no contact with their infants during the three weeks of special care; the remaining mothers were admitted to the nursery and encouraged to touch and handle their babies. During the first month post-discharge mothers were not observed to differ significantly in their parenting skill but separated mothers, especially primiparas, were less confident in their own parenting abilities. Two years later, five out of the 21 families who had been separated from their infants were divorced. In the 22 families with premature infants who had had contact one was divorced. By including mothers in the caretaking team the hospital was acknowledging the mother's strengths as a parent. With this recognition mothers, and also fathers, when included, presumably have a firmer base from which to adjust to the stress of a premature birth.

Hospital procedures which positively evaluate fathers as well as mothers will strengthen parenting resources within the family. Recent research indicates that fathers play an important role in infancy. Fathers respond to newborn babies as sensitively as mothers do[7] and their infants show strong attachment to them in the first year.[8] Early on fathers emerge as important play partners to their infants: they have been found to devote more time to play than mothers[9,10], offer a different style of play[8,11] and infants show a stronger preference for them as playmates.[8,12] Through a supportive relationship with the mother, the father also contributes to a more successful mother-infant relationship.[13]

It is anticipated that if fathers are given early support to value their own as well as their partner's role, there will be consequent benefits to the parent-infant relationship. Procedures in hospital which give fathers more opportunity to be with their infant and practice caretaking skills during the postpartum hospital period have been found to increase their involvement at home.[14,15] These fathers also indicated more positive adjustment to parenting, expressing less resentment and concern about the disruptive impact of an infant on their lives.

Although hospital procedures can help parents adjust to parenthood and feel more adequate in their role, considerable care must be taken when implementing support systems. Too often procedures which are introduced to give parents more support are associated with improvement and become standards which are used to evaluate future parents. The task is to help all parents make their individual adjustment to parenting. In terms of postnatal care, for instance, being supportive may involve very different care for different mothers. One mother may benefit from being mothered as she adjusts to the responsibility of a new baby. Another may benefit from staff immediately sharing the excitement of her baby with her. For the first mother early rooming-in may be overwhelming; for the second mother rooming-in would be an obvious immediate support for attachment. Similarly with fathers, more participation in the postpartum period may cause difficulties in well-established and satisfying role definitions in some families. The goal should be supportive care where parents feel that their contribution is valued and their individual needs are given primary recognition. This is especially important because it is *against this background* that parents not only care for but also learn about their new baby.

## HOSPITAL PROCEDURES AND THEIR INFLUENCE ON THE DEVELOPMENT OF A MUTUALLY REWARDING PARENT-INFANT RELATIONSHIP.

**Attachment will be enhanced if hospital practices become geared to both the infant and the parent as interactive persons who from the very first moment of birth are negotiating this important relationship.**

### The Socially Competent Newborn

Following a *normal* delivery, infants are exquisitely sensitive to their new surroundings. Many of the babies' early behaviours may help mothers and fathers feel close to them. Wolff has established that the infant may be in a prolonged alert state following birth, something which is most unusual for the rest of the postnatal week.[16] During this time the infant can focus and follow and prefers face-like configurations to all others.[17] The eye-to-eye contact afforded by the baby's alert behaviour would appear especially rewarding to parents. Mothers are particularly interested in their baby's eyes.[18,19] When given their infants after birth they positioned their baby so they could look into his eyes and some said that once the infant looked at them they felt closer to him in later interactions. Fraiberg has described how difficult it is for mothers of blind babies to feel close to their infants.[20] "Without the affirmation of mutual gazing mothers feel lost and like strangers to their babies until both learn to substitute other means of communication."[18]

The infant can also hear at birth and is attracted to human speech. Even in the first few hours of life, the infant moves in rhythm to his parent's speech.[21] The infant's grasp and ability to mould when cuddled are behaviours which also work to capture parents' affections. For mothers all these rewarding behaviours may be expected to be important in breast-feeding.

These early behaviours may help mothers and fathers respond in a more sensitive way to their babies. Parents may perceive their infant's alert, responsive behaviour as characteristic of a "real person" and be more often guided by their baby when reaching decisions on his care. Studies that have pursued the effects of early and extended postpartum contact consistently indicate more *reciprocity* in the mother-infant relationship: mothers given time with their babies after birth appear more sensitive to the infants' individual response style and infants show more enjoyment of their mothers.

*Early and Extended Postpartum Contact and Reciprocity in the Parent-Infant Relationship*

De Chateau and Wiberg's studies indicated that breast-feeding proceeded more smoothly when mothers experienced early contact with their infants.[22,23,24] Primiparous mothers with contact were much more like multiparas in the handling of their infants, and their babies were more content than infants whose mothers did not have early contact. Breast-feeding was significantly prolonged in early contact mothers and they also gave night feedings for a considerably longer time and experienced less problems with night feeding compared to controls. In other care-giving they were significantly less likely to commence early toilet training. In short, early contact mothers gave the impression of more sensitively adapting their behaviour to that of their infants. At three months the majority of these mothers reported that settling in with their infants had been easy, compared to only a minority of routine care mothers who had help at home for a considerably longer period. De Chateau has been unable to find any constitutional differences between mothers to explain these findings. An alternative explanation is that early contact encouraged maternal sensitivity, which in turn enhanced the quality of the mother-infant relationship.

Whiten studied two groups of English middle class mothers comparable in all respects except early separation from their infants.[25] Continuous contact mothers had their infants with them from birth. Separated mothers were apart from their infants from two to ten days because their babies had minor ailments like mild jaundice. When observed three weeks postpartum, contact infants were more content and their mothers were more responsive when they did cry. Over the next two months contact mothers and infants looked and smiled and vocalized in response to each other more often and social smiling appeared sooner in these babies. In play with toys at four months, the contact mother was more likely to offer the toy so that the infant had to reach or grasp it. Mothers who were separated from their infants were more likely to place the toy in their infant's hands. It is as if contact mothers were creating more possibilities for their infants at an age where the children were learning so much about reaching and grasping. Although subtle, these findings suggest that early contact helped mothers to be more responsive to their individual infants and contributed to a more rewarding relationship.

When disadvantaged, low socio-economic status mothers are given the opportunity to room-in with their babies, there appears to be significant, advantageous consequences for the mother-infant relationship. Klaus and Kennell compared 14 primiparous mothers, mainly young, poorly educated and single, who experienced extended contact with their infants, to 14 similar mothers whose infants were brought to them only for feeding.[18] The mothers given early contact were more responsive to their infants' cries at one month[26] and one year.[27] Observation of a subsample of these mothers and babies indicated that mothers were more verbally responsive toward their infants at two years[28] and their infants showed enhanced language development when assessed at five years.[29] The large follow-up study of O'Connor and Vietze which showed a reduction in child abuse cases in children where there was rooming-in is described in the next chapter. It is well established that poorer, less well educated parents, teenage mothers in particular, are less knowledgeable about infants and hold more unrealistic developmental expectations and less desirable child-rearing attitudes.[30,31] For these parents, early contact with their babies may foster more reciprocal attitudes and help them to become more sensitive towards them.

### The Maternal Sensitive Period

Klaus and Kennell suggest a period of close contact between mother and infant immediately after birth facilitates the establishment of a close bond.[18] They and others observed that mothers who were given extended contact with their newborns following birth were more affectionate toward their infants later on, compared to mothers who received routine care and were not given their babies immediately.[22,32,33] Klaus and Kennell considered the mother's early affectionate response to have a biological basis, and postulated the maternal sensitive period.

Most recently it has been observed that when fathers were also allowed extended contact with their infants at birth, they were also more affectionate toward their infants later on.[34] At six weeks postpartum they touched their infants more and vocalized more often to them, similar to the affectionate behaviour observed for mothers. Furthermore, study of paternal behaviour at birth[35] has shown that fathers greet their newborns with much the same sequence of behaviours as mothers, exploring through touch then increasing eye-to-eye contact with their baby. These observations suggest that maternal hormonal changes may not necessarily trigger mother-to-infant attachment.

Attachment is a *mutual* process between parent and infant that begins *at birth*. From their earliest interactions parents and infants begin to learn about and from each other. Parent responsiveness enables the infant to form expectations about himself and his family that contribute powerfully to his overall development. He learns from his parent's contingent care that his behaviour causes things to happen. Feedback from the parent enables the infant to become more organized and predictable. From this experience the infant develops an expectation for being effective which enhances exploration and the practice of new skills and promotes autonomous development.

Infants who learn that their behaviour will be responded to and their needs met, develop certain expectations about their parents as well as their own mastery. They develop a "working model"[36] of their mother as generally accessible and responsive to them or as a person whom they can trust. In contrast, babies whose mothers appear to disregard their signals or respond to them belatedly or inappropriately may be seen to have no basis for believing their mother to be accessible or responsive; consequently, ". . . they are anxious, not knowing what to expect of her".[37]

In reciprocal fashion, infant responsiveness increases parents' responsiveness and affectionate ties to their baby. From the beginning parents value their infant's reactions, endowing behaviour with highly personal meaning which they react to effectively.[38,39] If the newborn is responsive "his very nature will be a source of self esteem".[40]

Hospital practices concerned with promoting attachment have focused on the parent's potential, usually the mother, for making this relationship and have neglected the infant and what impact his early responses have on the bond that is established. Little attention until now has been paid to how care of the infant in hospital can *also* promote attachment. This will be examined now with emphasis on both healthy infants and infants born at risk.

## THE VALUE OF INFANT RESPONSIVENESS

**As well as providing optimal conditions for the physical well-being of the infant, management in hospital which provides opportunities for infant behavioural organization will result in an infant with whom parents can function well.**

### The Healthy Newborn, Behavioural Organization and Reciprocity

With full-term, healthy babies the immediate task for parents is to help their infant become settled into a more predictable pattern. The ability to soothe their baby is one of the first challenges parents face in the earliest weeks of life. Their success or failure might be expected to have an impact on the beginning parent-infant bond.

Research conducted at Foundation 41[41,42] suggests that medication given during labour can interfere with the infant's early state regulation or organization of waking, sleeping and crying periods. For the first few days following birth, babies whose mothers received epidural anaesthesia were more irritable and less predictable in their behaviour, compared to babies whose mothers received little (brief inhalation of nitrous oxide) or no medication. Although at one month the examiners observed few differences between the groups, mothers who received medication seemed to view their infants less favourably, appearing less responsive to their cries and in general found them more difficult to care for. At 12 month follow-up there was some evidence that these mothers paid less attention to their infants' individual behaviour — appearing less verbally responsive, a little "abrupt" in play and less aware of their infants' current needs and interests. Their infants, in turn, vocalized less, seemed less relaxed in play and were less advanced in their development at that stage.

Mothers' attitudes or education did not explain these patterns of interaction. Only when the baby's earliest behaviours were considered did substantial relationships emerge. In particular, mothers' perceptions of their babies at one month and mother-infant interaction at 12 months were related to many aspects of their babies' behaviour at one day. It is as if the baby's initial behaviour has shaped the mother's expectations and style of communicating with her infant. At birth all mothers equally believed in reciprocity or the view that babies could signal their needs and that parents should respond to them. Mothers of babies disorganized at the start, however, presumably found their babies' unpredictable behaviour difficult to "read" and respond to and were less likely to be rewarded with their infants' responses. They seem to have learnt from this early experience to rely less on their babies' signals when reaching decisions on their care. In contrast early experience with responsive infants appeared to help mothers to give more weight to their infants' behaviours, thereby facilitating reciprocity in the mother-infant relationship.

What has been described by Klaus and Kennell[18] as a critical period for maternal bonding may, as well, be a sensitive period for the transfer of knowledge to a mother about her baby. Initial exchanges may be far less important for multiparous mothers[6,22] but for primiparas early interactions seem to constitute important "transactions"[43] which influence how rewarding they find their babies and how they communicate with them later on. In terms of obstetric care in labour and delivery, the implications are that anaesthetic interventions may interfere with the infant's early responsiveness which may, in turn, affect the mother's attempts to get to know her baby. Although it is at times necessary and beneficial for some mothers to receive medication during childbirth, it could be recommended that the elective use of these procedures be minimized. In this area there needs to be more research to examine whether various delivery procedures, like use of forceps or caesarean section, and other medication given during labour might indirectly affect the developing parent-infant relationship.

Postnatal care can also influence the way a mother settles in with her infant. Sander found that infants who roomed-in with their mothers and were fed on demand, cried less and established a day-night rhythm more quickly than in the traditional nursery setting, where the mother and a number of nurses cared for the baby and fed four hourly.[44] In another aspect of his study, infants who were to be fostered spent their first ten days in the nursery and then roomed-in with one of two nurses over the next three weeks. Babies who roomed-in with the first nurse began to cry less than in the nursery, those with the other nurse cried as they did before. Differences in care-giving explained the more settled behaviour of babies in the first group. The nurse with the less settled babies felt that the best care was to love the babies. Although she perceived individual differences among the infants in her care she did not often draw on this information in dealing with them. The first nurse, on the other hand, paid keen attention to the individual differences and tried out different ways of care-giving to suit particular infants' needs.

In order to facilitate synchrony between mother and infant, staff must look at the mother's care-giving in the context of the particular infant she is caring for. There are enormous individual differences in newborns and handling is more effective if it is in response to the individual infant. A recent study reports that self-regulated non-nutritive sucking is effective in settling restless newborns.[45] Over the first four days restless infants were given a pacifier if they needed it following feeds. Infants using the pacifier engaged in more regular sleep and in less waking activity and vigorous crying. Similarly, Chisholm and Richards have found that swaddling active babies results in the infants sleeping more, startling less and being less reactive to stimulation.[46] The prolonged settling of these very young babies may prevent or ameliorate colic and sleep problems which can interfere with parent-infant attachment.

*The Infant Born at Risk, Behavioural Organization and Reciprocity*
The technology of the special care nursery and the infant's early appearance can heighten parents' perception of their infant as fragile and interfere with their responsiveness towards their baby. Minde found that infants with serious neonatal complications were significantly less active while ill, than were infants who had few complications.[47] Mothers of these infants perceived them as more ill than they actually were. Their care-giving in the nursery and at home over the first three months correlated more highly with their perception of their particular infant's illness than his actual medical condition. Despite their infants' recoveries mothers remained less responsive — they touched, smiled and vocalized less to their infants, both in the nursery and at home.

Nursery care which leads to more responsive babies will positively affect how parents relate to their baby. As with healthy infants, care that is sensitive to and in response to the individual infant has been found to facilitate behavioural organization in premature and sick babies.[48,49,50]

Several studies have shown how many infants are able to organize themselves around rhythmic stimulation or handling that supports their biological rhythms. Korner randomly assigned infants on ventilation for severe respiratory distress to either water beds oscillating in the rhythm of maternal respirations or to a control group.[51] Infants on the water beds showed more modulation in their movements, were more alert and responsive and were less often irritable or hypertonic. In another group very low birthweight infants (600-1000 grams) on water beds were found to have significantly fewer apnoeic spells, especially the most severe apnoea associated with bradycardia.[52] The soft support of the water beds also reduced the incidence of the infants developing asymmetrically shaped heads.

Barnard found that rhythmical stimulation, including rocking and a heart beat sound, helped premature infants to become more organized in their sleep.[49] The stimulation increased the time the babies spent in quiet sleep without affecting the amount of time in quiet wakefulness. When awake these infants were more alert, their sucking reflexes were stronger and clinically they seemed to be easier to feed than the control infants. Others have found that when premature infants are given pacifiers to suck during tube feedings they more quickly begin to bottle feed, show greater weight gain, fewer postnatal complications and leave hospital sooner.[53,54]

Early positive changes or gains in the infant's behaviour are not only significant in terms of the infant's immediate recovery, but have the potential for strengthening the early parent-infant relationship. Behavioural changes like faster weight gain, more settled sleep and increased alertness and less irritability may have an enduring effect on parental attitudes. Parents are likely to perceive these changes as indictors of their infant's robust development and more settled behaviour. The infant's more organized behaviour will also give parents a better focus for their parenting. When infants can signal their needs clearly, parents can respond more promptly and appropriately, contributing to a more rewarding relationship.

*Intervention Programmes Which Help Parents Adjust to their Infant's Different Behaviour*

At a more general level the professional (paediatrician, psychologist, physiotherapist, occupational therapist) has the opportunity, in talking about the infant's behaviour with his parents, to reinforce them for seeing their baby as a functioning person. This is especially useful when an infant is born at risk: "Instead of wishing for and grieving for the lost perfect baby, (parents) can see his strengths as an individual by seeing his responsive behaviours."[55]

We and others have used the Brazelton scale[56] in hospital to confirm for parents the contribution that the infant is making to the relationship, and parents feel less anxious in their parenting once the strengths in their baby are acknowledged. The Brazelton scale is beautifully adapted to be shared with parents because the behavioural observations that the scale uses to assess the infant's integrity are the same observations that parents use and attach meaning to when responding to their infant's behaviour. The infant is observed sleeping and the effects of intrusions on his sleep are assessed. Next the baby is uncovered and undressed and his reflexes examined. These are equivalent to daily handling like nappy changing or preparing the infant for the bath. When the infant is alert, his attention to objects, faces and voices is noted, similar to a play period at home. The examination tracks the infant's negotiation of these manoeuvres, noting how well he can organize himself around positive stimulation, like alerting or consoling to a soft voice, and protect himself from negative stimulation, like blocking out the sound of a sharp noise. For the examiner these behavioural observations reflect the integrity of the infant's central nervous system, in particular the infant's interactive and motor organization, state of control and physiological response to stress. For parents these observations have meaning for care-giving, alerting them to what may upset and what is enjoyable for their baby and what the infant can handle easily and what will still tax him.

Widmeyer and Field have found Brazelton demonstrations useful in helping teenage mothers attach to their premature infants.[57] Performance on the Brazelton scale was used to reinforce the infants' early responsiveness. This demonstration helped to confirm for mothers what they valued in their infants and placed importance on their own responsiveness to their babies' behaviours. At 12 months infants showed enhanced development and mothers were more sensitive in their early relationship with their babies.

Our programme at Foundation 41 was designed to foster the early parent-infant relationship for both mothers and infants and fathers and infants in hospital.[58] The infants included full-term infants and premature babies, both first born and later born. It was thought that parents experiencing a premature birth and who could not room-in with their infant, and parents having their first baby might benefit most from this support.

Intervention was conducted at discharge. At this time parents completed a questionnaire version of the Brazelton Scale for their infant[59] and we talked with parents about our assessment, making use of a videotape of their infant's behaviour. In these sessions our role was the ally of the parents, reinforcing their observations of their baby's behaviour, and the advocate of the infant, highlighting his strengths and needs.

Following intervention, parents and infants were seen at six months. It was often found that with or without support, parents of premature babies and parents of first borns get off to a good start if they have an "easy" baby. Babies were classified as easy or difficult according to their state of organization at the time of discharge.[60] Easy babies were likely to respond reliably and predictably to handling and when upset were responsive to efforts to comfort them. Presumably these babies' early responsive behaviours were easy to respond to and learn from. Parents of "difficult" babies, however, appeared to benefit dramatically from early support. Their infants' behaviour was either flat and sleepy, or labile and irritable. At the follow-up at six months, parents of these babies who received support were more sensitive and positive in their relationship with their infants. Compared to mothers without early support, intervention mothers were more affectionate and verbally responsive toward their infants and more aware and active in meeting their infants' developmental needs. They were more reciprocal in play and more responsive to their infants' cries. Results are less consistent for fathers, but fathers receiving support appeared to be more involved with their babies, to the extent that in daily care-giving they were more likely to find things for their infants to do and provided a greater variety of toys.

With "difficult" infants it may be most critical to share the infant's difficult behaviour with parents. Sameroff points out that when infants do not fit the normative pattern, serious problems can arise in the parent-infant relationship.[61] When infants do not produce the responses parents expect (for instance, when the infant cries constantly despite the mother's hugging and rocking) parents are likely to question their own efforts or label their baby as different. Parents of children admitted to hospital for failure to thrive or child abuse are often the successful parents of other children. In many cases parents attribute their failure with the one child to their inability to reach that child or for that child to reach them from the very beginning.

Helping parents to see their baby's difficult behaviour as distinct from their own and specific in time will enable them to work more constructively with their infants. Brazelton has worked in this way in hospital with parents of small-for-gestational age infants.[55] Because of their more fragile central nervous system organization, these babies can have very disturbing behaviour and are easily overwhelmed. Early on, parents' normal attempts to interact with their infant are met with exhaustion as the baby's whole behaviour signals "please leave me alone". Later on these infants may cry intensely to block out the stimulation, leaving their parents feeling helpless and out of control. By discussing these aspects of the infant's behaviour with parents, Brazelton was able to facilitate parents' earlier adjustment to their babies. The demonstration freed parents from the feeling that the difficult behaviour was their own fault and enabled them to express their responsiveness through changes in their care-giving to enhance the infant's organization. By regulating the intensity of their care — for instance, using one modality at a time (rocking or talking) to soothe or stimulate — they were able to contain their infant. Once they had achieved this, their baby became more organized and gradually became more responsive, proving to be more rewarding for parents. For Brazelton, "the critical aspect of this demonstration seemed to be that we gave them (parents) credit for being equal to this job and important to the baby".[55]

## *An Expanded Model for Hospital Care*

The hospital is the usual, and acknowledged safest setting for the birth of a baby. Along with the procedures it adopts is the earliest opportunity to unite the family and help mother, father and infant get off to the best possible start. To do this, hospital practices need not only to be concerned with a safe delivery and optimal physical care, but also to be sensitive to parents' and infants' responses as adaptations to their new roles. If hospitals anticipate that parents will be responsive and responsible then they will add to the parents' feelings of importance to their baby; if hospitals can provide opportunities to build on the infant's responsiveness, parents will be even more likely to do so.

---

The authors' research presented in this paper was funded by Foundation 41 and a Health Service Development grant from the Commonwealth Department of Health. The authors are grateful for the support of the medical and nursery staff of The Women's Hospital (Crown Street) and to Marion Pozniak and Yvonne Molloy for clerical assistance. Special thanks to co-investigator Beulah Warren, who contributes valuable clinical skill in our work with parents and infants in hospital. Third author's current address: Research Division, Boys Town Institute for Communication Disorders in Children, Omaha, Nebraska, USA.

## Notes

1   S Doering and D Entwistle, "Preparation During Pregnancy and Ability to Cope with Labour and Delivery" (1975) *Am J Orthopsychiat* **45**:824-37

2   J Lumley and J Astbury, *Birth Rites, Birth Rights* (Thomas Nelson, Sydney, 1980)

3   J Astbury, "The Crisis of Childbirth: Can Information and Childbirth Education Help?" (1980) *J Psychosomat Research* **24**:(1)

4   N Newton and M Newton, "Mothers' Reactions to their Newborn Babies" (1962) *JAMA* **181**:206-11

5   R Sosa, J Kennell, M Klaus, S Robertson and J Urrutia, "The Effect of a Supportive Companion on Perinatal Problems, Length of Labor, and Mother-Infant Interaction" (1980) *N Engl J Med* **303**:597-600

6   M Seashore, A Leifer, C Barnett et al, "The Effects of Denial of Early Mother-Infant Interaction on Maternal Self-confidence" (1973) *J Personality Soc Psychol* **26**:369-378

7   R Parke and S O'Leary, "Father-Mother-Infant Interaction in the Newborn Period: Some Findings, Some Observations and Some Unresolved Issues" in K Riegel and J Meacham (eds) *The Developing Individual in a Changing World Vol 2: Social and Environmental Issues* (The Hague Mouton, 1976)

8   M Lamb "Father-Infant and Mother-Infant Interaction in the First Year of Life" (1977a) *Child Dev* **48**:167-81

9  M Kotelchuck, "The Infant's Relationship to the Father: Experimental Evidence" in M Lamb (ed) *The Role of the Father in Child Development* (J Wiley and Sons, New York, 1976)

10  F Pederson and K Robson, "Father Participation in Infancy" (1969) *Am J Orthopsychiat* **39**:466-72

11  M Lamb, "The Development of Mother-Infant and Father-Infant Attachments in the Second Year of Life" (1977b) *Devl Psychol* **13**:637-49

12  A Clarke-Stewart, "And Daddy Makes Three: The Father's Impact On Mother and Young Child" (1978) *Child Dev* **49**:466-78

13  F Pederson, "Mother, Father and Infant as an Interactive System", Paper presented at the Annual Convention, American Psychological Assoc (Chicago, 1975)

14  R Lind, "Observations after Delivery of Communications between Mother-Infant-Father". Paper presented at the International Congress of Pediatrics (Buenos Aires, 1974)

15  R Parke, S. Hymel, T Power et al, "Fathers and Risk. A Hospital Based Model of Intervention" in D Sawin and R Hawkins (eds) *Psychosocial Risk During Pregnancy and Early Infancy* (in press)

16  P Wolff, "Observations on Newborn Infants" in L Stone, H Smith and L Murphy (eds) *The Competent Infant* (Tavistock Publications, London, 1974)

17  T B Brazelton, "Behavioural Competence of the Newborn Infant" (1979) *Seminars in Perinatology* **3(1)**:35-44

18  M Klaus and J Kennell, *Maternal-Infant Bonding* (The C V Mosby Co, Saint Louis, 1976)

19  A MacFarlane, *The Psychology of Childbirth* (Fontana, London 1977)

20  S Fraiberg, "Blind Infants and their Mothers: An Examination of the Sign System" in M Lewis and L Rosenblum (eds) *The Effect of the Infant on its Caregiver* (J Wiley and Sons, New York, 1974)

21  W Condon and L Sander, "Neonate Movement is Synchronized with Adult Speech: International Participation and Language Acquisition (1974) *Science* **183**:99-101

22  P de Chateau and B Wiberg, "Long-term Effect on Mother-Infant Behaviour of Extra Contact During the First Hour Postpartum. I. First Observations at 36 Hours" (1977a) *Acta Paediat Scand* **66**:137-44

23  P de Chateau and B Wiberg, "Long-term Effect on Mother-Infant Behaviour of Extra Contact during the First Hour Postpartum. II. A Follow-up at Three Months" (1976b) *Acta Paediat Scand* **66**:145-51

24  P de Chateau and B Wiberg, "Long-term Effect on Mother-Infant Behaviour of Extra Contact during the First Hour Postpartum. III. One Year Follow-up" *Devl Med Child Neurol* (in press)

25  A Whiten, "Assessing the Effects of Perinatal Events on the Success of the Mother-Infant Relationship" in H Schaffer (ed) *Studies in Mother-Infant Interaction* (Academic Press, London, 1975)

26  M Klaus, R Jerauld, N Kreger et al, "Maternal Attachment — Importance of the First Postpartum Days" (1972) *N Eng J Med* **286**:460-3

27  J Kennell, R Jerauld, H Wolfe et al, "Maternal Behaviour One Year after Early and Extended Postpartum Contact" (1974) *Devl Med Child Neurol* **16**:172-9

28    N Ringler, J Kennell, R Jarvelle et al, "Mother to Child Speech at Two Years — Effect of Early Postnatal Contact" (1975) *J Pediatrics* **86**:4

29    N Ringler, M Trause and M Klaus, "Mother's Speech to her Two-year-old; its Effect on Speech and Language Comprehension at 5 Years" (1976) *Pediat Research* **10**:307

30    T Field, S Widmeyer, S Striager and E Ignatoff, "Teenage, Lower-class Black Mothers and their Preterm Infants: An Intervention and Developmental Follow-up" (1980) *Child Dev* **51**:426-436

31    A Epstein, "Pregnant Teenagers' Knowledge of Infant Development". Paper presented at the biennial meeting of the Society for Research into Child Development (San Francisco, 1979)

32    S Carlsson, H Fagerberg, G Hornerman et al, "Effects of Various Amounts of Contact Between Mother and Child on the Mother's Nursing Behaviour" (1978) *Devl Psychol* **11**:143-50

33    P de Chateau, "Parent-Infant Relationship after Immediate Postpartum Contact" in *Proceedings of the Second International Congress on Child Abuse and Neglect* (London, 1978)

34    W Keller, K Hildebrandt and M Richards, "Effects of Extended Father-Infant Contact". Paper presented at the biennial meeting of the Society for Research in Child Development (Boston, 1981)

35    M Rodholm and K Larsson, "Father-Infant Interaction at the First Contact after Delivery" (1979) *Early Human Dev* **3**:21-7

36    J Bowlby, *Attachment and Loss Vol 1: Attachment* (Basic Books, New York, 1969)

37    M D S Ainsworth, "Infant-Mother Attachment" (1979) *Am Psychologist* **34(10)**:932-7

38    T B Brazelton, B Koslowski and M Main, "The Origins of Reciprocity. The Early Mother-Infant Interaction" in M Lewis and L Rosenblum (eds) *The Effect of the Infant on its Caregiver* (J Wiley and Sons Inc, New York, 1974)

39    K Robson and H Moss, "Patterns and Determinants of Maternal Attachment" (1970) *J Pediatrics* **77**:976-85

40    A Korner, "Conceptual Issues in Infancy Research" in J Osofsky (ed) *Handbook of Infant Development* (J Wiley and Sons, New York, 1979a)

41    A Murray, R Dolby, R Nation and D Thomas, "Effects of Epidural Anesthesia on Newborns and their Mothers" (1981) *Child Dev* **52**:71-82

42    R Dolby and B English, "Do first Impressions Persist? Consequences of Obstetric Medication on Newborn Behaviour and the Mother-Infant Relationship at 12 Months". Paper presented at the 51st ANZAAS Congress (Brisbane, 1981)

43    A Sameroff and M Chandler, "Reproductive Risk and the Continuum of Caretaking Casualty" in F Horowitz (ed) *Review of Child Development Research* Vol 4 (University of Chicago Press, Chicago, 1975)

44    L Sander, G Stechler, P Burns and H Julia, "Early Mother-Infant Interaction and 24-hour Patterns of Activity and Sleep" (1970) *J Am Acad Child Psychiat* **9**:103-23

45    G Anderson, A Grant and U Vidyasagar, "Self-regulatory Non-nutritive Sucking (SNS): Effects on Arousal and Feeding in Restless Newborn Infants." Paper presented at the biennial meeting of the Society for Research in Child Development (Boston, 1981)

46   J Chisholm and M Richards, "Swaddling, Cradleboards and the Development of Children" (1978) *Early Human Dev* 2:255-74

47   K Minde, J Brown and A Whitelaw, "The Effect of Severe Physical Illness on the Behavior of Very Small Premature Infants and their Parents." Paper presented at the biennial meeting of The Society for Research in Child Development (Boston, April 1981)

48   H Als, E Tronick, B Lester and T B Brazelton, "The Brazelton Neonatal Behavioral Assessment Scale (BNBAS)" (1977) *J Abnorm Child Psychol* 5:215-31

49   K Barnard, "Sleep Organization and Motor Development in Prematures" in E Sell (ed) *Follow-up of the High Risk Newborn — A Practical Approach* (Charles C Thomas, Springfield, 1980)

50   P Gorski, M Davison and T B Brazelton, "Stages of Behavioral Organization in the High-risk Neonate: Theoretical and Clinical Considerations" (1979) *Seminars in Perinatology* 3(1):61-72

51   A Korner, T. Forrest and P Schneider, "Development of a Longitudinal Neurobehavioral Assessment Procedure for Preterms: Preliminary Results from an Intervention Study." Paper presented at the biennial meeting of The Society for Research in Child Development (Boston, April 1981)

52   A Korner, "Maternal Rhythms and Waterbeds: A Form of Intervention with Premature Infants" in E Thomas (ed) *Origins of the Infant's Social Responsiveness* (J Wiley and Sons, New York, 1979b)

53   T Field, S Stringer, E Ignatoff and G Anderson-Shanklin, *Effects of Non-nutritive Sucking on Preterm Infants* (Unpublished manuscript, 1979)

54   C Porter and G Anderson-Shanklin, *Non-nutritive Sucking during Tube Feedings: Effect Upon Clinical Course in Premature Infants* (Unpublished manuscript, 1979)

55   T B Brazelton, Forward in E Sell (ed) *Follow-up of the High-risk Newborn — A Practical Approach* (Charles C Thomas, Springfield, 1980) p 15

56   T B Brazelton, "Neonatal Behavioral Assessment Scale" *Clinics in Developmental Medicine* No 50 (Spastics International Medical Publications with Heinemann Medical Books, London, 1973)

57   S Widmeyer and T Field, "Brazelton Demonstrations for Mothers; Their Effects on Preterm Infant Development at One Year." Paper presented at the biennial meeting of the International Conference on Infant Studies (New Haven, 1980)

58   R Dolby, B English and B Warren, "Brazelton Demonstrations for Mothers and Fathers: Impact on the Developing Parent-Infant Relationship" (Paper in preparation)

59   T Field, J. Dempsey, N Hallock and H Shuman, "The Mother's Assessment of the Behaviour of Her Infant" (1978) *Infant Behaviour and Dev* I:156-67

60   H Als, B Lester and T B Brazelton, "Dynamics of Behavioural Organization of the Premature Infant: A Theoretical Perspective" in T Field (ed) *Infants Born At Risk* (Spectrum Publications Inc, New York, 1979)

61   A Sameroff, "Theoretical and Empirical Issues in the Operationalization of Transactional Research." Paper presented at the biennial meeting of the Society for Research in Child Development (San Francisco, 1979)

Chapter 7

# Rooming-in as a Factor in Reducing Parenting Inadequacy

Susan O'Connor and Peter Vietze

Rooming-in refers to an arrangement whereby the newborn infant remains with his mother in her room during the postpartum hospital stay. The alternative to rooming-in, widely practised until recently in the United States, is collective nursery care of infants who are permitted to be with their mothers only briefly every four hours for feedings until discharge two or three days after birth. Rooming-in is properly called extended mother-infant postpartum contact which may or may not include early mother-infant contact during the first several hours after delivery. There is a growing, controversial, body of data which suggests that some form of extra postpartum contact may have a beneficial influence upon certain mother-infant relationships. The concept of rooming-in to facilitate parenting was first championed in the United States in the 1940's by Faith Jackson[1,2], a child psychiatrist at the Yale-New Haven Medical Center, and a group of psychologists and physicians known as the Cornelian Corner.[3] However, it took two decades for investigators to begin to examine this idea with scientific rigour. Several detailed critical reviews of these studies are available[4,5], including Earl Siegel's review in the following chapter. Most of these investigators have concentrated on early contact during the first three postpartum hours rather than on rooming-in.[6,7,8,9,10,11,12] The results of these studies have varied, possibly because socio-economic status of subjects differed among studies and low-income mothers may be more vulnerable to harsh hospital birth policies than mothers from the middle income bracket. There have been only three studies of extended postpartum contact, and all have found some degree of impact of extended contact upon the mother-infant relationship. All three studied low-income mothers. Details of two of these[13,14,15,16] appear in the chapter by Earl Siegel, and the third will be described here. First, however a caveat: conclusions from research usually should not be accepted as fact until concurring replication studies have been done. None of the extended contact studies have yet been replicated. Failure to observe this precaution has resulted in widespread fervour for "bonding", a slang term for extra contact, as necessary for normal development of a mother's attachment to her baby. The result of this in some cases has been further imposition upon newly delivered mothers under pressure from hospital personnel to "bond" with their newborns even when they have quite lucid and normal reasons for wanting their infants to spend some time away from them in the nursery. Worse, mothers quite firmly attached to their children but who for some reason such as premature birth, a surgical delivery or hospital policies were separated from them perinatally have been made to feel guilty that their effectiveness as parents has somehow been compromised. The pendulum has swung from enforced postpartum separation to excessive enthusiasm for "bonding". Either extreme may be deleterious to a mother and her baby. Even if these extended contact studies are successfully replicated, newly delivered mothers and infants should be handled delicately with flexibility rather than merely adding "bonding" to the technical assembly-line of hospital care.

## PARENTING ADEQUACY FOLLOWING ROOMING-IN

The idea for this study of rooming-in occurred to us after we learned the early results of Klaus and Kennell's work.[13,14] They followed mother-infant pairs to 12 months after early and extended versus limited postpartum mother-infant contact. Their findings suggested that early and extended contact mothers were more involved with and attached to their infants than controls. We reasoned that, if Klaus and Kennell were correct, then rooming-in should reduce the frequency of parenting disorders such as child abuse and neglect. At that time we were working in a city hospital for a low-income and indigent population in which child maltreatment and poor parenting techniques were common. It was also hospital routine at that time to separate mother and infant completely for at least the first 12 postpartum hours and then to allow contact only every four hours for 30 minute feedings. These circumstances were ideal for a test of this hypothesis; and so, after receiving permission from the Vanderbilt Human Experimentation Committee, we initiated the first of a series of randomized, prospective, double-blind studies. These will be discussed generally; full details are available elsewhere.[17,18,19,20]

Subjects included in the first study were 143 primigravidas who had completed their pregnancies with vaginal deliveries without any perinatal complications.[17] The mothers averaged 18 years old with ten years of education. About 40 per cent were single, and 40 per cent were black. Only 14 per cent intended to breast-feed. Half of the infants were male. The 158 control mothers and their infants experienced the hospital routine of limited contact. The 143 rooming-in pairs were together during the day after the first seven postpartum hours and averaged 9·3 more hours together than controls during the first 48 hours after delivery. Rooming-in mothers also could be visited by the infant's father or grandmother while their infants were with them, while for the control group visiting was limited to two hours daily and only when infants were in the nursery. After discharge from the hospital, subjects were followed through medical records and Protective Service reports for child maltreatment. When the children averaged 17 months old, 7 per cent of the control versus 1·5 per cent of the rooming-in children had suffered from non-organic failure-to-thrive, abuse, hospitalization due to inadequate parental care, neglect, or abandonment. While this was a significant difference only five of the control children actually received caretaking sufficiently alarming to provoke a Protective Services referral, and one of the rooming-in children was also referred for physical abuse. We therefore concluded that rooming-in apparently favourably influenced overall parenting adequacy but the results were not sufficiently strong to confirm the hypothesis that the frequency of physical child abuse was reduced. Note also that the findings cannot be attributed only to the extended mother-infant contact as rooming-in mothers also received expanded visiting privileges, and this support from relatives during the post-partum period might have played a role in determining outcome.

## MOTHER-INFANT INTERACTION AND CHILD DEVELOPMENT AFTER ROOMING-IN

Ordinarily these findings would have made it impossible to continue studying rooming-in in our hospital because the ethical mandate for universal rooming-in would eliminate a control group. In this case, however, the second study of mother-infant interaction following rooming-in was completed before results from the first study were known. The second study utilized the same experimental design except that mothers of any parity were included and outcome was measured by direct observation of mother-infant interaction at 48 hours, 1, 3, 6, 12 and 18 months postpartum.[18,19,20] Infant develop-ment was also tested at 9 months. The 152 mothers in this study averaged 21 years of age, 10 years of education, and 2 previous births; 73 per cent were white, 63 per cent were married, and 19 per cent intended to breast-feed. Their infants averaged 3300 grams birthweight, and half were males. These mothers were randomly assigned to rooming-in (N=62) or control (N=90) groups which did not differ for any of these independent variables.

Each mother-infant interaction observation lasted 60 minutes and included a feeding.[21] The trained interaction observers maintained acceptable agreement reliabilities throughout the study. Information recorded during mother-infant interaction observation are listed in the table. The first category of data in the table describes the context or setting in which interaction occurred: mothers' mode of activity with her child (feeding, cradling, caretaking other than feeding, or no caretaking), the infant's state of arousal ranging from sleep to crying, and mother's proximity to her child. The second category of data collected describes the actual content of the interaction: maternal and infant behaviours expressed. Numerical codes for recording combinations of mother and infant behaviours were made and the information analysed by computer. This process yielded information about duration of mother and infant behaviours during observation. After observation at 48 hours, and one, three and six months postpartum a set of rating scales[22] for the mother, infant, and home (excluded at the 48 hour observation) were completed by the observer.

TABLE I

INFORMATION RECORDED DURING MOTHER-INFANT INTERACTION
OBSERVATIONS

I DATA DESCRIBING THE CONTEXT IN WHICH
INTERACTION OCCURRED

| Maternal Caretaking Setting | Maternal Proximity To Infant | Infant State |
|---|---|---|
| Feeding | Out of the Room | Asleep |
| Cradling | In the Room But Distant | Drowsy |
| Caretaking | Within Arm's Reach | Alert |
| No Caretaking | Holding | Fussing |
| | | Crying |

II DATA DESCRIBING THE CONTENT OF THE
INTERACTION

| Maternal Behaviour | Infant Behaviour |
|---|---|
| Looking at Infant | Looking at Mother |
| Vocalizing to Infant | Vocalizing |
| Smiling at Infant | Smiling |
| Touch Playing | Crying |
| No Interactive Behaviour | No Interactive Behaviour |

Results at 48 hours postpartum revealed only differences which might be expected due to the circumstances of rooming-in. Rooming-in mothers spoke more softly to their newborns and tended to perform a greater variety of caretaking beyond simple feeding and cradling. Their infants spent more time asleep while control newborns were more alert. These findings could be anticipated since control infants were brought to their mothers for feeding and were fed only at those times. They were therefore hungry during observation at 48 hours and their mothers eager to encourage feeding, so it was not surprising that control infants were more alert and that their mothers spoke to them more loudly. On the other hand, rooming-in allowed flexibility of feeding and caretaking, so it would be expected that rooming-in neonates would sleep more during observation at 48 hours and that their mothers would have more time to do more expanded infant care procedures. The findings at 48 hours postpartum do not indicate any enhanced maternal attachment to the newborn during rooming-in. This differs from studies testing not rooming-in but only early mother-infant contact during the first few postpartum hours where differences in maternal affectionate behaviours have been found as early as 36 to 96 hours after birth.[6,7,8,9,10] The present findings in this study of predictable differences descriptive of the circumstance of rooming-in suggest that rooming-in may influence later parenting style in ways which differ from the effects of very early mother-infant postpartum contact upon maternal attachment behaviours.

Results after 48 hours postpartum varied with infant age, and it appeared that the earliest consequences of rooming-in centred around mutual mother-infant regulation of the context within which their relationship would develop. At one month after delivery rooming-in and control interaction did not differ in actual content of maternal and infant behaviours, but they did differ in contextual factors of maternal caretaking mode, proximity to the infant, and infant state. Control mothers spent more time doing non-feeding caretaking of their infants while rooming-in mothers were physically closer to their children. Control infants experienced noisier homes and cried more while rooming-in infants were more drowsy. By six months postpartum, differences in specific behaviour exchange began to emerge. Rooming-in mothers looked at their children more, while control mothers tended to spend more time not interacting with their infants. Rooming-in mothers showed a shorter latency in response to infant distress signalling and tended to show more appropriate feeding techniques. Contextual differences persisted at this time, however. As was true at one month, control mothers spent more time physically distant from their children, entirely out of the room. Their infants again cried more, while rooming-in children tended to spend more time alert. When the children were 12 months old, differences in behavioural exchange predominated. Rooming-in mothers smiled at their children more and tended to look at and speak to them more. Control infants spent more time not interacting with their mothers, who spent more time engaged in activities unrelated to infant care. At nine months rooming-in children were more advanced in motor development than controls.[19]

Not all findings favoured rooming-in. At three months, few differences were found but those present contradicted the remainder of the results. Although mean scores for both groups were in the desirable range, rooming-in mothers expressed more negative emotion toward their infants and tended to have longer latency in response to infant distress signalling. Control infants tended to be less irritable than the rooming-in children. The explanation for these findings at three months is not clear, although the later results suggest that this was a transition period which was successfully traversed by the rooming-in mothers and infants.

Despite the unexpected direction of findings at three months, the overall sequence of results suggested to us that rooming-in initiates a serial effect beginning with facilitation of early mother-infant adjustment leading to an expanded repertoire of favourable mother-infant interaction. This pattern of mutual exchange could influence parenting style through positive reinforcement. No differences were found, however, at 18 months. The next series of analyses were done in part to see if the effects of rooming-in truly disappeared by 18 months and also to substantiate our impression that rooming-in perpetuates a cascade of influences upon the mother-infant relationship.

## RESPONSIVITY DURING MOTHER-INFANT INTERACTION FOLLOWING ROOMING-IN

Results of mother-infant interaction observation described in the previous section provide information about duration and kind of maternal and infant behaviours displayed. These duration data, however, do not capture the reciprocal nature of normal mother-infant exchange. The data indicate, for example, that the infants vocalized and the mothers looked at their infants for certain percentages of observed time; yet it is not clear whether each did these things in response to the other or whether maternal and infant behaviours were expressed haphazardly and without mutual co-ordination. An alternative approach to data analysis is needed to measure the responsive quality of mother-infant interaction. One method for doing this labels any maternal behaviour (look, vocalize, smile, touchplay) as "mother signalling" and the absence of any one or more of these behaviours as "mother not signalling". The same process for infant behaviours (look, vocalize, smile, cry) renders two infant conditions: "infant signalling" and "infant not signalling". Thus converted, mother-infant interaction becomes a sequence of four possible combinations: both mother and infant simultaneously signalling; mother alone signalling while infant is not; infant alone signalling while mother is not; and neither partner signalling. These four conditions may be termed "dyadic states" since they describe the state of interactive behaviour for teach member of the mother-infant dyad. Having done this with the interaction observation record, it is then possible to examine transitions between dyadic states. For example, if infant alone is signalling and mother responds, this would be a transition from the dyadic state, infant alone, to the dyadic state, both responding. It is also possible to calculate the probability of transition between these dyadic states. For example, suppose that during an interaction observation the dyadic state of both mother and infant signalling simultaneously occurs 100 times. Suppose then that 50 of these times are followed five seconds later by the dyadic state of infant alone signalling (ie, mother ceases signalling). Then the probability of transition from both signalling to infant alone equals 0·50. Once probabilities for transition between dyadic states have been calculated statistical procedures may be computed to determine whether experimental groups differ significantly in response transition probabilities. In this study [19], 12 response transitions were examined in this way.[23] Four of these reflect maternal responsivity to the infant: mother joins in response to infant's signals (transition from state of infant signalling alone to mother and infant signalling together); mother stops signalling (transition from state of both infant and mother signalling to infant signalling alone); and no response from mother (transition from either infant signalling to infant or from infant signalling to neither party signalling). Four describe infant responsivity to mother: infant joins in response to mother's signals (mother to both), infant stops leaving only mother signalling (both to mother), and no response (mother to mother, mother to neither). The last four indicate mutual responsivity: coacting continues (both to both), coacting stops (both to neither), and coacting never achieved (mother to infant, infant to mother). These last three response transitions are very abrupt and rarely seen in normal mother-infant interaction.[24] Mother to infant and infant to mother by definition indicate temporal separation of maternal and infant behaviours since both partners are acting sequentially but in isolation. Both to neither is known to differentiate dyadic interaction of pairs subsequently to be involved in child maltreatment from that of normals.[25]

Results indicated that rooming-in influenced responsivity during mother-infant interaction, especially at 12 months postpartum. Two of the differences in infant responsivity to mother persisted to 18 months. At 3, 6 and 12 months control mothers were more likely to cease interacting (both to infant). At three months control mothers were more likely not to join their infants (infant to infant). At 12 and 18 months rooming-in children were more likely to respond to their mothers (mother to both). At 6, 12 and 18 months control infants were more likely not to respond to their mothers (mother to none). At 12 months, rooming-in mothers and infants were more likely to continue an interaction (both to both). At 6 and 12 months control dyads were more likely to abruptly stop exchange (both to none). At one and 12 months, control dyads were likely not to enter mutual exchange (mother to infant). The only finding which contradicts the positive influence of rooming-in in this series of analyses again occurred at three months, when rooming-in mothers were more likely not to respond (infant to none).

## CONCLUSION

The findings reported above suggest that rooming-in many enhance parenting adequacy and that this is accomplished through a series of intermediary effects upon mother-infant interaction. The earliest influence appears to be facilitation of mother-infant adaptation during the period when each is learning the cycles of daily activities of the other. The next phase, possibly developing from this early mutual regulation, seems to be an expanded repertoire of behaviours which are thought to reflect attachment, that is looking, smiling and amount of time given to mutual exchange. This apparently leads in turn to greater responsivity during mother-infant interaction. Our most recent work in this area, however, indicates that rooming-in influences outcome differently depending upon initial characteristics of the mothers.[26] When mothers have many characteristics known to be associated with child abusers (eg, a non-nurturing childhood, stress, little support), parenting adequacy and child development are most affected by rooming-in. When mothers are low risk for child maltreatment, predominant influences from rooming-in appear in observed mother-infant interaction. It appears, therefore, that outcome following extended postpartum mother-infant contact will vary depending upon maternal risk status and measures used for evaluation.

There is sufficient evidence to support liberalized hospital policies allowing mothers to be with their newborns after delivery. Child maltreatment is a complex problem requiring multifactorial solutions. Rooming-in may be one of these factors.

The authors thank Victoria Henderson, certified nurse mid-wife, for reviewing this manuscript.

This research was supported by the William T Grant Foundation; The National Centre of Child Abuse and Neglect/Children's Bureau Administration of Children, Youth and Families grants ≠90-c-419 and 90-CA-2138; and The National Institute for Mental Health grant ≠2RO1 MH 31195.

## Notes

1   E B Jackson, "The Initiation of a Rooming-in Project at the Grace-New Haven Community Hospital" in M J E Senn (ed) *Transactions of First Conference on Problems of Early Infancy* (The Josiah Macy, Jr, Foundation, New York, 1948)

2   S O'Connor, P M Vietze, H M Sandler, K B Sherrod and W A Altemeier, "Quality of Parenting and the Mother-Infant Relationship following Rooming-in" in P M Taylor (ed) *Parent-Infant Relationships* (Grune and Stratton, New York, 1980)

3   J C Moloney, "The Cornelian Corner and its Rationale" in M J E Senn (ed) *Transactions of First Conference on Problems of Early Infancy* (The Josiah Macy, Jr Foundation, New York, 1948)

4   P H Leiderman, "Human Mother to Infant Social Bonding: Is there a Sensitive Phase?" in K Immelmann and G Barlow et al (eds) *Ethology and Child Development* (Cambridge University Press, Cambridge, 1980)

5   P M Veitze and S O'Connor, "Mother-to-infant Bonding: A Review" in N Kretchmer and J Brasel (eds) *The Biology of Child Development* (Masson Publishing Inc, New York, 1981)

6   D J Hales, B Lozoff, R Sosa et al, "Defining the Limits of the Maternal Sensitive Period" (1977) *Devl Med Child Neurol* **19**:454-61

7   P de Chateau and B Winberg, "Long-term Effects on Mother-Infant Behaviour of the Extra Contact during the First Hour Postpartum. I. First Observations at 36 hours" (1977) *Acta Paediat Scand* **66**:137-44

8   S G Carlsson, H Fagerberg, G Horneman et al, "Effects of Amount of Contact between Mother and Child on the Mother's Nursing Behaviour" (1978) *Devl Psychol* **11**:143-50

9   J Hittleman, A. Parekh, S Zilkha et al, "Enhancing the Birth Experience: Assessing the Effectiveness of the Leboyer Method of Childbirth and early Mother-Infant Contact" (1980) *Pediat Research* **14**:434 (Abstract #52)

10  E G Lipper and E M Anisfeld, "Effects of Perinatal Events on Maternal-Infant Interaction" (1980) *Pediat Research* **14**:435 (Abstract #57)

11  S B G Campbell and P M Taylor, "Bonding and Attachment: Theoretical Issues" in P M Taylor (ed) *Parent-Infant Relationships* (Grune and Stratton, New York, 1980)

12 M J Svejda, J J Campos and R N Emde, "Mother-Infant "bonding": Failure to Generalize" (1980) *Child Dev* **51**:775-9

13 M H Klaus, R Jerauld, N C Kreger et al, "Maternal Attachment: Importance of the First Postpartum Days" (1972) *N Engl J Med* **286**:460-3

14 J H Kennell, R Jerauld, H Wolfe et al, "Maternal Behaviour One Year after Early and Extended Postpartum Contact" (1974) *Devl Med Child Neurol* **16**:172-9

15 N M Ringler, J H Kennell, R Jarvelle et al, "Mother to Child Speech at Two Years: Effect of Early Postnatal Contact" (1975) *J Pediatrics* **86**:141-4

16 E Siegel, K E Bauman, E S Schaefer et al, "Hospital and Home Support during Infancy: Impact on Maternal Attachment, Child Abuse and Neglect, and Health Care Utilization" (1980) *Pediatrics* **66**:183-90

17 S O'Connor, P M Vietze, K B Sherrod, H M Sandler and W A Altemeier, "Reduced Incidence of Parenting Inadequacy Following Rooming-in" (1980) *Pediatrics* **66**:176-82

18 S O'Connor, P M Vietze, W A Altemeier et al, "Extended Postpartum Contact: I. Observation of Maternal-Infant Interaction over the First Year following Rooming-in". (Submitted to *Pediatrics*)

19 S O'Connor, P M Vietze, H M Sandler et al, "Extended Postpartum Contact: II. Responsivity of Maternal-Infant Interaction following Rooming-in". (Submitted to *Pediatrics*)

20 S O'Connor, P M Vietze, H M Sandler et al, "Extended Postpartum Contact: III. Maternal and Infant Behaviour during Rooming-in". (Submitted to *Pediatrics*)

21 B Anderson, P M Vietze, G Faulstich et al, "Observation Manual for Assessment of Behaviour Sequences between Infant and Mother: Newborn to 24 Months" (1978) *JSAS Catalog of Selected Documents* **8**:31

22 L J Yarrow, J L Rubenstein and F A Pedersen, *Infant and Environment: Early Cognitive and Motivational Development* (Halsted, New York 1951)

23 M Lewis and S. Lee-Painter, "An Interactional Approach to the Mother-Infant Dyad" in M Lewis and L A Rosenblum (eds) *The Effect of the Infant on It's Caregiver* (Wiley and Sons, New York, 1974)

24 R Bakeman and J Brown, "Behavioural Dialogues: An Approach to the Assessment of Mother-Infant Interaction" (1977) *Child Dev* **48**:195-203

25 S O'Connor, W A Altemeier, S. Gerrity et al, "Mother-Infant Interaction before ID of Abuse, Neglect, or Nonorganic Failure-to-thrive" *Pediatric Research* (Abstract, in press, 1981)

26 S O'Connor, P M Vietze, H Sandler et al, "Mother-Infant Interaction and Child Development after Rooming-in: Comparison of High Risk and Low Risk Mothers" *Prevention and Human Services* (in press)

Chapter 8

# A Critical Examination of Maternal-Infant Bonding — Its Potential for the Reduction of Child Abuse and Neglect

Earl Siegel

A critical examination of studies of maternal-infant bonding may be viewed as straight forward, non-controversial and fully documented by many. But, for others the relationship between early and extended contact and its potential for reducing child abuse and neglect have raised difficult issues. Indeed, a muted backlash, particularly coming from some neonatologists and developmental psychologists, questions the effectiveness of early and extended contact interventions.

Boundaries for this critical review included the following: First, it was restricted to prospective studies with experimental research designs. Second the designs employed early and/or extended postpartum contact between mother and infant as the intervention variable. Third, full-term, essentially normal infants comprised the samples. Finally, it was assumed that the term *bonding studies* refers to close postpartum contact that occurs during a *sensitive period* shortly after birth and that the contact affects favourably the quality of subsequent mother-to-infant behaviour, with the potential of reducing child abuse and neglect.

With these boundaries, a systematic identification of key methodological considerations can be undertaken.

## CONCEPTUALIZATION

The first reported research on humans, by Klaus and Kennell suggested that early and extended contact promoted maternal-infant bonding.[1] In 1976 they presented a detailed review of the animal and human studies supporting the hypothesis of a sensitive period for maternal-infant bonding and its consequences.[2] Figure I reproduces their conceptual model. It indicates that a large number

**FIGURE I**

MAJOR INFLUENCES ON MATERNAL BEHAVIOUR AND THE RESULTING DISTURBANCES

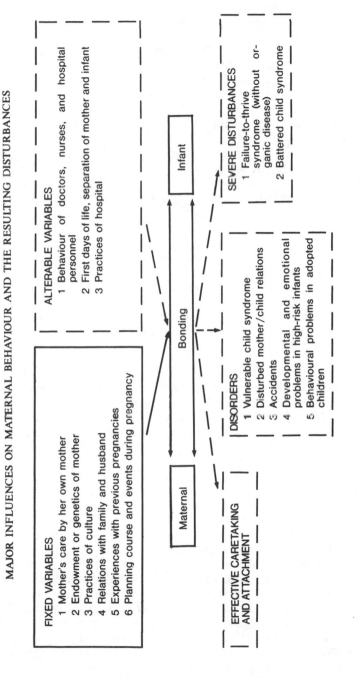

FIXED VARIABLES
1 Mother's care by her own mother
2 Endowment or genetics of mother
3 Practices of culture
4 Relations with family and husband
5 Experiences with previous pregnancies
6 Planning course and events during pregnancy

ALTERABLE VARIABLES
1 Behaviour of doctors, nurses, and hospital personnel
2 First days of life, separation of mother and infant
3 Practices of hospital

Maternal

Bonding

Infant

EFFECTIVE CARETAKING AND ATTACHMENT

DISORDERS
1 Vulnerable child syndrome
2 Disturbed mother/child relations
3 Accidents
4 Developmental and emotional problems in high-risk infants
5 Behavioural problems in adopted children

SEVERE DISTURBANCES
1 Failure-to-thrive syndrome (without organic disease)
2 Battered child syndrome

Source: Marshall H Klaus and John H Kennell: *Maternal-infant bonding* (C V Mosby Co, St Louis, Missouri, 1976)

of variables, in addition to early and extended contact, influence parent-infant interaction and subsequent events relevant to child development, including the most severe disturbances — abuse and neglect. But, emphasis was placed on "alterable" as contrasted to what was labelled "fixed" influences, with the former framed in dotted and the latter in solid lines. It was inferred that the reciprocally directed arrows between the "parent" and "infant" blocks represent a bonding process. Referring to the schematic diagram, the authors stated: "It is our hypothesis that this entire range of problems — the caretaking and attachment continuum — may result largely from separation and other unusual circumstances which occur in the early newborn period as a consequence of present hospital care policies. This position was endorsed by professional and consumer groups, and changes in hospital practices to initiate early and extended contact were recommended."[3,4,5]

Despite inclusion of the "fixed" influences in the model, little importance was attached to them when results of early and extended contact studies were reported. Further, the role of events that followed early and/or extended contact received virtually no attention in study designs. In considering the methodological issues, we shall build a case for a revised conceptualization, based on the results of reported maternal-infant bonding studies.

RESEARCH DESIGNS

Research designs have varied substantially in relation to sample characteristics, sample size, outcome measures and confounding variables included in data collection and analysis. However, all cited studies assigned mother-infant pairs randomly to experimental and control groups. In fact, few perinatal procedures have benefited from as many randomized clinical trials as have been applied to bonding research.

More complicated theoretical and practical questions relate to types of early and/or extended contact. Several studies employed *combined* early and extended contact that is at least 45 minutes of skin-to-skin contact within the first three hours after birth and five hours of additional contact during each postpartum hospital day. Most studies, however, provided *only early* contact during the first several hours after birth. In one study a third type of intervention, extended contact, occurred after an average delay of eight hours and consisted of six additional hours of rooming-in during days 1 and 2.[6,7] In order to clarify the importance of immediate contact, Hales and her associates attempted to assess how long the hypothesized "sensitive period" lasts.[8] Their findings suggested it may be of brief duration.

Thus, the "treatment" variable, though restricted to the first postpartum hours or days, has been modified from one study to the next, making it difficult to determine the precise timing of a "sensitive period".

## SAMPLE CHARACTERISTICS

Study samples have included mother-infant pairs from a number of different hospital settings in various countries. Most samples were drawn from low socio-economic status populations, and all studies but one were limited to primiparous mothers. To assess maintenance of comparability of experimental and control groups, almost always their socio-demographic and occasionally their health characteristics were compared. Few differences between them were found, tending to confirm that random assignment produced groups that were not different with respect to the control variables measured.

Sample sizes varied considerably, with numbers as low as Klaus and Kennell's original 14 experimental and control pairs to samples of 148 experimental and 153 control subjects. Inevitably, sample attrition occurred when outcomes were measured beyond the postpartum period. Where sample sizes were small or attrition great, there was the hazard that, despite random assignment, factors other than early and/or extended contact contributed to observed outcome differences.

## IMMEDIATE AND SHORT RANGE OUTCOMES

The bonding studies that observed maternal-infant behaviour during the first postpartum days provide immediate and short range outcome measures. Based on findings of replicated, carefully controlled investigations it appears that early contact, irrespective of its supplementation by extended contact, favourably affects maternal behaviour towards the infant during the first postpartum days.[8,9,10,11]

A recently published study is the only one that has failed to demonstrate an effect of early and extended contact at 36 hours.[12] However, in this study, there were only 15 mothers. They were all middle class, had 12 or more years of education, were married, had received prenatal education and their husbands were available during labour and delivery. These mothers, as suggested by the authors, may have been "near ceiling for maternal interest and responsiveness", particularly at a day and a half after delivery.

## INTERMEDIATE RANGE OUTCOMES

It seems clear that there is a significant relationship between early contact and the duration of breast-feeding. In Sweden, Brazil, Guatemala and Jamaica the effects of early contact were clinically and statistically significant when measured at two to three months and even at one year.[9,13,14,15,16]

Observations of maternal-infant behaviour at several months also seem to support a "sensitive period". But, there are fewer such studies. In addition they often report *only* statistically significant observations and are limited to bivariate analysis techniques. Reported positive findings associated with early and/or extended contact include specific maternal affectional behaviour such as increased eye-to-eye contact, smiling, singing, kissing and vocalization.[1,16,17,18] Infants have been reported as significantly more responsive and alert.[17,18]

Detailed results from a bonding study carried out in Greensboro, North Carolina will be presented below. Favourable effects were found at four months in a regression analysis that controlled for major socio-demographic and psychological variables.[19]

## LONG RANGE OUTCOMES

To date four studies have reported outcomes beyond several months:
   (1) Follow-up at two and five years for the original Klaus and Kennell groups;[13,20,21]
   (2) O'Connor's study of extended contact or rooming-in[6,7] which is amplified in the preceding chapter;
   (3) An early contact Swedish investigation;[22,23] and
   (4) the Greensboro results.[19]

Since much of the controversy regarding bonding derives from issues related to long range effects, these studies warrant careful examination.

Of the Klaus and Kennell 14 experimental and 14 control children, nine and ten respectively were observed at two years in five separate situations.[20] Differences between the groups, favouring mothers and children who received early and extended contact, were found but were limited to increased maternal language stimulation, observed in only one of the situations. Findings from observations made in the other four situations have not been reported. Initial small sample sizes and sample attrition suggest caution when interpreting the two year observations and their potentially favourable consequences.

At five years the nine experimental and ten control children were given three standardized IQ and linguistic functioning tests.[21] Within the early and extended contact group, the more "stimulating" language the mother used with her child at two years, the higher the child's speech and language comprehension scores at five years.

The Greensboro study will serve as a frame of reference for further assessment of long range impact. Although only partially pertinent to this review, the research also tested the effects of an intensive paraprofessional home visitor intervention during the first three months of life. Systematic observations of the mother-infant behaviour were made at four and twelve months. Reports of child abuse and neglect and health care utilization data were collected on all infants until they reached one year.

Subjects included in the study were 202 low income women, approximately one-quarter of whom were white and about one-third were currently unmarried. They averaged 0·8 babies before the index pregnancy, had attained 11 years' education and averaged 21 years of age. All had experienced uncomplicated pregnancies and were randomly assigned to four intervention groups: early and extended contact plus home visits; only early and extended contact; only home visits and controls. Follow-up observations, made in the home at four and twelve months, included 30 items of specific mother-infant attachment behaviour. Two observers independently recorded their ratings immediately after each of mother-infant interaction situations of bathing, dressing, feeding and play. Ratings on a 92 item Attachment Inventory also were completed after the home observations. Utilizing factor analysis, all of the observations were aggregated and organized into factor scores.[22] At four months three factors emerged: "Acceptance"; "Interaction/Stimulation" and "Consoling of Crying Baby". At twelve months, "Acceptance" and "Interaction/Stimulation" also emerged, but "Infant's Positive versus Negative Behaviour" replaced the "Consoling" factor.

Unique to the Greensboro study was the use of multiple regression analyses. Maternal background variables: race, marital status, parity, education, age and a Peabody Picture Vocabulary Test Score, were obtained from interviews conducted in the third trimester of pregnancy. The multiple regression analysis strategy had an important methodological advantage. It allowed assessment of the relative contribution of the interventions, after the socio-environmental background variables had explained variance in the dependent maternal-infant attachment variables.

Results of the multiple regressions on the three attachment factors at four months are shown in Table I. Almost 22 per cent of the variance in "Acceptance" was accounted for by the background variables ($p < ·0001$), early and extended contact added 2·5 per cent to the amount of variance explained ($p < ·04$), but neither the home visit nor home visit interaction with early and extended contact increased the amount of variance explained. Although the background variables were related to "Interaction/Stimulation" ($< ·0001$), none of the interventions improved the prediction of this attachment factor. Slightly more than 10 per cent of the variance in

"Consoling of Crying Infant" was explained by the background variables (<·03), early and extended contact added 2·5 per cent (p<0·5), but again neither home visit nor home visit interaction with early and extended contact increased the amount of variance explained.

TABLE I

REGRESSION ANALYSIS OF SELECTED VARIABLES ON ATTACHMENT FACTORS AT FOUR MONTHS OF INFANTS NOT PLACED IN OBSERVATION NURSERY DURING FIRST 24 HOURS OF LIFE (N=149)

| Attachment Factors | Variable* | | | | |
|---|---|---|---|---|---|
| | Background† | Home Visit | Early and Extended Contact | Home Visit Plus Early and Extended Contact | Total Model |
| Acceptance | 0.217 (p<.0001) | 0.221 (NS) | 0.245 (p<.04) | 0.258 (NS) | p<.0001 |
| Interaction/ Stimulation | 0.198 (<.0001) | 0.198 (NS) | 0.203 (NS) | 0.209 (NS) | p<.0002 |
| Consoling of crying Infant | 0.102 (p<.03) | 0.110 (NS) | 0.135 (p<.05) | 0.136 (NS) | p<.02 |

* Cumulative variance and significance levels (significance level of the increase in predicted variance).
† Race, marital status, parity, education, age, and Peabody Picture Vocabulary Test.

Source: E Siegel, K E Bauman, E S Schaefer, et al: "Hospital and Home Support During Infancy: Impact on Maternal Attachment, Child Abuse and Neglect, and Health Care Utilization" (1980) *Pediatrics* **66**:183.

The 12 months results are shown in Table II. Neither background nor intervention variables were significantly related to "Acceptance". The background variables were related to "Interaction/Stimulation" (p<·0001), but none of the interventions explained additional amounts of variance in that factor. Early and extended contact was the only variable significantly related to the "Infant's Positive/ Negative Behaviour" (p<·04), explaining 3·2 per cent of the variance.

Table III displays the number of hospitalizations, number of emergency room visits, mean number of preventive care visits, and

## TABLE II

REGRESSION ANALYSIS OF SELECTED VARIABLES ON ATTACHMENT
FACTORS AT TWELVE MONTHS OF INFANTS NOT PLACED IN
OBSERVATION NURSERY DURING FIRST 24 HOURS OF LIFE (N=149)

| Attachment Factors | | Variable* | | | |
|---|---|---|---|---|---|
| | Background† | Home Visit | Early and Extended Contact | Home Visit Plus Early and Extended Contact | Total Model |
| Acceptance | 0.084 (NS) | 0.085 (NS) | 0.085 (NS) | 0.091 (NS) | NS |
| Interaction/ Stimulation | 0.190 (p<.0001) | 0.193 (NS) | 0.201 (NS) | 0.203 (NS) | p<.004 |
| Infant's positive/ negative behaviour | 0.046 (NS) | 0.046 (NS) | 0.078 (p<.04) | 0.078 (NS) | NS |

* Cumulative variance and significance levels (significance level of the increase in predicted variance).
† Race, marital status, parity, education, age, and Peabody Picture Vocabulary Test.
Source: E Siegel, K E Bauman, E S Schaefer, et al: "Hospital and Home Support During Infancy: Impact on Maternal Attachment, Child Abuse and Neglect, and Health Care Utilization" (1980) *Pediatrics* **66**:183.

## TABLE III

HOSPITALIZATIONS, EMERGENCY ROOM VISITS, PREVENTIVE CARE
VISITS, AND IMMUNIZATIONS BY HOSPITAL AND HOME VISIT
INTERVENTION AT AGE 12 MONTHS*

| Type of Intervention | Hospital-izations | Emergency Room Visits | Preventive Care Visits | Immuniz-ations |
|---|---|---|---|---|
| Early and Extended Contact Plus Home Visit (N =47) | 4 | 9 | 3·8 | 4·7 |
| Early and Extended Contact (N=50) | 1 | 13 | 3·8 | 4·4 |
| Home Visit (N=53) | 4 | 11 | 4·1 | 5·1 |
| No Early and Extended Contact and No Home Visit (N=52) | 3 | 13 | 4·1 | 4·5 |

* No statistically significant differences were observed between groups for these variables.
Source: E Siegel, K E Bauman, E S Schaefer, et al: "Hospital and Home Support During Infancy: Impact on Maternal Attachment, Child Abuse and Neglect, and Health Care Utilization" (1980) *Pediatrics* **66**:183.

**TABLE IV**

REPORTS OF CHILD ABUSE AND NEGLECT BY HOSPITAL AND HOME VISIT INTERVENTION

| Type of Intervention | Child Abuse and Neglect | | |
|---|---|---|---|
| | No Observation Nursery | | Total |
| | Reported | Not Reported | |
| Early and Extended Contact Plus Home Visit | 4 | 43 | 47 |
| Early and Extended Contact | 3 | 47 | 50 |
| Home Visit | 7 | 46 | 53 |
| No Extended Contact and No Home Visit | 3 | 49 | 52 |
| Total | 17 | 185 | 202 |

Source: E Siegel, K E Bauman, E S Schaefer, et al: "Hospital and Home Support During Infancy: Impact on Maternal Attachment, Child Abuse and Neglect, and Health Care Utilization" (1980) *Pediatrics* **66**:183.

**TABLE V**

COMPARISON OF PARENTING INADEQUACY FOR EXTENDED CONTACT AND CONTROL CHILDREN

| | Extended Contact (N=143) | Controls (N=158) |
|---|---|---|
| Families with Parenting Inadequacy | 2 (1·5%) | 10 (7%)* |
| Substantial | 1 (0·7%) | 9 (6·3%)† |
| Minor | 1 | 1 |
| Children Hospitalized with Parenting Inadequacy | 1 (0·7%) | 8 (5·6%)* |
| Children Referred to Protective Services for Maltreatment | 1 (0·7%) | 5 (3·5%) |
| Children with Non-Parent Caretakers | 0 | 5 (3·5%)* |

* p <·05:   † p <·02

Source: S O'Connor, P M Vietze, K B Sherrod, et al: "Reduced Incidence of Parenting Inadequacy Following Rooming-in" (1980) *Pediatrics* **66**:176.

mean number of immunizations at age 12 months. There is no indication that a relationship exists between type of intervention and the health care utilization variables measured.

The distributions of reports of abuse and neglect are found in Table IV. The data show no relationship between the type of intervention and reports of abuse and neglect.

Another study which assessed long range effects reported strikingly different results. One hundred and forty-three low income Nashville women were assigned randomly to an additional 8½ hours of contact, but only after the infant was at least seven hours old (range 7-21 hours); 158 mother-infant pairs received routine contact.[6,7] Sample characteristics were similar to those in the Greensboro groups. Outcome measures were obtained at a mean age of 17 months (range 12-21 months) and consisted of data from reports to Protective Services and from Nashville General Hospital medical records. Using stringent criteria such as physical abuse, surrender of child, or nonorganic failure to thrive, families with substantial parenting inadequacy were ascertained. The parenting inadequacy results are shown in Table V. Two extended contact and ten control children experienced inadequate parenting. One extended contact and eight control children were hospitalized for these problems. One extended contact and five control children were reported to Protective Services for maltreatment. No extended contact and five control children were cared for by adults other than their own parents. Although no extended contact and five control infants had a diagnosis of one of the classical exanthematous diseases of childhood ($\leq .05$), no significant differences were found in health care utilization, infestations and gastroenteritis, or accidents.

Several major methodological contrasts between the Greensboro and Nashville studies stand out. The type of intervention varied, with the Greensboro experimental groups receiving early contact and the *same* extended contact for a slightly greater number of days. Data regarding reports to Protective Services seem to have been collected with comparable completeness in both studies. Although in Greensboro there was some difficulty assessing the children's medical care records, a complete search was conducted, and it was felt that all relevant information was obtained. All infants were followed systematically to 12 months of age in Greensboro; the Nashville sample was followed to an average of 17 months, with varying periods of risk that ranged from 12-21 months.

Identification of differences in study designs and data collection methods appear insufficient to explain sharp discrepancies in results between the two studies. Re-examination of the outcome measures and sample sizes may be useful. Observations and ratings of maternal-infant behaviour in the Greensboro research were intended to assess attachment, a proxy for parenting inadequacy and perhaps a precursor in some instances of abuse and neglect. Systematic measurement in four situations, for the entire visit and on the total sample of mothers and infants represents a considerably more detailed assessment than is permitted by the review and abstraction of medical records. Nevertheless, ascertainment of gross parenting inadequacy may require access to, and indepth study of the child's *complete* medical records. Also, the Nashville study, with a larger sample size, generated greater power in its analyses of reports of abuse and neglect. The methodological problem resides in the relative infrequency of abuse and neglect, making adequate sample size useful in avoiding a Type I error — acceptance of the null hypothesis.

The last study examined limited early contact to 15-20 minutes of skin-to-skin contact and suckling following delivery for 22 primiparas while 20 served as controls.[22,23] Significant differences in maternal behaviour between the early contact primiparas and controls were observed at 36 hours, the differences being greater for the behaviour of boys and their mothers than for girls. Others[24,25] also have noted sex differences in the development of maternal-infant bonding, warranting careful attention in future studies.

At three months early contact mothers spent significantly more time looking en face as well as kissing their infants and cleaned them less frequently. The infants cried less and smiled or laughed more than the controls (Table VI). These findings also were more pronounced for boys than girls. As Table VI indicates, however, a number of the attachment behaviour items were not significantly related to early contact.

Extensive studies on 18 of the 22 early contact mother-infant pairs and 17 of the 20 controls were carried out at one year.[23,26] During a physical examination in an outpatient clinic, early contact mothers held their infants with close body contact for a larger proportion of the total observation time, touching and caressing them more often and were more inclined to comfort their children with words. Differences again were greater for boys than girls.

Because the investigators had their greatest experience with the Gesell Development Test, they preferred it for study of the children's development at one year. They reported that the "main differences were found in gross-motor, fine motor and social development", but given the data presented, statistical and clinical significance of the findings appear unclear.

TABLE VI

COMPARISON OF EARLY CONTACT AND CONTROLS AT THREE
MONTHS (MEAN FREQUENCY AND P VALUES)

| | Mean Frequency | | |
| Observation | Early Contact (N=21) | Controls (N=19) | P Value |
|---|---|---|---|
| **Infant Behaviour** | | | |
| Eyes closed | 0 | 1·1 | 0·1 |
| Eyes open | 10 | 8·9 | 0·1 |
| Crying | 0·2 | 1·2 | 0·02← |
| Smiling/laughing | 2·7 | 1·4 | 0·02← |
| Looks at mother | 7·5 | 7·3 | 0·7 |
| Plays with hands | 0·6 | 0·8 | 0·7 |
| Plays with toy | 3·9 | 4·7 | 0·4 |
| Holds mother's hand | 1·1 | 0·8 | 0·5 |
| **Maternal Behaviour** | | | |
| Leaning on elbow | 0·3 | 1·1 | 0·3 |
| Looks en face | 3·1 | 0·8 | 0·008← |
| Smiles | 5·5 | 4·5 | 0·2 |
| Laughs | 0·9 | 0·5 | 0·5 |
| Kisses | 1·1 | 0·3 | 0·009← |
| Cleans | 0·1 | 0·5 | 0·05 ← |
| Gives toy | 4·6 | 4·0 | 0·5 |
| Rocking infant | 0·1 | 0·5 | 0·1 |
| Others present | 3·6 | 2·5 | 0·5 |

Source: P de Chateau: "Parent-infant Interaction and its Long-term Effects" in E
Simmel (ed): *Early Experiences and Early Behaviour: Implications for Social
Development* (New York, Academic Press, 1980) pp 109-79.

A 15 question, semi-structured interview, covering socio-economic
and occupation circumstances, health, some child rearing practices
and the fathers' participation in the daily care of the children also
was administered. Four significant differences were obtained.
Control mothers had more frequently returned to professional work
and started bladder training of the infant but less frequently had
arranged for them to sleep in their own rooms. Control fathers more
frequently engaged in daily care of their infants. The author
speculates about the clinical significance and implications of these
findings. But, the differences seem marginal and items for which no
significant differences were obtained are not consistently reported.

CONCLUSIONS

The critical examination of maternal-infant bonding research has
offered a kaleidoscopic view of all identified reports. However, a
number of questions remain. What is well documented and what do

we need to find out? What is the theoretical basis for a maternal-infant bonding construct? What is the relationship between bonding and attachment? What mechanisms link brief early and/or extended contact to subsequent outcome measures, including the most severe disturbance — child abuse and neglect?

An undeniable impact of early contact on a series of affectionate maternal behaviours during the first postpartum days has been documented, especially among low income women. Mechanisms for such behaviours, though fragmentary, appear reasonable. Lozoff and colleagues thoroughly reviewed the literature pertinent to development of mother-infant relationships, specifying unique infant and maternal postpartum attributes.[27] It has become well-known over the past decade that the newborn infant is in an unusually aroused state during the first several hours after birth. The mother at the same time is especially responsive to her infant. Animal studies by Rosenblatt[28] continue to give a careful picture of the interplay of hormones and infant contact which in combination help to determine maternal behaviour. His work has recently been extended by evidence that oestrogen primed rats, when administered oxytocin, became fully maternal, while no controls were so affected.[29] These hormones are at substantially increased levels in the immediate postpartum period, and one might assume operate in human situations to mediate the "high" that many mothers experience. Hormonal data on human mothers is needed, but a biologically determined maternal-infant bonding hypothesis appears confirmed by the experimental human studies presented and the supporting rationales just cited.

It seems plausible that early and/or extended contact facilitates an initial sensitive period, enhancing synchrony between the newborn's signals and the mother's responsiveness. As they experience contingently satisfying interactions, the synchrony or reciprocity grows. It is the strength and ongoing success of such a "match" which many investigators feel is crucial to subsequent development of positive maternal-infant relationships[30,31], reducing the probability of later abuse and neglect. However, care must attach to the relative strength and durability that these early effects predict.

The Klaus/Kennell model shown in Figure I was appropriately conceptualized, but too often studies of maternal-infant bonding restricted data collection and analyses to a single "alterable" variable, that is early and/or extended contact. Outcome measures also are influenced by a number of confounding variables, partially represented in the "fixed" variable box. For example, we know, and the model indicates, that a mother's own care as a child and her past cultural as well as prenatal and other intrapartal experiences also explain variance in maternal-infant behaviour. The behaviours are further influenced by such variables as the infant's temperament, sex and birth order as well as the mother's temperament, and perceptions of her infant. Thus, variation in maternal-infant bonding is multifactorial. Early and/or extended contact, given its potential for reduction of abuse and neglect, must be researched and programmatically approached with these co-variables specifically incorporated.

Having accepted that prior experiences and early contact together determine maternal-infant bonding, it is suggested that an evolving process ensues as shown in an adapted model (Figure II). Maternal-infant bonding and maternal-infant attachment are conceptualized as continuing but discrete longitudinal behavioural phenomena. Attachment, though influenced by early bonding, also is substantially affected by a number of intervening variables. The "fixed" variables continue to play major roles and indeed may change over time. These are joined by socio-environmental and psychological factors such as those reflected by the Greensboro study background variables.

Reported long range outcomes at one year and beyond are contradictory and come from only a few studies. Nonetheless, some residual effects of early and extended contact on parenting behaviour seem to persist, but inconsistently. It appears that advocates of early and extended contact have over-interpreted modest long range outcomes, setting themselves up for criticism, even by supportive investigators.

What, in closing, is the practical significance of the studies that were examined? Institutional and professional practices that enhance close contact between parents and their infants during the postpartum period are simple, safe, inexpensive and have documented short and intermediate range impacts. We need to maximize their availability to all parents and infants, but we must recognize that basic antecedents to favourable parent-infant relationships begin prior to the time of early and extended contact. Therefore, we need to employ the full range of activities that may affect the known co-variables. Important interventions include family planning and comprehensive prenatal care, with family supports to reduce socio-environmental and psychological stresses being of special importance. Despite disappointing home visitor results in Greensboro, several recent, methodologically strong studies initiated their home visitor interventions during the prenatal period and continued them through the first year, with encouraging effects on parent-infant behaviours and suggesting a modality for reducing child abuse and neglect.[31,32,33]

# FIGURE II

## MAJOR INFLUENCES ON MATERNAL-INFANT BEHAVIOUR AND SUBSEQUENT PARENTING INADEQUACY

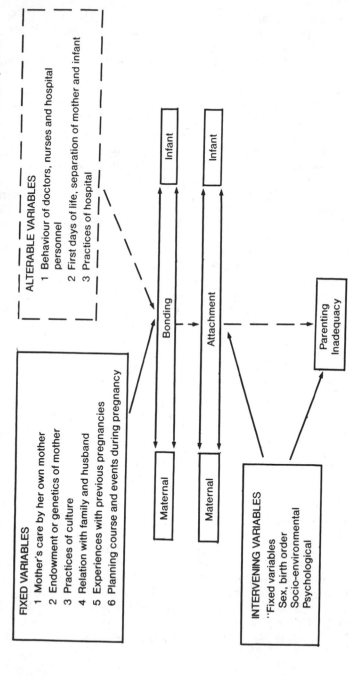

Adapted from: Marshall H Klaus and John H Kennell: *Maternal-infant bonding* (C V Mosby Co, St Louis, Missouri, 1976).

The intertwined, longitudinal experiences that affect parenting behaviour are complex. Early and extended contact is an efficient procedure which must be widely supported, with the explicit acknowledgement that simple solutions and quick fixes directed at reducing child abuse and neglect run the risk of serious disillusionment.

Adapted from: E. Siegel, "Early and Extended Maternal-Infant Contact: A Critical Review" (1982) *Am J Dis Child* **136(3)**:251-7

## Notes

1   M H Klaus, R Jerauld, N C Kreger et al, "Maternal Attachment: Importance of the First Postpartum Days" (1972) *N Engl J Med* **286**:460

2   M H Klaus and J H Kennell, *Maternal-Infant Bonding* (C V Mosby Co, St Louis, Missouri, 1979)

3   American Medical Assoc, *Statement on Parent-Infant Bonding* (House of Delegates, Washington DC, 1977)

4   Interprofessional Task Force on Health Care of Women and Children: Joint Position Statement on the Development of Family Centered Maternity/Newborn Care in Hospitals, American Medical Association, American Academy of Pediatrics, American College of Obstetricians and Gynecologists, American Nurses Association, American College of Nurse Midwifery, Washington DC, American College of Obstetricians and Gynecologists (1978)

5   American Public Health Assoc: Family-Centered Care in Hospitals With Maternity Services, Policy Resolution (Washington DC 1978)

6   S O'Connor, K B Sherrod, H M Sandler et al, "The Effect of Extended Postpartum Contact on Problems with Parenting: A Controlled Study of 301 Families" (1978) *Birth and the Family J* **5**:231

7   S O'Connor, P M Vietze, K B Sherrod et al, "Reduced Incidence of Parenting Inadequacy Following Rooming-in" (1980) *Pediatrics* **66**:176

8   D J Hales, B Lozoff, R Sosa et al, "Defining the Limits of the Maternal Sensitive Period" (1977) *Devl Med Child Neurol* **19**:454

9   P de Chateau and B Wiberg, "Long-term Effect on Mother-Infant Behaviour of Extra Contact during the first hour Postpartum. I. First observations at 36 hours" (1977) *Acta Paediat Scand* **66**:137

10   S G Carlsson, H Fagerberg and G Horneman, "Effects of Amount of Contact between Mother and Child on the Mother's Nursing Behavior" (1978) *Devl Psychobiol* **11**:143

11   F A Jones, V Green and D R Krauss, "Maternal Responsiveness of Primiparous Mothers during the Postpartum Period: Age Differences" (1980) *Pediatrics* **65**:579

12   M J Svejda, J J Campos and R N Emde, "Mother-Infant 'bonding': Failure to Generalize" (1980) *Child Dev* **51**:775

13   J H Kennell, R Jerauld, H Wolfe et al, "Maternal Behavior One Year after Early and Extended Contact" (1974) *Devl Med Child Neurol* **16**:172

14   N W Johnson, "Breast-feeding at One Hour of Age" (1976) *Am J Maternal Child Nursing* **1**:12

15   R Sosa, J H Kennell, M Klaus et al, "Breast-feeding and the Mother: The Effect of Early Mother-Infant Contact on Breast-feeding" (1976) *Ciba Foundation Symposium* **45**:179

16   Z Ali and M Lowry, "Early Maternal Child Contact: Effects on Later Behaviour" *Devl Med Child Neurol* (in press)

17   P de Chateau and B Wiberg, "Long-term Effect on Mother-Infant Behavior of Extra Contact during the First Hour Postpartum. II. Follow-up at Three Months" (1977) *Acta Paediat Scand* **66**:145

18   D Kontos, "A Study of the Effects of Extended Mother-Infant Contact on Maternal Behaviour at One and Three Months" (1978) *Birth and the Family J* **5**:153

19   E Siegel, K E Bauman, E S Schaefer, et al, "Hospital and Home Support during Infancy: Impact on Maternal Attachment, Child Abuse and Neglect, and Health Care Utilization" (1980) *Pediatrics* **66**:183

20   N M Ringler, J H Kennell, R Jarvella, et al, "Mother-to-child Speech at Two Years — effects of Postnatal Contact" (1975) *J Pediatrics* **86**:141

21   N M Ringler, M A Trause, M H Klaus and J H Kennell, "The Effects of Extra Postpartum Contact and Maternal Speech Patterns on Children's IQ's, Speech and Language Comprehension at Five" (1978) *Child Dev* **49**:862

22   E S Schaefer, K E Bauman, E Siegel, et al, "Measurement, Stability and Predictability of Maternal Attachment to the Infant." Presented at the Annual Meeting of the American Health Assoc (Los Angeles, California, 18 October, 1978)

23   P de Chateau, "Parent-Infant Interaction and its Long-term Effects" in E Simmel (ed) *Early Experiences and Early Behavior: Implications for Social Development* (Academic Press, New York, 1980) pp 109-179

24   H A Moss, "Sex, Age and State as Determinants of Mother-Infant Interaction" (1967) *Merrill-Palmer Quarterly* **3**:19

25   P H Leiderman, A Leifer, M. Seashore, et al, "Mother-Infant Interaction: Effects of Early Deprivation, Prior Experience, and Sex of Infant" (1973) *Early Dev* **51**:154

26   P de Chateau and B Wiberg, "Long-term effect on Mother-Infant Behavior of Extra Contact during the First Hour of Postpartum. III. One Year Follow-up" *Devl Med Child Neurol* (in press)

27   B Lozoff, G M Brittenham, M A Trause, et al, "The Mother-Infant Relationship: Limits of Adaptability" (1977) *J Pediatrics* **91**:1

28   J A Rosenblatt, "Prepartum and Postpartum Regulation of Maternal Behaviour in the Rat" in *Ciba Foundation Symposium 33: Parent-Infant Interaction* (Associated Scientific Publishers, New York, 1975) pp 17-37

29   C A Pedersen and A J Prange, "Induction of Maternal Behavior in Virgin Rats after Intracerebroventricular Administration of Oxytocin" (1979) *Proceedings National Acad Sciences* **76**:6661

30   E Tronick, H Als, L Adamson, et al, "The Infant's Response to Entrapment between Contradictory Messages in Face-to-Face Interaction" (1978) *J Am Acad Child Psychiat* **17**:1

31   R Schaffer, *Mothering* (Harvard University Press, Cambridge, Massachusetts, 1977)

32   J Gray, C Cutler, J G Dean and C H Kempe, "Prediction and Prevention of Child Abuse and Neglect (1977) *Child Abuse and Neglect* **1**:45

33   C P Larson, "Efficacy of Prenatal and Postpartum Home Visits on Child Health and Development" (1980) *Pediatrics* **66**:191

# Chapter 9

# Comments on Studies of Maternal Attachment

## Marshall H Klaus and John H Kennell

It is important to note that the results reported by O'Connor in Chapter 7 and Siegel in Chapter 8 disagree. Siegel did not note a significant difference in parenting disorders, finding ten in the control and seven in the extended contact. On the other hand, O'Connor found a significant difference in parenting disorders, child abuse, neglect and abandonment, finding ten infants in the control group and two infants who were given extended contact with their mothers.

In commenting on these differences it is worth noting a statement by Bateson on discussing a sensitive period. He stated: "The extent to which a sensitive period is replicated may frequently depend on the degree to which the conditions in which it was first described are copied. Even small changes can cause the evidence to evaporate." Close inspection of the many studies of this issue reveals many differences "such as the presence of the father, whether the mother and/or baby were nude and so forth". What at first glance appears superficial may significantly alter the outcome.

Even with slight differences in study design, in 9 out of 13 studies in which the effects of early contact only in the first hour were studied, later differences in the behaviour of the experimental group of mothers were observed when compared with the control group. However we are in complete agreement with Doctors Siegel and O'Connor that the long-term effects have yet to be well documented. The most important contribution of the Siegel study was the exploration of the variance contributed by the intervention or, to put it simply, the power of early and extended contact to influence maternal attachment behaviour. The investigators calculated that 3 per cent of the variance could be explained by early and extended contact whereas somewhere between 10 and 22 per cent could be explained by background variables such as the mother's economic status, race, housing, education, parity and age. The Siegel study emphasizes the contribution of background variables that are not easily changed. But it is also significant that it shows the advantages of extra contact. Although early and extended contact contributes a much smaller amount of the variance than might be expected it can still be arranged for all parents at no additional cost.

It is important to comment about the study of Campbell and Taylor in Pittsburgh[1] and the study by Svejda et al in Colorado.[2] These studies did not show any difference between the control and experimental groups in the hospital or one month later. It should be noted however that in both of these studies the control mothers received their infants for five minutes in the first hour of life. At present there are no appropriate studies to tell us the length of time required in the first hour after delivery to produce an effect on the mother's behaviour if there is a sensitive period. Could these small differences in study design result in the effects of the sensitive period for both groups? That is, is five minutes long enough to affect the mother's later behaviour with her infant? To consider this matter further the patients in both the experimental and control groups in these two studies were well prepared and motivated middle class mothers who delivered in a highly supportive environment. In addition, an interested, motivated mother can in five minutes see that she has produced a beautiful, healthy baby. This can trigger feelings of accomplishment, ecstasy and a series of interactions with the baby. In a large number of maternity units, a control or routine mother who has been totally separated from her child after birth is not sure if the baby is healthy or even alive. She has not experienced the flood of positive feelings that the beauty and responsiveness of her baby might have released and she may feel lonely, empty, and deprived. The whole question is whether five minutes might have altered the behaviour of the control group bringing the behaviour of the control and experimental groups close together.

Dolby and her colleagues in Chapter 6 attempt to understand the mechanisms by which early interventions for the mothers of premature infants alter later behaviour. They observed at six months that parents of babies who received support were more sensitive and positive in their relationship to their infants compared to the mothers without early support. Intervention mothers were more affectionate and verbally responsive to their babies. There was more reciprocal play. O'Connor and Vietze also extended their creative work attempting to understand the mechanism by which rooming-in affected later parenting behaviour. They noted that at six months mothers in the rooming-in group looked at their children more, while control mothers tended to spend more time not interacting. Rooming-in mothers showed a shorter latency in response to infant's distress signals and tended to show more appropriate feeding techniques. As was true at one month, control mothers spent more time physically distant from their infants and entirely out of the room. These two studies suggest the mechanism by which early interventions for either parents of premature or full-term infants in the first days of life, might alter later behaviour. What is unknown is how significant this effect is on the incidence of child abuse, accidents and failure to thrive. Disagreement between the results of the Siegel and O'Connor studies concerning whether additional early contact dicreases parenting failure is an area of high priority for further research.

It must be emphasized that a large patient population will be required in future studies. For example, if we assume that 12 hours of additional early rooming-in does significantly reduce the incidence of child abuse by 50 per cent, from 6 per cent to 3 per cent, at least 1500 patients would have to be admitted to have an 80 per cent chance of finding this improvement in any controlled randomized study. Although close detailed follow-up studies such as these are difficult and time consuming to perform, and the incidence of parenting disorders is relatively low, further investigations of this matter must be carried out. The desire to prevent or eliminate parenting disorders might be compared to a similar goal for paralytic polio. Preventive measures may decrease or eliminate the potential difficulty. However, in both situations once the problem has developed, there is a devastating effect on the individual and the family, and a mammoth expenditure of professional time and effort is required. Even under the best circumstances, the final outcome can never be as satisfactory as the initial prevention.

We would agree with Adler's comment in Chapter 5 that the first feelings of love for an infant are not immediate, like instant glue. The relationship between the time when a mother falls in love with her baby and a sensitive period is not clear at present. Several mothers have shared with us their distress and disappointment when they did not experience feelings of love for their babies in the first minute. It should be reassuring for them and mothers like them to learn about two studies of normal, healthy mothers in England. MacFarlane and associates[3] asked 97 Oxford mothers: "When did you first feel love for your baby?" The replies were as follows:

(a) During pregnancy — 41 per cent; at birth — 24 per cent;
(b) in the first week — 27 per cent; and
(c) after the first week — 8 per cent.

In a study of two groups of primiparous mothers Robson and Kumar noted on 112 and 41 mothers that 25 per cent recalled that the predominant emotional reaction on holding their babies for the first time was one of indifference.[4] Most of the mothers in both groups had developed affection for their babies within the first week.

They noted that maternal affection after childbirth was more likely to be delayed if the membranes were ruptured artificially, if the labour was painful or if they had been given a generous dose of pethidine.

We faced a real dilemma in deciding how strongly to emphasize the importance of parent-infant contact in the first hour. Obviously, in spite of the lack of contact experienced by parents in hospital births in the past 30 to 40 years, almost all of these parents became bonded to their babies. The human is highly adaptable and there are many fail-safe routes to attachment. Sadly, some parents who miss the bonding experience have felt that all was lost for their future relationship. This was and is completely incorrect, but it is so upsetting that we have tried to speak more moderately about our convictions. Unfortunately, this, we have found, has led some sceptics to discontinue the practice of early contact or make it a slapdash charade, often without attention to details. There are still large hospitals that have never provided for early contact. Mothers who miss out are often those at the limits of adaptability and who may benefit the most; the poor, the single, the unsupported and the teenage mothers. At the writing of this report there is a hospital in the United States with nearly 9000 deliveries where healthy mothers never care for or see their normal, full-term infants until discharge, except through a glass window.

At present we believe that there is evidence from many studies for a sensitive period in the first hours and days of life. This does not imply that every mother and father develops a close tie to their infants in the few minutes of first contact. Each parent does not react in a standard or predictable fashion to the multi-environmental influences that occur during this period. This fact is not evidence against the sensitive period but more likely represents multiple individual differences of mothers and fathers. When we make it possible for parents to be together with their baby in privacy throughout the hospital stay starting in the first hour, we establish the most beneficial and supportive environment for the beginning of the bonding process.

## Notes

1   S B G Campbell and P M Taylor, "Bonding and Attachment: Theoretical Issues" (1979) *Seminars in Perinatology* 3:3-13
2   M J Svejda, J J Campos and R N Emde, "Mother-Infant Bonding: Failure to Generalize" (1980) *Child Dev* 51:775-9
3   D M MacFarlane and D H Garrow, "The Relationship between Mother and Neonate" in S Kitzinger and J A Davis (eds) *The Place of Birth* (Oxford University Press, Oxford, 1978)
4   K M Robson and R Kumar, "Delayed Onset of Maternal Affection after Childbirth" (1980) *Br J Psychiat* 136:347-53

# Chapter 10

# Risk Factors Associated with Child Abuse

R Kim Oates

The goal of predicting which families in the community are likely to abuse and neglect their children and then to take measures to prevent this from happening is a laudible one. Much work has been done in this area but the situation is still far from being clear cut. A major problem is that many of the features that have been described as being characteristic of abusive families also occur in families where child abuse has not occurred. It has been shown that only 10 per cent of battering parents have a psychiatric illness.[1] It is clear that many of the associations found in abusive families, such as disruption of the mother-infant bonding process due to prematurity or neonatal illness and the social problems found in many abusive families also occur in some families who are very successful in child-rearing, despite these difficulties.

Prematurity has been associated with a higher incidence of child abuse since Elmer and Gregg showed that in a sample of 20 child abuse cases from the Chicago area there was a 30 per cent incidence of prematurity.[2] They suggested that the mother may have perceived the child as being abnormal simply because it was premature. Klein and Stern in a review of 88 child abuse cases at the Winnipeg Hospital found a 12·5 per cent incidence of prematurity and in their review of 51 battered children at Montreal found that 23·5 per cent of these children were of low birthweight compared with 9-10 per cent of Montreal newborns.[3]

The question has been raised as to whether the increased incidence in premature infants is associated with an increased level of illness and abnormalities in this group. Hunter and colleagues studied 282 infants admitted to a Newborn Intensive Care Unit.[4] On review, when the group was at a mean age of twelve months, ten of the infants had been reported for child abuse and neglect. In these children there was a statistically higher incidence of birth defects and prolonged stay in hospital compared with the premature infants who had not been injured. The battered infants when in the Neonatal Unit had been visited less by friends and relatives, and their families were characterized by social isolation with poor support systems, inadequate child spacing, marital problems, a precarious financial situation and serious consideration of abortion early in the pregnancy. There had also been a family history of child abuse and neglect, inadequate child care arrangements and poor use of medical services. The parents were characterized by either an immature, dependent personality style or an apathetic, futile personality style. These authors also showed that, at the time the child was admitted to the Newborn Intensive Care Unit, an interview could establish if the family was in an "at risk" group. At follow-up all battered children had been in the group which had been regarded initially as at high risk for child abuse. However it is noteworthy that there were also 31 families thought to be at high risk who did not abuse their children. It is also interesting that in the abusive families, contrary to much that has been written about these families, there was no significant association with inexperience in child care, major life stresses during the pregnancy, unrealistic expectations of the infant, prison or police record or drug and alcohol abuse.

Studies of abused children show an increased incidence of physical and mental handicap. What is difficult to be sure about is whether these handicaps were factors that were present before the abuse and perhaps added to the parental stresses that finally resulted in abuse or whether the handicaps were the result of abuse.

Johnson and Morse found that of 79 abused children nearly 70 per cent had either mental or physical abnormalities prior to the reported abuse.[5] Gil found that in his nationwide study in the USA of a sample of 12,000 children, 22 per cent of the abused children were suffering from a deviation in physical or intellectual function[6] while Ounsted and colleagues reported a higher incidence of unrecognized physical handicaps in abused children.[7]

Several studies have reported an increased incidence of mental retardation in abused children but again it is difficult to prove a cause and effect relationship because of other factors involved. Elmer found that 55 per cent of children in her sample from 50 families had an IQ of less than 80.[8] Morse found 43 per cent of her sample had an IQ of less than 80 although most of these were thought to be retarded prior to the abusive incident.[9] This is in contrast to the findings of Brandwein who feels that the mental retardation is secondary to the abusive incident.[10] Martin also expresses the view that the developmental problems of battered children are secondary to the abusive incident and states that only between 2 per cent and 5 per cent of abused children in his experience have a significant medical or developmental problem of a congenital nature.[11] Sandgrund and colleagues in 1974 showed that there was a higher incidence of mental retardation in abused children compared with controls and concluded that this higher incidence was difficult to attribute to the abuse incident alone.[12] However these authors later failed to substantiate these findings when they performed a multivariant analysis of risk factors associated with children in their series.[13] It has been suggested that child-produced stress on the parents is probably a factor in some cases.[14] Certainly the work of Brazelton has shown that some babies are more adaptable and easier to live with and care for than other babies.[15] It would seem that temperamental factors in the baby as well as other difficulties such as medical illness, mental handicap or birth defects are additional risk factors in families where there is already a distorted parent-child interaction. These additional risk factors may, in some cases be enough to tip the balance towards child abuse.

More recently workers have started to look at ways of predicting, particularly during pregnancy and the neonatal period, families where there is thought to be an increased risk of child abuse. Lynch showed that abnormal pregnancy and labour, neonatal separation and other separations in the first six months of life, illness in the mother and illness in the infant in the first year of life correlated with an increased incidence of child abuse.[16] Lynch and Roberts, looking at families in the maternity hospital, found five factors which distinguished the control group from the abusive group: more abusive mothers were under 20 when their first child was born, they were more likely to have signs of emotional disturbance recorded in the maternity notes, they were more likely to have been referred to a hospital social worker, the babies were more likely to have been admitted to the special care nursery and the mothers were more likely to have evoked concern from the staff over their mothering capacity.[17]

Using predictive factors found during the pregnancy, neonatal period and infancy there has been some success in predicting those families where abuse[18] and severe parenting difficulties[19], are likely to occur. It has also been shown that health visitors, visiting parents in the first year of life are able, with reasonable reliability to predict families likely to be in the group at risk for child abuse and neglect.[20]

However a word of caution is expressed by Daniel and colleagues who point out that child abuse screening programmes are likely to give a large number of false negatives and that the large social cost of this type of labelling is likely to make such an approach unacceptable.[21]

Characteristic features of the families have been well described in early papers by Kempe[22] and Elmer.[23] These authors pointed out the high incidence of divorce, separation and unstable marriages as well as minor criminal offences. Young added to Kempe's list lack of roots in the community, lack of immediate support from extended families, social isolation, high mobility and unemployment.[24] However it must be remembered that the majority of deprived families do not abuse their children although they too are exposed to the social and economic stresses that authors have described in abusive families. Steele and Pollock, in a sample which was mainly middle and upper-middle class abusive families say that social stresses would only incidentally intensify more deep-rooted personality factors.[25]

Smith showed that abusive parents had significantly lower IQs than control groups and had a significantly greater number of personality abnormalities, usually neurosis, than the controls.[26] This difference in intelligence testing was not confirmed by the National Society for the Prevention of Cruelty to Children (NSPCC) Battered Child Research Team who found that there was no difference in intelligence between abusive and control families.[27] However this group did show that the abusive parents were less able in verbal skills than the controls and that the abusive parents, on a personality measure were found to be consistently more reserved and detached with poorer emotional control than the control parents.

Because of the very few control studies available comparing characteristics of families of abused children with a matched group where abuse has not occurred, a study was carried out at the Royal Alexandra Hospital for Children to review 56 children and their families one to three years after their initial presentation with abuse and neglect. Each mother participated in a structured interview which enquired into the obstetric history, experiences with the child during the neonatal period, the parents' child-rearing practices and their expectations for the child. Problems of family health, housing, finance and domestic friction were explored and each child's development was estimated using the Denver Developmental Screening Test. Each family was compared with a control family matched for education, employment, socio-economic status, nationality, marital status of the parents and age, sex and health of the child. The mothers in the control group were not aware that they were being compared with abusive families but agreed to be interviewed as part of a survey looking at child-rearing practices.

The results showed that mothers in the two groups perceived their childhood quite differently. Seventy-nine per cent of the mothers from the child abuse and neglect group described their own childhood as lacking in affection from their parents compared with only two per cent of controls. Thirty-seven per cent of these mothers described their own mother's attitude as being one of rejection compared with two per cent of controls.

There was no significant difference between the ages of the mothers in the two groups when the index child was born. Fathers from the abuse and neglect group were younger than the control fathers; 25 per cent of fathers from the abuse and neglect group were between 16 and 21 years of age compared with 4 per cent of fathers in the control group. There were significant differences in the pregnancies of the two groups. While 52 per cent of pregnancies were unplanned in the abuse group, 27 per cent were unplanned in the control group.

The mothers in the abuse and neglect group were less likely to have made preparations, such as purchase of nappies and clothing for the baby's arrival; 46 per cent of the study group had made preparations compared with 81 per cent of controls. The control family was more likely to have chosen a name for a boy and a girl during the pregnancy whereas the abuse and neglect family seemed to have expectations for the child even before birth, by more often choosing a name for only one sex. The father's reaction to the news of the pregnancy, as described by the mother, was less favourable in the abuse group; 36 per cent of these fathers were reported to be displeased about the pregnancy compared with 12 per cent of control fathers.

The births of the babies in the abuse group were reported as being more difficult and less pleasant. Obstetric complications, including prolonged labour, forceps delivery, unusual presentations, caesarian section or a combination of these factors occurred in 55 per cent of the abuse group compared with 37 per cent of controls. The birth was described as being difficult or a bad experience by 64 per cent of the mothers in the abuse group compared with 27 per cent of controls.

Prematurity or postmaturity occurred in 54 per cent of the babies from the study group and in 13 per cent of controls. Medical problems in the first week of life, ranging from respiratory distress syndrome, apnoea and infection through to mild jaundice and feeding problems occurred in 52 per cent of the babies from the abuse group and in 9 per cent of controls. These factors may have

contributed to the lower incidence of attempted breast-feeding in the
study group, which was 20 per cent compared with 66 per cent of
controls.

To find out what sort of experiences the mothers had with their
children in the first few months of life, they were asked to rate their
memories of the child as a baby on a scale ranging from ideal to
very poor. While the control mothers tended to think that their
babies had been at least reasonable (27 per cent) and often above
average (70 per cent), in the abuse and neglect group 45 per cent of
mothers perceived their babies as being below average. When asked
if they enjoyed caring for their child, 34 per cent of mothers from
the abuse group stated that they did not. This response was not
made by any mothers from the control group.

The expectations the two groups of parents had for their children,
were compared by asking about toilet training and behaviour. The
parents from the abuse and neglect group commenced toilet training
much earlier often before 12 months of age, than the control parents,
who were more likely to commence toilet training after 18 months
(Table I).

In addition to the high expectations for toilet training, punishment
in trying to achieve bowel control was used much more frequently
in the abuse group who often made the child sit on the pot for long
periods and meted out punishment for soiling (Table II).

There were significant differences between the two groups in the
use of physical punishment for discipline. Fifty-four per cent of
mothers in the abuse and neglect group said that they used physical
punishment frequently compared with 11 per cent in controls. When
verbal punishment was used, the children from the abuse group were
told that they were bad or not loved in 41 per cent of cases,
compared with this approach in 2 per cent of controls. Control
mothers were more likely to deal with temper tantrums by going to
another room and leaving the child (55 per cent compared with 29
per cent from the abuse group) whereas the study mothers were more
likely to react to temper tantrums by screaming back at the child or
hitting him (55 per cent compared with 12 per cent of controls).

When children from the abuse group were good, they were rarely
praised for it. Table III shows that the children from the control
group were likely to be praised readily by their parents when they
were good compared with children in the abuse group who were
rarely praised for good behaviour.

Parents in the abuse and neglect group described themselves as
being stricter than the control parents, however they were less likely
to know what their children were doing at a particular moment and

## TABLE I

### AGE OF COMMENCEMENT OF TOILET TRAINING

| Age Toilet-Training Commenced | Under 6 Months | 6-11 Months | 12-17 Months | 18-23 Months | 24 Months and Over |
|---|---|---|---|---|---|
| Abuse and neglect (56) | 25% | 23% | 20% | 11% | 21% |
| Controls (56) | 0% | 5% | 20% | 46% | 29% |

$x^2 = 33 \cdot 32$     $p < \cdot 0001$

## TABLE II

### DEGREE OF STRICTNESS OF TOILET TRAINING

| Method of Training | Left on Pot for Long Periods, Accidents Punished | Put on Pot Regularly, Moderate Disapproval for Accidents | Trained when Child Seems Ready, No Scolding |
|---|---|---|---|
| Abuse and neglect (56) | 30% | 50% | 20% |
| Controls (56) | 0% | 50% | 50% |

$x^2 = 24 \cdot 41$     $p < \cdot 0001$

## TABLE III

### AMOUNT OF PRAISE FOR GOOD BEHAVIOUR

| Praise given | Rarely | Sometimes | Readily |
|---|---|---|---|
| Abuse and neglect (56) | 45% | 37% | 18% |
| Controls (56) | 0% | 27% | 73% |

$x^2 = 44 \cdot 84$     $p < \cdot 001$

## TABLE IV

### AMOUNT OF SUPERVISION PROVIDED BY MOTHERS

| Supervision | Checks Frequently | Checks Fairly Often | Practically Never Checks |
|---|---|---|---|
| Abuse and neglect (56) | 21% | 38% | 41% |
| Controls (56) | 62% | 36% | 2% |

$x^2 = 31 \cdot 44$     $p < \cdot 001$

checked on their whereabouts and activities less frequently than the control mothers who provided a higher level of supervision (Table IV).

The mothers in the study group thought highly of their partners in 7 per cent of cases and 54 per cent of them thought poorly of their partner. This compares with the control group where 43 per cent thought highly of their partners with 11 per cent holding their partners in poor regard.

When the mothers were asked how the child's father got on with the child, 48 per cent of fathers in the abuse and neglect group were said to be not interested in the child. Table V shows the differences in the mother's perception of how the fathers in the two groups related to their children.

TABLE V

DEGREE OF FATHERS' INTEREST IN THEIR CHILDREN

| Fathers' Interest in Child | Very Fond of Child | Quite Fond of Child | Rejects Child or Not Interested |
|---|---|---|---|
| Abuse and neglect (56) | 14% | 38% | 48% |
| Controls (56) | 69% | 20% | 11% |

$$x^2 = 37 \cdot 07 \qquad p < \cdot 001$$

The mothers from the abuse and neglect group had social contact with people less frequently than the controls. While 59 per cent of controls had daily social contact this was so for only one third of the study group and many of the mothers had very little social contact at all. Opportunities to get away from their child for short periods were less common in the study group; 48 per cent used baby-sitters compared with 85 per cent of controls. Differences between the two groups were found in finance, housing, domestic friction and health in the family. In the abuse and neglect group financial problems were twice as common, problems of inadequate housing were four times as common and serious domestic friction was reported as being ten times as common. Poor health occurred 11 times more often in the mothers and other members of the family were four times more likely to have health problems than the control families.

An estimate of the developmental level of each of the two groups of children, using the Denver Developmental Screening Test showed that children from the child abuse and neglect group were more likely to have two or more delays in the various sub-tests. This was particularly marked in the language sub-test with 36 per cent showing two or more delays compared with 8 per cent of controls.

These findings suggested that there were clear differences between the families of abused children when compared with control families. These differences were particularly obvious in the areas of the mothers' perception of problems at birth, the parental perception of the child, the high expectations and standards expected of the child, the lack of outside family supports and the high degree of minor health problems in the family. It was particularly disturbing to see the developmental delays in these children, particularly the delays in language development.

In 1981, five to seven years after this group of children had been first diagnosed as suffering from child abuse and neglect, 39 of the original group of 56 children were able to be traced and were again reviewed and were compared with a matched control group of 39 children. Now that the children were older, increased emphasis was placed on their development, their personalities, their social maturity, intelligence and reading ability. The personalities of the parents were also assessed.

The mean intelligence quotient for the control children, using the Wechsler Intelligence Scale for Children (WISC)[28] was 107 compared with a mean of 95 for the controls. There were no significant discrepancies between the verbal and performance scores on the WISC, in contrast to the significant differences reported for children with non-organic failure to thrive.[29]

The Vineland Social Maturity quotients[30] for the study and control groups were 103 and 105 respectively. However it was the impression during interviews with the mothers and children that the study group had, of necessity to develop some of the social skills which were being tested. For example in many of these families the children were given a large amount of responsibility, often in caring for other children, in preparing their own meals and in getting up in the morning and getting themselves off to school.

A standard reading test[31] and a test of language development[32] were given to each child. The control group on average had a six months delay in their reading age when compared with a normal population. The difference in the abused children was much greater with an average delay in reading age of 15 months. There were also differences in the language abilities of the two groups with the abused children having a language quotient on the Verbal Language Development Scale[32] of 92, compared with an average language quotient of 100 in the control children.

On personality testing using the Piers-Harris Childrens Self-Concept Scale[33] both groups had scores between the 31st and 70th percentile which is considered to be the normal range for the test. However, the abused children had an average percentile score of 44, which is towards the lower end of the normal range of self-esteem while the control children had an average percentile score of 60, at the upper end of the normally accepted range of self esteem. This is in contrast to Elmer's findings of no differences between a study and a control group using this measure of self-concept.[34]

Using the Childrens Personality Questionnaire (CPQ)[35], the abused children showed a greater tendency to be serious, shy, restrained and inhibited in interpersonal contacts compared with the controls who were more socially outgoing, less inhibited and better at interpersonal contacts.

When the mothers of both groups were studied using the Sixteen Personality Factor Questionnaire (16PF)[36], the mothers of the abused group, had significantly higher scores than the controls on factor L of the 16PF which relates to suspicion and jealousy.

The most interesting results were obtained using Rutter's Behaviour Questionnaire.[37] This questionnaire was designed to be completed by teachers and when scored, divides children into those with either normal or abnormal behaviour, the abnormal group being further divided into a predominantly neurotic, a predominantly antisocial or a predominantly undifferentiated group. In a general population, Rutter found that 11 per cent of boys and 3·5 per cent of girls obtained abnormal scores.[37] In the present study it was found that when the children's teachers were asked to complete the questionnaire, 15 per cent of the control group had abnormal scores compared with 56 per cent of the abused group. Of the children in the abused group who had abnormal scores, three fifths were predominantly antisocial.

The parents of both groups were then asked to complete the Rutter behaviour questionnaire on their own child to see if the parental perceptions were similar to those of the teachers. The parents in both groups perceived their children as having more deviant behaviour than the teachers with 34 per cent of parents in the control group and 81 per cent of parents from the abuse group completing the questionnaire in a way which gave their child an abnormal score. Of the abused children who had abnormal scores, almost two thirds were in the antisocial group.

## SUMMARY

Although the two groups of families were superficially similar in terms of marital status, nationality, socio-economic and employment status there were marked differences in a number of areas. These included the mother's childhood and her experiences during pregnancy and the perinatal period, the family's expectations for the child, child-rearing techniques, family and community support, health of the parents and development of the child.

In a study such as this it is difficult to be sure about the validity of retrospective information obtained from mothers about their pregnancy, the neonatal period and the child's early development. Whether the material that was recalled was quite accurate or not is less important than the fact that these mothers, when compared with the controls, perceived the birth as being difficult, the father as being unsupportive and the child as being difficult to manage.

As these children develop in infancy, they seem to be seen by their parents as comparing unfavourably with other children. Child-rearing techniques seem to be strict although there is little positive encouragement or supervision of the child. This puts the child in the difficult position of being supervised infrequently by parents who have high expectations and who are more likely to punish the child when he gets into trouble, even though this behaviour may result from lack of supervision. These high expectations are exemplified by the approach to toilet training, which is commenced early and is likely to be punitive.

The spouse is likely to be held in low regard by the other partner, contact with other adults outside the family is infrequent and there are few opportunities to be relieved from the burden of constantly caring for a child who is seen as unrewarding. Problems of poor health in the parents and other family members are particularly common. Maternal ill health has been shown to be a factor that correlates with child abuse[16] and this study shows that health problems are more common in all family members when compared with controls.

When these children were reviewed five to seven years after the abusing event it was found that problems were still present. They were seen by their teachers and parents as having undesirable personality characteristics, their language development and reading ability was delayed compared with controls and, in comparison with the control group had lower self esteem and were more inhibited in their interpersonal contacts.

Van Staden has shown that on reviewing abused children in infancy using the Griffiths Scales they were lower on all parameters apart from locomotor performance.[38] The development of abused children is discussed more fully in Chapter 13 by Harold Martin but the picture that emerges from this group is a gloomy one which may well manifest itself as parenting problems in the next generation.

Although in individual families all of the factors described as being commoner in abusive families may occur in families where abuse does *not* occur it does appear that in larger groups of families the factors described above do correlate closely with child abuse. This is not to suggest that all families identified by these factors are liable to child abuse. However it is possible that many of the abusing families within the community will be located within the large group identified by these factors. As medical, social work and community support resources will always be limited it does seem that they could profitably be directed towards providing support for the group which could be identified by the risk factors described in these studies.

Some of the work described in this chapter was done with the aid of a grant from the Children's Medical Research Foundation, Royal Alexandra Hospital for Children.

## Notes

1   B F Steele and C B Pollock, "A Psychiatric Study of Parents who Abuse Small Children" in R E Helfer and C H Kempe (eds) *The Battered Child* (University of Chicago Press, Chicago, 1968)

2   E Elmer and G Gregg, "Developmental Characteristics of Abused Children" (1967) *Pediatrics* **40**:596

3   M Klein and L Stern, "Low Birth Weight and the Battered Child Syndrome" (1971) *Am J Dis Child* **122**:15

4   R S Hunter, N Kilstrom, E N Kraybill and F Loda, "Antecedents of Child Abuse and Neglect in Premature Infants: A Prospective Study in a Newborn Intensive Care Unit" (1978) *Pediatrics* **61**:629

5   B Johnson and C Morse, "Injured Children and their Parents" (1968) *Children* **15**:147

6   D Gil, *Violence Against Children* (Harvard University Press, Cambridge, Massachusetts, (1970)

7   C Ounsted, R Oppenheimer and J Lindsay, "Aspects of Bonding Failure: The Psychopathology and Psychotherapeutic Treatment of Families of Battered Children" (1974) *Devl Med Child Neurol* **16**:447

8   E Elmer, *The 50 Families Study: Summary of Phase I: Neglected and Abused Children and their Families* (Children's Hospital of Pittsburgh, Pittsburgh, 1965)

9   C Morse, O Sahler and S Friedman, "A Three Year Follow-up of Abused and Neglected Children" (1970) *Am J Dis Child* **120**:439

10  H Brandwein, "The Battered Child: a Definite and Significant Factor in Mental Retardation" (1973) *Mental Retardation* **11**:50

11  H P Martin, "Children Who Get Abused" in H P Martin (ed) *The Abused Child* (Ballinger, Cambridge, Massachusetts, 1976)

12  A Sandgrund, R W Gaines and A H Green, "Child Abuse and Mental Retardation: a Problem of Cause and Effect" (1974) *Am J Ment Defic* **79**:327

13  R Gaines, A Sandgrund, A H Green and E Power, "Etiological Factors in Child Maltreatment: a Multivariant Analysis" (1978) *J Abnorm Psychol* **87**:531

14   R J Gelles, "Child Abuse and Psychopathology: A Sociological Critique and Reformulation" (1973) *Am J Orthopsychiat* 43:611

15   T B Brazelton, "Neonatal Behavioural Assessment Scale" *Clinics in Developmental Medicine No 50* (William Heinemann Medical Books, London, 1973)

16   M A Lynch, "Ill Health and Child Abuse" *Lancet* 2:317

17   M A Lynch and J Roberts, "Prediction of Child Abuse: Signs of Bonding Failure in the Maternity Hospital" (1977) *Br Med J* 1:624

18   J D Gray, C A Cutler, J G Dean and C H Kempe, "Prediction and Prevention of Child Abuse and Neglect" (1977) *Child Abuse and Neglect* 1:45

19   D C Geddes, S M Monaghan, R C Muir and C J Jones, "Early Prediction in the Maternity Hospital: The Queen Mary Child Care Unit" (1979) *Child Abuse and Neglect* 3:757

20   J G Dean, I A G Macqueen, R G Mitchell and C H Kempe, "Health Visitors Role in Prediction of Early Childhood Injuries and Failure to Thrive" (1978) *Child Abuse and Neglect* 2:1

21   J H Daniel, E H Newberger, R B Reed and M Kotelchuck, "Child Abuse Screening: Implications of the Limited Predictive Power of Abuse Discriminants from a Controlled Family Study of Pediatric Social Illness" (1978) *Child Abuse and Neglect* 2:247

22   C H Kempe, F N Silverman, B F Steele, P W Droegemueller and H K Silver, "The Battered Child Syndrome" (1962) *JAMA* 181:17

23   E Elmer, *Children in Jeopardy: a Study of Abused Minors and their Families* (University of Pittsburgh Press, Pittsburgh, 1967)

24   L Young, *Wednesday's Children: a Study of Child Abuse and Neglect* (McGraw-Hill, New York, 1964)

25   B F Steele and C B Pollock, "A Psychiatric Study of Parents who Abuse Infants and Young Children" in R E Helfer and C H Kempe (eds) *The Battered Child* (University of Chicago Press, Chicago, 1968)

26   S M Smith, R Hanson and S Noble, "Parents of Battered Children: A Controlled Study" in A W Franklin (ed) *Concerning Child Abuse* (Churchill Livingstone, London, 1975)

27   E Baker, R L Castle, C Hyman, C Jones, R Jones, A Kerr and R Mitchell, *At Risk* (Routledge and Kegan Paul, London, 1976)

28   D Wechsler, *Wechsler Intelligence Scale for Children* (Psychological Corpn, New York, 1949)

29   I W Hufton and R K Oates, "Non-organic Failure to Thrive: a Long-term Follow-up" (1977) *Pediatrics* 59:73

30   E A Doll, "Measurement of Social Competence" (American Guidance Service Inc, Minnesota, 1953)

31   A J Schonnell and F E Schonnell, *Diagnostic and Attainment Testing* 2nd ed (Oliver and Boyd, Edinburgh, 1952) p 38

32   M J Mecham, *Verbal Language Development Scale* (American Guidance Service Inc, Minnesota, 1958)

33   E V Piers, *The Piers-Harris Children's Self-Concept Scale* (Counselor Recordings and Tests, Nashville, Tennessee, 1976)

34   E Elmer, "A Follow-up Study of Traumatized Children" (1977) *Pediatrics* 59:273

35   R B Porter and R B Cattell, *Handbook for the Childrens Personality Questionnaire (CPQ)* (Institute for Personality and Ability Testing, Champaign, Illinois, 1979)

36   R B Cattell, H W Eber and M M Tatsuoka, *Handbook for the Sixteen Personality Factor Questionnaire (16PF)* (Institute for Personality and Ability Testing, Champaign, Illinois, 1970)

37   M Rutter, "A Children's Behaviour Questionnaire for Completion by Teachers" (1967) *J Child Psychol Psychiat* **8**:1

38   J T Van Staden, "The Mental Development of Abused Children in South Africa" (1979) *Child Abuse and Neglect* **3**:997

## Chapter 11

# Failure to Thrive — Part of the Spectrum

R Kim Oates

Growth failure was first recognized to be associated with emotional deprivation in institutionalized children. Although these children lived in hygienic conditions and were given adequate food, they received a minimum amount of "mothering", failed to gain weight, had increased susceptibility to infections, were lethargic in their behaviour and retarded in their developmental milestones.[1] In 1915 Dr Henry Chapin reported on ten infant asylums in different cities in the United States. In all but one institution, every infant under two years of age had died.[2] The Benevolent Society home in New South Wales between 1850 and 1858 had a somewhat better record with an 18 per cent mortality of children under 12 months compared with a 6 per cent mortality in children under 12 years.[3]

Failure to thrive in infancy can be divided into two broad groups: an organic type, in which an abnormality can be found and which usually responds to a specific treatment; and a non-organic type, in which no specific abnormality can be found and which responds to a combination of providing an adequate caloric intake and providing for the child's emotional needs. It is likely that this latter group is the largest. In distinguishing these two broad groups of failure-to-thrive from each other the laboratory investigations that are required are relatively few[4,5] and the single most important initial step is the taking of a careful medical and social history. An infant should be regarded as failing to thrive if the growth progress fails to keep up with a previously established growth pattern. It is therefore important to plot the child's weight on a standard growth percentile chart and to see how far he deviates from the normal range.

If at all possible previous weights should be obtained and plotted out to show the curve of the child's growth pattern. It is also necessary to plot the height and head circumference and to compare these with the weight percentile. The child's weight will be the parameter which deviates the most from normal. If linear growth is also affected it suggests that the condition has been present for a longer time. It is quite unusual for head circumference to be affected in failure-to-thrive except in those cases where the growth failure has been very long-standing. Children with advanced failure-to-thrive may look at first sight as if they have enlarged heads because their other bodily proportions look small in relation to their head size. The pattern usually found on the percentile charts is for the head circumference to be normal and for the weight to be reduced out of proportion to any reduction that there may be in length.

Non-organic failure to thrive in infancy is a complex problem. One point of view is that the growth failure is solely due to emotional deprivation despite adequate intake[6] while the study of Whitten and associates in 1969 showed that adequate caloric intake alone was enough to increase the growth rate in deprived children, even though the same level of deprivation continued during the study.[7] Modern ethical considerations would not make it possible for Whitten's study to be repeated. The likely explanation is that the growth failure is due to a combination of emotional and caloric deprivation. Severe growth failure due to cult diets and parental food fads has also been reported as an extreme example of a cause of failure to thrive.[8]

In 1967 Powell and associates described 13 young children with severe growth retardation, developmental delay and bizarre behaviour who had histories suggestive of emotional deprivation.[9] These children were found to have hypopituitrism which resolved with an improvement in their environment.[10] Catch-up in physical and emotional growth in these children was often dramatic. One other study showed a decrease in pituitary function in 14 of 28 children with failure to thrive and in several of these children, pituitary function improved with an improvement in the environment.[11] The concept of functional pituitary insufficiency may only be of academic interest as it is clear that as soon as the environment improves for these children there is an improvement in growth and development.

In 1959 Williams, from Melbourne, was one of the first to recognize that when considering the various causes of growth failure in infancy, inadequate care in the family and inadequate nutrition was a major factor.[12] He noted that in these families adverse social circumstances and emotional deprivation were often found and also noted that at times differences in the temperament of the infants may add to the problem. He emphasized the importance of the history, including a history of the pregnancy and labour, of observing the mother and infant together and noted that only simple laboratory tests were necessary in most cases. In following years the syndrome was thoroughly investigated and the status of the child and the family at the time of hospital admission or shortly after, the presence of environmental deprivation, low socio-economic class and marital instability were documented.[13,14,15,16,17,18]

Children with this form of failure to thrive have been described as sad, apathetic, having cold hands and feet, being over-familiar with strangers and indiscriminate in their seeking of attention and affection.[19] The voracious and perverted appetites that are sometimes found in these children have been thought to be due to the fact that they eat large amounts of food when admitted to hospital and from this point on their growth starts to increase. Hopwood and Becker, in a review of 35 children, showed 86 per cent had polyphagia, 54 per cent a bizarre oral intake and 48 per cent were found to steal or hoard food.[11] This group also had a high incidence of behavioural problems. These workers noted that the children had an increased incidence of difficulties in pregnancy, at birth and a high incidence of neonatal illness. There was also an increased incidence of delay in speech and motor milestones. What is particularly noteworthy is that 13 of the 35 children they studied had a prior history of physical abuse.

Studies of the families, particularly the mothers have shown a common theme. There has been a high incidence of family separation, unemployment, financial difficulties and poor communication between parents,[11] maternal depression and suicide attempts.[20] In a psychological study of the mothers there was found to be a common theme of profound emotional and physical deprivation in their own early childhood.[17] The mothers at the time of study had very poor impulse control and in particular had difficulty dealing with their sexual and aggressive impulses. These mothers were described as having little to spare from their own meagre stores of affection to pass on to their own offspring.

Fischoff and Whitten described a character disorder in ten of the twelve mothers they studied.[21] They believe that the finding of character disorders rather than psychoneurotic personalities in the mothers is the result of character disorders being a constellation of features which are more conducive to inadequate mothering. These include a limited ability to accurately perceive and assess the environment, their own needs and the needs of their children; a limited ability to adapt to changes in the environment; an adverse affective state; defective object relationships and a limited capacity for concern. These authors believe that this finding has implications for treatment.

A problem-solving approach is appropriate for treating a psychoneurotic problem where the mother has the capacity for introspection and instruction. However a mother with a character disorder has a limited ability to perceive and assess the environment and the needs of her children. Her patterns of thought are literal and concrete and therefore the emphasis on treatment should be on providing basic help in all phases of her life with practical help in feeding, child-rearing and other general aspects of child care.

It is clear that there is not just one single pattern of non-organic failure to thrive. Non-organic failure to thrive can also occur in stable, intact families with favourable economic circumstances[14,15] and there is a range of different findings in the children in follow-up studies.[22] Jacobs and Kent suggest that the mothers fall into three groups: a group deficient in basic mothercraft skills; a group who have these skills but who are passive with low affect and overwhelmed by family problems so that they could not respond to their infant's needs; and a third group with a significant psychological disorder and/or drug and alcohol abuse. They suggest that this classification will be helpful in planning treatment programmes.[23]

The earlier treatment approach of excluding organic disease, keeping the child in hospital until a good weight gain has been achieved and then discharging the child to the same situation is of short-term benefit only. When these children are taken from their mothers, cared for by other females who are efficient and competent, and have their nutrition brought up to normal, this may be a demonstration to the mother that others have been able to manage where she has failed and is likely to reinforce her feelings of inadequacy. Part of the management of non-organic failure to thrive should be to involve the mother in the care of the child right from the start. The mother should be encouraged to be involved in the care and feeding of her child in hospital and should receive support from social work staff and help in learning to relate to her child. She should be praised for her efforts and be given the credit for the progress that the child makes. This warm, supportive relationship should be continued at home. These parents have difficulty in keeping appointments so community resources should be utilized to co-operate with the hospital in providing continuing care. Through-out, the emphasis should be on supporting the mother and child together.

Ayoub and colleagues, in a review of 100 cases, emphasized the importance of helping the mother to develop a positive relationship with the infant and working to increase the mother's confidence in her own mothering abilities.[24] Part of their programme includes teaching the mothers to play with their infants. They report that mothers fall into the three groups previously described by Jacobs and Kent and report that the first two groups (those deficient in basic mothercraft skills and those with low affect and overwhelmed by family problems) respond to their treatment programme but that the response to this programme is poor from mothers in the third group which is characterized by significant psychological disorder.[23]

Because of the size of the problems and because it is unlikely that there will ever be enough professionally trained workers to meet the needs of these families the Denver group have successfully used the Volunteer Parent Aide concept in providing practical help and friendship for these mothers.[25]

The follow-up studies of these children generally give depressing results. There is some evidence that severe and prolonged malnutrition during the first year may lead to a decrease in intellectual functioning[26,27,28] but what is probably more important is the fact that the child's development is most likely to be impaired if he remains in an unstimulating and unsupportive environment.

Most of the follow-up studies have looked at subsequent growth, intellectual functioning and personality of the children. Patten and Gardner felt that these children may be limited in their ability to regain a normal growth pattern.[29] However their series was small (only six cases) and their follow-up was reported at less than one year. Prader and Tanner found that catch-up growth following starvation or severe illness can often restore the situation to normal in a pre-pubertal child.[30] However Chase and Martin in a follow-up study of 19 children seen at a mean of three and a half years after presentation found that 68 per cent were still below the third percentile in weight and 53 per cent below the third percentile in height.[26] These children were also behind in their developmental scores. A study of 40 children followed up at a mean of three years five months showed that 17 of the group were still below the third percentile for either height, weight or both parameters.[16] These workers noted behaviour disorders in some of the children with six having borderline or retarded intelligence.

They also found that a third of the families had severe social pathology. However they noted that a third of the children had no detectable physical, emotional or psychological abnormalities and concluded that not every case of non-organic failure to thrive results in severe pathological sequelae even without specific treatment. This last point would support Rutter's assertion[31] that some children are particularly resilient and do surprisingly well despite adverse social circumstances. The review by Elmer's group of 15 children reviewed at a mean of 15 years after hospitalization showed that seven were still below the third percentile in both height and weight with over 50 per cent showing some degree of intellectual retardation.[15] Hopwood and Becker's review of 35 children at a mean of 2.6 years was particularly gloomy.[11] Only seven of these children remained in their natural homes and they noted that those children who had been adopted had made the best adjustments. These workers reported that catch-up growth was uncommon when the children remained in their natural home and recommended that in general these children should be put in foster care until they reached the third percentile which they suggest may take between one and a half and two years. In general they are gloomy about their ability to help these families in contrast to the optimistic report from Ayoub and Pfeiffer who report that, in a study of 100 cases with an intensive supporting approach on follow-up after discharge from hospital, weight gain and developmental gains continued over a 14 month follow-up period.[24] They report that 85 per cent of children in this intensive treatment programme were doing well on follow-up. However they report that in a small group who had less intensive follow-up, two thirds were re-admitted to hospital with a recurrence of failure to thrive and 13 per cent of this group were physically abused. This link between non-organic failure to thrive and physical abuse has been described by other authors[22,32] and suggests that non-organic failure to thrive and child abuse are in many instances, different parts of the same spectrum.

At the Royal Alexandra Hospital for Children a study of non-organic failure to thrive commenced in 1969. The results of the 12 year follow-up have recently become available and provide additional information about the long-term results of this problem.

In 1970 a review of 24 children seen in 1968 and 1969 with non-organic failure to thrive was made.[18] In this review we showed that it was usually the youngest child in the family who failed to thrive and that this child had usually been born within 18 months of a sibling, suggesting that this extra child was often more than the mother's over-burdened resources could manage. The siblings were nearly all of normal size. We found that preventive health care in these children was poor, less than half of them being fully immunized.

In the 1970 review we found that half of the children had already grown to be over the tenth percentile for weight but a third had delayed development and three quarters had an abnormal personality profile. Details of the pregnancy, neonatal period and family circumstances were similar to those described by other authors.

The majority of these children were lost to regular long-term follow-up but in 1975, 22 of these families were traced and a further review was undertaken at an average time of six years and four months after the initial presentation.[20]

At first sight the health and growth of the children looked encouraging. Only a quarter of the group were below the tenth percentile for weight and only five percent were below the tenth percentile for height. However it was found that a quarter had been admitted to hospital since the last review. One of these admissions had been for a fractured skull and another was for a broken arm which had occurred in suspicious circumstances. Another child had died at home following convulsions and autopsy on this child showed head injuries. These were thought to have been caused by the mother's de facto husband. It is noteworthy that on the initial review in 1970 one child was found to have been severely bruised by his father and another child from this group was found to have died following a beating from a family member.

Although physical growth seemed to catch up in this group, there were educational, intellectual and behavioural problems. Half of the group were described by their teachers as being below average in school performance and almost a quarter had an intelligence quotient of less than 90. A third of the group had a verbal IQ 20 points or more below their performance IQ suggesting that their deficient language may possibly be secondary to being raised in an understimulating, non-verbal environment, two thirds had a reading age below their chronological age, half of this group being more than two years behind their actual age in reading. School teachers of these children completed a personality assessment which showed that half of the children scored in the abnormal range.[33]

We postulated that perhaps these children, like physically abused children may be perceived differently by their mothers. If their mothers perceived them as difficult, unrewarding and even unpleasant children, this may account partly for their emotional and nutritional deprivation early in childhood and may have partly explained the delay in language skills and the personality problems which persisted in later childhood even though growth became normal.

To look at this we asked the mothers to complete the same personality assessment on their own child and compared the scores with the teachers' assessments. While the teachers gave 50 per cent of children an abnormal score, 89 per cent of the mothers perceived their own children as being abnormal. The mothers also reported a high proportion of other undesirable characteristics such as temper tantrums, lying, nervousness, bed-wetting, over-activity, attention seeking behaviour and stealing.

A fifth of the mothers had abnormal profiles on the Minnesotta Multiphasic Personality Inventory[34] and over two thirds described themselves as being nervous or depressed. It was also found that the high incidence of family problems present in the 1970 review had increased.

In 1981 fourteen of these children were able to be traced and again reviewed, 12 years after the initial presentation. This time the group was compared with a control group of families matched for education, socio-economic status, marital status, employment status and social class, with emphasis in the assessment on peronality, behaviour, intelligence and language development.

The mean intelligence quotient using the Wechsler Intelligence Scale for Children (WISC)[35] in the control group was 103 compared with a mean of 93 in the failure to thrive group. The control group had no significant differences between their verbal and performance scores, while the failure to thrive group had a lower average verbal score (90) compared with an average performance score of 98. This discrepancy between verbal and performance scores is much less marked than when the group was reviewed in 1975.[20]

The failure to thrive group had a Vineland social maturity quotient[36] of 98 compared with an average quotient of 107 in the control children. The Verbal Language Development Quotient[37] which is adopted from the Vineland scale revealed a mean quotient of 80 in the study group compared with a mean of 91 in the controls.

Both groups were given the Schonnell reading test.[38] The control children were all behind the normal population in their reading age, having an average deficit of 17 months. However the reading age of the failure to thrive group was significantly more retarded, being an average of 45 months behind the general population.

The Piers-Harris Children's Self Concept Scale[39] did not show any differences between the two groups, with a mean score for self esteem within the normal range for both the study and control groups. Similarly, there were no significant differences found between the two groups using the Childrens Personality Questionnaire[40] and the High School Personality Questionnaire.[41]

There were however, marked differences between the two groups on Rutter's Behaviour Questionnaire.[33] This questionnaire, which was designed to be completed by school teachers, divides children into groups with normal or abnormal behaviour and further divides the abnormal children into predominately antisocial, neurotic or undifferentiated groups. The teachers of the children in both groups were asked to complete the questionnaire. Twelve of the fourteen children in the control group were rated as normal when the teachers' results were scored, however 50 per cent of the failure to thrive group were rated by the teachers to give an abnormal score. The parents of both groups were then asked to complete the behaviour questionnaire on their own child to see if parental perceptions between the two groups differed. The parents in both groups rated factors which scored their children as being more deviant than the teacher's scores. In the control group 29 per cent of parents gave scores which rated their children as abnormal, while 64 per cent of the parents whose children had suffered from non-organic failure to thrive gave scores which led to their children receiving an abnormal behaviour rating.

It is clear that non-organic failure to thrive has serious long-term complications. Although growth failure is likely to cease to be a problem, many of these children are left with residual problems in language development, reading abilities and behavioural disorders.

Very little was known about the consequences of failure to thrive when this group was first studied in 1969. There was little information about the need to do anything other than provide adequate nutrition until the child made a good weight gain in hospital. It is clear now that non-organic failure to thrive is a complex problem with many features of these children and their families that are common to abusive families. It is now recognized that non-organic failure to thrive and physical abuse may occur in the same child at different periods and that non-organic failure to thrive is often one part of the spectrum of the child abuse syndrome.

Some of the work described in this chapter was done with the aid of a grant from the Children's Medical Research Foundation, Royal Alexandra Hospital for Children.

## Notes

1   H Bakwin, "Emotional Deprivation in Infants" (1949) *Pediatrics* 35:512

2   H D Chapin, "A Plea for Accurate Statistics in Infants Institutions" (1915) *Transactions of the American Pediatric Society* 27:180

3   B Gandevia, *Tears Often Shed: Child Health and Welfare in Australia from 1788* (Charter Books, Sydney, 1978)

4   R K Oates, "The Child Who Fails to Thrive" 1977 *Med J Aust* 1:300

5   R H Sills, "Failure to Thrive: The Rate of Clinical and Laboratory Investigation" (1978) *Am J Dis Child* 132:967

6   E M Widdowson, "Mental Contentment and Physical Growth" (1951) *Lancet* 1:1316

7   C F Whitten, "Evidence that Growth Failure from Maternal Deprivation is Secondary to Undereating" (1969) *JAMA* 209:1675

8   I F Roberts, R J West, D Ogilvie and M J Dillon, "Malnutrition in Infants Receiving Cult Diets: A Form of Child Abuse" (1979) *Br Med J* 1:296

9   G F Powell, J A Brasel and R M Blizzard, "Emotional Deprivation and Growth Retardation Simulating Idiopathic Hypopituitarism I. Clinical Evaluation of the Syndrome" (1967) *N Eng J Med* 276:1271

10  G F Powell, J A Brasel, S Raitis and R M Blizzard, "Emotional Deprivation and Growth Retardation Simulating Idiopathic Hypopituitarism II. Endocrinologic Evaluation of the Syndrome" (1967) *N Engl J Med* **276**:1279

11  N J Hopwood and D J Becker, "Psychosocial Dwarfism: Detection, Evaluation and Management" (1979) *Child Abuse and Neglect* **3**:439

12  H E Williams, "Failure to Grow or Thrive in Infancy" (1959) *Med J Aust* **2**:345

13  F S Leonard, J P Rhymes and A J Solnit, "Failure to Thrive in Infants: A Family Problem" (1966) *Am J Dis Child* **111**:600

14  E Shaheen, D Alexander, M Truskowsky and G J Barbero, "Failure to Thrive — A Retrospective Profile" (1968) *Clinical Pediatrics* **7**:255

15  E Elmer, G S Gregg and P Ellison, "Late Results of the 'failure to thrive' Syndrome" (1969) *Clinical Pediatrics* **8**:584

16  H J Glaser, M Heagarty, D M Bullard and E C Rivchik, "Physical and Psychological Development of Children with Early Failure to Thrive" (1968) *J Pediatrics* **73**:690

17  M Togut, J E Allen and L Lelchuck, "A Psychological Exploration of the Non-organic Failure to Thrive Syndrome" (1969) *Devl Med Child Neurol* **11**:601

18  R K Oates and J S Yu, "Children with Non-organic Failure to Thrive: A Community Problem" (1971) *Med J Aust* **2**:199

19  D McCarthy, "Deprivation Dwarfism Viewed as a Form of Child Abuse" in A W Franklin (ed) *The Challenge of Child Abuse* (Academic Press, London, 1977)

20  I W Hufton and R K Oates, "Non-organic Failure to Thrive: A Long-term Follow-up" (1977) *Pediatrics* **59**:73

21  J Fischoff, C F Whitten and M G Pettit, "A Psychiatric Study of Mothers of Infants with Growth Failure Secondary to Maternal Deprivation" (1971) *J Pediatrics* **79**:209

22  R K Oates and I W Hufton, "The Spectrum of Failure to Thrive and Child Abuse: A Follow-up Study" (1977) *Child Abuse and Neglect* **1**:119

23  R A Jacobs and J T Kent, "Psychosocial Profiles of Families of Failure to Thrive Infants — Preliminary Report" (1977) *Child Abuse and Neglect* **1**:469

24  C Ayoub, D Pfeifer and L Leichtman, "Treatment of Infants with Non-organic Failure to Thrive" (1979) *Child Abuse and Neglect* **3**:937

25  R S Kempe, C Cutler and J Dean, "The Infants with Failure to Thrive in C H Kempe and R E Helfer (eds) *The Battered Child*, 3rd ed (University of Chicago Press, Chicago, 1980)

26  H P Chase and H Martin, "Undernutrition and Child Development" (1970) *N Engl J Med* **282**:491

27  M Hertzig, H G Birch, S A Richardson and J Tizard, "Intellectual Levels of School Children Severely Malnourished during the First Two Years of Life" (1972) *Pediatrics* **49**:814

28  M B Stock and P M Smythe, "Fifteen Year Development Study on Effects of Severe Undernutrition during Infancy on Subsequent Physical Growth and Intellectual Functioning (1976) *Arch Dis Child* **51**:327

29  R G Patten and L I Gardner, "Influence of Family Environment on Growth: the Syndrome of Maternal Deprivation" (1962) *Pediatrics* **30**:957

30  A Prader, J M Tanner and G A von Harnack, "Catch-up Growth following Illness or Starvation" (1963) *J Pediatrics* **62**:646

31  M Rutter, "The Long-term Effects of Early Experience" (1980) *Devl Med Child Neurol* **22**:800

32  B S Koel, "Failure to Thrive and Fatal Injury as a Continuum" *Am J Dis Child* **118**:565

33  M Rutter, "A Children's Behaviour Questionnaire for Completion by Teachers" (1967) *J Child Psychol Psychiat* **8**:1

34  S R Hathaway and J C McKinley, *Minnesota Multiphasic Personality Inventory* (Psychological Corp, New York, 1967)

35  D Wechsler, *Wechsler Intelligence Scale for Children* (Psychological Corp, New York, 1949)

36  E A Doll, *Measurement of Social Competence* (American Guidance Service Inc, Minnesota, 1953)

37  M J Mecham, *Verbal Language Development Scale* (American Guidance Service Inc, Minnesota, 1958)

38  A J Schonnell and F E Schonnell, *Diagnostic Attainment Testing*, 2nd ed (Oliver and Boyd, Edinburgh, 1952) p 38

39  E V Piers, *The Piers-Harris Children's Self-Concept Scale* (Counselor Recordings and Tests, Nashville, Tennessee, 1976)

40  R B Porter and R B Cottell, *Handbook for the Children's Personality Questionnaire (CPQ)* (Institute for Personality and Ability Testing, Champagin, Illinois, 1979)

41  R B Cottell and M D L Cottell, *Handbook for the High School Personality Questionnaire (HSPQ)* (Institute for Personality and Ability Testing, Champaign, Illinois, 1975)

Chapter 12

# A Comprehensive Child Sexual Abuse Treatment Programme

Henry Giarretto

A father-daughter incestuous relationship usually is extremely damaging to the victim, the offender, and the entire family, both during the sexual phase and after it ends. The daughter suffers emotional trauma which often leads to self-abusive behaviour that may last a lifetime, the father's life goes into sharp decline; and the marriage, weak to begin with, becomes intolerable and often ends in dissolution. If the situation is reported to the authorities, reactions may aggravate the family's troubled state even more. The victim's accusations are often ignored by law enforcement officials if the evidence is weak and the parents deny the charges, leaving the child feeling betrayed both by her parents and by the community. On the other hand, the officials become harshly punitive if they have a court provable case. They separate the child from her mother and family and incarcerate the father, often for several years. This way of coping with father-daughter incest prevails in most communities in the United States and was the way officials reacted in Santa Clara County, California before the Child Sexual Abuse Treatment Programme (CSATP) of that county was started and proven effective.

This chapter will discuss the three components of the CSATP and the processes of case management and treatment.

THE CSATP

In 1971, I began to counsel sexually abused children and their families for the Juvenile Probation Department of the county. During the first year, 26 cases were referred. I soon discovered that the traditional weekly session was inadequate and that each family needed much more attention than I could provide alone. It was this realization that led to the development of the community-based effort which was eventually named the CSATP. In 1978, the programme provided services to more than 600 families, receiving by far the largest number of referrals recorded by any comparative population area in the country. This sharp increase in the referral rate must be attributed to the growing reputation of the CSATP as a resource for help rather than punishment for sexually abusive families. In all the CSATP has served more than 2000 families. Of those families who received full treatment and formally terminated, about 90 per cent of those children have been reunited with their families, and the recidivism rate in these is less than one per cent. I mention these figures to urge other communities to set up their own CSATPs. I estimate that more than a quarter million children are being molested in their own homes each year and that most of the molestations would stop if a CSATP were established in every community in the country.

The CSATP is composed of three interdependent components: a professional staff, a cadre of volunteers, and self-help groups which together provide services responsive to the special needs of sexually abused children and their families. All three components are necessary — together they generate the humanistic community rooted climate in which sexually abused children, perpetrators, and other family members are supported during the crisis period and go on to learn the attitudes and skills needed to lead self-fulfilling lives and social responsibility. The CSATP copes with all forms of child sexual abuse, both familial and extra-familial, including not only children recently molested but also adults molested as children. However, the majority of the clients referred to the programme are for father-daughter incest under current investigation.

## The Professional Component

The professional component of the CSATP includes all the officially responsible members of the community: police, social workers, mental health workers, probation officers, defence and prosecuting attorneys, judges and rehabilitation officers. To enable the community to treat abusive families successfully (humanely and economically) this group must agree in substance on a consistent treatment approach and work co-operatively to implement this approach. Inter-agency co-operation does not come about by chance. Someone has to take the lead in convincing the other interveners by sound rationale and demonstration that a CSATP approach is more effective than a punitive one in coping with parental child molestation. That person is usually a member of the county agency officially responsible for the child-victim, such as Child Protective Services. In a few instances CSATPs have been started by mental health people. Regardless of how they begin, all CSATPs must eventually win recognition and support from the local child protective service agency and the criminal justice system.

Typically, the child protection service worker, acting as co-ordinator, begins a CSATP by forming a core group composed of other child protection workers and counsellors from the mental health agency and/or private agencies. Eventually they meet with representatives of juvenile and adult probation, policemen assigned to sexual assault cases, and deputies of the district attorney's office. As the programme gains strength and credibility, interagency co-operation is gradually achieved. Concurrently the self-help component is formed, and as the caseload increases, the core group begins to organize a cadre of volunteers.

It must be stressed that a typical CSATP does not supplant or interfere with the functions of existing official agencies. Rather, the paid staff of a CSATP is drawn from these agencies and taught to perform their tasks in a more productive manner. Thus, a CSATP can be organized and operated with little additional cost to the community. As the caseload increases, new hires may be necessary, but these added costs are easily offset by considerable savings in welfare payments, upkeep of offenders in gaols, payments to temporary shelters, foster homes, and group homes.

### The Volunteer Component

The volunteer staff of the Santa Clara Country CSATP consists of about forty people. One-fourth of this number are administrative interns, usually undergraduate students who perform office duties, provide transportation to the children, and in general relate to them as big brothers and sisters. The balance of the staff is made up of graduate students working towards licences in marriage, family, and child counselling. They are supervised by the licenced counsellors and frequently see the clients in their own homes. A few of the volunteers are seasoned members of Parents United whose dedication exceeds that of the average member. They provide countless hours of intense companionship to the new clients and perform a variety of administrative tasks. The volunteers, ranging in age from the early twenties to late fifties, do much to give the CSATP its community-based character.

### The Self-help Component

Parents United and its adjunct, Daughters and Sons United (PU/D&SU), constitute the self-help component of the CSATP. A Parents United chapter is usually started the way the one in Santa Clara County was started. In 1972, I asked the mother of one of the first families treated to make a telephone call to another mother who was caught in the early throes of the crisis. The ensuing conversations went on for several hours and had a markedly calming effect on the new client. I continued to couple old and new clients by telephone, and a month later three of the mothers met together for the first time. As expected, they found it very helpful to talk things out personally with others who had been through the same experiences, and they began meeting regularly in their homes with a juvenile probation officer, a public health nurse, myself, and my wife, Anna.

At one point, I suggested that these women get together with the mother of a physically abused child; perhaps they could start a chapter of Parents Anonymous in San Jose. The women found, however, that although they could discuss general family problems with this other woman, they did not feel completely at ease discussing intimate details of their particular problem of incest with her. Their own weekly sessions continued, however, with rewarding results. After a few more such meetings, to which several other women were invited, the group known as Parents United was formally designated and launched. To celebrate this event, the three charter mother-members wrote the following creed:

To extend the hand of friendship, understanding, and compassion, *not* to condemn.
To better our understanding of ourselves and our children through the aid of the other members and professional guidance.
To reconstruct and channel our anger and frustrations in other directions, *not* on or at our children.
To realize that we *are* human and do have angers and frustrations; they are normal.
To recognize that we do need help, we are all in the same boat, we have all been there many times.
To remember that there is no miracle answer or rapid change; it has taken years for us to get this way.
To have patience with ourselves, again and again and again, taking each day as it comes.
To start each day with a feeling of promise, for we take only one day at a time.
To remember that we *are* human, we will backslide at times.
To remember that there is always someone willing to listen and help.
To become the *loving, constructive* and *giving parents* or *persons* that we wish to be.

The primary purpose of the meetings was group therapy, but from the very beginning the group performed many other important functions. For example, as the members became aware that some of the new mothers did not have jobs, money, or transportation, they investigated resources to fill those needs and invited different agency people to come talk to their group. As people from various agencies found out about the small group and what they were trying to do, they would ask the mothers to speak to their groups. This public relations function of Parents United is now known as the Speakers

Bureau. Besides the obvious benefit of spreading the word about the programme, it gives client-members an important opportunity for social action. Many of them have been loners and have limited social skills. They have felt helpless and unable to have any effect on "the establishment". Through Parents United they know that they can have a definite, positive effect on the community and can pave the way for helping other troubled families.

An important development in the history of Parents United came when fathers began to enter the group. The first father to do so was serving a sentence at a rehabilitation centre. The father's rehabilitation officer became interested in what the CSATP and particularly Parents United were accomplishing and started meeting with them. He was instrumental in gaining permission for the father to be allowed to meet with the mother's group. This development, in late 1972, opened the way for other fathers from the rehabilitation centre to attend the meetings.

The Santa Clara County chapter of Parents United has grown rapidly. The chapter now has over 200 members with an average attendance of 125 members at the weekly meetings.

Meetings begin with a group centring exercise, followed by a brief conference to discuss progress in growth and effectiveness. The membership then breaks up into smaller groups jointly led by a staff member and a trained member of Parents United. The smaller groups include five couples groups limited to five pairs each, a men's group, a women's group, a mixed gender group, an orientation group primarily for new members but including older members as well, a group for women who were molested as children, a social skills group, and a group for training group leaders. The number and focus of the small groups change periodically according to the needs expressed by the membership. The groups are started at the same time and run for eight sessions after which the members are encouraged to join other groups.

The group process provides clients an opportunity to compare their view of reality with that of their peers, since all clients in the group have a common, highly stigmatized problem. This peer interaction also has the effect of emphasizing increased self-direction and personal accountability instead of reliance on authority figures who will "cure" them. To prepare members for positive social attitudes and confidence in their ability to effect changes in the attitude of the official community toward families troubled by incest, Parents United welcomes police, probation officers, prosecuting and defence attorneys, judges, and other professional interveners to the meetings.

Parents United provides for many of the urgent emotional and practical needs of its members. The independent evaluation team who studied the CSATP estimated that incoming families receive an average of 20 hours per week of support over the crisis period by Parents United members. In some areas, such as babysitting transportation for the non-driving parent, members of the programme are able to assist one another directly. Parents United keeps a list of jobs available for women who have been out of the work force for many years; it also helps them brush up on job skills or obtain training for new vocations. The group also maintains a list of companies who are willing to hire a parent with a felony record and uses its influence to help get work furloughs approved.

Parents United has drafted a form letter to send to lawyers who exploit the vulnerable emotional state of the offender by inflating their fees. The letter protests the exorbitant fee, suggests a fair fee, and insists that the fee be adjusted either voluntarily by the attorney or by determination by the Santa Clara County Bar Association. Parents United now has a list of lawyers with proven competence who charge reasonable fees. The organization has outgrown its present quarters and will soon move into a facility especially renovated for its requirements. To reduce the rent on these new quarters, the members have contributed over 5000 hours of labour to the renovation project. One of the members has opened his home to fathers who may not live in their own homes. About six members live on the average in his home, and the men are on call on what in effect is a 24-hour hotline. These are a few examples of the many ways Parents United helps its members help themselves through this difficult passage in their lives.

The following statement describes the impact of parents United on a new member:

HELLO ME!

Hello Me seems like a strange thing to be saying, especially when you're saying it for the first time to the person that's lived inside you for almost 38 years.

As far back as I can remember, I've felt dislike, disgust and displeasure. Hell! I downright hated myself most of the time.

Oh, I managed to project a desirable image of myself which I considered socially acceptable — self-confident, dependable, understanding, honest, brave — a lily white pillar of respectability. That was me.

Suddenly! Out of nowhere, I had been discovered, my protective covering had been penetrated. The world would know who and what I really was. I would be destroyed. There I stood naked and ugly, the likeness of a Dorian Grey. I wanted to hide, to run, to somehow disintegrate.

The phone rang. "Hello, I'm with Parents United. I'm a member of a group of people who've been through the same thing you're going through."

"My God," I thought, "not only am I not the only one this has ever happened to — Hell! They've got their own club." The voice on the phone continued, "We understand your pain. We share your pain with you. We want to help you." I didn't believe any of this was possible. How could anyone understand my pain? How could anyone want to help me?

What I could have easily believed was that this Parents United was a colony on an island off the coast of somewhat like a leper colony where they sent people like me so we wouldn't be able to contaminate the rest of the people in the world.

Well, I came to Parents United's Wednesday night meeting. I don't have to tell any of you what I expected to find. However, what I found was a room full of normal, everyday looking people — hugging and kissing, smiling and greeting each other as if they were all family and hadn't seen each other for years.

What I discovered that first night was that they were a family, a very special family held together by a common bond of unconditional love and understanding, of honest truth and caring. I began to feel warm inside. I felt alive again. I began to feel that "I, too" might be a worthwhile person.

The success of the self-help component of the CSATP is a tribute to the power of, and the need for, caring; it is due most of all to the dedication of its members to fellow human beings in crisis. That so many members remain to help others even after their own treatment has been successfully completed underscores the vigour of the self-help concept as defined by Parents United. Again, it must be stressed that Parents United/Daughters and Sons United is not as autonomous as other self-help groups such as Alcoholics Anonymous and Parents Anonymous. Parents United/Daughters and Sons United is an organic part of the CSATP and grows as the CSATP grows.

In June 1975, Parents United became incorporated and gained status as a non-profit organization. Formal bylaws were written and a Board of Directors was formed. The directors include several Parents United members, some representatives of other chapters, a member of Daughters and Sons United, two lawyers, three psychiatrists, two members of the San Jose Police Department, and two community leaders. The Santa Clara chapter of Parents United continues to grow, with about six new families joining each week. In addition, the chapter has had a major role in the formation of 23 new chapters in California and several throughout the nation.

## DAUGHTERS AND SONS UNITED

This organization, an adjunct of Parents United, is composed of children five to eighteen years of age, the majority of whom are girls. The two organizations work together and share many similarities. I formed the first DSU group in 1972, a play therapy group for children up to the latency period and the other one for adolescent girls. Both were co-led by juvenile probation officers. The children's groups require much more professional attention and guidance than the adult groups, which of course, are more self-sufficient. Because of the press of an increasing case-load on a small staff, the children's group did not grow as rapidly as the adult group. However, since late 1977, two young interns were assigned the task of improving and expanding DSU. Since then the membership of DSU has grown to about 120 members, and its organizational structure has been considerably strengthened.

DSU's decision-making body is the Task Force Committee. The Committee is composed of six members who meet weekly with a Parents United representative and the Daughters and Sons United coordinators. The committee establishes goals and projects geared to enhance the development and unity of the DSU programme. The DSU co-ordinators and the interns under their supervision implement the Task Force Committee's decisions. The self-expressed goals of the committee are:

(1) to alleviate trauma experienced by the victim through intensive emotional support during the initial crisis;

(2) to facilitate victim and/or sibling awareness of his/her individual feelings;

(3) to promote personal growth and communication skills;

(4) to alleviate any guilt the child may be feeling as a result of the sexual abuse;

(5) to prevent subsequent destructive behaviour such as running away, heavy drug abuse, suicide, child prostitution, and promiscuity;

(6) to prevent repeats of the offences by increasing victims' independence, assertiveness, and self-esteem;

(7) to prevent subsequent dysfunctional emotional/sexual relationships; and

(8) to break the multi-generational abusive and dysfunctional pattern which is evident in many of these families.

The Task Force Committee assessses all new group formats and sees to it that the group facilitators who work with the professional group leaders are carefully selected and trained. DSU helps to organize and conduct an adolescent girls' orientation group, four adolescent girls' groups, an adolescent boys' group, a pre-adolescent girls' group, a pre-adolescent boys' group, a play therapy group, and a transitional group for young women.

DSU provides or participates in the following services:

(1) a Children's Shelter Liaison, which makes initial contact within one or two days after admission for crisis intervention, introduces the children to DSU groups, and continues to provide support and counselling throughout protective custody;

(2) a Juvenile Hall Liaison, which performs the same function for children in Juvenile Hall;

(3) Home Liaisons, in which DSU co-ordinators make initial contact during the crisis period with those children who remain in the home; and

(4) a Sponsorship Programme, in which seasoned members facilitate new members' entry into the group;

(5) a Time-Out Corner, which is an area designed specifically for DSU members where resources and reading materials are available to enhance the children's understanding of drug abuse, birth control, and other adolescent problems;

(6) supportive people who accompany the children through the various steps in the criminal justice system process;

(7) a Big Sister/Big Brother Programme, which provides one-to-one friend relationships for those children demonstrating the need for sustained support; and

(8) transportation for about 30 children to weekly groups and counselling sessions.

The DSU task force also organizes fund-raising activities and administers the money collected. The members are active in the public education effort of the self-help component by participating in talks to schools and private organizations, appearing on radio and television, and publishing and distributing various information packages. To build esprit de corps, birthdays are celebrated and visits are arranged to entertainment and cultural centres. The members are becoming increasingly assertive in defence of children's rights in general; they often come to the adult groups to argue fo their specific rights within the CSATP. It is gratifying to see that DSU does not regard itself as the lesser half of the self-help component but as a full partner in the aims and purposes of the CSATP.

## WOMEN MOLESTED AS CHILDREN

The CSATP has treated many women, molested as children by their fathers, who were not helped during childhood. Their stories of lives devastated by parental rejection, promiscuity, drug addiction, inability to keep jobs, and broken marriages are repeated in the several hundred letters we have received from women with similar childhood histories. In each of these letters is the message explicitly stated or implied: "Where were you when I needed you?" The women molested as children who come to the CSATP receive individual counselling and couple counselling if they are married or living with someone. if their parents are available, they come for joint sessions with their fathers and mothers. These sessions occur infrequently and only later in the therapeutic process. The most progress usually develops in the group sessions of Parents United, first in the group made up exclusively of women molested as children and later in the orientation group where they gradually learn to understand the confusion and guilt suffered by mothers and father-offenders of sexually abusive families. In role-playing exercises with these parent members, the women prepare themselves for future confrontations with their real parents.

It seems that alienation from one's parents is intolerable at any age and is particularly painful when the mother-daughter bond is broken. In the women who eventually are able to re-establish emotional ties with their parents, a remarkable transformation takes place. Their life postures, formerly withdrawn and fear-ridden, are now patently confident, even exuberant. The changes are clearly manifested in the improvement in their marriages and careers. When this breakthrough occurs, they usually want to help others and several of these clients work with young victims individually or serve as facilitators in the group sessions of Daughters and Sons United and Parents United, recognizing that helping others is an important phase in their own therapeutic process. Another critical step in this process is the realization that their present ability to identify sensitively with the feelings of others and to articulate them precisely is in large part a compensatory reaction to the severe trauma they had experienced during childhood. One such client, Donna, has been in the programme for about two years. Donna was molested as a child, and the situation had not been exposed and dealt with. Her adolescent and early adulthood periods were marked by typical self-destructive behaviour including promiscuity, drug abuse and sabotage of intimate relationships, schooling, and career. She was in her early thirties and still in the self-abusive phase when she joined CSATP and PU. Since then Donna has received in-depth individual counselling and participated in the group for women molested as children and in the group which is made up of current offenders and their spouses. She now serves as a volunteer counsellor and a few months ago she took another big step when she enrolled in a graduate programme leading to a masters degree in marriage, family, and child counselling. The following are excerpts from a paper Donna wrote for a classroom assignment:

This paper and my 35th birthday coincided. The combination promoted a long reflection. Who am I, who was I, what do I need, what do I have to give, what do I require of myself, of others, of life? I'm in charge of my life for the first time this past year. I'm a real neophyte in the world of the really living. I still have to assure myself I'm no longer the young woman who lay in bed for days at a time, refused to drive a car, couldn't operate a washing machine, was terrified to live so decided not to. I have freed myself from practically a lifetime career of sitting on the secret that I was an abused child. Keeping a secret and living a lie is a true energy drainer. The stamina I expended projecting the image I wanted passersby to see was tremendous. I now spend that stamina building brick by brick a constructive, honest, serene life . . . I'll keep taking in as much of the world and as much experience as my energy limits allow, because I'm determined to make up for all those wasted years when I was Sylvia Plath's understudy.

Donna began to turn away from her self-sabotaging behaviour when she was finally able to fly home and to confront her mother successfully. Past attempts had failed because she had met with both parents and was angrily accusative and vindictive towards both. She would become incoherent when her father denied the charges and her mother supported him, both countering that Donna's disastrous marriage and career were the true cause of her craziness. This time Donna took my advice and talked to her mother alone. She was able to communicate her story clearly, incontrovertibly, and with sadness rather than anger at her mother's inability to see what was going on right under her nose and at her father's obsessive but unconscious need to exploit her sexually. That encounter went on for hours, ending with the embrace and the plea for forgiveness that Donna had long sought from her mother. Later they met with the father, who, seeing that his wife now believed Donna's story, acknowledged that something must have happened between him and Donna because he couldn't remember a thing about that period of his life, probably because he had been drinking heavily at that time.

Donna's relationship with her father remained partly unresolved, but in being able to re-establish her bond with her mother, she returned to the programme truly a new woman. She continued to communicate with her parents by telephone and letters. Recently her parents came to visit her in California and, as a result of counselling sessions in which they all participated, the father finally was enabled to face his fear and guilt. He recovered his memory and made a full admission of his offences to his wife and daughter. This encouraging outcome, however, probably would not have taken place if Donna had not prepared herself with the co-operation of Parents United members. In the group sessions, she was able to ventilate her terrible anger towards her parents. Once this was discharged, she gradually began to realize that the parents of sexually abusive families are themselves victims of a dysfunctional family system.

It is heartening to know that lives blighted by untreated incest can be salvaged with the help of the CSATP. However, far more rewarding is the knowledge that the victims and their families can be spared long years of alienation and pain if they are treated while the victims are still children. During the early stages of treatment, some of the adolescent girls, in particular those who feel they have been abandoned by their mothers, begin to manifest the anticipated self-abusive behaviour: truancy, promiscuity and drug abuse. Girls rejected by mothers who deny the charges or blame their daughters for the incestuous situation are the most difficult to treat. But here, too, the maladaptive behaviour usually stops largely through the influence of the adolescent group sessions which are often attended by women molested as children; the extra individual attention given by the staff and volunteers; and, in essence, the surrogate family formed around the girls by foster parents, the CSATP staff, and members of PU/DSU. A surrogate family, of course, is a poor substitute for the child's natural family, and if there is any hope at all of reuniting the child with her mother and family, the CSATP perseveres toward that end.

## THE TREATMENT PROCESS

### The Humanistic Attitude

The success of a CSATP depends on how well the leaders have internalized what may be called a humanistic attitude in coping with sexually abusive individuals and families and how well they are able to transfer this viewpoint to co-workers, the various official interveners, and the clients. Because this attitude has been discussed in previous articles[1,2] it will only be summarized here.

Persons who form abusive relationships with their mates, children, and other important people in their lives do so because they are incapable of developing trusting and mutually beneficial relations. Abusive parents typically were raised by punitive and generally uncaring parents. As children and later as adults they seem to court rejecting and even hostile responses from siblings, relatives, acquaintances, teachers, and others. They persevere in this lifestyle when they form their own families. Abusive parents are incapable of leading self-fulfilling lives. Consequently, they stew in a state of chronic resentment which can be discharged only through hostile acts *unconsciously* intended to be self-punishing.

It must be emphasized that this essentially self-abusive behaviour is an *unconscious* reaction to inner malaise. The sexually abusive father does not use his child primarily for sexual gratification but principally as a means of reconfirming and discharging his low self-worth. He approaches his child sexually without full awareness of the needs, drives and motives fueling his behaviour, nor of its consequences to his child, family and himself. The negative emotional energy that impels parental child abuse is similar to that which leads to substance abuse. Conversely, the greatest personal rewards come from satisfaction (not negation) of traditional human values: we would all prefer to be loved and respected by our children, mates, and peers. When we can't attain these commonly desired goals, we simply are incapable of doing what we must do to attain them; they are beyond our present life coping abilities. When abusive parental behaviour becomes severe enough to warrant intervention by the authorities, and they react by harshly punishing the offender, his self-hate/destructive energy syndrome is reinforced once more.

Despite their schooling, members of the helping professions are not entirely free of punitive emotional reactions to abusive parents. The image of a five year old child performing fellatio on her father in submission to his parental authority does not engender compassion for the parents. Instead, the images evoke spontaneous feelings of revulsion and hatred that shatter any reason and capacity to function as a therapist. CSATP counsellors still experience these feelings when they read the details of the offences in police reports despite the large number of cases that have come to their attention over the past eight years. Although these feelings are normal reactions, if they persist, the counsellor cannot hope to help the clients. He cannot claim to be working for the best interests of the child-victim, if he destroys her father. Normally a positive direction is given towards family reconstitution when the counsellor actually faces the father and senses his desperate helplessness and confusion. The hateful reactions of the counsellors toward abusive parents must be replaced with productive interventions based on understanding of the complex psychological dynamics that led to the abusive acts.

Another key realization that came during the early stages of the CSATP was that although traditional counselling is important, one person cannot attend to the multitudinous needs of the family. Many persons took part in the negative socialization of the family, and many must contribute to the positive resocialization process. People immobilized in low self-worth can be taught the attitudes and skills for high self-esteem and thereby the ability to lead self-fulfilling lives. This aim is best accomplished if such people are given the opportunity of helping one another towards that end by professionals who themselves take part in the process.

## Case Management

The case management of a family referred to the CSATP for father-daughter incest illustrates how the professional, volunteer, and self-help components work together. The procedure is more or less replicated in the other CSATPs in California, with the exception that child protective service workers perform the duties of the juvenile probation officers in Santa Clara County.

The initial referral of the sexually molested child in Santa Clare County often comes to the patrolman on duty within the jurisdiction where the child lives. The child may go to her mother, relative, or friend who usually report the situation to the police. If she relates her plight to a school nurse or another professional, all are required by law to call the police department. A patrolman is on round-the-clock duty to receive and immediately respond to these referrals. The officer takes the initial statement from the girl and any witnesses concerning what has happened, and, if he believes that the child is in jeopardy, places her in protective custody in the Children's Shelter. That occurs much less frequently than it did before the CSATP got started. A police officer from the Sexual Assault Investigation Unit of the San Jose Police Department, who has had special training in sexual abuse cases, investigates the case to decide whether or not there is sufficient evidence to warrant an arrest and referral to the District Attorney for prosecution.

An intake juvenile probation officer may also receive the referral directly via a telephone call from the school, a neighbour, or another agency person and takes appropriate action for the child. The juvenile probation officer is a member of a special unit specifically set up to investigate cases of child neglect and abuse. The probation officer may bring the child to the attention of the Juvenile Court by filing a petition under Section 600 of the Juvenile Court Law, which applies when the minor resides in a home "which is unfit by reason of depravity".

Generally, the police and probation officers work together during the investigative stages, co-ordinating their efforts to minimize the trauma to the child and family during this process and to maximize services to the family. The Juvenile Probation Department completes an exhaustive inquiry into the family situation to determine if the case requires the attention of the juvenile court.

The family is referred to the programme co-ordinator of the CSATP, who assigns the family to a counsellor. The counsellor and the responsible juvenile probation officer confer and agree on a plan of emergency and long-range supportive action for the family. Thereafter, they meet when necessary. It is important for the CSATP to maintain continual contact with the policeman and the juvenile probation officers servicing the cases.

About 40 per cent of referrals to the CSATP come from the clients directly. Prospective clients, who are often very upset, call in for information about the programme. The programme co-ordinator usually takes these calls although other staff members and Parents

United members may get them. The callers are listened to carefully and given information about the programme and the services available to them. However, no identifying information is taken until they agree that the situation must be reported. Those who do not want to report are listened to, talked to about their alternatives, and asked to call back if they want further help. If they decide to come forward, they are given the names of agency persons such as the juvenile probation officers and police officers to contact for reporting purposes. They are given a counselling appointment as soon as possible. If a client is very disturbed and needs immediate services, a counsellor or intern and a Parents United member are assigned to the family and particularly to the victim during or immediately after the reporting interview.

When girls are placed in the Children's Shelter, they also often need immediate services, and an intern or staff member tries to go out right away to see them. In cases where the situation is not critical, the girl will see a counsellor in a few days and is invited to come to the girls' group. An intern trained as a liaison worker between the CSATP and the Children's Shelter goes twice weekly to see the girls.

As much as it is possible, crisis needs are met immediately. These initial crisis interventions markedly influence the way clients orient themselves to the programme.

**Order of Treatment**

The counsellor's first step is to design a treatment programme for the family. Conjoint family therapy was found to be inappropriate for families in the early throes of the crisis, but the fundamental aim of family therapy which is to facilitate a harmonious familial system has not been discarded. Incestuous families are badly fragmented as a result of the original dysfunctional family dynamics, which are further exacerbated upon disclosure to civil authorities. The child, mother, and father must be treated separately before family therapy becomes productive. Consequently, the treatment procedure is usually applied in this order: (1) individual counselling, particularly for the child, mother and father; (2) mother-daughter counselling; (3) marital counselling, which becomes a key treatment if the family wishes to be reunited; (4) father-daughter counselling; (5) family counselling; and (6) group counselling. The treatments are not listed in order of importance, nor followed invariably in each case, but all are usually required for family reconstitution.

The length of treatment varies from family to family, but in general the objective of the treatment plan is to rebuild the family around the essential mother-daughter core. The counsellor usually meets first with the mother to help her deal with her distraught state and to assure her that the CSATP will help her through her family's crisis, and in time hopes to bring her family together.

The mother, and in most cases, the father are contacted by telephone by a member of Parents United. The purpose here is to put the parents in touch with a "sponsor" who has been through a similar experience. In addition to personal contacts, the sponsor invites the clients to Parents United and prepares them for the initial group sessions.

In the first meeting with the child, the counsellor helps to quiet down her fears, assures her that she has a responsible and sympathetic team working for her, and arranges the important early counselling sessions between the child and her mother. The child is also assigned a sponsor and invited to attend one of the groups conducted for DSU. If necessary, transportation is provided by interns.

Mother-daughter counselling is the key first step towards re-establishing a sound mother-daughter relationship. The child's overwhelming fear is that she has placed her father and family in serious jeopardy. The thrust at this point is to return the child to her home and her mother as soon as possible.

With few exceptions, most child victims wish to return to their mothers who in turn want them back. This may not be apparent at first because the child often feels she has betrayed her mother and family just as she feels anger for having been betrayed. The mother too often feels badly let down by her daughter. In some cases the alienation between them is so acute that the child and mother must be counselled several times separately before they can be brought together for treatment. The aim of the early counselling sessions is to convince the child that she indeed was victimized by her father and that it was her mother's duty to protect her. She must hear this not only from the counsellor but convincingly from her mother before she'll be ready to return home. She must also learn from her mother that her father has assumed full responsibility for the sexual activity. If the mother-daughter relationship cannot be resolved and it is necessary to place the child in a foster home, she is still persuaded to attend group sessions and individual counselling. Persistent effort is maintained to return her to her home.

While working with the mother and the daughter, the counsellor also sees the father as soon as he is free on bail or placed on his own recognizance. Generally the father is not allowed to make contact with the daughter at this point, but in most instances it is possible to start marriage counselling. In any case, it is important to provide therapy to the father as quickly as possible during the pretrial period. If the offender is discouraged by his lawyer from attending counselling sessions because this may be construed as an admission of guilt, the lawyer is contacted and usually convinced that it is to his client's advantage to come for counselling. It will help his marital and familial relationships and this in turn will have a positive effect on the decision of the juvenile probation officer and the courts regarding the return of the child-victim to the home and of the adult probation officer regarding his recommendations to the court. The father continues with his treatment throughout the prosecution period. The counselling continues by special arrangement with the rehabilitation centre even if he is given a gaol sentence. Counselling and participation in Parents United goes on after the sentence is served; participation in the CSATP is often a condition of his probation or parole.

By now the mother and the daughter usually are re-united in the home. The main thrust of the counselling at this point is to save the marriage and get the father back into the home. It must be repeated that this is not desirable if the child still feels that her parents are blaming her for the family's crisis. When the child and her father are ready to confront each other, counselling sessions are scheduled. The sessions eventually include the mother, and, finally, the entire family.

The professional counsellors supervise the treatment plan and use PU/DSU members and counsellor interns to assist them in providing services to the family. The counsellor determines on an individual basis whether or not to release the family to an intern for gradual termination of the counselling. The counsellor continues to be responsible for monitoring the progress of the family and to determine when the family can be released from treatment.

## The Court Process

During the early parts of this procedure, the father is facing the court process which lasts, on an average, about three months. If the offender is charged with a felony (usually the charge is child molestation or statutory rape; incest is seldom the charge), he is instructed to contact two court-appointed psychotherapists to determine if he is a mentally disturbed sex offender. If, on the basis of their reports, the judge finds the offender to be mentally disturbed, the offender is sent to the psychiatric state facility for chronic sex offenders. Incest offenders in Santa Clara County, however, are now rarely diagnosed as mentally disturbed, owing to the growing acceptance of the CSATP by the psychiatrists and judges as an effective alternative to the psychiatric facility. If the offender is judged not to be mentally disturbed, then he can be sent to a state prison, but this has never happened to a CSATP client. As a rule the offender is given a suspended sentence or is sentenced to the local rehabilitation centre for a few months. His rehabilitation officer is contacted and urged to hasten the client's work furlough and to permit him to come for individual counselling and to the Parents United weekly meetings. The officials at the rehabilitation centre have been releasing offenders who have employment immediately upon incarceration and also allowing attendance at counselling sessions and Parents United meetings. In a growing number of cases the judges, in lieu of gaol, order the offenders to contribute several hundred hours of work to Parents United.

### Criteria for Termination of Treatment

If the client or family remains in counselling with the CSATP, then the decision to terminate the case takes these criteria in consideration:

(1) Is a court order for counselling still in existence?

(2) Does the family, in particular the parents, feel they have made sufficient progress in their communication, parenting, and self-management skills to need no further regular counselling?

(3) Does the counsellor who has been seeing the family feel they have made sufficient progress to terminate counselling?

(4) If a supervising probation officer or social worker is involved, does he or she feel the family has progressed sufficiently to recommend termination of the counselling to the court?

The following questions are usually considered to determine "sufficient progress":

(1) Is a molestation likely to recur? In other words, has the marital and home situation improved enough to prevent recurrence of molestation and ensure a safe home environment for the child-victim?

(2) Has the offender taken responsibility for his/her behaviour and become aware of the formerly largely unconscious impulses which preceded the molestation of his/her child? Is the offender able to control them if they recur?

(3) Have the feelings and conflicts between family members (mother, daughter, father, siblings) been dealt with openly and completely so that the family environment is nurturing for the child and other family members?

In cases where only the adult is being counselled as in the case of an adult woman who was molested as a child or in cases where only the child victim is being seen, perhaps in conjunction with his or her foster family, these questions will be considered but in relation to the client's particular circumstances.

If there is an existing court order, that order must be modified before termination. The court usually respects the recommendation of the CSATP counsellor in this regard. If no order exists, the decision is made jointly by the client, counsellor, and supervising agency. The above description of case management describes the treatment cycle for most incest cases. Generally family members receive intensive individual, couple, and family counselling as well as group counselling in PU/DSU. The average family stays in the CSATP for about nine months. The family is encouraged to stay with the program as long as it is deemed necessary.

## GROWTH AND ACCOMPLISHMENTS

The success of the Child sexual abuse Treatment Programme can be assessed by the rate of increase of referrals and by the percentage of families who are helped. As mentioned in the introduction to this chapter, the referral rate has increased dramatically since 1971. Since it is reasonable to suppose that the actual rate of incest itself has not changed appreciably in Santa Clara County during the past few years, the significance of this growing referral rate is all the greater. It means that many families are now receiving help who would not have received such help were it not for the CSATP and its ability to gain the co-operation of the criminal justice system and a positive reception by the press and public. Hundreds of families being treated each year for a family problem that has always plagued society but has heretofore largely been ignored.

In 1977, the success of the CSATP was measured by the staff, and the findings were considered by some to be questionable because of potential bias. In mid-1977, however, a review committee appointed by the California State Director of Health assigned an independent investigator to collect and analyse data on the performance of the CSATP. A evaluation team, led by Dr Jerome A Kroth, surveyed comparable groups of clients at three stages in the treatment programme: intake, mid-term, and near termination. *"The evaluator's overall conclusion is that the impact of CSATP family therapy in the treatment of intrafamilial child sexual abuse is positive, conclusive and unmistakable."* [3]

The following are some of the evaluation team's key findings.

### The Daughter

Child victims of incest in Santa Clara County who were removed from their mothers by the authorities are being returned to their mothers much sooner than they were before the CSATP was formed and sooner than in other communities throughout the county. Based on a sample of 127 active cases, the median time out of the home for these girls was 90 days, and 92 per cent could be expected to return home eventually .

Although not objectively measured, it was clearly apparent to the staff that there was a decline, both in intensity and in duration, in the typical self-abusive behaviour of child victims. It appeared that the co-ordinated approach of the CSATP prevents truancy, decline in school performance, promiscuity, and heavy drug use, by helping the girls overcome their strong feelings of betrayal and guilt. The evaluator measured this absence of self-abusive behaviour as a "failure to deteriorate". He found, from a sample of 70 incest victims, that during the prior two months only four per cent had gotten drunk or high on drugs; only three per cent had shown signs of sexual promiscuity; only one per cent had stayed out overnight without permission or run away from home; and only six per cent had become involved with the authorities. These figures are extremely low compared with any other figures in the literature of child sexual abuse.

Put, perhaps, in strong terms, if one supposes that children who experience incest have an increasing tendency toward social maladjustment and are, as a consequence of the molest, more prone toward delinquency, sexual acting-out, substance abuse, etc, receiving family therapy intervention entirely contradicts such a prognosis.[4]

The psychological health of the girls also improved during the course of the treatment. The percentage with symptoms such as bedwetting, nail biting, and fainting declined from 47 per cent at intake to six per cent by termination. The girls' relationships with their peers and the other members of their families, particularly their fathers, showed marked improvement. Whether these gains can be sustained remains to be seen.

As an indication of the CSATP's success in achieving the goal of repairing the relationship between father and daughter, *no recidivism has been reported among the more than 600 families who have received a minimum of ten hours of treatment and whose cases have been formally terminated.* Kroth determined that the overall recidivism rate for CSATP client families was 0·6 per cent and, compared this rate to the two per cent rate reported by two other studies, cited by Maish (1972) and a 20 per cent rate reported in a study by Gebhard (1965)[5] It must be noted that the typical recidivism rates reported in professional journals are based on institutionalized offenders of whom the majority do not return to their families whereas about 85 per cent of the offenders treated by the CSATP do return to their families. Kroth believes, however, the recidivism rate is not as significant as the number of the referrals to the CSATP.

However admirable the recidivism rate may be at CSATP or elsewhere, it is difficult to place a great deal of emphasis on such small percentages and draw substantial conclusions from them. With or without therapy, it appears that 98 per cent of incest offenders will not repeat the offence *once coming to the attention of the criminal justice system.* In effect the single most important statistic which reflects on the efficacy of treatment is not recidivism or anxiety level, or the grade point averages of victims in treatment, but the rate at which victims, offenders and families come forward! In this regard the CSATP referral record is superb ... Since 1974, for example, there has been *an average increase of about 40 per cent in the number of clients coming forward each year, and it is likely 98 per cent of these new clients will not repeat the offence merely on the basis of the fact* that the molest has been reported and the family secret broken.[6]

## The Father

The father-offender in the incestuous family has also benefited greatly from the Child Sexual Abuse Treatment Programme. Men who formerly would have received long prison sentences are now being given shorter terms or even suspended sentences as a result of increasing reception of the CSATP by the judiciary as an effective alternative to incarceration. Indeed, many fathers initially come to the CSATP primarily because they assume that participation in the CSATP and in Parents United is likely to soften the court's decision on their sentence. Before long most realise that the CSATP tries to keep them out of gaol so that they can be taught to become effective husbands and parents and, in general, to lead more rewarding lives.

For successful treatment to take place, the father must accept full responsibility for the molestation. In the evaluator's sample, 89 per cent are ready to accept most or all of the responsibility for the molestation at termination of the study period. Significant, too, is the finding that feelings of extreme general guilt are reduced at the same time. The number of parents feeling "strong guilt" declined from 65 per cent of the sample at intake to 24 per cent near termination. This ability to distinguish between responsibility and guilt is one of the important goals of therapy. The former is necessary for self-management; the latter is only destructive.

The CSATP has significantly speeded up the process of rehabilitation for the offender. Before the programme started, individual or marriage counselling did not occur, if at all, until after the offender was released from gaol. Now counselling is started soon after his arrest and continues during and after incarceration. It is reasonable to assume that this early counselling has been vital in helping to return valuable men to society. For example, CSATP personnel were effective in helping to restore the licences of two pilots and two real estate men, to reinstitute the secret clearances of two engineers in the aerospace industry, to have a discharged postal service employee return to his civil service position, to save the jobs of several men in private industry, and to save the careers of four military servicemen.

Even more important in terms of the victims and their fathers, the CSATP has been successful in developing normal relationships between them. This goal, once considered by many to be undesirable and/or impossible, has proven to be vital to the future mental health of the parent, child and family as a unit. The evaluation found, in a sample of 23, that worsening relationships between father and daughter decreased from 17 per cent to 4 per cent, while improving relationships increased from 22 per cent to 50 per cent.

## The Mother

In the typical incestuous family treated by the CSATP, the mother is the first to receive tangible help, in the form of immediate counselling and emergency assistance with housing, employment, and financial aid. Before the programme existed, mothers usually found themselves alone and devastated. The bureaucracy was badly fragmented, and the mother had no guidance in securing the various kinds of help available. The CSATP has been able to mobilize typically disjointed and often competitive services into a co-operative effort.

While the mother's strong sense of guilt declines during the course of treatment, as does the father's, she too learns to accept her share of responsibility for the conditions leading to the molestation. By termination, 50 per cent of the evaluator's sample admit that they were "very much responsible" as opposed to none who admitted this at intake. This change of attitude comes from learning that incest is in large part due to a failing marriage for which both spouses are responsible.

## The Marriage and the Family

The positive effect of the CSATP on both parents is revealed in the evaluator's measure of "attitudinal changes". Near termination, 82 per cent of the parents agreed with the statement "I feel more open, honest, and in control of myself", and all affirmed that "Things are a lot better than they used to be". The percentage of those who disagreed with the statement "Right now I feel devastated emotionally" rose from zero per cent at intake to 76 per cent near termination. Similarly, the percentage of those who felt "not close at all" to a nervous breakdown rose from 12 per cent to 88 per cent.

Near termination, 59 per cent of the sample reported that their relationships had improved, whereas only six per cent reported that their relationships had deteriorated. They reported that their sexual activity increased both in frequency and quality. There is a corresponding marked improvement in the husband's sense of his own sexual health. Those marriage partners who argued "quite a lot" at the beginning of the study argued much less at the end; the decrease in arguments ranged from 38 per cent at intake to zero per cent near termination. In many instances, the husbands and wives confided that their relationships are better now than they were before the crisis, or, for that matter, better than they have ever been. As one couple put it: "This is the first time in our marriage that we have ever been able to communicate."

In the future, it will be possible to measure the success of the CSATP's case management in terms of quantitative data. A computerized system for data collection has been developed and is now being tested which allows the CSATP to gather a wealth of demographic and case history information at intake on each family referred to the programme. The present system is designed for intake information only; but the use of data processing has opened up the possibility of future computer programmes which will be able to monitor the progress of each case to termination.

The need for computerized data collection in the field of child sexual abuse is great. Until now there has been no effective way to gather information on incest, and the statistics offered by the literature have been speculative, inconclusive, conflicting, and biased by meagre samples. Weinberg's study[7] for example, although it was based on a retrospective survey of 203 cases (an exceptional number when compared to the majority of other studies), led to conclusions that already appear deceptive in light of the extensive first-hand experiences of the CSATP. Undoubtedly other treatment programmes will emulate this system and improve on it, making possible a network of reliable and valid data on child sexual abuse.

## CONCLUDING REMARKS

This article has described the approach developed by the Child Sexual Abuse Treatment Programme of Santa Clara County, California, for treating the casualties of father-daughter incest — the victims, the offenders, and their families. My faith in this method leads me to hope that one day CSATPs or agencies like them will be common-place, so that all families — not only those troubled by incest — will have available to them a humanistic, caring environment in which to rebuild their lives.

Reprinted with permission from P B Mrazek and C H Kempe, *Sexually Abused Children and their Families* (Pergamon Press, Oxford, 1981)

# Notes

1   H Giarretto, "Humanistic Treatment of Father-Daughter Incest" in R E Helfer and C H Kempe (eds) *Child Abuse and Neglect: The Family and the Community* (Ballinger, Cambridge, Massachusetts, 1976)

2   H Giarretto, A Giarretto and S M Sgroi, "Co-ordinated Community Treatment of Incest" in A W Burgess, A N Groth, L L Holstrom and S M Sgroi (eds) *Sexual Assault of Children and Adolescents* (Lexington Books, D C Heath and Co, Lexington, 1978)

3   J A Kroth, *Child Sexual Abuse: Analysis of Evaluation Report on the Child Sexual Abuse Demonstration and Treatment Project* (Office of Child Abuse Prevention, California Dept Health, Sacramento, 1979) p 137

4   J A Kroth, ibid, p 100

5   J A Kroth, ibid, p 124

6   J A Kroth, ibid, p 125

7   S K Weinberg, *Incest Behaviour* (Citadel, New York, 1955)

# Chapter 13

# Abused Children — What Happens Eventually

Harold P Martin

For the first ten years after child abuse became a widely recognized clinical phenomenon,[1] there was little attention paid to the morbidity in the surviving abused child. The effects of the physical attack on the child at most were considered worthy of description, although not even those immediate biological consequences were rigourously studied. Finally, the work of Elmer and Gregg emphasized startlingly high neurological, developmental, and psychological disabilities.[2,3,4] Since those landmark studies, increasing attention has been paid to this issue.

Rather than hypothesize on the reason so little attention was paid to the morbidity of the abuse syndrome for so long, one might more profitably wonder what motivates researchers and clinicians now to attend to this important question. Certainly the child clinician is impressed and both professionally and personally moved by the neuro-developmental and psychological deviancy seen in so many mistreated children. While some of the injuries to children are serious and even lethal, more often the bruises, burns, and fractures of long bones do not carry serious biological prognoses. Rather, it is the longer-term consequences which concern one. A corollary of this is the clinician's convictions that the whole pattern of parenting and family life in the abusive home is what takes such serious and long lasting toll on the child.

There may be an intuitive feeling that mistreated children will grow up to be adults who may threaten the peacefulness and security of society. One cannot help but feel that there may be a warping of children's lives by being unloved, neglected and physically abused. This may increase that child's chances of growing up to be an unhappy adult who may play out his anger and hurt by striking out at others.

There may be more personal reasons to study the effects of abuse on children. After all, all of us were children ourselves some years ago. We may recall our reactions to the physical and psychological injustices we endured. So one may empathize with the mistreated child. We know from our own experiences as children that even occasional or mild mistreatment of children takes its toll. Further, many of us are parents. As we think back on the times we became angry and had impulses to strike our own children, the question of what harm might have been done arises.

There is increasing concern about violence in general in our societies. This may take the form of group movements surrounding spouse abuse, police brutality, increased use of violence by criminals, terrorism, or aggression by the state. It may also translate into concern about the consequences of violence towards children. For in this syndrome, one finds the quintessence of violence towards the unprotected, weak and powerless members of society.

Finally, some clinical researchers are basically interested in child development. They must be intrigued by knowing what the effects of such parenting styles are on these children. This is so much more compelling and socially pertinent than looking at more subtle factors in the rearing of children, for example effects of mothers working outside the home, effects of divorce, effects of using a pacifier, etc.

I intend no cynicism in this discourse on why the question is posed as to what eventually happens to abused children. Most of the answers have not come from the researcher's laboratory, but have come from the observations and research designs of clinicians, workers in the field. These have mostly been professionals who have been genuinely moved by the plight of abused children. There need be no besmirchment of noble motives to acknowledge that our own life's experiences and professional interests may sharpen the edge of our interest and concern about the future adjustment and lives of abused children.

This author will review what is known about the consequences of abuse to children, artificially dividing these into short-term and long-term effects. For there is interest in how abuse affects infants and children as well as what effects may be seen in the adolescent and adult who were abused in childhood.

## INFANCY AND CHILDHOOD

Little detail need be given the types of wounds and injuries immediately suffered through physical abuse. Standard texts and papers describe these quite nicely.[5,6,7,8,9] In addition to soft tissue damage, burns, fractures, brain injuries and damage to other internal organs, the physician has been cautioned regarding the "hidden" wounds of damage such as intracranial bleeding from shaking of infants, retinal hemorrhage, etc.

## Health Problems

Abused children may be anaemic. Ebbin reported 50 per cent of their cohort of abused children were significantly anaemic.[10] Dietrich found that abused infants in his study had a mean haemoglobin level of 9.9 grams per cent while the control infants had levels of 12.07.[11] Other authors have suggested that abused children may have increased incidence of illnesses of a variety of sorts.[12,13,14,15]

Another consequence of the abusive environment may be undernutrition. Koel dramatized this by reporting on three infants with failure-to-thrive who were later re-admitted to hospital with physical abuse, from which two of the three died.[16] This report helped refute the earlier view that abuse and neglect rarely co-existed. Johnson reported that 50 per cent of her 101 abused children had undernutrition or failure-to-thrive[17]; Ebbin's 50 abused Los Angeles children had a 30 per cent prevalence of growth retardation[10]; Morse indicated that over 50 per cent of her reported children had delayed heights and/or weights[18]; Martin reported 33 per cent of 42 abused children had failure to thrive at the time of diagnosis[19] and 36 per cent of a separate group of 58 abused children had growth failure.[20] Inasmuch as neglect (including nutritional neglect) may accompany abuse, there should be no surprise in finding undernutrition in many physically mistreated children.

Less well documented are increased risk of infection, dental problems, visual and hearing deficits, greater risk of accidental ingestions, and inadequate health care in the past.[3,8]

Some health problems may actually *precede* the abuse. Hunter and colleagues showed abused children to be of lower birth weight and to have three times the incidence of medical problems at discharge from nursery than the comparison group.[21] Lynch and Roberts reported at the Third International Congress that abused children had almost twice the incidence of neurological abnormalities as their non-abused siblings, with four times greater incidence of visual problems.[22] Nakou lists more perinatal problems, poorer nutrition, and more illnesses in infancy in 50 abused children than their 53 non-abused siblings.[23] A recent book written for physicians and nurses regarding the health problems of abused and neglected children addresses the incidence and treatment of these problem.[8] Lynch and colleagues earlier presented data on 25 abused children and their 35 non-abused siblings.[24,25] She said 60 per cent of the abused children had been significantly ill in infancy while the siblings had been outstandingly healthy. Oates and colleagues similarly found that 52 per cent of their abused sample had been ill in infancy while only 9 per cent of the control children had had similar ill health.[26]

## Neuro-developmental Disabilities

More impressive are overwhelming data demonstrating that mistreated children are at considerable risk of mental retardation, brain damage, language delays, preceptual-motor immaturity, and learning disabilities. The earliest descriptions of seriously abused children reported developmental morbidity of 88 per cent.[1,2,3] Subsequent studies also documented retardation and other developmental disabilities in large percentages of abused children.[17,18,19,20,27,28,29] These data are summarized in two recent publications.[30,31] Most of the early research was retrospective, descriptive, or anecdotal, had no or inadequate control groups, and had inadequate sample selection for generalizability to most other groups of abused children. Besharoff faults child abuse research on theoretical grounds,[32] and Plotkin and Twentyman roundly criticize the methodology of 250 published articles they reviewed.[33] Yet to this author, it seems that the research of the past few years had improved in quality and is more convincing to the scientific sceptic. These more recent data make the validity of earlier studies more convincing through more rigorous research methodology.

Applebaum demonstrated mental scores on the Bayley at a mean age of 14.7 months to be 31 points lower in abused infants than in a control group ($p < .001$).[34] Motor scores were even more discrepant. Denver Developmental Screening Tests (DDST) on the children found significant delays in motor and language development in the abused infants.

Hay and Hall found similar results in 2-6 year olds.[35] Scores on the DDST and the Stanford-Binet were lower in abused than control children ($p < .05$). They found the lower scores to be primarily due to deficiencies in language and fine motor abilities. Oates and colleagues have consistently found mistreated children to function significantly lower on developmental tests and in language, as well as to have more learning disabilities as compared to control groups.[36,37,38,39]

The sample of abused children one chooses to study will alter how serious the effects of abuse seem. Barahal and colleagues studied a group of 17 abused 6-8 year olds and compared them to a very closely controlled group of non-abused children.[40] While the IQ's of both groups were in the normal range (perhaps due to the researchers deliberately excluding any child with neurologic abnormality), the abused children's scores were ten points lower than the control group ($p < .02$). On the other hand, Buchanan and Oliver looked at all of the admissions to a residential treatment centre for retarded in England.[41] They pointed out that 22 per cent of these 140 children had evidence of physical assault prior to admission to hospital. At least three per cent were retarded because of assault, and another 11 per cent were suspected of being retarded because of physical abuse, but evidence was not definitive. Even more shocking was the finding that 41 per cent of the incoming retarded children had been exposed to a habitual pattern of neglect with 24 per cent having neglect as a contributory factor in reducing intellectual potential.

Even when mental abilities are normal, learning disabilities are frequent. Kline was one of the first to show that there is a high frequency of learning disabilities in abused populations.[42] In a followup study of 58 abused children, 27 per cent of the school-aged children were having learning problems that were not the result of mental deficiency.[43] Hufton and Oates suggested that 66 per cent of neglected children had reading disabilities.[39] An unpublished study in Boulder, Colorado, revealed that there were more than four times the proportion of abused or neglected children in special education classes than in the regular classrooms.[44]

While data are lacking to accurately prognosticate the chances of developmental disability in an individual abused child, there seems no question that what eventually happens to a large number of abused children is to be handicapped by some variety of neuro-developmental delay. Retardation, learning disability, motor delay and inco-ordination (both gross and fine motor), and language disability are common problems that abused children must endure.

### Emotional Problems

There are also risks of psychiatric problems for the infant and child. The clincian cannot escape noting the psychological price(s) which are paid by being raised in an abusive and/or neglectful home. There is no one specific personality profile seen in abused children. Rather, the child's personality will be shaped by a number of factors, including the type of parents, the developmental stage(s) when abuse occurred, innate factors within the child, who the perpetrator of abuse was, the type of parenting behaviors to which the child was exposed, and the type of treatment offered the child and the family.

As with the developmental studies, early reports were often descriptive and were poorly controlled. However, more and more reports tend to corroborate these early descriptions. When Kinard reviewed nine studies of the mental health needs of children he found impressive congruency.[45] While faulting the methodology of eight investigators in addition to his own work (Rolston[46]; Green[47,48,49,50]; Baher[51]; Kent[52]; Martin[43,53]; Elmer[54,55]; Reidy[56]; Berkley Planning[57]; and Kinard[58]) he still found that most of these reports agreed that abused children are unusually aggressive, have poor self-concept, lack a capacity to trust, have deviant interpersonal relationships, and have unusual attachment and detachment behaviours. Martin and Beezley's description of 50 abused children[43] emphasized extremes of behaviour, for example, the child may have excessive stranger anxiety, or may be indiscriminate in affection to all; there may be oppositional behaviour or co-operative obsequious responses.

There has been considerable focus on the aggressivity of abused children. Green and colleagues have emphasized this, noting that sometimes the aggression is turned outward, and just as often inward. Indeed, in one report, he notes that slightly more than eight percent of children with a mean age of 8.5 years had attempted suicide and that 20 per cent had self-mutilative behaviour. Bakan had earlier commented on self-abuse being more common in abused children.[58] In addition to the findings of Kent and Reidy mentioned above, a more recent controlled study of 1-3 year olds showed that abused pre-schoolers were more assaultive than their peers.[59] Only in the abused toddlers were assaults and threats directed towards care-givers. Further, the abused children responded to friendly overtures by avoidance or by combining approach and avoidance behaviours.

The latency aged child also bears psychological scars. Lynch and Roberts considered how teachers view abused children.[60] Twenty-five per cent of the 49 abused children were viewed as maladjusted by their teachers. Parenthetically, most of these children had learning disorders despite adequate intelligence.

Barahal's study, previously noted,[40] found that abused children had a much greater tendency to have external locus of control than non-abused control children. This was especially significant for negative or bad events, and remained statistically significant when intelligence was controlled for. The ability of the abused latency aged child to take the perspective of others and to be sensitive to other's feelings were less well developed. Comprehension of social roles of children and adults was less well understood.

Kinard reported data on 30 abused children and a comparison group which was carefully controlled for age, sex, race, birth order, number of children in the family, SES, and neighbourhood.[61] The abused children were more sad, unpopular, and had significantly lower scores on five other items from the 80-item test. Factor analysis suggested that abused children did more poorly on conformity-happiness scales. They were more outwardly directed in their aggression. On projective testing, the abused children scored lower in socialization with peers and trust in other people.

Anne Cohn reviewed three demonstration treatment programs for abused children in the United States.[62] She notes that 70 per cent of the children did not relate well with peers and 57 per cent had deviant interrelationships with adults. Over one-half of the children had poor self-concepts and had difficulty in giving or receiving affection. The children were described by workers as being generally unhappy with over 40 per cent exhibiting aggression or apathy and having difficulty in reacting to changes in their environment.

And so it would seem that Kinard's conclusions are repeatedly being borne out:[45] abused children are likely to be aggressive, have poor self-concepts, have deviant object relations and impaired ability to trust and attach to people. Inasmuch as these traits are similar to the characteristics described in abusive adults, it gives some credence to the hypotheses of Barahal, Waterman and Martin that one might expect to see the early appearance of the abusive adult's character traits in the child who is identifying with an modelling after an abusive parent.[40]

## Transactional Paradigm

A bit more needs be said about the difficulties in interactions between abused children and their parents. Often it is not clear which member of the relationship is having the difficulty. Indeed, more and more papers focusing on interaction, or the transactional paradigm, point out that both partners play their role in deviant relating. Gaensbauer observed approximately 100 abused and non-abused children between 6 and 36 months of age.[63] He found that the mistreated children had distortions in communicating intent and affects, thereby interfering with mutual engagement. Work such as that of Hunter point out that there are differences in the babies *and* in the abusive mothers as compared to the 245 non-abusive dyads.[21]

Burgess and Conger recorded over 20,000 interactions in abusive, neglectful and control families.[64] While they found the role of the mother to be central in abuse and neglect, they also noted that the abused children were less compliant and more aversive, while the neglected children had extreme negativity and a low rate of positive interactions. Bee and colleagues noted that abusive mothers were different than non-abusive mothers when teaching their toddlers a task, but also noted that the abused children lacked clarity in their cues and were less responsive to their parents.[65] Hay noted that abused children vocalized less and had more proximity to their mothers *without* initiating contact.[35] Egeland and Brunnquell pointed out that babies of abusive mothers were less able to orient themselves to stimulae, were more irritable, and had less social responsiveness.[66] This is reminiscent of George and Main's findings of abused pre-schoolers responding to friendly overtures by avoidance or by combining approach and avoidance behaviours.[59]

A recent presentation from Wales reinforces this interactive paradigm by finding both infant characteristics and family stress to correlate with later abusive behaviour in a retrospective study of 80 abused five year olds and 80 control children.

Despite this author's enthusiasm for the transactional paradigm to explain much of the deviant behaviour in the abuse syndrome, one must be cautious. One must not necessarily consider parents' reports about their children's behaviour as valid. O'Connor and Altemeir showed in their prospective Nashville study that while mothers of failure-to-thrive babies scored their children as more difficult than did control mothers, there were *no* differences on the Brazelton tests with both groups of infants.[68] This fits Hinchy's findings that abusive mothers are less empathic to their children than a control group.[69] Frodl showed that abusive mothers react differently to a baby's cry and smile than a control group.[70] The former showed more annoyance, less patience, and had greater cardiac rates. This makes one cynical about the validity of the parents' reports in Herrenkohl's study of abused children and their non-abused siblings.[71] In this paper, parents recalled their abused children as having been more difficult and quite different from the 284 non-abused siblings.

The transactional approach is important from several perspectives. At least one thing to be learned is that abused children may not relate well with adults other than their parents. Whether the child's deviancy in relating is congenitally temperamental in nature, or a reflection of reinforcement of mildly deviant infantile behaviour, or is strictly learned from months and years of deviant parenting behaviour is not fully answered. But, it is clear that the high rate of foster-placement failure is partly due to the contribution of the abused child to unsatisfactory object relations.

## ADOLESCENTS AND ADULTS WHO WERE ABUSED IN CHILDHOOD

Data on long-term effects of the abusive environment are less systematic. There are no prospective longitudinal studies of abused children which follow them into adult life. One is left with retrospective studies of special groups of people such as delinquents, criminals, school drop-outs, teenage parents, and abusive parents. There seems little doubt that there is a real risk of abused children taking one of these socially deviant pathways. What is not clear is just what the statistical risk is for the individual child.

An example of this dilemma resides in the risk of growing up to be an abusive parent. The generational transmission of abuse and neglect was described early on by Steele and Pollock.[72] They felt that almost all abusive adults were mistreated themselves as children. This understandably would raise considerable concern in any adult who was abused as a child as to whether or not they have the capacity to avoid a repetition of this pattern of parenting. Hunter's study of 255 mothers who gave birth to premature babies sheds some light on this concern.[21] Nine of ten mothers who mistreated their children during the first year of life had histories of being abused or neglected themselves as children, while only 17 per cent of the other 245 mothers had such a history. This difference in abuse rates was highly statistically significant (p<.0005). The casual reader might well assume that being abused put one at a very high risk of becoming an abusive parent. However, one must also realize that the 17 per cent figure for the non-abusers works out to a total of 42 mothers who had histories of being abused who did *not* mistreat their children versus nine mothers with similar histories who *did* mistreat their children. This suggests that only about 20 per cent of the women with histories of being abused, mistreated their children, at least in the first year of life. And so the seeming paradox: being abused as a child greatly increases the risk that one will be abusive as an adult; and yet the majority of abused children will not follow that course.

The finding of aggressivity in abused children and infants finds its parallel in studies of adolescents and adults who were abused during childhood. Lewis correlated aggressive, assaultive behaviour in delinquents with a history of being abused.[73] Further, his group shows that there is an even higher correlation with having witnessed violence in their homes. Earlier studies from this investigator reviewed medical records and found that in those delinquent adolescents with more violent offences, there were more histories of injuries about the face and head during childhood.[74,75] Bradley feels that many adolescents with borderline personality disorders had early maternal deprivation, without any information whether physical abuse was part of the depriving environment.[76]

Rogers and Leunes compared juvenile delinquents who were abused as children with other delinquents without any such history.[77] The former group were less flexible, less socially mature, and had less satisfactory home relationships than the latter group. In comparing college students who had been abused with a control group, Chan and Perry found the previously abused young adult had lower self-esteem and was less satisfied with their social support systems.[78] They then compared the college students with a history of being abused, dividing them into those with low and those with high self-esteem. The pertinent differences in the two groups seemed to relate to the type of family environments in which they were reared.

The consequences of abuse on children and infants, noted in the previous section have some prognostic value in considering the adolescent and adult years of life. Impaired learning, retardation, langugage and motor disabilities will not spontaneously disappear in adulthood. This relates to this author's experience that a most distressing long-term effect of maltreatment is a life of incompetence and failure. One certainly sees this in the abusive adult who was the victim of maltreatment as a child. Such adults repeatedly give histories of job failures, school failures, and repeated failures in marriages or romantic liaisons. This would follow if low self-esteem, impaired interpersonal relationships, and external locus of control persist from childhood. If, as Steele feels, most mistreated children who grow up to be abusive are borderline or narcissistic personality disordered people, it would follow that lack of competence or success would prevail in their lives.[79]

It is clear that what eventually happens to abused children need not be so grim a picture. There will always be some subset of persons who were exposed to stressful and noxious experiences who do quite well. Or, the prices that these individuals pay are in developing characteristics which may be painful to the individual, but are not viewed as deviant by the society, for example, compulsive behaviour, an insatiable drive to succeed, etc. It is of some interest to speculate on why some abused children fare so well.

It may be that in some individuals, some very potent therapeutic experiences occurred. This may take the form of specific treatment programs instituted to help the abused child. Or it may be serendipity which provided a child with some parent surrogate, or alternate life's experiences which muted the effects of abusive parenting. It is clear that in some relatively unscathed children, there was an abundance of love and nurturing during the earliest years. Abuse by parents may have developed later in response to a specific developmental stage of the child, or abuse or neglect may have occurred at some point later when the parent(s) was under special external or psychological stress.

There must be characteristics or temperamental traits of individuals, probably congenital, which make that person more or less vulnerable to abusive or neglectful parenting. It is known (and was reinforced by Brazelton's work) that there is variability in newborns ability to adapt to painful or noxious stimulate such as light, sound, or pain.[80] Some babies are more capable than others, some more able to soothe themselves, and some more socially responsive than others. It is posited here that these variations in coping or adaptation to the world continue beyond the newborn period, indeed become more prominently varied as life progresses.

It would be naive to assume that nothing can make a difference in what eventually happens to an abused child. Even primate research shows the modifying effect of the social surround. For example, gorilla research shows that even when a female was poorly parented herself the gorilla mother's abuse decreases when another familiar adult is put in the cage with her and her infant.[81] The whole underpinnings of programs such as Parent's Anonymous, the lay-health visitor, or any number of other preventive strategies is that with proper suport and help, many at-risk adults who were mistreated themselves can be aided to prevent the onset of abuse and neglect. Many of the therapeutic approaches to abusive parents not only can result in better psychological health in these adults, but concretely help in job placement, interpersonal relationships, crisis resolution, and general increases in satisfaction with life.

## SUMMARY

And so the question of what eventually happens to abused children can be answered only by pointing out various pathways the child, adolescent and adult may take. At best, one can know that the abused child is at increased risk of various problems. For the surviving abused child, the risks are great for various forms of neuro-developmental delay or disability. With or without such consequences, a most grim picture is for the child to grow up to be much like his parent. Unfortunately the child may even fare worse by becoming more socially and psychologically deviant. And yet one must end on a note of optimism, or at least of therapeutic and preventive pragmatism. These are not irrevocably certain outcomes. The course and future of the abused child can be affected and altered.

What eventually happens to the abused child will in large part depend on the professionals who plan treatment for that child. We must be sure that specific treatment plans for every abused child are considered, discussed, and implemented. What eventually happens to the abused child will also depend upon our finesse in avoiding more trauma to the child via our therapeutic efforts. While the child may need to be hospitalized, separated from parents, or put into alternate home care; the psychological trauma of these stresses can be greatly diminished by preventive efforts of the abuse team. Treatment for developmental deviancy, attention to associated medical problems, and therapeutic intervention for the psychological scars the child has suffered can make a difference in prognosis.

When the parents can respond to treatment, it must include efforts at changing the attitudes and behaviour towards the child. When change in the parents is minimal, prompt action to find a permanent family for the child must be a high priority so that the child does not suffer more damage from years of foster placements.

The frequency of child abuse is considerably greater than professionals would have imagined a few years ago. The morbidity for the surviving child victims can be quite high and life-long. To stress in this chapter the risks for abused children throughout their lives is to build a platform for emphasizing the need for sensitive treatment modalities to be provided these children. Without treatment, the chances of these mistreated children growing up socially, developmentally, and personally deviant and unhappy are high.

## Notes

1   C H Kempe, F Silverman, B Steele, W Droegmueller, and H Silver, "The Battered Child Syndrome" (1962) *JAMA* **181**:17-24

2   E Elmer, *Children in Jeopardy* (University of Pittsburgh Press, Pittsburgh, 1967)

3   E Elmer and G S Gregg, "Development Characteristics of Abused Children" (1967) *Pediatrics* **40**:596-602

4   G S Gregg and E Elmer, "Infant Injuries: Accident or Abuse" (1969) *Pediatrics* **44**:434-439

5   B Schmitt and C H Kempe, "Neurological Aspects of the Battered Child Syndrome" in Vinker and Bruyn (eds) *Handbook of Clinical Neurology* (North Holland Publishing Co, Amsterdam, 1974)

6   B Schmitt and C H Kempe, "The Battered Child Syndrome" in Kelley (ed) *Brennemann-Kelley Practice of Pediatrics* (Harper and Row Publishers Inc, New York, 1974)

7   B Schmitt, "Battered Child Syndrome" in Kempe, Silver and O'Brien (eds) *Current Pediatric Diagnosis and Treatment,* 6th ed (Lange Publishers, Los Altos, California, 1980) pp 120-126

8   N Ellerstein (ed), *Child Abuse and Neglect: A Medical Reference* (J Wiley and Sons, New York, 1981)

9   R S Zimmerman, L T Bilanink, D Bruce, L Schut, B Uzzell and H I Goldberg, "Computed Tomography of Craniocerebral Injuries in the Abused Child" (1979) *Radiology* **130**(3):687-90

10  A J Ebbin, M H Gollub, A M Stein and M G Wilson, "Battered Child Syndrome at the Los Angeles County General Hospital" (1969) *Am J Dis Child* **118**:660-67

11  K M Dietrich, *The Abused Infant: Developmental Characteristics and Maternal Handling* (Masters thesis, Wayne State University, Detroit, Michigan, 1977)

12  B Johnson and H Morse, *The Battered Child: A Study of Children with Inflicted Injuries* (Denver Dept of Welfare, Denver, March 1968)

13   C W Morse, O J Z Sahler and S B Friedman, "A Three-Year Follow-up Study of Abused and Neglected Children" (1970) *Am J Dis Child* 120:439-46

14   J T Kent, "A Follow-up Study of Abused Children" (1976) *J Pediat Psychol* 1(2):25-31

15   H P Martin, *Treatment for Abused and Neglected Children* (DHEW Publication # (OHDS) 79-30199, August 1979)

16   B S Koel, "Failure to Thrive and Fatal Injury as a Continuum" (1969) *Am J Dis Child* 118:565-7

17   B Johnson and H Morse, *The Battered Child: A Study of Children with Inflicted Injuries* (Denver Dept of Welfare, Denver, March 1968)

18   C W Morse, O J Z Sahler and S B Friedman, "A Three-Year Follow-up Study of Abused and Neglected Children" (1970) *Am J Dis Child* 120:439-46

19   H P Martin, "The Child and His Development" in Kempe and Helfer (eds) *Helping the Battered Child and His Family* (Lippincott, Philadelphia, 1972) pp 93-114

20   H P Martin, P Beezley, E F Conway and C H Kempe, "The Development of Abused Children — Part I: A Review of the Literature, Part II: Physical, Neurologic, and Intellectual Outcome" (1974) *Advances in Pediatrics* 21:25-73

21   R S Hunter, N Kilstrom, E N Kraybill and F Loda, "Antecedents of Child Abuse and Neglect in Premature Infants: A Prospective Study in a Newborn Intensive Care Unit" (1978) *Pediatrics* 61:629-635

22   M A Lynch and J Roberts, "The Importance of Neurological Assessment" (April 1981) *ABSTRACTS: Third International Congress on Child Abuse and Neglect* 89:60-61

23   S Nakou, H Adam and H Agathonos-Marouli, "Health Status of Abused and Neglected Children Compared with Their Siblings" (April 1981) *ABSTRACTS: Third International Congress on Child Abuse and Neglect* 84:57

24   M Lynch, "Risk Factors in the Child: A Study of Abused Children and Their Siblings" in Martin (ed) *The Abused Child: A Multidisciplinary Approach to Developmental Issues and Treatment* (Ballinger, Cambridge, Massachusetts, 1976) pp 43-56

25   M Lynch, "Ill Health and Child Abuse" (1975) *Lancet* 2:317-19

26   R K Oates, A A Davis, M G Ryan and L F Stewart, "Risk Factors Associated with Child Abuse" *ABSTRACTS: Second International Congress on Child Abuse and Neglect* (Pergamon Press, London, 1978) p 171

27   S M Smith and R Hanson, "134 Battered Children: A Medical and Psychological Study" (14 Sept 1974) *Br Med J* pp 666-70

28   R G Birrell and J H W Birrell, "The Maltreatment Syndrome in Children: A Hospital Survey" (1968) *Med J Aust* 2:1023-29

29   A Sandgrund, R W Gaines and A H Green, "Child Abuse and Mental Retardation: A Problem of Cause and Effect" (1975) *J Mental Deficiency* 19:327-30

30   H P Martin, "The Consequences of Being Abused and Neglected: How the Child Fares" in Kempe and Helfer (eds) *The Battered Child,* 3rd ed (University of Chicago Press, Chicago 1980) pp 347-65

31   H P Martin, "Neuro-Psycho-Developmental Aspects of Child Abuse and Neglect in N S Ellerstein (ed) *Child Abuse and Neglect: A Medical Reference* (Wiley and and Sons, New York, 1981) pp 95-120

32   D J Besharov, "Toward Better Research on Child Abuse and Neglect: Making Definitional Improvement a Research Priority" (April 1981) *ABSTRACTS: Third International Congress on Child Abuse and Neglect,* **9**:5

33   R C Plotkin, S T Azar and C T Twentyman, "A Critical Evaluation of the Research Methodology Employed in the Investigation of Causative Factors of Child Abuse and Neglect" (April 1981) *ABSTRACTS: Third International Congress on Child Abuse and Neglect* **15**:9

34   A S Applebaum, "Developmental Retardation in Infants as a Concomitant of Physical Child Abuse" (1977) *J Abnorm Child Psychol* **5(4)**:417-423

35   T F Hay and D K Hall, "Behavioral, Psychological and Developmental Differences Between Abusive and Control Mother-Child Dyads" in *Abstracts of Society for Research in Child Development* Vol 3 (University of Chicago Press, Chicago, 1981) p 129

36   R K Oates, A A Davis, M G Ryan and L F Stewart, "Risk Factors Associated with Child Abuse" (1979) *Child Abuse and Neglect: The International J* **3(2)**:547-54

37   M G Ryan, A A Davis and R K Oates, "187 Cases of Child Abuse and Neglect" (1977) *Med J Aust* **2(19)**:623-8

38   F Grunseit, R K Oates and G Angel-Lord, "The Hidden Face of Child Abuse" (April 1981) *ABSTRACTS: Third International Congress on Child Abuse and Neglect* **73**:51

39   I W Hufton and R K Oates, "Non-Organic Failure to Thrive: A Long Term Follow-up" *Pediatrics* **59**:73-77 (1977)

40   R Barahal, J Waterman and H P Martin, "Social-Cognitive Functioning in Abused Latency-Aged Children" (1981) *J Consult Clin Psychol* **49(4)**508-16

41   A Buchanan and J F Oliver, "Abuse and Neglect as a Cause of Mental Retardation" (1977) *Br J Psychiat* **131**:458-67

42   D F Kline, "Educational and Psychological Problems of Abused Children" (1977) *Child Abuse and Neglect: The International J* **1**:301

43   H P Martin and P Beezley, "Behavioral Observations of Abused Children" (1977) *Devl Med Child Neurol* **19**:373-87

44   J Wilkinson and P Donaruma, "Incidence of Abuse and Neglect Among Children in Special Education Versus Regular Education" (unpublished report, Family Resource Center, Boulder, Colorado)

45   E M Kinard, "Mental Health Needs of Abused Children" (1980) *Child Welfare* **59(8)**:451-62

46   R H Rolston, "The Effect of Prior Physical Abuse on the expression of Overt and Fantasy Aggressive Behavior of Children" (Doctoral Dissertation, Louisiana State University, 1971) *Dissertation Abstract International* **32**:3010 (University Microfilms #71-29,389)

47   A H Green, "The Child Abuse Syndrome and the Treatment of Abusing Parents" in S A Pasternak (ed) *Violence and Victims* (Spectrum, Holliswood, NY, 1975)

48   A Green, "Self Destructive Behavior in Battered Children" (1978) *Am J Psychiat* **138(5)**:579-82

49   A Green, "Psychopathology of Abused Children" (Winter 1978) *J Am Acad Child Psychiat* **17(1)**:92-103

50    A H Green, "Psychiatric Treatment of the Abused Child" (1978) *J Am Acad Child Psychiat* **17**(2):356-71

51    E Baher et al, *At Risk: An Account of the Work of the NSPCC Battered Child Research Team* (Routledge and Kegan Paul, Boston, 1976)

52    J T Kent, "A Follow-up Study of Abused Children" (1976) *J Pediat Psychol* **1**(2):25-31

53    H P Martin (ed), *The Abused Child: An Interdisciplinary Approach to Developmental Issues and Treatment* (Ballinger, Cambridge, Massachusetts 1976)

54    E Elmer, "A Follow-up Study of Traumatized Children" (1977) *Pediatrics* **59**(2):273-79

55    E Elmer, *Fragile Families, Troubled Children: The Aftermath of Infant Trauma* (University Pittsburgh Press, Pittsburgh, 1977)

56    T J Reidy, "The Aggressive Characteristics of Abused and Neglected Children" (1977) *J Clin Psychol* **33**(4):1140-45

57    Berkley Planning Associates, *Evaluation of Child Abuse and Neglect Demonstration Projects 1974-1977 Volume 11: Child Impact* (US Dept of HEW, National Center for Health Services Research, Hyattsville, Maryland, 1978)

58    E M Kinard, "Emotional Development in Physically Abused Children: A Study of Self-Concept and Aggressions" (Doctoral Dissertatrions, Brandeis University, 1978) *Dissertation Abstract International,* 39:2964B; University Microfilm –78-21, 706

59    Carol George and Mary Main, "Social Interactions of Young Abused Children: Approach, Avoidance, and Aggression" (1979) *Child Dev* **50**:306-18

60    J Roberts and M Lynch, "A Follow-up Study of Abused Children and Their Siblings — How Their Teachers See Them" Presentation at the Second International Congress on Child Abuse and Neglect (15 September 1978 Abstract, Pergamon Press, London, 1978) p 191

61    E M Kinard, "Emotional Development in Physically Abused Children" (1980) *Am J Orthopsychiat* **50**(4):686-96

62    A H Cohn, "An Evaluation of Three Demonstration Child Abuse and Neglect Treatment Programs" (1979) *J Am Acad Child Psychiat* **18**(2):283-91

63    T J Gaensbauer and K Sands, "Distorted Affective Communications in Abused and Neglected Infants and Their Potential Impact on Caretakers" (1979) *J Amer Acad Child Psychiat* **18**(2):236-50

64    R L Burgess and R D Conger, "Family Interaction in Abusive, Neglectful, and Normal Families" (1978) *Child Dev* **49**:1163-73

65    H L Bee, M A Disbrow, N Johnson-Crowley and K Barnard, "Parent-Child Interactions During Teaching in Abusing and Non-abusing Families" *ABSTRACTS: Society Research Child Development* Vol 3 (University Chicago Press, Chicago, 1981) p 17

66    B Egeland and D Brunnquell, "An At-Risk Approach to the Study of Child Abuse" (1979) *J Am Acad Child Psychiat* **18**(2):219-35

67    J R Sibert, J F Murphy, J Jenkins and Newcombe, "Objective Birth Data and the Prediction of Child Abuse" (April 1981) *ABSTRACTS: Third International Congress on Child Abuse and Neglect* **95**:63

68    S M O'Connor and W A Altemeier, "Prospective Study of Non-organic Failure to Thrive" (March 1979) *ABSTRACTS: Society Research Child Dev* Vol 2 p 152

69   F S Hinchey and J R Gavelik, "Empathic Responding in Children of Battered Mothers" (April 1981) *ABSTRACTS: Soceity Research Child Dev* Vol 3 p 135

70   A Frodi, J Schima and R Ohman, "Child Abuser's Responses to Infant Smiles and Cries" (March 1979) *ABSTRACT: Society Research Child Dev* Vol 2 p 74

71   E C Herrenkohl and R C Herrenkohl, "A Comparison of Abused Children and Their Non-abused Siblings" *J Am Acad Child Psychiat* **18(2)**:260-69

72   B V Steele and C B Pollock, "A Psychiatric Study of Parents Who Abuse Infants and Small Children" in R Helfer and C H Kempe (eds) *The Battered Child*, 2nd ed (University Chicago Press, Chicago, 1974) pp 89-134

73   D O Lewis, S S Shanok, J H Pincus and G H Glaser, "Violent Juvenile Delinquents, Psychiatric Neurological, Psychological and Abuse Factors" (1979) *J Am Acad Child Psychiat* **18(2)**:307-19

74   D O Lewis and S S Shanok, "Medical Histories of Delinquent and Non-Delinquent Children: An Epidemiological Study" (1977) *Am J Psychiat* **134**:1020-25

75   D O Lewis, S S Shanok and D A Balla, "Perinatal Difficulties, Head and Face Trauma, and Child Abuse in the Medical Histories of Seriously Delinquent Children" (1979) *Am J Psychiat* **136**:419-23

76   S Bradley, "Relationship of Early Maternal Deprivation to Borderline Personality in Adolescence and Children" (1979) *Am J Psychiat* **136**:424-26

77   S Rogers and A Leunes, "A Psychiatric and Behavioral Comparison of Delinquents who were Abused as Children and Their Non-abused Peers" (1979) *J Clin Psychol* **35(2)**:470-72

78   D A Chan and M A Perry, "Child Abuse, Discriminating Factors Toward a Postive Outcome" *ABSTRACTS: Society Research Child Development* Vol 3 (University Chicago Press, Chicago, 1981)

79   B Steele, Personal communication (Denver, Colorado, October 1981)

80   T B Brazelton, *Neonatal Behavioral Assessment Scale: Clinics in Developmental Medicine* No 50 (J B Lippincott, Philadelphia, 1973)

81   M A Rock, "Gorilla Mothers Need Some Help from Their Friends" (1978) *Smithsonian* **9(4)**:58-62

Chapter 14

# A Response to Mandatory Reporting — The Child Life Protection Unit

## Jan Shier and Jane Brazier

The early recognition and reporting of suspected child abuse or neglect is the first essential step in preventing further maltreatment.[1]

To be an effective tool in meeting the needs of the child at risk, reporting must be accompanied by:

(1) The maintenance of a central register of notified cases of child abuse and maltreatment.

(2) A specialized, qualified and co-ordinated Child Protection Service.

(3) A well equipped Children's Court for cases where court action is necessary.

It is with reluctance that a society moves towards the curtailment of parental power. As Kempe points out: "The question of the rights of parents to be left alone must be weighed against the rights of the child to be protected from parents unable to cope at a level assumed to be reasonable by the society in which they reside."[2] Fontana argues that: "Society has to face the reality that not all parents can or will care for their children properly. Indeed some parents will place their children at risk. In such circumstances children are entitled to the protection of the State."[1] We would add that they are also entitled to the development of a wide range of services which give expression to that entitlement.

The realization that many children at some point in their lives are in need of protection from a wide range of situations which could be detrimental to their emotional and physical well being came only recently to the State of New South Wales. While the State has long been responsible for the supervision of neglected children, and for the provision of care for such children, when directed by the Children's Court, only recently has this State taken on a responsibility for establishing formal procedures for the monitoring of parents care of, and behaviour towards their children. In 1977, developments in Child Welfare legislation made provision for mandatory reporting. This led to the maintenance of a central register; the development of a range of specialist services across government departments and voluntary agencies to deal with children and families at risk; the development of clear co-ordinated policy guidelines for the Police Department, the Health Commission, and the Department of Youth and Community Services; and the development of the Children's Court as a therapeutic tool of intervention on behalf of a child.

## MANDATORY NOTIFICATION

In July 1977, in New South Wales, legislation was passed to amend the Child Welfare Act of 1939 which made mandatory the notification by medical practitioners, of children suspected to have been abused. This law protects such persons who notify cases, from any possible legal action and ensures the confidential nature of such reports. This law also regards the future of mandated persons to notify such cases, as an offence punishable with a fine of up to $1000.

The reaction to the implementation of mandatory notification was widespread and various, with the strongest opposition being voiced by those directly effected by the provision. Many doctors perceived the law was threatening to their relationship with their patients and suggested it would be an active deterrent to parents seeking medical assistance for their children.

"When parents faced with child abuse and neglect problems do not seek help on their own, the responsibility to take protective action rests with others."[3]

This point of view from the United States of America is reflected in the implementation of mandatory provisions, for a wide range of professionals, in every State. The belief is held that reports are vital in order to identify children in need of protection. Of commensurate importance is the capacity of protective services to respond to the needs of such children and their families. No law is the ultimate answer to any problem, and resistance to the law is often based on a lack of understanding of the intention behind the law. Although the intention of the law in New South Wales was primarily to ensure a child's safety, there was a recognition by the Department administering the Act, that such legislation must be followed closely by the development of a range of services to children at risk and their families.

"Ultimately, the prevention and treatment of child abuse and neglect depends less on laws, and more on the existence of sufficient and suitable helping services for children and parents."[3]

In Australia, legislation in regard to mandatory notification varies from State to State, not only in regard to compulsory notification but also in respect to those professionals legally obliged to make reports.

The effect of the legislation in New South Wales was a rapid increase in the numbers of notifications of children abused or suspected to have been abused. Notifications were received from a wide range of professionals and non-professionals, from persons within the community and from parents themselves.

The number of notifications suggest that medical practitioners in hospitals and community health centres are more willing to make use of the mandatory provisions than are their colleagues in private practice. We believe the only effective method of encouraging more extensive reporting will be to extend our education programmes to reach those working in the private sector.

## CHILD PROTECTION SERVICES

The major goals of a child protection service should include analysis of situations in which children are at risk and the development of a range of intervention techniques and services designed to deal effectively with these situations.

At one end of the continuum child protection involves the child who may require temporary or permanent removal from his family. At the other end of the continuum child protection involves working with families to enable parenting and child care to reach levels that are minimally detrimental to the child.

A child protection service on one level therefore involves the skilful and sensitive use of statutory authority in order to protect the rights of the child. In a broader sense however, the service includes the development of structures within a community to enable early identification, management and ongoing support for cases of children at risk, and for the co-ordination of a wide range of services to these children and their families.

The Department responsible for administering Child Welfare legislation in New South Wales is the Department of Youth and Community Services. It provides specialist services to children and families at risk through three Child Protection and Family Crisis Units and provides a range of specialist and generalist services to families in the community through a network of district offices in urban and rural New South Wales.

In 1977 the Department's total response to legislation was the establishment of a specialist Child Life Protection Unit in metropolitan Sydney. The views of the Unit at the time of its establishment were optimistic:

In the early days we talked a lot about protection and preserving the rights and dignity of the whole family with particular emphasis on the parent. We believe if we offered ourselves as human lifelines and poured the bulk of our energies into working with adults who had suffered at the hands of their own impoverished families; then the therapeutic benefits would logically pass onto their own children. In this way the cycle would be broken.[4]

Since 1977 there have been significant changes in the goals and objectives of the service.

It is our opinion that, in part, these changes reflect a process of developmental maturation characteristic of many child protective services and the personnel that are involved in their delivery.

We now know that the needs of abusive parents are far greater than we could have imagined. We have learned that a therapeutic relationship alone is unable to compensate for the extensive personal, social economic neglect and deprivation that a great many abusive families experience.

In practical terms this shift in philosophy has seen the decentralization of child protection workers away from a specialist facility into the District Office and therefore into the community. The role of these workers has been broadened from providing only a specialist case worker to including the development of community resources to monitor and review notifictions of children at risk, and the provision of consultation and support for generalist departmental field staff and other workers in the community.

Now, in 1982 the original specialist Child Life Protection Unit aims to provide a multidisciplinary service which is complementary to those other services provided by the Department of Youth and Community Services and to other key resources in the State such as the Police Department, the Health Commission and community-based facilities.

The specialist Unit is responsible for the receipt of all notifications of children at risk, for the referral of such cases for initial investigation by workers in the field and for the maintenance of a central register of substantiated cases of abused children. The Unit also provides a 24 hour telephone counselling and crisis intervention service, a multidisciplinary residential assessment for children and families and a range of group and individual programmes for parents and children.

The aim of the service is to maintain the family unit where possible. There are families who agree to accept the support services necessary to maintain the child's safety in his home. There will always be those families for whom voluntary supervision and support is not acceptable, and there will be those families where the termination of parental rights is essential to the future safety of the child. The protective service agency must then resort to the ultimate use of authority invested in the Children's Court as an integral part of a treatment plan.

A well equipped Children's Court is able to make a variety of decisions in regard to a child's future. These range from commital to wardship, with long term foster placement, release to parents on probation and supervision, commital to the care of a voluntary organization or a remand for further evaluation of the situation. These decisions are of vital importance to the individuals before the courts as not only do they affect the child in his own right but they affect future generations of parents and children. There is a growing awareness amongst magistrates, and child protection service and departmental field officers in New South Wales that only a thorough assessment of the family and child will enable the fullest consideration of the need for a particular decision to be taken.

Decisions that are taken by a Children's Court and the recommendations that arise out of a multidisciplinary assessment are appropriate tools only if consideration is given to the resources available to the family in its own community and to the family's own ability to utilize these resources.

Any response to mandatory notification is only effective if it is backed by appropriate specialist services, community education programmes, training that looks to the needs of workers in the field and constructive and sensitive handling of the problem by the media. To develop a service whose prime focus is but any one of these features is to deny their interrelatedness and will miminize the effectiveness of mandatory legislation.

## Notes

1   V J Fontana, *Somewhere A Child Is Crying* (Macmillan, New York, 1973)

2   C H Kempe, "Recent Developments in the Field of Child Abuse" (1978) *Child Abuse and Neglect* 2:261

3   US Dept of Health Education and Welfare National Center on Child Abuse and Neglect, 1977

4   G Winkworth, "Role of a Statutory Agency" in *Proceedings of Conference, Community Encounter, Co-operation or Conflict* (Royal Alexandra Hospital for Children, Sydney, 1980)

# Further References

Bersharov D J, "Building a Community Response to Child Abuse and Maltreatment" (1975) *Children Today* 5

Brazier J, Davis A and Shier J, "Montrose Child Life Protection Unit, A Treatment and Assessment Model in Child Abuse Intervention" in *Proceedings of Second Australasian Conference on Child Abuse* (Queensland Government Printer, 1981)

Brazier J, "A Residential Care Programme as a Specific Service in the Field of Child Protection" in *Proceedings of Second Australasian Conference on Child Abuse* (Queensland Government Printer, 1981)

Dickens B, "Legal Responses to Child Abuse (1978) *Family Law Quarterly* Vol XII, No 1

Reinhert J B and Elmer E, "The Abused Child, Mandatory Reporting Legislation" (1964) *JAMA* **188**:358

Chapter 15

# After Recognition, What Next? — The Role of the Community Nurse

Alison Davis

Long-term treatment is an essential component of any adequate intervention programme for child abuse and neglect. Many services are, of necessity, geared to crisis intervention to alleviate the immediate stresses for the child and family. Without adequate ongoing care, and, when necessary, early intervention, few changes or growth will occur; the abused child will remain unprotected.

Community health nursing has great potential for intervening in the child abuse and neglect cycle. Treatment, or tertiary prevention, begins after the identification of abused or neglected children. The main goal of tertiary prevention is to help abusive and neglectful parents relinquish their current child-rearing practices and replace them with methods of child care that are more conducive to optimal development of the child and, at the same time, satisfying to the parents.

Recent studies clearly indicate that most mistreated children frequently have characteristics that place them in a high risk category for abuse and neglect.[1,2] These studies include an over-representation of children with low birth weights, major or minor congenital abnormalities, and illnesses in infancy. Such conditions affect the child's behaviour and further compound an already stressful situation for parents who have experienced difficulties in their own childhood. Such difficulties are internalized into their own child-rearing practices, when they, in turn become parents — and these entrenched behaviours are very resistant to those changes sought by professional intervention.

Although nurses are often the most non-threatening professionals with whom families come in contact, they may still meet with resistance from abusive and neglectful parents. These parents frequently have learnt such behaviour over several generations and therefore are unlikely to relinquish their current parenting practices and behaviour without appropriate intervention. For some families intervention must include court action. Contrary to popular belief, legal intervention does not mean that a child will automatically be removed from his biological family, although long-term separation must be an option. Once the case has been established, the Children's Court can make a decision to place the child in care or to return the child to his parents, either on remand or probation. Conditions are often included in the remand or probation orders.

These conditions may include counselling for the parents, regular pre-school kindergarten attendance for the child, direct therapeutic intervention for the child, speech therapy, medical and dental treatment orders, as well as close monitoring of the situation by the Child Protection Service. If the conditions are not adhered to the case may be taken back to the Children's Court for review.

In the course of court action nurses often provide the Children's Courts with evidence that will assist the court to make the best decisions for the abused child and his family. However legal education in nursing curricula has usually been confined to legal practice in the hospital environment. Rarely has it included training in documentation and preparation of evidence in Child Protection. This lack of relevant legal training is probably not confined just to the nursing discipline.

The Community health nurse's responsibility in the provision of care to the abused and neglected child and family includes several areas. Care includes the recognition of an abused or neglected child; notification to the Child Protection Service; when necessary the provision of accurate, well documented evidence for the Children's Court; an assessment of the child's needs and developmental status; plus long-term follow-up for the child and his family members.

Each Community nurse has an excellent opportunity to observe children who are in need of more appropriate parenting, or are simply not safe in their home environment. Once she has identified these children she is in a position to initiate the process of protection that provides for adequate intervention, in co-operation with other qualified members of multidisciplinary and interagency teams.

## NURSING PROCESS

When working with families who have an abuse and neglect problem it is practical to use the nursing process.[3] The nursing process has five elements:

(1) establishing rapport
(2) assessment
(3) planning and setting goals
(4) implementation of goals
(5) evaluation

### Establishing Rapport

This usually is not easy with abusive parents who are likely to have poor self-esteem, inability to trust, low sense of self-worth, neediness, loneliness and dependency.[4] It takes time and frequent, consistent effort. The author believes that the community nurse must make a decision as to wherether she sees the child or the parent as her client. Preferably she should undertake a joint visiting arrangement with another worker. Frequently, a community nurse is perceived as a "friend" by her clients. While this is true up to a point, it hinders the development of a healthy relationship if the therapeutic element of her visits are not defined to the family members. Nurses working in community agencies require a heightened awareness of the abusive parent's ability to manipulate, giving the information they believe the worker wants to hear, for example, "everything is all right", and to play one worker off against the other, given the opportunity.

### Assessment and Screening

Community nurses are usually seen as non-threatening members of the community and because of their training they are good listeners. They also have a working knowledge of the local "grape-vine", and can receive information in quite unorthodox ways. When the community nurse has information about suspected abuse and/or neglect she has an obligation to assess the situation and notify the Child Protection Service of her findings. The community nurse also has a duty then to continue to monitor these situations.

Although there is a degree of role overlap with other disciplines a community nurse is equipped with special health related skills that enable her to intervene in the abusive cycle in her own right. These skills include an understanding of child development, nutrition, the physical growth and development of children, plus their health care requirements.

Growth and developmental lags in infants and young children may be indicators that a child is in an unsuitable environment for healthy emotional development.[5] It is important to make an initial assessment of the child's bare weight, height and head circumference as a baseline. Subsequent monitoring of physical growth patterns should be plotted on percentile charts. When looking at physical status the child's skin and hair condition is of significance.[6] All of this information is helpful in forming an overall picture of the child and family which can assist in the assessment of the degree of risk present.

A large proportion of growth problems can be attributed to inadequate kilojoule intake, often associated with an environment that is not conducive to an adequate nutritional intake.[7] In instances of growth failure, it should be a routine part of the assessment to elicit a detailed feeding history. In non-organic failure to thrive, the history which the parent gives and believes to be true, may not fit the picture seen on direct observation.[8] The feeding history should be coupled with a history of the pregnancy, birth, developmental and special medical history. The psychosocial history of the family is usually gathered by the social worker, and shared at a case conference.

Developmental screening, using the Denver Developmental Screening Test (DDST) can be helpful in highlighting delays and the child's ability to perform age-appropriate activities.[9] This may indicate understimulation due to inadequate parenting. The most frequently occurring developmental delays are in the areas of language and gross motor development.[1] On occasions, delayed language may be associated with a diet that is too sloppy for the child's chronological age, thus inhibiting the child's opportunity to develop the muscles necessary for speech. Language delays are also attributable to parents who speak to their children only in demands, or simply are unable to communicate with their child. One parent of a two year old remarked: "I simply can't wait until he goes to pre-school, so he can learn to talk to me." This parent had never had her own needs met, was unable to meet her child's needs, and found the child unrewarding. The child did not have any language and was fed a nutritionally inadequate, sloppy diet. His teeth were in poor condition as a result of the "bottle-mouth" syndrome[10] which exacerbated his inability to speak. This little boy was a typical "milk-aholic" — that is when he was fretful he was put in his cot with a bottle of milk. As a result of his iron-deficient diet he was anaemic, lethargic and apathetic.

**Planning and Setting Goals**

Once the needs of each family member are assessed, the next step is to formulate a case plan. A comprehensive management plan should incorporate time related goals for the family to achieve. These goals must be realistically based on the family members' ability to achieve them. The child's safety and the long-term effects of intervention are implicit in setting goals. Case plans are best formulated at a case conference; ideally a conference that involves the parents although this is not possible, or even desirable, in every case.

**Implementation of Goals**

The community nurse's responsibility in child protection does not end with recognition. Rather, identification is the beginning of long-term involvement with these children and their families. The community nurse can provide frequent and predictable home visits and act in a co-ordinating role. It is usually necessary for more than one worker to be involved, in order to meet the multiple needs of abusive and neglectful families. Work in child protection requires all the elements of an equally shared responsibility. The nurse requires support and back-up, and must use the resources of her own agency and interact with other agencies for this purpose.

Community nurses who work in a defined geographical area are in a position to be aware of community resources and can introduce their clients to these services. Often it is difficult for dysfunctional, isolated parents to join community groups, or to accept that they have parenting and relationship problems. When a community nurse works with these families she can support the child and parents through the process of becoming involved in groups and supportive intervention.

### Evaluation

Throughout this process it is essential for the nurse to document the findings of her assessment, the treatment goals and details of her work with the family for ongoing effective evaluation. It is especially important to document observations of objective data such as percentiles and DDST results, any injuries to a child, or new information elicited. Good documentation contributes to the monitoring process and allows appropriate intervention to be planned. When the case is scheduled for review the nurse can prepare her written report for presentation from her documentation. This report is vital to the re-establishment of goals or upgrading the case plan.

## CHILDREN'S COURT PROCEEDINGS

When court action is taken it should not be seen as an isolated event in child protection, but rather as an integral part of the overall case plan. Court action enhances the effectiveness of treatment plans, and particularly supports the third element of the nursing process, planning and setting goals. Just as nurses have a responsibility to be involved in the recognition, assessment and management services for abused children, they also have an equally important responsibility to participate in court proceedings when required. Giving evidence in a Children's Court need not be a traumatic experience. Much depends on the worker's confidence prior to the hearing, adequate preparation and documentation of the evidence, and familiarization with the court process prior to the hearing. When possible, together with the support of a team member, it is wise to share the contents of the nursing report with the parents prior to the hearing. This is because it is more productive to ongoing case management if the evidence is not a surprise to them. It is often helpful if the nurse talks to the parents at the court prior to and after the hearing. The nurse should remember that the parents are often frightened and lonely people at this stage. Children's Court proceedings are not for the purpose of reinforcing the parent's already poor self-image, even though, on occasions this is the outcome. Children's Courts are primarily for:

(1) Protecting the child.
(2) Placing the child in the best available environment for his development.
(3) Setting limits for parents unable to set their own limits.
(4) Initiating treatment plans.
(5) Reviewing treatment progress for both the child and his family.

## CONCLUSION

I have discussed the community nurse's role in dealing with abusive and neglectful families. Although many of these responsibilities are parallel with those of other child protection team members, some functions provide a special focus for the community health nurse. To enhance the effectiveness of case plans, community nurses should also participate in the legal intervention process which includes giving evidence in the Children's Court jurisdiction. This is essential when the community nurse has provided care, assessment and intervention to families with whom the child protection team is involved.

## Notes

1    R K Oates, A A Davis, M G Ryan and I F Stewart, "Risk Factors Associated with Child Abuse" (1979) *Child Abuse and Neglect* 3:547

2    M G Ryan, A A Davis and R K Oates "187 Cases of Child Abuse and Neglect" (1977) *Med J Aust* 2:623

3    A F Neilson, "Why Do We Need the Nursing Process?" (30 November 1978) *Nursing Times* 1974-7

4    H P Martin, "The Consequences of Being Abused" in C H Kempe and R E Helfer (eds) *The Battered Child,* 3rd ed (University of Chicago Press, Chicago, 1980)

5    J Money, "The Syndrome of Abuse Dwarfism" in G J Williams and J Money (eds) *Traumatic Abuse and Neglect of Children at Home* (John Hopkins Press, Baltimore, 1980)

6   C Cooper, "Symptoms Signs and Diagnosis of Physical Abuse" in V Carver *Child Abuse: A Study Text* (Open University Press, Milton Keymes England, 1978)

7   C L Bridges, "The Nurse's Evaluation" in B D Schmitt (ed) *The Child Protection Team Handbook* (Garland Press, New York, 1978)

8   R S Kempe, C Cutler and J Dean, "The Infant with Failure to Thrive" in C H Kempe and R E Helfer (eds) *The Battered Child,* 3rd ed (University of Chicago Press, Chicago, 1980)

9   G M Bryant, "Use of Denver Developmental Screening Test by Health Visitors" (1980) *Health Visitor* **53**:2

10  M Rabinovitz, "Why Didn't Anyone tell me about Bottle-Mouth Cavities?" (1974) *Children Today* 3:18

## Further References

Ayoub C and Pfeifer D R, "An Approach to Primary Prevention: The 'At-Risk' Programme" (1977) *Children Today* 3:14-17

Frew M J and Alden E R, "Role of the Pediatric Nurse Clinician in Early Identification of Potential Child Abuse" (May 1978) *Military Medicine* 325-27

Learoyd S and Williamson B A, "Nursing Care" (June 12, 1975) *Nursing Times* **12**

Savino A B and Sanders R W, "Working with Abusive Parents, Group Therapy and Home Visits" (1973) *Am J Nursing* **73**:482-4

Chapter 16

# The Planning and Development of a Community Child Abuse Management Programme — The Tasmanian Experience

Ian C Lewis

Tasmania is one of the six States which with the Northern Territory constitutes the Commonwealth of Australia. It is a roughly heart-shaped island of some 68,000 square kilometres below the south-eastern part of the mainland between the 40° of latitude. It represents less than one per cent of the total land mass of Australia and has a population of only 413,680 (mid-1978). The ethnic background of the community is nearly all European with the large majority being of British descent. The island is one of the most mountainous in the world and although the mountains are not high, few being over 1,500 metres, they are numerous, widespread and often rugged. The population density is only six per square kilometre but a quarter of the island is uninhabited and at least another quarter is sparsely populated because of the nature of the terrain. Most of the population live on the northern fringe and the eastern and south eastern part of the island with a few small mining towns on the midwestern side. Many people are involved in occupations related to primary production but there are quite a number of secondary industries too.

Tasmania was settled by Europeans less than 20 years after Sydney and at one time rivalled New South Wales in importance. In the present century, population growth has been much slower than the rest of Australia with fewer migrants choosing to settle there. The State has good roads and an internal air service. The health, education and welfare services are well developed.

The history of the development of a programme to recognize, to manage and to prevent child abuse in Tasmania has followed what seems to have become a fairly classical path. In 1970 the problem could no longer be ignored, or rather left to haphazard handling, by the existing medical and welfare services. The State Minister for Health at that time, acting on advice, brought together interested parties which included the medical profession, the welfare services represented by hospital and community social workers and the legal profession. The latter included a magistrate and representatives from the Attorney-General's department. There followed a series of meetings over the next two years which resulted in a Childhood Injury Investigating Committee being established in the capital, Hobart.[1] It was multidisciplinary and chaired by the State Attorney-General or his deputy. The selection of a lawyer to head the committee overcame professional jealousies existing between medical and social work personnel. The advantage of this move and also of holding meetings on "neutral" territory cannot be overstressed in the light of problems which have arisen in other cities where co-operation has not always been satisfactory between hospital and welfare based child protection units.

The committee met regularly over the next three years but, being purely advisory and having no clearly recognizable status in the eyes of established services and institutions, it soon became clear that a statutory body with defined powers was required.

A special committee helped draft legislation to give greater protection to children and greater powers to personnel in caring and welfare situations and this resulted in the Child Protection Act 1974. This Act required the State Governor to appoint a Child Protection Assessment Board to be chaired by a legal practitioner and having a paediatrician, a psychiatrist, a social worker and one other person as members.

Under the Act, certain professional groups could be named by the governor as specified classes of persons who were required to notify suspected cases of child abuse although no penalties for non-compliance were specified. Notifications were to be made to authorized officers appointed by the Board and an authorized officer was empowered to have the child examined by a paediatrician. A court could make a 30 day child protection order which might be extended for a further 30 days on sufficient evidence. An early amendment allowed a child to be retained in hospital for 72 hours against the parents' wishes on the authorization of the medical superintendent of that hospital. A later amendment allowed any authorized officer to issue a 72 hour order.

The definition of child abuse in the Act was very broad:

For the purposes of this Act, a child may be regarded as having suffered cruel treatment notwithstanding that the treatment was not intended to be cruel or was not intended to result in injury to the child, and the neglect, or failure to perform any act required for the welfare of the child may constitute cruel treatment of that child.

Specific classes of persons were named in 1975 with the aim of involving all those professionals having contact with children and their families. They included medical practitioners, community nurses, some welfare officers and social workers, principals of primary schools, kindergarten teachers, persons in charge of creches and nurseries, school guidance officers, child welfare officers and probation officers. It should be noted that doctors agreed to be included after discussions between members of the Child Protection Assessment Board and representatives of the Tasmanian Branch of the Australian Medical Association. As well as having specified classes of persons who must notify cases, the Act states that anyone was entitled to report child abuse to an authorized officer either verbally or in writing.

A network of authorized officers was appointed covering all the major areas of population in the State. Board members and several senior welfare and probation staff members were selected for this role initially but later hospital matrons and social workers have also been included. A list is available of all these persons with their occupations, work and home telephone numbers and addresses.

The Child Protection Act gave complete legal protection to anyone notifying a suspected case of child abuse in good faith. It was recommended that a report should be made to an authorized officer as early as possible. The notifier thereafter was not required to take any further part in the subsequent proceedings. The authorized officer was to arrange for the child to be examined by a paediatrician and he or she could obtain police assistance by obtaining a warrant if necessary. The authorized officer was expected to furnish a report to the Board.

The vacancy on the Board was filled by the Director of Social Welfare as his department worked in close relationship with the Board and most of the management of abusing families was carried out by the officers of that department.

It has been evident from the beginning that effective management was not possible when centrally controlled, so committees were recruited in the four main population concentrations namely Hobart, Launceston, Devonport and Burnie. The composition of these regional committees was not defined. The only stipulation was that they should be multidisciplinary and composed of people with a definite interest in child abuse. Their mode of operation was left to their chairmen but the Board insisted on receiving the minutes of each meeting and the Board's social worker attended regional meetings periodically to advise on procedures. The Board was able to concentrate on administration and policy making.

Amendments to the Act were passed late in 1978. These strengthened the powers of the Board and defined its function more clearly. It empowered the Board to establish committees and to delegate duties to them so that the regional committees already functioning in Hobart, Launceston, Devonport and Burnie were given legal recognition. The Board could arrange legal representation for children in court proceedings. The Board could now take action in at risk situations whereas prior to these amendments children had to have been actually abused before anything could be done. The Board could undertake community education and there were also several changes in procedural matters.

During the last six years the relationship with the State police force has caused concern on occasion as by tradition and training police officers uphold the law at all times and view with suspicion any organization which appears to condone criminal acts. Child abuse can be a serious criminal act and their viewpoint is readily understood from a strictly legalistic angle. Police cadets are now lectured on child abuse by a paediatrician who stresses the aetiological factors and methods of management of the child and the family. The decision to have police representation on management committees is left to each region and at present only one committee includes a police officer. Over the years there has been a steady improvement in the relationship between the Board and its officers on the one hand and the police force on the other. This has resulted from a better understanding of each organization's role in the community and of the needs of families in which child abuse has occurred.

The analysis of the statistics on child abuse from the Tasmanian scene reveals some interesting trends. It is nearly nine years since

## TABLE I

### CHILD ABUSE IN TASMANIA

### REFERRALS BY REGION

|  | Hobart & SE (population — total 196,000 percentage 47) | | Launceston & NE (population — total 113,000 percentage 27) | | N & NW (population — total 104,000 percentage 25) | |
|---|---|---|---|---|---|---|
|  | No | (%) | No | (%) | No | (%) |
| 1972-74 | 36 | (63) | 10 | (17) | 11 | (19) |
| 1975-77 | 127 | (65) | 33 | (17) | 33 | (17) |
| 1978-80 | 193 | (65) | 50 | (17) | 53 | (18) |

records were kept of child abuse notifications from all over the state and it is convenient to break this period into three triennial segments the last one being incomplete by two months in 1980. These segments coincide with the initial period of planning, the introduction of the Child Protection Act and finally the 1978 major amendments.

Despite the publicity given to child abuse and a greater professional awareness over the last six years in Tasmania, the biggest percentage of cases still comes from the major population centre and the area it serves although there has been a general increase in notifications (Table I). It is hard to account for this other than the fact that the Board itself sits in Hobart and perhaps its mere presence stirs memories and precipitates action.

The Board made the decision initially to concentrate its activities mainly on the physical types of abuse and leaving children who fail to thrive and children who are emotionally abused to other agencies except in unusual circumstances. This policy was necessary because of the sheer size of these problems and the Board's inability to cope with the numbers involved. Information and education activities conducted by the Board include these two areas however. The types of abuse being notified are shown in Table II.

### TABLE II

### CHILD ABUSE IN TASMANIA

### INCIDENCE OF SOME TYPES OF ABUSE

| Type | 1972-74 | 1975-77 | 1978-80 |
|------|---------|---------|---------|
| Physical | | | |
| serious* | 19 | 19 | 21 |
| mild | 15 | 74 | 107 |
| Sexual | 1 | — | 27 |
| Preventive** | 13 | 50 | 99 |
| Others (including incipient or threatened)*** | 18 | 67 | 138 |

   * injuries requiring hospitalization
  ** children seen to be at risk
*** children felt by parents or guardians to be at risk

This table reveals that while the numbers of seriously injured children have stayed the same there has been a sharp rise in the mildly injured group. This could be put down to greater professional awareness. The large numbers of children now coming under preventive observation also represents professional awareness. The many parents or guardians now coming forward for help because they feel that they cannot cope with, or fear they will injure, their children is a most desirable trend. Such persons not only have some insight into their problems but they are also likely to co-operate with helping agencies.

There have been changes in the ages of children being notified too with many more of the older ones aged from two to twelve years being involved (Table III).

**TABLE III**

CHILD ABUSE IN TASMANIA

AGE AT NOTIFICATION

| Age in Years | 1972-74 | | 1975-77 | | 1978-80 | |
|---|---|---|---|---|---|---|
| | No | (%) | No | (%) | No | (%) |
| 0-1 | 15 | (27) | 44 | (29) | 60 | (18) |
| 1-2 | 16 | (29) | 24 | (16) | 44 | (13) |
| 2-5 | 12 | (22) | 50 | (33) | 87 | (25) |
| 5-12 | 10 | (18) | 31 | (20) | 142 | (42) |
| over 12 | 2 | (4) | 2 | (1·3) | 49 | (2·6) |

Notifications come from several different sources. Over the years the numbers from each agency have risen except from the police. The greatest increases have come from the education services, self referrals and community referrals (Table IV).

This description of a system designed to manage child abuse in a total community is presented not because it is thought to be ideal but more to allow those areas which have yet to attempt to introduce a widespread management scheme to see one alternative to those based on hospitals or welfare departments.

**TABLE IV**

CHILD ABUSE IN TASMANIA

REFERRING AGENCIES

|  | 1972-74 | | 1975-77 | | 1978-80 | |
|---|---|---|---|---|---|---|
|  | *No* | *(%)* | *No* | *(%)* | *No* | *(%)* |
| Health services (doctors, hospitals and nurses) | 22 | (39) | 82 | (42) | 115 | (30) |
| Welfare services | 8 | (14) | 35 | (18) | 70 | (18) |
| Education services | 3 | (5) | 17 | (9) | 47 | (12) |
| Police | 14 | (25) | 8 | (4) | 4 | (1) |
| Self referral | 1 | (2) | 12 | (6) | 43 | (11) |

## Note

1   M G Everett, I C Lewis, Catherine H Mair, G C Smith and D McK Stranger, "The Battered Baby Syndrome: the Tasmanian Approach" (1973) *Med J Aust* **2**:735

Chapter 17

# Involving the Community — The Child Abuse Prevention Service CAPS

Dorothy Ginn

On each day of the year, including especially those days when only the most essential public utilities are working, members of CAPS, a group of ordinary people in the community, are available to their fellow community members should they need help. This help is given free of charge and provided at a very small cost to the community it serves. It is, in effect, a coming together of community members trying to resolve a community problem.

As is often the case, this service came into existence simply because it was needed. It began when the present director, then working in a crisis centre in Sydney's Kings Cross, was brought to the realization of the special and often long-term difficulties facing people caught up in this problem. Over the eight years of its existence, Prevention (as it is colloquially known) has grown from this small beginning to its present organization of more than 40 counsellors working from a control office in a community centre. It covers the entire metropolitan and nearby country areas. As it grew, the name "Child Abuse Prevention Service" was adopted and the organization registered as a charity in New South Wales.

Its name has always implied "prevention" and its work is based on the premise that social problems are not necessarily "sick" problems. Isolation and loneliness, two of the oft-stated causes of child abuse, are not sick problems by themselves automatically needing medical or other professional care. On the other hand, the causes and results of these social problems, if not coped with, may require professional help for resolution. The old adage that "prevention is better than cure" was never more true than in this case, not only from the human aspect, but from the viewpoint of cost to the community.

PHILOSOPHY
The evolution of CAPS has been a filling out of the service to better handle the problems presented. Originally, all team members were

mothers who had reared their families and thus had lived through, and were able to understand or empathize with child-rearing problems of others. Although most CAPS workers must still be in this category, others who have not been parents but have relevant skills or special insights, have found a place in the organization. Four of the present team are males and provide a necessary balance.

Advertising the organization's existence and its desire to help, with a strong accent on anonymity and confidentiality, provided stressed parents with an attractive outlet. Although CAPS is not the only agency working in this field (the New South Wales Department of Youth and Community Services provides a 24 hour service) it remains the alternative for those who do not wish, for one reason or another, to contact officialdom. This is particularly so in the case of an anxious, isolated mother of a continuously crying baby, who has not yet abused her child but is experiencing frustration and angry feelings and realizes she could be in danger of losing control. It applies also in the case of professional people, whose lives are severely threatened by any possiblity of losing face in the community and who can also use this service before control is lost.

When considering CAPS' emphasis on anonymity, our primary aim must be remembered. It is to prevent or alleviate abuse of the *child*. The *child's* interest and safety are of paramount concern, and if this involves quick referral to the government's Child Life Protection Unit, this is done.

Our overall philosophy is strongly related to the United Nations Declaration of the rights of the child and in particular to the following excerpts from the preamble:

Whereas the child, by reason of his physical and mental immaturity, needs special safeguards and care ...

Now therefore the General Assembly proclaims this Declaration of the Rights of the Child to the end that he may have a happy childhood ... and calls upon governments and voluntary organizations ... to recognize these Rights and strive for their observance ...

(General Assembly Resolution 1386:xiv)

The following extracts echo principles which challenge CAPS members to spend themselves in the service not only of children who have been abused (or who are at risk) but also of their families.

... The child, for the full and harmonious development of his personality, needs love and understanding ...

... He shall, wherever possible, grow up in the care and under the responsibility of his parents ...

... A child of tender years shall not, save in exceptional circumstances, be separated from his mother ...

... The child shall, in all circumstances, be among the first to receive protection and relief ...
... The child shall be protected against all forms of neglect, cruelty and exploitation ...

Since in most cases, the child will remain with his parents, CAPS works for the well-being of the child through the parents.

On the subject of exploitation, it is a matter of concern that the media are tending to sensationalize this problem under the guise of community welfare or education. The tendency is to encourage parents to appear in personal interviews "letting it all hang out". The harm which invariably comes from such exploitation, *over which the child has no control,* is best illustrated by the child who said "Mum, why do you have to tell everyone what you do to me? It hurts more than the hits and the kids poke fun at me at school and say awful things about you."

There is always pressure on CAPS to produce "an abusive mother or two" for a brief interlude of community distraction. We abhor this form of abuse which can sometimes be more distressing to the child than the original hurt. We deprecate such acts of exploitation by any other organization, irrespective of whatever guise or rationale is put forward as a cover for so doing.

## HOW CAPS WORKS

Based at the central office, the organization's counsellors work from their homes scattered throughout the whole metropolitan area of Sydney. The counsellors are loosely grouped under three supervisors for case control, relief and mutual support.

A Diverte-phone in the office enables a 24 hour 7 day service to function. The CAPS phone number is published in the "Help Reference" pages of the Sydney Telephone Directory. This number is connected to the office switch during office hours and diverted to duty counsellors after hours.

As a general rule, callers are extremely agitated when they ring CAPS and very isolated or lacking in trust. Their first need is to establish a secure relationship between client and first-met counsellors before this relationship can be broadened to include others. However, broadened it must be as soon as possible. Clients are then able to contact their own counsellor (or alternative) or the duty counsellor at any time. People who call for help give many reasons. Some common points made are:

I don't trust officialdom.
I don't trust anyone.
I am afraid of records.
I can't bear a "Psych" to look at me.

I have had bad experiences when I've tried before.
How far will this information go?
What will happen to my children.

Whatever the source of referral, each case must be assessed quickly to decide the level and type of support needed. Help by CAPS ranges from brief crisis aid to years of long-term support involving many agencies in conjunction with CAPS.

The kinds of people who contact CAPS come from all suburbs, all classes and all backgrounds. Poor people cannot always cope with society because of ignorance and fear, while rich people have difficulty in being able to ask for help.

Because CAPS is involved on a personal contact basis and not merely by telephone, the geographical spread of counsellors is practical and useful, since the area to be covered is large and distances can be very long in the early hours or in a crisis.

As soon as possible at least two counsellors become involved in any case which is indicated as likely to be difficult or long term. We have found that a ratio of two counsellors to four clients is better than 1:2. Two counsellors can provide relief for each other. One can be on tap if the other is ill or away while even a break from the same set of problems and woes becomes necessary over time.

It is mostly the mothers who call, often without the husband's knowledge. Our "little boys don't cry" society makes it unmanly for men to seek help with family affairs. CAPS experience has always been that clients with serious problems need great support, and counsellors are trained to use all relevant supports available in the community. After all, it is a community problem being dealt with. As an example of this support, the case of "Daphne" is illustrated.

Daphne, a lone mother of two (pregnant again) almost starved one of her children. Her case has been a long one and CAPS has been with her throughout arranging supports including the following:

Two hospitals
Paediatricians
Psychiatrist
Karitane Mothercraft Home
The State Government Child Life Protection Unit
Parents-in-law
Day Care
Legal Aid
Housing Commission of New South Wales

It will be readily apparent from the above that CAPS members need careful selection and thorough training.

## Selection

The formation of the CAPS team has been a matter of steady growth. Not all volunteers who join remain. Wastage occurs through various causes, including moving, family needs and illness, but also inability to cope with the extra strain caused by CAPS work. Generally speaking, growth of the team is by natural selection with only those suited to the work remaining. This becomes clear because of the long training programme. Out of two intakes per year each of about 30 volunteers, approximately one third to one half are still active at the end of their training. At the end of 12 months this fraction is still further reduced, but out of those who then remain, the turnover is small and one finds that they are invariably warm, tolerant people, with life experiences behind them, a common sense approach, the ability to accept dependency without seeking it, and possessing a keen sensitivity to peoples' needs but without overwhelming needs of their own. In short they are very special "ordinary" people.

## Training

We have used the word "counsellor" to describe a team member who operates in the field on behalf of CAPS, but in CAPS it has not the same connotation as in other organizations. We have found that the somewhat artificial relationship with clients often found in the counselling area is an anathema to those who seek our help. Most probably they have experienced the "counselling technique" over and over again and we find its use can be quite counter-productive. Therefore, the first step in training is to let new members know that they will not be taught to "counsel in six easy lessons", as they invariably expect, but that the emphasis will be on self-development, broadening of acceptance and absorption of relevant knowledge of community resources.

Training begins with a three day workshop where new members learn the organization's concepts and guidelines and work though problems connected the child abuse. The remainder of the six months, one day per week, is taken up with films, guest speakers, role plays and exercises. The availability and use of community resources is thoroughly covered. Case discussions with the counsellors involved are on-going, and first names only are used to preserve confidentiality. Visits are arranged to other organizations and centres. This period is more one of adjustment to the problem of child abuse over a period than a quick learning about it. We also believe that, in working in the humanities area, whilst it is difficult to be over-educated, it is easy to be over-schooled.

Trainees also learn the value of sometimes doing nothing — as opposed to other times needing to move quickly to protect a child — and that the time to assess the real needs of a case is generally not at the time of the crisis but later.

## Things Counsellors Need to Know

Parents ring CAPS to load us with their bad feelings until they feel safe enough to show the good, but sometimes, until they feel safe enough, they may only show their nice side.

Clients must understand that our acceptance is for *them* and not their *abuse*; for their feelings and not their *actions* and that we will help them to stop doing what they themselves are not wanting to do.

Counsellors also need to know about child development, about the stresses a young baby may produce in a mother, how hyperactivity and other difficult behaviours may trigger abuse, how drug and alcohol use can cause abuse, even if this only takes the form of inability to meet the child's needs, how lack of nutrition may effect the child's behaviour and details of the sorts of injuries children are likely to suffer.

Counsellors also need to realize that their clients are likely to become dependent on them and they need to be aware of the potential difficulties in these situations.

A certificate is presented to each new member who completes the course.

## Guidelines

These have been mentioned as an important aspect of training. They are the putting-into-effect of lessons hard-learned over years. One guideline which may initially appear strange is that a team member should not become a friend of the client being helped. The reasons are simple enough. For example, if the circumstances of the helper are much better than those of the helped, envy, inadequacy and dissatisfaction can get in the way of progress. (The opposite circumstance can equally apply). Again the simple kindness of taking children at risk (often deprived) into a home which may be comfortable, and spacious, perhaps with a swimming pool, may cause friction with child and parent after the child returns to its own home which may be lacking in such amenities. Quite often the care, love and lack of severe restrictions shown a child can engender feelings of inadequacy in a parent, who may be jealous of the attention shown the child, while she may feel deprived of affection. This can be particularly so if the child involved is a "disliked" one. There is a paradox here that the child whom the parent may "want out" can also be the one she may wish to see deprived, but also to hang on to.

On the other hand the relationship is a caring one, which is different from being a friend. However, humans being what they are, exceptions to the rule can occasionally occur and a firm friendship between helper and helped can develop as things improve. This has happened with excellent results.

Another guideline is that the counsellor's family must always come first — another reason for having more than one counsellor involved for each serious case. The counsellor's family is part of the community too and has its own needs and priorities.

## Use of Community Resources

CAPS works to support clients while also introducing them to whatever other community resources are applicable to each case. These include professionals of all types, marriage guidance, child guidance, play centres, daycare centres, foster care, occasional care, mothercraft homes, nursing mothers association, community nurses, alcoholics anonymous, drug referral units, institutions, hospitals, community health centres, police, Youth and Community Services and ministers of religion.

While using any of the above (which also act as a safety valve for CAPS and spread the responsibility for at-risk families) CAPS remains a 24 hour contact for many reasons, for example to help clients to make or keep appointments, to accompany them on first or other visits, to give an explanation of what to expect before a visit takes place and to act as a contact/catalyst between client and professional. Very often clients do not want to go back for a second visit through misinterpretation or poor communication. This is particularly applicable when clients are involved in psychiatry or child guidance areas. It was in this way that CAPS first made an important finding — not previously documented — that the undergoing therapy, or the examination of one's self and one's relationships, at times lays added stress onto already highly stressed people and may exacerbate or precipitate the abuse we are trying to avoid. On the other hand, similar treatment with other clients can bring relief and amelioration of the abuse problem. No two cases can ever be regarded by us as completely similar, but the need for the therapist to be aware of the abuse problem is real and the need for feedback is, in our opinion, extremely important in the client's treatment.

## Difficulties With the Use of Community Resources

Set hours are a problem, as crises coming into CAPS rarely obey any fixed times. In fact, they have a tendency to occur during holidays, weekends and early mornings. Professionals and most resources are not always available at the times mentioned.

Another problem facing volunteer organizations is that clients will not always accept referral to agencies and persuasion is the only way to get them there. But perhaps the greatest difficulty of all stems from attitudes. The word "volunteer" is often a definite bar and two unwelcome results can occur. First, great difficulty can be met in persuading people or institutions to accept referral until the bonafides of the organization or that of a member of it are established, and this can take some time. The word "volunteer" seems to be the "turn-off" point. Such an attitude is, of course, quite understandable and even justifiable when one considers the proliferation of volunteer organizations staffed with well-meaning but often completely untrained people. But in the midst of a crisis, when time is of the essence, such negative attitudes can be most disconcerting. Secondly, the CAPS member involved is often excluded after referral is arranged. Better results are gained, it seems to us, when CAPS is included while treatment continues.

## Load on Counsellors

The load on volunteers must be constantly monitored for the good of all concerned. An overloaded counsellor will soon neglect her/his own family with adverse effects. The clients will suffer if the counsellor cannot give them enough time and will soon lose contact, whereupon CAPS fails in its aim. The self-esteem and feeling of being welcome are never very strong in most contacts. It takes little to turn them off. Thus reviews of caseloads must take place with other members being brought in. Other team members who may not be counsellors can also assist. Such members can act as child minders, grannies etc and provide valuable help and insights to counsellors. There is a wealth of untapped natural talent in the community only waiting to be asked, and more importantly, organised. This resource, moreover, is unimpaired by restrictions and taboos which will always plague professionals or institutions in some way or another.

## Dangers in Using the Telephone

To assess where problems in a family lie, it is necessary to visit the family. For example, a mother can sound very plausible on the telephone relating a tale of violence, often using reference to good agencies or the police, because she is trying to make a case against her husband for divorce purposes. Some can be made violent by *passive* aggression by the marriage partner, while in other cases a husband may be goaded to violence by his wife. It is so easy to listen and judge and easy to be horrified.

## Sexual Abuse

Children call CAPS when they have been subjected to sexual abuse. Their case is special because:

— They are generally terrified of the result of telling this information to their family. They have often been threatened with dire consequences by the abuser.
— Some, in their ignorance, have initially thought the sexual behaviour to be "normal".
— Mothers often cannot or will not believe their daughters when they tell them that there has been sexual molestation by their father.
— Nuisance and fun calls need sorting out.
— Every case must be treated seriously and the ramifications are wide.

Our counsellors are trained not to go deeply into details or question the child too much. The same attitude is applied to mothers who ring. They are advised not to cross-question the child but to accept what has been reported then ring and seek help. Similarly they are helped to remain as calm as possible with the child until appropriate help can be obtained. The point in all this is to avoid worsening the child's guilt and trauma. Of course, where the abuse has been serious with physical damage, then the need is for quick action to help the child.

We have found sexual abuse to be widespread, though naturally well-hidden, and not only within families. Calls have involved external pederasts, baby sitters, pseudo-doctors and so on. In our experience it is unrelated to class or area.

## Blackmail

While our emphasis is on empathy and tolerance, with most clients responding to this and after a period of time relating in a similar manner to their children, there are those who use this acceptance and tolerance as a licence to abuse. Some claim to have abused to gain attention even though they have not done so, while others actually abuse, feeling that this is the only way they can get people to respond to *their* needs. While these types are few, the team have to be able to recognize and cope with them.

## Advantages and Disadvantages of Using Volunteers

The advantages will be listed first. There are disadvantages, but if the advantages did not out-weigh them, CAPS would not have come into existence nor grown.

*Advantages*

*Time and Conditions:* CAPS volunteers are where they are, doing what they are doing, because they want to, rather than because they have to. They are generally not interested in the number of hours they work or the times when they work these hours. Similarly, the conditions under which they work are not matters of confrontation.

*Parenting:* As a general rule, our volunteers have been through a parenting experience. While others may argue that there are good and bad aspects of this, it is important to note that the client is often relieved to know that the counsellor is a parent. An example from CAPS files illustrates this.

A mother called late one night from a public telephone box, quite distraught and claiming to be unable to go back to her house. She was persuaded to return home but to avoid going to the room of the infant, whom she had just realized with horror, that she "hated", until a CAPS member arrived. Twenty minutes later that CAPS member was confronted with a heavy, locked door and the mother telling her to go away because "you will only take my child from me". After some time and a lot of persuasion the team member was allowed in, only after she confided that "I could understand how you feel because I've had six of my own". Both mother and child were taken to hospital for safety that night as the child was also ill. Later the mother accepted professional help with constant support from two team members and now after two years is developing a good relationship with her child and can say, to her own amazement "I really like her".

*Training:* Our volunteers often have a broad training in their pre-CAPS lives that is their education has not only been in one narrow specialty, but can include experiences in teaching, welfare, social work and nursing as well as in life's ups and downs.

*Cost to Community:* One can achieve so much more with volunteers. The total grant on which CAPS exists, provides a 24 hour 7 day service by 40 people including paying for advertising, phone bills and other expenses. Through the team, a great many more people and resources can be brought to bear on problem cases. On a full-time basis, this grant could provide salaries only for one or two professionals working normal office hours. Where today, can one expect to obtain the services of an intelligent, capable person at any hour of day or night for out-of-pocket expenses of about $5.00 per week?

*Acceptance of Help:* Volunteers have no inhibitions about asking for or accepting help in line with their interest or in referring cases onward for their own good.

*Veneer:* Volunteers can be quite natural and have no need to adopt any veneer of officialdom or professionalism. Such a veneer or even an atmosphere or place can erect a barrier between client and helper.

*Age or Physical Ability no Barrier:* We have had a blind mother with very good ears and perception and a paraplegic (who incidentally had been a professional) with all the time in the world on her hands. In our work, such people find great satisfaction and perform wonderfully within their limits.

## Disadvantages

There are other advantages, but, as always, there is another side. Volunteers can opt out easily. They can ignore times and have no financial or contractual commitment. They may lack self-discipline which is generally a very strong characteristic in the professional. Lack of remuneration, though a plus as mentioned above, can be of detriment in that many good people just cannot continue since they must accept other employment to live.

### Attitude of One Volunteer — Patsy Gibb

It is a few years now since I learned about the CAPS team, and it is difficult to recall exactly why I felt the goosebumps that told me this was the kind of involvement I had been looking for. Years ago I had considered training as a Mental Health Association Team Leader, but the timing was wrong; I had heavy family ties at that stage and so had kept it in the back of my mind for "one day". As my tertiary training was nil, apart from business college, the few jobs I had taken since marriage had been secretarial/clerical, and whilst I had enjoyed being out in the world, that kind of work palled quickly. By the time I joined "Prevention" I was fortunate to be in a financial situation and one with fewer family responsibilities which enabled me to become involved with reasonable freedom.

I quite forget what my expectations of CAPS were, but I know now that I was in for many surprises. The first necessity for making a decision to give one's time and efforts to the community is the preparedness of one's family, and in particular one's spouse, to accept the commitment. I took many months of easing mine into the Prevention outskirts before I was brave enough to go in "boots and all", and there are still occasional fragile periods in our life.

The fact that Prevention is a 24 hour crisis intervention service means that once we accept the caring of a mum who is at risk of abusing, we accept her dependency 24 hours a day for as long as she needs us. The first marvellous reward from Prevention, however, was the total team spirit that develops from a group with a common bond of caring. Immediately a team member's case load becomes too heavy, or her/his family begins to suffer, the team closes in and accepts that member's role while she/he takes a "breather". Belonging to a group composed of a cross section of the metropolitan community, and concerned with learning, listening and empathizing with the problem of child abuse is such a constant source of stimulation and joy to me that though there are anxieties and fears connected with the case calls and their follow-ups, I have grown in so many directions. For one, my mind has been cleared of very many prejudices and it constantly broadens as I see the many problems, persecutions, angers, inhibitions and battered backgrounds, that other people have. My middle-aged brain seems to have recaptured elasticity, and it stretches a little each day. If the elasticity gives way, is this what they call the social worker's "Burn-Out"?

The reward of hearing a mum who has been weeping on the phone with anger and frustration, after maybe listening to her and murmuring understanding and "stroking" words for an hour or so, say "Oh, I've stopped shaking — isn't that funny, how much better I feel from just talking to someone" is so good.

The process of eliminating prejudices starts with one's team mates, and an important part of our training programme is working at getting to know one another, our backgrounds, reasons for joining, and dissolving negative feelings, personality clashes, various feelings of inadequacy and discomfort connected with other team members. This process then broadens with each speaker, who comes to tell us of ways of life we previously had shut out of our minds. By the time we "graduate" as counsellors we have come a long way towards ignoring the client's particular way of life, its associated moral values, and looking at the presenting problem.

The next step in our Prevention education, and also in the *developing of our character,* is freeing oneself of the urgent impulse to interrupt another person's story — with probably the best intentions; the feeling that you can solve that person's problems. I discovered that by allowing the client to hand those feelings to me to hold, she can take back those she wants and hopefully throw away the others, and in the process sort out her own solution — thereby building her self esteem and restoring self confidence.

A great bonus to me is developing the patience to listen, sometimes for great lengths of time, to someone who is pouring out problems which totally clash with my own ideas, beliefs and moral values, and to keep remembering that these are not the important things, but the anger and frustration accompanying them are, and once those feelings can be shown to be acceptable to the caller, the feelings themselves seem miraculously to de-fuse.

My coping capabilities have been strengthened in so many ways. There are the mums who ask you to set up any manner of appointments with the best recommended professional help, and fail to keep these appointments, without any feeling of conscience about your embarrassment and trouble. Coping with cooking dinner for a tired husband, when that is the very time a distraught "client" calls, requires ever-developing tact and diplomacy — to say nothing of manual dexterity. All these things sound like masochistic exercises to most of my friends, but I find them very consolidating for me, and if I should find the going rough — even to the point of giving it up some later time, I will always have been thankful that I took the step to join this team.

In summary, one could say that the value of a good professional worker in this area complements that of a good volunteer. The value of the volunteer to the community lies in the number available and the low cost of their services.

## Funding

Although it makes small claim on community monies, CAPS needs enough funds to pay a small full-time staff in the central office, the administrative costs which go with this and to reimburse the expenses of its volunteers. The only constant support to date has come from the Office of Child Care (Department of Social Security) in the form of a small grant. Public fund raising is not easy for an organization working in this area, because of the misconceptions about child abuse. While almost anyone is prepared to dip into his pocket for the blind or paralysed, very few wish to help an organization which helps "handicapped" parents not to abuse their children. The community at large tends to think of all child abusers as being like those who make the tabloid headlines by killing or maiming small children. They also equate "helping" with the parent, rather than with the child.

The general community does not accept that 90 per cent of abuse happens down any street of any town, suburb or village. However, until there is a better way of communicating this, donations to help organizations like CAPS will be slow in coming. But it gratifies us to find that there *are* organizations, individuals and companies who *do* understand and help in a small way. The fact that they understand and try to help makes our efforts on the community's behalf more worthwhile.

## CONCLUSION

CAPS exists because the community needs it, because there are sufficient understanding and caring people who are prepared to give their time and themselves to meet the community's need and because enough professionals and institutions recognize that CAPS performs a vital function in this area alongside themselves and perhaps in ways not open to them.

Indeed, a number of out-of-work professional people including psychologists and social workers, have gained valuable field experience and subsequent employment through the time spent and knowledge gained working in this service.

The service CAPS can provide, in spread and quality, is circumscribed only by the funding and people available. Make no mistake, there are people in need of a CAPS — like service in every corner of our country who would make use of the service if they knew of it, or could reach it.

CAPS very simply, cares for the family. It is a family-support service to ordinary parents and children, for those who are stressed by circumstances beyond normal limits. Whilst some who come to us often trigger our frustration and sorely try our patience, the great majority of those who turn to CAPS for help are caring people — ordinary community members, "beside themselves" at the thought at what they are doing or might do. CAPS team members have amassed a great storehouse of admiration and respect for those who have shown the courage to seek a way out of this temporary hell which they feel they must at all costs hide from their neighbours and from the community which, as yet, does not fully understand their problem.

# Chapter 18

# Family Day Centres and Child Abuse

Jan Carter

One of the most controversial issues in the development and care of the young child has been the question of the impact of offering the child day care outside the family. Ever since the World Health Organization claimed that day care had a particularly negative and permanently damaging effect on young children,[1] the question of substitute child care by the day outside the family has been of great interest to researchers and practitioners. The debate about day care has been summarized by Michael Rutter who said: "The concerns over day care stem from the fear that if the child has prolonged daily separations from his parents and if caretaking is divided among a large number of different adults, then either the bonding process may be impaired or the attachments formed will be in some way, less secure or less effective in bringing comfort and security."[2]

In the past decade, a body of research work on day care in the United Kingdom and the United States has accumulated and the findings and the issues they raise have been summarized by Rutter.[2,3] The opinions about the long-term damage to the child are clearly shown to be exaggerated and good quality day care does not disrupt a child's emotional bonds with his mother, nor does it usually result in emotional disturbance for even a very young child, say under three years of age. But we are still none the wiser, as Rutter has said, about what type of care is most suitable for which children under what circumstances. Further, in most western countries — and certainly in Britain and Australia — there is a plethora of types of day care for the pre-school child, offered by both private, voluntary and public services. To take Britain as an example, there is the private sector, which offers nursery schools and child minders, at market rates. Then the voluntary agencies offer family centres and play groups, often on a subsidized basis. Then the public sector can be subsidized into the provision of health agencies (specialist psychiatric day care and health visitor-sponsored ad hoc playgroups), the contribution of the educational services (nursery schools) and that of the local authority social services departments (day nurseries). To confuse the subject even further, some leisure and recreational services also offer facilities to mothers and young children. In Australia, where provision varies from state to state, the details differ but the subject is equally complex, although it is possible that the private sector is larger. The criteria for admission to day care in Australia are as complicated as in Britain; for example, children are admitted by parental wishes to facilities such as kindergarten and early childhood educational equivalents or by the "need" of the child or family to subsidized child care places. Some day care provision is sponsored by commonwealth and state governments, or by a combination of both.

Three matters are frequently overlooked in reviews of day care for young children. First, not all day care is provided primarily for the child — some of the criteria for admission are based more on the parental needs than on the child's requirements; although the assumption is that in meeting the needs of the parents (often in relieving a stress of a certain kind) there will be a spin-off for the child too. Second, not all day care for young children automatically involves a separation between parent and child; although certainly most day care settings invoke the idea of multiple caretaking, with other persons, either staff or parents, taking care of the child. Examples of day care settings where the parent and child are not separated, are playgroups and family day centres. The third distinction is the type of setting. Some day care takes place at home in domiciliary settings and other day care takes place in non domiciliary centres. In the United Kingdom, day care at home is known as child minding, whilst in Australia, confusingly, it is known as family day care.

The purpose of this chapter will be to discuss day care where parents are present in a *non-domiciliary* setting in family day centres. What contribution can they make to the development of both parents and children who have problems relating to non-accidental injury? Some of this information comes from a survey of family day centres carried out in England and Wales in 1976[4] and the results of this study will be discussed in the light of other information available.

Family day centres offer a relatively new form of child care by the day. All the centres located in England and Wales in a national survey of all forms of day care provision for adults had opened since 1970.[4] As already discussed, most child care provision, whether day care or residential, assumes that parent and child should be separated in the interests of one or the other, although a small amount of residential provision has been established where both parent and child can be admitted together: examples in non-accidental injury cases are the Park Hospital, Oxford, and the Triangle, Amsterdam. This type of residential family care acknowledges that it is not always appropriate to separate the parent and child. But at the same time, it may not always be strategic to remove a family from familiar surroundings into a "foreign" residential environment, with all the artificial protection from the "real" world that this implies.

At present, when day care is used as a method of intervention in child abuse cases, it is often done with the purpose of providing the child with a safe place for, say 40 hours of the week and to offer the mother a break from the child.[5] Now, while it is known that a time in a day centre does not actually appear to weaken the child's attachment behaviour and bonds to the mother[3], the reverse does not apply and separation of the child into a day care centre is not likely to enhance automatically a fragile mother-child connection. On the other hand where the mother-child connection does not seem to be overly fragile and where the risk of abuse relates more to the social stresses experienced by the family,[6] than to a lack of attachment, the more conventional form of day care which involves separation of parent and child might be advisable. Of course, these two groups are not easy to distinguish clinically and frequently overlap. But these criteria suggest the desirability of making a detailed and accurate assessment before recommending the use of either child day care or family day centres.

One difficulty about conventional day nursery provision is that staff in some centres have ambivalent, or negative attitudes to parents.[7,8] Staff sometimes want to substitute for parents and to exclude them from the nursery, clearly a disadvantage in child abuse cases. So a number of commentators have written about the usefulness of *family* day centres in managing child abuse cases. Bentovim describes a family day centre in a psychiatric department in a London children's hospital, where one or two days per week attendance is offered to a family and where individual work, family therapy and marital therapy takes place "in a setting of insight, understanding and containment", a modified therapeutic community.[9] Similarly, the National Society for the Prevention of Cruelty to Children (NSPCC) special unit in Northamptonshire, gives family day centre support to families who acknowledged a problem and who wished to change: three days a week are offered for six months and transport to the centre is provided.[10] In a Birmingham day centre where children are placed full time, parents attend for one day a week for activities based on learning social and cognitive skills. The goal is to avoid admission of the child to residential care.[11]

Family day centres have also developed within the past decade in Australia. For example, several child care agencies sponsored by voluntary organizations in Melbourne have turned former children's institutions into family day centres which cater for families tempted to hurt their children. This has demanded a complete re-organization of philosophy, staffing and programme; altering a nursing model of care to one of a type of therapeutic community. (This is discussed more fully in Carter, 1981.) Such an instance is the Copelen Street Family Centre, formerly a mother and baby home, which now helps family members suffering from chronic social stresses living in underprivileged areas of the city.[12] Arnion House, another Melbourne centre, takes on families with problems of abuse who are often turned away from other agencies because of their extreme disorganization and their unacceptably high level of demands for service.[13] In Sydney, Wiley Park Centre offers a pre-school programme for 25 children and their parents while in Perth the Fremantle Parent Education Centre caters for single parents. Most of these centres have been evaluated by external investigators and whilst none of their sampling nor their study methods are strictly comparable with each other, or with the United Kingdom day care study, the impression is that the Australian centres have a high complement of professional staff; that their multi-disciplinary emphases are well developed; that the facilities for children are well integrated with nursery or pre-school programmes and that most centres are also prepared to offer a service to parents and children in their own homes as well as at the centre, whether via social workers, or family aides, or both. In other words, the Australian centres appear to have a more central role in service delivery when compared with their British counterparts, partly because the emphasis on local authority social services development in the United Kingdom has meant a huge growth of "field" social services, with day care as a peripheral adjunct, rather than as the central core of service delivery.

Involvement by parents at a number of levels are issues in Australian family day centres. This extends from offering mutual aid one to the other, making choices about the activities of the Centre and at Copelen Street, to membership of the Board. The type and degree of parent participation are also issues in family day centres in the UK. Langtry Young Family Care Centre in London Borough of Camden pioneered the use of the "New Careers" method in family day care; the system whereby staff members are recruited from the client group to work in the centre and eventually seconded to professional training courses.[14] However, the most notable example of parent participation in a family day centre is that of the Brotherhood of St Laurence in Melbourne. This long established professional social work agency serving an underpriveleged group (although not solely child abusers) turned its operation into a family day centre and gradually withdrew its professional staff until the agency was totally parent-controlled and operated by its clients.[15]

Thus for parents who need to work intensively to improve their relationship with a child, family day centres are a hopeful resource. The discussion which ensues will be an attempt to provide information from a largely descriptive study, where measures of evaluation come from reports provided by parents. The centres discussed were located in the course of a national study of adult day care carried out in England and Wales between 1974 and 1979.[4] This survey covered all forms of mental disorder and handicaps as well as provision for the aged and young families. Thirteen areas of the country were selected at random and 290 day units of all types were located in these areas.

## A SURVEY OF FAMILY DAY CENTRES

Six family day centres were located and all had been established to cater for young families and multiple social problems, where the risk of abuse was thought to exist. The centres were sponsored either by local authority social service departments or voluntary agencies and were small in size, with between 8 and 18 parents, plus their pre-school child or children attending each day. The centre was usually located in a house in a street, or in an adapted building. A random sample of 29 parents, whose average age was 29 years was interviewed. Nearly all parents were mothers, half were the head of single parent families and two-thirds relied on state benefits as their sole income. Forty per cent of parents had been in the centre for six months or less and over a quarter for longer than a year. On average the parents attended two days per week and half the centres offered a time-limited service.

This survey was designed to collect information about the adults in family day centres and parents underwent an extensive interview. The children were not assessed, but a detailed battery of questions aimed at assessing mood state indicated that nearly half the parents in the family day centres confessed to having trouble in controlling their tempers. Nearly two-thirds had felt upset and irritable with those around them. Two-thirds were rated as depressed and of this group, a third were rated by independent assessors as "severely" depressed. This was proportionately more than the users interviewed in psychiatric day hospitals in the same study. A third of the parents had actively contemplated suicide within the past month.

As well as having difficulty in controlling themselves and their tempers, a third of the parents nominated a further problem as that of having difficulty in controlling their children. A twenty-two year old mother of two, separated from her husband, explains:

I just could not control my little boy. He had been back to and fro from his dad and I just did not know if I was coming or going. I could not understand why he was taking it out on me. I can understand better since I've been coming here why children do things now. Before they were aggressive and they'd tear the wallpaper down [at home]. Here they tell you how to understand it and they suggest ways to get them to do certain things. Since coming here I can cope with life better, before I just wanted to get out of it — [she had taken an overdose] — now I can cope.

A third of the parents indicated that they had difficulty in controlling their own surroundings. Amongst their problems were outstanding material needs, such as requiring better housing, or play facilities for the children, or dealing with the restrictions imposed by a particular location, such as the way that heavy traffic cut off access for play in a local park.

How did these centres go about meeting the needs of the parents? Each centre offered the parents and children a range of activities and the parents were asked to rate the things they spent most time at in the centre. Chatting to each other was the time consuming activity for most users, followed by attendance at groups, either discussion or treatment groups. Participating in formal activities, such as arts and crafts programmes, or educational groups was infrequent, compared with other branches of adult day care. Thus there was a strong emphasis on interpersonal contact, both between parents and with staff, at the expense of the provision of more instrumental activities, such as arts and crafts programmes, or provision of educational skills.

Detailed interviewing and ratings indicated that all parents, with one exception, were satisfied with the programme offered by the centres. In the parents' view, what they got most out of their day centre was, first, the contact it provided with other parents, second, its impact on modifying their children's behaviour and third, the practical services it offered. These points will be discussed in detail.

First, two thirds of the parents delineated the benefits of meeting with others and pointed out that sharing common experiences with each other appeared to lighten the burden. It was the impact of meeting with people in the same situation which was pertinent and in this sense, family day centres offer a benefit similar to the impact of self-help programmes.

It's helped me to make friends which I can't do on my own.

It's given us a family life.

Working with other people in a group has given my life a focus.

When I started coming here it was the high spot of my week. My marriage had broken up. It was so important to me — I've made a lot of friends.

Second, half the parents spontaneously commented on the help of the centre, either in improving their children's behaviour or in contributing to their own confidence in feeling that they could manage the children. The experience of observing other adults handle their children suggested new approaches and allowed for practise of new ideas in a safe setting.

Now he eats his meals which he didn't before.

It helps me to cope with the children better.

It's helped me with Thomas and his potty training: if you have a problem with the children they help you out. Everything they have spoken to me about has worked out all right.

Third, a fifth of the parents said that the day centre had provided or arranged special practical help for them, and their comments indicated that the relief of financial or material stress did both demonstrate interest on the part of staff and also prevented parents taking out extant stressors on their children.

A twenty-five year old father commented:

I've had a lot of help with family problems. When my son was in hospital they arranged for us to be taken and brought back. They helped me to sort my bills out and with information, how to get extra time. For me it couldn't have done more as it has helped me to adapt and talk my problems out about John and see how others are in the same way.

The parent's assessments of the staff are of interest, because repeatedly they emphasized the staff's ability to handle people and suggested that they offered important behavioural models. Comments about their approachability were made by almost all parents. For example:

They're not stuck up here, they don't class themselves better than the likes of me.

The thing is, they're not snobs. They have to talk proper and work with people. They are polite and when you come in they always give you their attention. They have to understand people and not lose their temper.

Further, the facility of staff in getting on with children in a family day centre was noted. "Relating to the little ones" was a critical form of credibility of the staff whose work in a day centre is always visible.

The staff need to be loving and affectionate to all the kids and that's what they are down here all the time. Some of the children are really wild and need a lot of patience.

Tommy was very crabby but the social workers didn't mind that. Everything they have tried to help me with has worked out all right. They are good with children ... they help you with anything you can't do and find a way around it for you. They have to know what to expect from children.

The impact of attendance at the family day centre was rated. If the attendance at the centre seemed to have enabled a parent to perform an activity, or a behaviour which was not possible before he/she came to the unit, "improvement" was said to have taken place. On the other hand, if attendance had kept a parent going in personal or social ways, "maintenance" was the outcome rated. But if an adverse expected event, such as removal of the child into care had not occurred, the case was rated as "prevention". On this basis, five families were rated as "improved" (17 per cent); two thirds or slightly more (68 per cent) as "maintained"; and two families (7 per cent) were rated that "prevention" had taken place.

Other measures indicated that parents had started to talk to each other for the first time and that other parents become confidants. One mother commented: "We begin to depend on each other: that's what friends are for." As half the families never had visitors, nor did they visit other people, nor could they rely on relatives in an emergency, the family day centre was important in providing a function akin to the extended family.

All but one of the parents would recommend family day centres to other parents. A twenty-three year old mother of three said:

I'd recommend this centre, because I know how much it has helped me — it has eased my mind over Sam's eating and helped me to sort out my bills. It's helped me to relax. I used to be a nervous person and it took me a while to know others. Others probably feel the same way.

## DISCUSSION

Most parents, (93 per cent), were satisfied with the service offered by family day centres. Their opinion about what the centre had done for them centred on, first, the benefits of meeting with other parents; second, the improvement to their children's behaviours and third, the practical help the centre had offered them. This outcome suggests that there could be a slight lack of perspectives between the aims of family day centres, as seen by staff, compared with the things that families actually perceived as helpful. The more common emphasis on family day centres is to offer a therapeutic milieu where psychological growth can take place and where parents view psychological change as a priority.[9,10] However, it is well known that parents with child abuse problems do not readily see the necessity for personal change and the information of this chapter suggests that more modest aims, those of meeting the parents' needs for companionship and friendship, helping them to cope with their children and offering practical help may be more basic than attempting to climb the Everest of achieving psychological insight and maturity.

Many parents in family day centres are isolated socially and also severely depressed. The chance to meet fraternally with other parents appears to be important in the matter of establishing a confidant. It is known from other social research that a reliable confidant is a protection against breaking down when under adverse stress[16] and it is clear then, that the establishment of social bonds with others in a family day centre might carry far reaching psychological implications for parents.

The regimes of the family day centre have been dealt with elsewhere,[4] but one feature of the centres discussed in this study was the blurring of the distinction between staff and parent and the democratic method of decision making in the centres. This democratic approach can, perhaps, be contrasted with the professionalized model of family day centres[9,10] where the assumption is that the highly trained staff, rather than the users, are the therapists and where the aim is the fostering of therapeutic insight as defined by the staff. Thus approaches to organizing family day centres may be defined according to the degree of parent control, as opposed to the degree of staff control.

Turning from parent-evaluated views of family day centres to professional evaluations produced paradoxical results. Sutton and Roberts[11] compared families who did and did not attend a family day centre on the question of whether or not the child went into residential care and found that attendance at the family day centre maintained children in the community. However, a study of the therapeutic effectiveness of the staff-controlled hospital day centre reported by Bentovim[9] suggested that when the progress of 25 children aged 2½-3½ years was compared over 12 months with 25 simililarly disturbed children in the community, that there were few differences in actual behavioural outcomes.[17] This review advocated the formulation of a specific treatment plan with carefully defined objectives, but did not tackle the subject of parent participation which may be an equally important objective from a treatment point of view. Critchley and Berlin[18] suggest that maximum parental involvement in the running of a day centre programme is one key to easing the child's disturbance. This accords with the implications of this chapter, where the help the parents gave each other and improvements of children were associated in the parents' minds, at least.

This suggests that family day centres can be a valuable resource to consider in cases where separation of a parent and child is not therapeutically desirable. Parents tempted to hurt their children appear to find these services helpful, especially their "mutual aid" component. But many questions are left unanswered. Can specific professional targets be pursued for both children and parents without disrupting the help parents give each other? Are professionalized approaches exclusive and contradictory to the self help ethos? Comparisons between highly professionalized family day centres with a low degree of parent participation and those centres with considerable parent participation, but minimal professional imput are necessary before such centres can reach beyond the experimental. But at the beginning of their life, family day centres suggest a promising innovation for the future for families where children are at risk.

## Notes

1  World Health Organization, Expert Committee on Mental Health, WHO (Geneva 1951)

2  M Rutter, *Maternal Deprivation Reassessed* (Penguin, Harmondsworth, 1972)

3  M Rutter, "Social-emotional Consequences of Day Care for Pre-school Children" (1981) *Am J Orthopsychiat* 51(1) January: 4-28

4  J Carter, *Day Services for Adults, Somewhere to Go* (George Allen and Unwin, London, 1981)

5  E Baher et al, *At Risk* (Routledge and Kegan Paul, London, 1976)

6  M A Straus, "Stress and Physical Abuse" (1980) *Child Abuse and Neglect, The International J* 4(2):75-88

7  C Garland and S White, *Children and Day Nurseries* (Grant Macintyre, London, 1980)

8  E Ferri, D Birchall, V Gingell and C Gipps, *Combined Nursery Centres, A New Approach to Education and Day Care* (Macmillan, London, 1981)

9  A Bentovim, "A Psychiatric Family Day Centre: Meeting the Needs of Abused or At Risk Pre-school Children and their Families" (1977) *Child Abuse and Neglect, The International J* 2-4:479-84

10  P Griffith, *The Provision of a Preventative, Protective and Treatment Programme in Northamptonshire, England* (1971). Paper presented to Second International Congress on Child Abuse and Neglect (London, September 1978)

11  A Sutton and E Roberts, "Day Care for Young Children who are Abused or Neglected" (1981) *Social Work Service* 25:29-33

12  P Tinney, *The Copelen Street Family Centre* (Methodist Department of Child Care, Melbourne, 1977)

13   Y Wadsworth, *A Family Kind of Place* (Melbourne City Council, 1979)

14   J Brill, "Langtry Young Family Centre, a Method of Intervention" in M R Olsen (ed) *Differential Approaches in Social Work with the Mentally Disordered,* BASW Occasional Paper No 2 BASW (1976)

15   M Lifeman, *Power for the Poor, The Family Centre Project, an Experiment in Self Help* (George Allen and Unwin, 1978)

16   G Brown and T Harris, *The Social Origins of Depression* (Tavistock, London, 1978)

17   S Woollacott, P Graham and J Stephenson, "A Controlled Evaluation of the Therapeutic Effectiveness of a Psychiatric Day Centre for Pre-school Children" (1978) *Br J Psychiat* **132**:349-55

18   D L Critchley and I Berlin, "Parent Treatment in Milieu Treatment of Young Psychotic Children" (1981) *Am J Orthopsychiat* **51(1)**:4-10

Chapter 19

# The Role of Media Campaigns in Preventing Child Abuse

Anne Harris Cohn

Child abuse is a community problem and can only be prevented if appropriate measures are taken at the local level. Because any action will be taken at the local level, however, community residents must be made aware of the seriousness of the problem of child abuse, why child abuse affects them and how they can help prevent it.[1,2,3,4] Until people know a problem exists — for themselves or for someone else — there is simply little hope for action. While there are many approaches to creating public awareness and to educating the public about these matters, the most direct route is by using the media — television, radio, newspapers, magazines, billboards. A media campaign — an orchestrated set of pre-arranged messages — can be a central feature of any child abuse prevention efforts. The purpose of this chapter is to discuss the positive influence of media campaigns in preventing child abuse while highlighting the potential negative effects of such campaigns.

## PURPOSE OF MEDIA CAMPAIGNS

Media campaigns generally have one of two complementary purposes.[5] The first is to bring parents the message that being a parent is not easy, that all parents experience stress in the parenting role and that it is all right to reach out for help. Through the media, parents can be provided with information on where to turn for help, particularly how to get in touch with local crisis care services. Such messages can also be geared to the adolescent or older child, helping a potential or actual victim of child abuse learn about how to get help. Media messages can also provide useful tips about parenting and family life. A second purpose of media campaigns is to mobilize concerned citizens to do something about the problem. Citizens may be given information about how to report a case of child abuse, how to help a neighbour and how to get involved in other ways to help prevent child abuse.

215

**Case History of One Media Campaign**

In 1976, the National Committee for Prevention of Child Abuse (NCPCA) in conjunction with the Advertising Council, Inc, launched its national public awareness campaign in the United States. A private advertising firm, the Campbell-Ewald Company, had volunteered its creative expertise in designing the campaign. All sectors of the media — television, radio, newspapers, magazines, as well as the billboard and transit companies — donated time and space for the campaign advertisements as a public service.

Prior to 1976, the United States public had sporadically been exposed to the child abuse problem primarily through sensationalized reporting of individual cases. The campaign, launched in 1976 was the first nationwide effort to systematically introduce communities across the country to the problem of child abuse. The purpose of the campaign was and is to increase the public awareness of the extent of the problem and the need to prevent it. A dream for the campaign designers was to educate the public sufficiently well about the problem so that in time the campaign could focus on specific actions concerned citizens could take to prevent it.

In the beginning, under the banner "Child Abuse Hurts Everybody", the campaign carried the message that child abuse is a

## FIGURE I

### CHILD ABUSE HURTS EVERYBODY

> Not so simple a statement, but very simply true.
> Child abuse hurts you, our country, everybody. It knows no boundaries of race, religion, income group or social status.
> You can see the hurt in our babies. Every year, an estimated one million children are injured by confused, abusive adults. Those million children don't go away. They are followed by at least a million more abused or neglected children a year.

big problem in the United States, a problem that cuts across all social, economic, racial and religious boundaries (Figures I and II). The following year, the campaign's message was "It Shouldn't Hurt to Be a Child". The public was introduced to ideas about how the hurt from child abuse could be reduced (Figure III). The subsequent campaign asked the public to "Help Destroy A Family Tradition", and pointed out that often abused children grow up to be abusive

## FIGURE II

# NO FAMILY IS SAFE FROM CHILD ABUSE. NOT EVEN YOURS.

Let's say you're lucky. Your family isn't one in which child abuse occurs.

But, because it is estimated that there are more than one million cases of child abuse in America each year, the chances are someone you know, or someone your child knows, is a victim of child abuse.

Child abusers are as much the victims of a vicious cycle as the children they abuse — whether the abuse is physical, sexual, emotional, or neglect. Abused children learn abuse as a way of life. When they become parents, they pass that learning on to their own children. If your child were to marry an abused child, you probably wouldn't know about it until your first grandchild was born. And then it might be too late, unless those parents receive help. Get more information, now, on how you can help break the cycle of child abuse.

**HELP DESTROY A FAMILY TRADITION. WRITE:**
National Committee for Prevention of Child Abuse, Box 2866, Chicago, Ill. 60690.

parents (Figure IV). Having told the public generally about the problem and its effect, the campaign sought, in the following years, to educate the public about the many different types of abuse — not

## FIGURE III

### IT SHOULDN'T HURT TO BE A CHILD

> But sometimes it does. Each year a million children feel the pain of child abuse. And we can do something about it. If we all do just one thing, no matter how small, we can help prevent child abuse. Below are a few suggestions. Commit yourself to at least one and help stop the hurt.

just physical abuse, but neglect, sexual abuse and emotional abuse as well (Figures V, VI and VII). The 1982 campaign asks the public to "Help Us Get To The Heart of The Problem" and explains the connection between child abuse and so many other social problems (Figure VIII). If public opinion polls continue to support the direction the campaign is taking, future campaigns will focus specifically on how to prevent child abuse.

Since 1976, over $100 million worth of advertising time and space have been donated by the media for this campaign. Print advertisements have appeared regularly in popular magazines, trade journals and newspapers throughout the United States and abroad. Billboards on America's highways and car cards on buses and subways in America's cities have carried the campaign's posters. National and local television and radio stations have played the audio visual spots at all times of day and night. Because all of the time and space is donated, the advertisements appear when and where the media chooses.

Although primarily designed as a national campaign, in keeping with the belief that child abuse is a community problem, the advertisements allow local organizations to tag on their own names and phone numbers and thereby localize the campaign. Hundreds of organizations across the country have chosen to do so.

### Responses to the Campaign

Beyond providing an educational message, campaigns have the option of calling people to action — and most do. "To report a case of child abuse, call us." "If you need help, contact us" or, "If you want more information on how you can help, write us." NCPCA's campaign thus far has asked readers or viewers to write to NCPCA for more information. Both the number and types of letters received suggest a great deal about a campaign's effectiveness.

## FIGURE IV

# HELP DESTROY
# A FAMILY TRADITION.

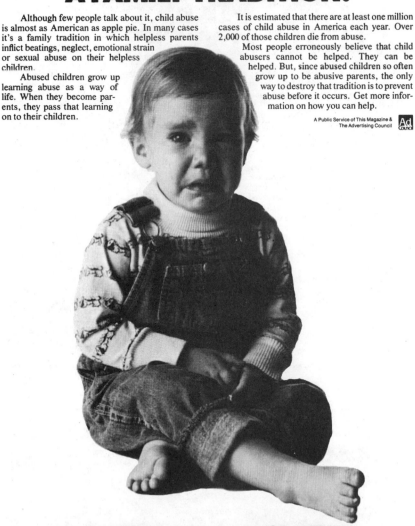

Although few people talk about it, child abuse is almost as American as apple pie. In many cases it's a family tradition in which helpless parents inflict beatings, neglect, emotional strain or sexual abuse on their helpless children.

Abused children grow up learning abuse as a way of life. When they become parents, they pass that learning on to their children.

It is estimated that there are at least one million cases of child abuse in America each year. Over 2,000 of those children die from abuse.

Most people erroneously believe that child abusers cannot be helped. They can be helped. But, since abused children so often grow up to be abusive parents, the only way to destroy that tradition is to prevent abuse before it occurs. Get more information on how you can help.

A Public Service of This Magazine &
The Advertising Council   **Ad** Council

### ✵ PREVENT CHILD ABUSE. WRITE:
National Committee for Prevention of Child Abuse, Box 2866, Chicago, Ill. 60690.

**FIGURE V**

# NEGLECT CAN KILL,TOO. IT JUST TAKES A LITTLE LONGER.

Mention the words "child abuse" and painful images of battered and beaten children probably come to mind. Rightfully so. Over 2,000 physically abused American children died last year. But the problem is more insidious than physical abuse. Much more.

The awful fact is that thousands of parents are abusing their children by leaving them alone. It's called neglect. A child growing up without parental love and attention will grow up bent and warped. Worse yet, a child who isn't provided necessary food, clothing and shelter can, and often does, die.

Physical abuse and neglect are at the opposite ends of the spectrum, but equally deadly. So are other types of child abuse, such as emotional damage, where a child is teased or belittled to the point of feeling inferior. Or sexual mistreatment, where children are abused by a friend, neighbor or close family member.

In all its forms, child abuse is an enormous problem. Each year one million children feel the pain in one way or another needlessly. Needlessly because child abuse can be prevented. If you help.

## Abused children are helpless. Unless you help.

**Write:** National Committee for Prevention of Child Abuse, Box 2866, Chicago, Ill. 60690

## FIGURE VI

# SEXUAL ABUSE OF CHILDREN. NOT TALKING ABOUT IT WON'T MAKE IT GO AWAY.

The act of sexually molesting children is unfortunately all too real. We would all perhaps like to deny it by not talking or even thinking about it. But the ugly fact remains: tens of thousands of children are sexually abused each year by a close friend, neighbor, parent or other member of the family. And it's only one form of the larger problem called child abuse.

Most people equate physical harm with child abuse. Rightfully so, but only part of the picture. Child abuse is also neglect; denying or ignoring a child's needs for proper food, clothing and shelter. It's also emotional abuse, where perhaps a child is belittled to the point he or she feels inferior. And child abuse is physical and sexual mistreatment. All forms of child abuse damage young personalities. They oftentimes result in death.

An estimated one million children suffered from abuse in America last year. A true tragedy because child abuse can be prevented. Not talking about it won't help. Finding out what you can do will.

# Abused children are helpless. Unless you help.

**Write:** National Committee for Prevention of Child Abuse, Box 2866, Chicago, Ill. 60690

## FIGURE VII

# FIND FAULT WITH A CHILD LONG ENOUGH AND HE'LL FIND FAULT WITH HIMSELF.

Children are impressionable. Their minds are open, sensitive to their environment and very fragile. Constant fault finding and belittling can convince a child that he is somehow inferior. It's emotional abuse and it is much more severe than it sounds. It warps children's minds and creates mental problems that will affect them the rest of their lives.

Thousands of children are emotionally abused every year. Unfortunately, that's only part of the whole child abuse problem. Physical harm is most commonly associated with child abuse. Sexual abuse is the molestation of children by an adult, usually a trusted friend or member of the family. And neglect is the failure to provide a child with the basic necessities of life. The number of cases reaches into the millions each year, when you put them together.

Today, five children will die from one of these abuses . . . five more will survive until tomorrow. Add up all the yesterdays and tomorrows and you'll begin to realize how desperate the problem really is. But, it's not hopeless. Over 80% of them can be helped. We know what to do. But we need your help. Please write and find out what you can do to prevent child abuse.

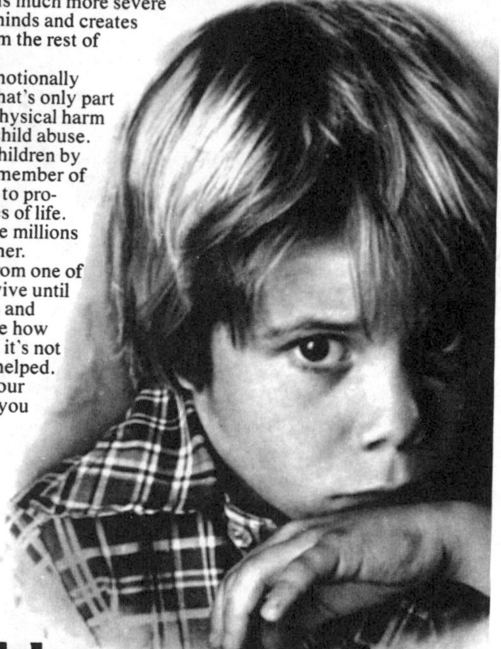

**Abused children are helpless. Unless you help.**

**Write:** National Committee for Prevention of Child Abuse, Box 2866, Chicago, Ill. 60690

A Public Service of This Magazine & The Advertising Council

## FIGURE VIII
### THE ABUSED CHILD WILL GROW UP
### SOMEDAY MAYBE

> Each year, over one million American children suffer from child abuse. Over 2000 children die from it. But what about those who survive? Statistics show that an abused childhood can affect a person's entire life. Many teenage drug addicts and teenage prostitutes report being abused children. So do juvenile delinquents and adult criminals. The fact is, a large percentage of many American social problems stem directly from child abuse. Yet child abuse *can* be prevented.
>
> HELP US GET TO THE HEART OF THE PROBLEM.

Since the beginning of its campaign, NCPCA has had a steady flow of correspondence from the American public. When the campaign was initially launched, correspondence was as high as 3000 letters a month. Discounting those initial months, NCPCA has received on an average somewhat more than 1000 letters a month over the lifetime of the campaign. The numbers vary somewhat from month to month depending upon when and where the media chooses to run the advertisements.

Most writers (76 per cent) simply ask for more information, often quoting the tag line from one of the campaign ads. (Figure IX). These writers receive standard NCPCA publications designed specifically to fulfill the promises of the media campaign to supply

## FIGURE IX
### TYPICAL DISTRIBUTION OF MAIL RESPONSES TO
### MEDIA CAMPAIGN

| | |
|---|---|
| Request for help | 7% |
| Offer to volunteer | 5% |
| Standard Request | 76% |
| Special Information on NCPCA | 3% |
| Career information | < 1% |
| Request for statistics | < 1% |
| Potential/Actual Contribution | 1% |
| Advertisements | 1% |
| Irresponsible letters | < 1% |
| Miscellaneous | 4% |

## FIGURE X

## SAMPLE "HELP" LETTER AND RESPONSES

Dear Sirs:

Almost three years ago we went to court against a woman who was abusing her daughter. Beating her and hitting her on the face and knocking her off cabinets and gave her a concussion. We had social workers who testified and said she was not mentally capable of taking care of her and a psychiatrist also testified against her and the judge *still* handed her (the mother) custody of the child. Now she's still being abused. You always say to report child abuse. What good does it do when the judge just hands her right back into her hands? What else is there to do? We had witnesses, doctors, social workers and everything and she still got away with it. I guess whenever she kills her then you guys will believe us. We have done everything we can do the rest is up to you.

Thank you.

Dear . . . . . :

Thank you for writing our organization explaining the child abuse case in your community. It sounds unfortunate that the decision of the judge was to return the child to the home. Even with testimony from neighbors and professionals, the final decision resides within the courts and sometimes we disagree with the judge's viewpoint. The situation you describe must be most frustrating and painful to watch.

However, we do encourage citizens to report suspicions of child abuse and to become involved as you did, because this is the most important means of aiding children and parents with problems. Laws sometimes need to be changed and judges sometimes need to be educated and this kind of advocacy happens when concerned citizens become involved. We still see abuse and neglect continue and children die, but our hopes are that with more public awareness and citizen involvement, parents can be helped.

If you are still in contact with the woman you mentioned, you might encourage her to join a group of Parents Anonymous (PA). This is a national self-help group for parents under stress who are abusers. Through weekly discussions members learn to handle their anger and frustrations in new ways. Enclosed is a PA brochure which lists a toll-free number you can call to locate a group in your community. You may also be interested in educating the judges in your county of this program. PA has a high rate of success in helping abusive parents, and some courts who are familiar with the program send abusers to PA groups for help.

We were sorry to hear of this case where the abuse continues. We hope that the mother has been helped by now. We also hope that you will not give up faith in the good work you have done and will continue to try to make changes. Continual reporting of abusive situations to your state agency is also critical. Thank you for continuing to care.

writers with additional information. The publications describe the magnitude and causes of the problem of child abuse and what can be done to prevent it as well as listing significant resource centres throughout the country where additional information can be obtained. The names and addresses of these letter writers are forwarded to state-wide child abuse agencies in their own states so that they will receive information about child abuse in their own states.

Although the campaign does not seek responses from people in need of help, approximately seven per cent of the letters are from individuals seeking help for themselves or another. As a group, these are the most challenging letters and the ones which require the promptest, most professional and most caring responses. Ten percent of these "help" letters are actually reports of child abuse. After some experimentation with different ways of handling these letters, NCPCA now forwards these reports by telephone to the appropriate state authorities to ensure a rapid response. In addition, a follow-up letter documenting the report is sent.

The remaining "help" letters are handled on an individualized basis. They come from abusive parents, abused children, grandparents of maltreated children and parents fearful of becoming abusive. Replies to each letter are written to respond specifically to the issues and concerns the letter writer raises. Every effort is made to refer the individual to helping resources in their own communities (Figure X).

Five percent of the letters are from individuals who want to volunteer their time to do something about the problem. These individuals are provided with specific information about programmes in their own state or community where they can volunteer their time. Where NCPCA has local affiliates, the writer's name and address is also sent directly to these programmes to increase the likelihood that the two will get together.

Three percent of the writers ask for more information about NSPCA, which is provided. Of the remaining letters most ask for selected information: "Where can I get statistics about child abuse?" "How can I set up a child abuse programme?" "I want to pursue a career in child abuse." Every reasonable effort is made to meet these specialized requests. Occasionally an envelope contains a contribution; just as frequently the letter writer is trying to sell something. And, a small number of the responses contain the unavoidable but always discouraging irresponsible letters.

The distribution of different types of letter responses to the campaign would appear to be rather typical. The distribution has remained generally the same over the period of the campaign.

Canadian government officials also report receiving generally the same type of distribution of letters in response to a media campaign on positive parenting.[6]

## Impact of the Campaign on Public Views

It is most difficult to assess what impact a campaign such as the one described has had on public attitudes. There are indications that over the lifetime of the campaign there has been a marked increase in the proportion of American adults who now acknowledge that child abuse is a significant problem in the United States. One informal survey suggests that before the campaign fewer than ten per cent of the adults in the United States thought of child abuse as a critical social problem and, after four years of the campaign, over 60 per cent of all adults recognized child abuse as a serious problem.[7]

Even if the findings of this informal study could be validated, it would still be difficult to determine specifically what role *this* campaign played in increasing public awareness, given the introduction of many other child abuse public awareness activities during the past half decade. Many states and community agencies have begun media campaigns to publicize reporting lines and local child abuse services. As awareness and reporting rates have increased so have coverage of child abuse episodes in the local and national press. Undoubtedly, this constellation of factors has contributed to increased public awareness of the problem.

Despite the challenges, in the interest of designing a national campaign which over time builds up the public's awareness of the problem, NCPCA continually seeks ways to assess what the public has learned and what the public is ready to learn. Recently the campaign's volunteer advertising firm, the Campbell-Ewald Company, conducted a study for NCPCA to develop some insights into the impact of the campaign on public opinions. The study, carried out in September, 1981, in Denver, Colorado and Detroit, Michigan, used a common advertising technique — focussed group opinion sessions. In depth discussions were held with groups of 8-12 parents representing different age ranges and socio-ethnic groups. The findings do shed light on how public awareness activities have influenced public opinion.

Most participants were aware of the magnitude of the child abuse problem. Most felt that the publicity associated with child abuse cases is a small percentage of the total number of incidents. While individuals could not approximate the number of abuse cases within the last year, no one seem shocked at its pervasiveness within our society.

"I think there is more than any of us know on our own streets."

"It is almost a national sickness."

Many questioned why more and more abuse cases are being reported today. They wondered: Is abuse increasing or are the number of publicized cases increasing?

Although an abusive parent was perceived as an uncontrollably angry parent, many people realize that this anger is a result of the person's inability to deal with stress.

... I think that until a person is a parent they are not really sympathetic or aware that they could potentially abuse a child. After a particularly stressful day you go into a situation tensed and if you are not in control, or unable to control yourself, you could be abusive to a child. If this person spanks once, I could see where one might lead to another and then another, and I could see it happening *given the right moment and the right person.* I have felt myself that it could happen, but I have been able to check it.

The majority of participants regarded child abuse as both physical and emotional. Physical abuse was easier for them to define. Very few participants suggested that neglect and sexual abuse were aspects of child abuse. Almost half of the participants showed an awareness of the more serious ramifications of child abuse — that the abused usually develop into abusers. While a few participants freely associated crime with child abuse, most people had difficulty dealing with crimes as a direct result of child abuse.

I am having a hard time relating to crime as a product of child abuse ... I never really thought of it in those terms.

The child is what he or she has been taught at home, and they have been taught through experience that violence is the name of the game.

I wouldn't even guess, I have never thought about it, never equated child abuse with crime.

NCPCA's ultimate goal for the campaign is to tell people specifically what activities they can get involved in to prevent child abuse. First, the public must be convinced that it is important to do something about child abuse. The focussed group opinion sessions showed NCPCA that the public still needed more information about the effects of the problem before learning about specific prevention strategies. The 1982 campaign has been designed accordingly.

## AREAS OF POTENTIAL PROBLEMS WITH MEDIA CAMPAIGNS

While the expense is usually the main barrier to the implementation of media campaigns, a number of potential hazards also stand in the way. (Figure XI)

Any media effort can result in unfortunate stigmatizing or labelling of the abuser or the abused unless great care is taken. For example, many professionals in the field believe that showing pictures of grossly abused children tends to cast unfortunately negative shadows over the abusive parent. And, some professionals have claimed that too much emphasis on the negative long-term consequences for the abused child could serve to so stigmatize the maltreated child as to create self-fulfilling prophecy. By only depicting one racial, ethnic or economic group in child abuse advertisements others argue that unsupportable stereotypes are created. Most organizations in the United States which have developed media campaigns have chosen not to depict actual abused children, to emphasize the message "child abusers may be just as helpless as their children" and to use a range of character types in visual advertisements.

### FIGURE XI

### POTENTIAL HAZARDS OF MEDIA CAMPAIGNS

Unfortunate stigmatizing of the abuser or the abused

Miscommunication or incomplete communication

Public overreaction leading to overlabelling

Lack of Control over use of media advertisements

Not being able to deliver what is promised

Alienating key people by not including them in planning and release

Selecting wrong theme

Media messages must, of necessity, be brief. They must use common, easy to understand language. The concepts presented, no matter how complex, must be presented in a simple manner. When simplified, messages about child abuse can never tell the whole story. And, as such, they can be misunderstood. For example, the message "child abusers may be just as helpless as their children" may be interpreted to mean that child abusers cannot be helped. NCPCA has choosen in its campaign to keep messages fairly narrow or specific from year to year and to encourage the public to write for more detailed information.

The most visible negative or problematic reaction to a media campaign about child abuse is one in which the public overreacts and as a result of the campaign begins to label all kinds of parental behaviour as abusive. By providing less than adequate information about how to identify an abused child or an abusive parent, the public may end up overlabelling. Every "isolated" adult, every "overly aggresive" child gets reported as being a potential abuser or potentially abused child. If a campaign is to encourage reporting, sufficient information must be provided to allow the public to do a good job of reporting.

Once an awareness campaign has entered the public domain, the designers and managers of the campaign lose a degree of control. This is particularly true of "public service" campaigns in which the media donates advertising time and space. Once released, a campaign may be run at any time or in any place the media desires. For example, NCPCA print advertisements have appeared in pornographic magazines. Television spots have been shown during children's Saturday morning programs as well as during Sunday afternoon football games and midnight movies. As long as the integrity of the advertisment is maintained, for example, it is not altered, this lack of control over where and when advertisements appear may not produce significantly negative results.

The most significant pitfall of any media campaign is offering more than can be delivered. A message such as "If you need help call us" must be connected with a service which can provide quality help to all those who choose to call. Advertising a phone number which will only bring to callers a busy signal or an untrained person who cannot offer any meaningful help can create more harm than good. It is hard to measure the extra frustration a person in need of help feels when he reaches out for help and receives none. That frustration must be considerable. The same is true of a reporting hotline which does not have the capacity to adequately investigate all reports received. Any service to be offered through a media campaign must be geared up to handle responses in a professional manner.

The launching of a media campaign, carries with it a significant public responsibility. Organizations, agencies or existing services which will in some way be directly affected by the campaign should be made aware of the campaign in advance. A campaign which might result in increased reports of abuse will have a direct impact local child abuse authorities. Without forewarning those authorities, not only does the campaign sponsor risk losing the good will and respect of those authorities, but the sponsor may also find out that the campaign offers more than can be delivered.

Finally, a media campaign can quite simply miss the mark. The campaign can carry a theme which the public does not want to hear or does not need to hear. For example, during very difficult economic times, the public may be uninterested in learning about new but costly solutions to the problem. During particularly stressful times, the public may need to know that: "Child abuse is a big problem, but we are beginning to make progress!" Assessing the economic, political and social climate is an important part of planning a successful campaign.

CONCLUSIONS

The media are a most powerful tool in communicating messages to the public. Just as the media can sanction violence of all forms, so too the media can be used to help prevent violence. Organized and thoughtful efforts to educate the public about child abuse and its prevention through the media offer a promising and quite likely essential avenue to reducing the amount of child abuse we experience in our societies.[8,9]

Altogether too little research has been done on different ways in which the media can be used to foster positive parenting, to help parents know that it is all right to reach out for help and to motivate concerned citizens to do something about the problem. Perhaps the experiences of the National Committee for Prevention of Child Abuse can be used as the starting point for creating a credible and useful literature on the subject.

## Notes

1  A H Cohn, *An Approach to Preventing Child Abuse,* National Committee for Prevention of Child Abuse (Chicago, Illinois, 1981)

2  R B Flanner Jr, "Primary Prevention and Adult Television Viewing: Methodological Extension" (1980) *Psychological Reports* **46(2)**:578

3  R E Helfer, "A Review of the Literature on the Prevention of Child Abuse and Neglect" (Michigan State University, unpublished paper, 1981)

4  G C M Lupton, "Prevention Recognition Management and Treatment of Cases of Non-Accidental Injury to Children: Arrangements in the United Kingdom." (1977) *Child Abuse and Neglect: The International J* 1(1):203-9

5  National Center on Child Abuse and Neglect, *How to Plan and Carry out a Successful Public Awareness Campaign on Child Abuse and Neglect* (DHEW Publication, No (OHD) 76-30089, 1976)

6  D Rudan, Ontario Provincial Government, Informal Communications December, 1981

7  Campbell-Ewald Company, Strategic Planning and Research Staff, "Focus Group Sessions Attitudes and Opinions about Child Abuse (Campbell-Ewald Company In-House Report, Warren, Michigan, September, 1981)

8  D H O'Brien, A R Schneider and H Traviesas, "Portraying Abuse Network Censor's Round Table" in G Gerbner et al (eds) *Child Abuse: An Agenda for Action* (Oxford University Press, New York 1980)

9  N Signorielli, "Covering Abuse: Content and Policy: Magazine Coverage" in G Gerbner et al (eds) *Child Abuse: An Agenda for Action* (Oxford University Press, New York 1980)

# Chapter 20

# Violence in Society

Anne Deveson

When Professor Henry Kempe defined the battered child syndrome in the early 60's, much of the public and professional press appeared to assume that this was some new evil of the twentieth century.

But historical and social records leave us in little doubt that child abuse is not a new problem. The fact that it is now a matter of public concern has come about partly because we are now more sensitive to human rights and partly because, as the nuclear family has become increasingly isolated, government and other external agencies have assumed many of the family's former functions and private life has become more public.

Kempe's and other early definitions of child abuse focused on very young children and on medical evidence of physical abuse. This meant that older children were excluded, as well as other forms of abuse, including less serious physical abuse. And, because it was the medical profession which had first labelled child abuse, it was the medical model which applied.[1]

People who abused children who were in their care were seen to be aberrant, psychologically abnormal, and in need of "cure". The climate tended to be a punitive one, and there was a marked division between those who abused, and those who didn't. The problem was seen as belonging mainly to the poor, because it was mainly the poor who came to the attention of public agencies and the law.

All this meant that there was little attempt to look beyond individual pathology and to question ways in which our whole environment might be providing a conducive climate for child abuse.

Many studies have explored varying theories about the nature of human aggression; put simplistically, they range from those which postulate an innate aggressive instinct, necessary for survival, to those which claim that humans are not normally aggressive, but only become so as a result of environmental frustration. This chapter is concerned with some of those external or structural characteristics which are believed to foster violent behaviour, and in particular, violence which is directed towards children.

American sociologist David Gil was one of the first to present a multi-level analysis of violence. Gil has defined violence as "acts and conditions which obstruct the spontaneous unfolding of innate human potential, the inherent drive towards development and self-actualization". He argued that such acts and conditions which "violate" the process of human development, may occur at interpersonal, institutional and societal levels, and referred to institutional and societal violence as structural violence. In his view, personal violence was usually reactive and rooted in structural violence, "since experiences which inhibit a person's development will often result in stress and frustration and in an urge to retaliate by inflicting violence on others".[2,3]

Most current literature acknowledges that violence is created and nourished by a confluence of internal and external characteristics and conditions. Cultural beliefs, attitudes and behaviours are learned within an environmental context, and for abusive patterns to develop within a family system, there must be cultural justification of forceful behaviours.[4]

The social acceptability of violence obviously varies between cultures, within cultures and across time, but if we take Gil's definition of violence, the most extreme threat to the process of human development that transcends all cultures and time, must surely lie in our relentless development of nuclear armaments.

Children today are born into anxiety which permeates our whole civilization. For the first time in history, the world is threatened with annihilation by the most grotesque kind of violence man has managed to devise. When world leaders rationalize such violence by talking about limited nuclear containment, and develop armaments which will destroy humans but preserve buildings, we have a chilling picture of the potential and extent of human aggression.

Violence in society is also evidenced by the rising incidence of homicide, suicide, crimes of violence, rape and road accidents. Television portrays this violence in living colour, and brings it into our living rooms, so that we can no longer cocoon ourselves from its reality. Fictionalized and cartoon violence augments and distorts the picture, so that for those who grew up with television and those who are heavy viewers, television does not mirror the world. It *is* the world.

The question is to what extent does such generalized exposure to violence lead to a lowering of sensitivity towards violence and to the attitude that problems in life can be more effectively solved by violence than by rational reasoning?

This is an important question with regard to the influence of television. The early years of life are critically important for a child's psycho-social development. This is the period when he is especially vulnerable to influence, whether for good or ill, and although infants are not directly influenced by television, by the age of two or three many children have begun to watch television regularly. Indeed, the Australian Senate Standing Committee on Education and the Arts (1978) has stated that television has clearly emerged as the dominant experience in the life of the average Australian child, monopolizing more of his time than any other single activity, apart from sleeping.[5]

Clearly, whether or not a child or an adult behaves aggressively does not depend solely on the television programmes that they view, and one of the problems inherent in research in this area is that the laboratory conditions required to measure aggressive behaviour provide a vastly different setting from what happens within the family home. However, in a review of research studies and commentaries, John Murray found a general consensus that increased aggressive behaviour can be produced under specific circumstances as a result of viewing various forms of televised violence. What researches do not agree upon is the seriousness of these affects.[6]

In one of the most important surveys undertaken in this field, under the auspice of the United States Surgeon General's Committee, it was stated: ". . . there is a convergence of the fairly substantial experimental evidence for *short-run* causation of aggression among some children by viewing violence on the screen and the much less certain evidence from field studies that extensive violence viewing preceded some *long-term* manifestation of aggressive behaviour. This convergence . . . constitutes some preliminary indication of a causal relationship".[7]

If we return to a consideration of Gil's definition of violence as acts and conditions which violate the process of human development, we can see that in Western industrialized societies, the dominant pressure to accumulate wealth, to compete, to succeed, results in inequalities, poverty and social alienation for a disturbingly high proportion of our society.

The Australian report to the International Conference on Social Welfare stated: "Economic development in Australia has been characterized by a relative heedlessness to the misfortunes of those 'left behind' in the name of progress, consequently the victims of such progress are still often seen as failures and drop-outs and a necessary unfortunate part of the cost of economic development."[8]

In Australia, the wealthiest 1 per cent of the population owns 22 per cent of the total wealth. The richest 2000 people own as much as the poorest 2·25 million.[9] The Poverty Survey found 10·2 per cent

of Australians to be "very poor", and this figure included nearly a
quarter of a million children.[10]

The gap is widening. Ten years ago, nine in every ten people in
Australia could afford to pay off a house. Now, only two in ten can
do so.[11] Unemployment has risen from 1·9 per cent in 1952 to 5·8
per cent in 1981. Moreover, it is structural unemployment, not
merely a problem of inflation or rising oil prices or seasonal
fluctuations.

A family with a very low income suffers the obvious disadvantage
of being able to purchase fewer material goods and services than
other families. What is not so obvious is the impact that poverty has
on the quality of family relationships. Life for one of these families
was described by a witness to the Royal Commission on Human
Relationships:

> Having no money or very little, can in fact, destroy family life ... It is
> not that we have no interest in one another. I think it is because you are
> so heavily burdened with the stress and strain of having nothing to feed
> your family on that you cannot think of anything else but that ... you
> cannot relate with one another because of that pressure. I think it destroys
> the relationship between parents and children too because of the same
> worry. Children cannot form a relationship with the schools because you
> are always on the move.[12]

The Commission report stated that violence towards children occurs
at the structural level when social institutions, policies and practices
inhibit the development of children to their fullest potential.
Equally, it manifests itself in statistics on infant hunger and
malnutrition, mortality, poverty, inadequate family services, poor
education and racial discrimination.

Structural abuse of children can also take place within our
institutions such as schools, children's homes, children's courts, child
care centres, hospitals and mental health establishments. For
example, the process of some of our children's courts has been
described as "generally rigid, pusillanimous, reactive and un-
principled".[13]

The way in which children are treated in our society relates to the
way we value children and the way we define their rights. As
Professor Peter Boss states in his book *On the Side of the Child*:

> When it is considered that social policies need not be the result of blindly
> determined economic and social conditions but rather can and should be
> the consequence of deliberate choices made by government on behalf of
> society, it is quite proper to assert that society, as a whole, can be accused
> of abusing its children, or some of them, if it fails to take account of the
> possibility of more equally allocating resources.[14]

Children's needs can only be met if parents are willing and able to be caring, and parental willingness and ability to be caring will depend heavily on the support and affirmation they receive from their environment.

By now, a number of studies have suggested that child abuse is perhaps more common where there is poverty, unemployment, poor housing, and domiciliary mobility. But most of this work is based on reported cases of abuse where there is a strong possibility of bias, just as there is in hospital studies. Middle class people are less likely to be reported, and more likely to go to private sources for help. They have more resources, more alternatives, and more escapes. But they are still just as vulnerable to the structural frailties of present-day family life. American psychiatrist and lawyer, Dr Judyanne Densen-Gerber, speaking in Australia in 1977, said:

I have given many speeches, and firmly believe that the nuclear family is the first act of violence in our society. I define the nuclear family as one adult male and one adult female (at best because sometimes it's a single parent family) chained to 2·4 muling and puking infants. No society was ever meant to be reared that way.[15]

This brings us to consider a growing contention that the family, far from being a haven of peace and happiness, is our primary training ground for violent behaviour. The family is the setting in which most people first experience physical violence, and also the setting which establishes the emotional context and meaning of violence.

Murray Straus sees three unintended consequences arising from the use of physical punishment within the family. The first of these unintended consequences is the association of love with violence, since parents are the first and usually the only ones to hit an infant; second, since physical punishment is used to train a child or to teach about dangerous things to be avoided, it establishes the moral rightness of hitting other family members; third, is the lesson that when something is really important it justifies the use of physical force.[16]

Physical punishment of children in our society is general and pervasive. It forms a strong element of our child-rearing practices.

At the second Australasian Child Abuse Conference in Brisbane in 1981, Jan Carter referred to a small pilot study of hers in Western Australia of interviews with 40 mothers with children in a range of occasional and permanent day care facilities. The women, who came from a wide range of social backgrounds, were asked what discipline methods they had used in the fortnight previous to the survey with a nominated child.

Nearly 85 per cent had smacked or hit a child; half had threatened hitting with an object, most commonly a wooden spoon, and half reported incidents where they had worried that they would go too far and hurt a child. The women "usually recognized that what they were doing was wrong, an were desperate for learning about alternative methods of coping."[17]

Physical punishment is also authorized in Australian schools. Australia is one of about ten countries left in the world which still permits this form of punishment. The Royal Commission on Human Relationships stated in its final report that as long as schools, and others to whom the care of children is committed, use physical means of punishment, this will convey subtle messages to parents that such methods are appropriate, and not so subtle messages to children that society approves of authority based on force.[18]

Few parents realize the risks involved in physical punishment of young children. Sometimes injury occurs when the parent, in the name of discipline, moves from what has been called "reasonable force" to unreasonable violence. Obviously there are degrees of punishment, but the most disturbing aspect of this feature of our child-rearing practices is that the use of physical punishment becomes so easily the norm rather than the exception.

For centuries, children and women were considered under the law to be possessions of the head of the household. Many women researchers contend that underpinning all family violence is the patriarchal structure of marriage and society.[19,20,21] The family is seen as a violent institution and this is born out by statistics which show that over half of all homicide victims were murdered by spouses or close kin.[22]

Violence towards children must necessarily be viewed within the total context of violence within the family. In Christina Gibbeson's study of 111 battered women at Elsie Women's Refuge in Sydney, 22 per cent of women said their children were attacked constantly, and 16 per cent said sporadically. In 32 per cent of the relationships, the children had intervened, physically or verbally. Over half the women said they always feared their children would be attacked. Seventy-five per cent said they thought there had been actual instances when there was danger they would harm their children. The instances were mostly related to feelings of inadequacy, depression and exhaustion.[23]

As the report of the Royal Commission on Human Relationships pointed out, the problems facing women in situations of domestic violence are very great. They have accommodation difficulties, financial problems, worries about bringing up their children single-handed, and they have to contend with a social climate which is unsympathetic. Many stay in situations of danger and conflict because they cannot see any other alternative. Their upbringing has trained them to be dependent.[24]

The patriarchal nature of Australian society provides a climate for family violence. Men are still encouraged to be aggressive and women to be passive. The male acts upon the world and the woman is acted upon. Furthermore, the male frequently acts upon the world in a way that is insensitive to the needs of women and children.

Inadequate child care centres, lack of family planning facilities, curtailment of family support programmes, closure of women's refuges, urban planning that neglects the needs of children, shrinking job opportunities for women, and a direction of government spending into resource development and big business at the expense of health, education and welfare, are the consequences of deliberate choices made by patriarchal governments which further lock women and children into violent situations from which there is little escape.

## Notes

1   Richard J Gelles, "The Social Construction of Child Abuse" (1975) *Am J Orthopsychiat* **45(3)**:363-72

2   David G Gil, "Unravelling Child Abuse" (1975) *Am J Orthopsychiat* **45(3)**:346-56

3   David G Gil, "Societal Violence and Violence in Families" *Family Violence, an International and Interdisciplinary Study* (Butterworths, Toronto, 1978)

4   J Garbarino, "The Human Ecology of Maltreatment, A Conceptual Model for Research" (1977) *J Marriage Family* **39**:721-34

5   Senate Standing Committee on Education and the Arts, *Children and Television* (AGPS, Canberra, 1978) p 18

6   John P Murray, "Violence in Childen's Television: Continuing Research Issues" *Media Information — Australia* **3 February 1977**:1-18

7   Surgeon General's Scientific Advisory Committee on Television and Social Behaviour, *Television and Growing Up: The Impact of Televised Violence* (US Government Printing Office, Washington DC, 1972)

8   Australian Council of Social Services, *The Making of Social Policy* Australian report to XVI International Conference on Social Welfare (The Hague, 1972)

9   P Raskall, *J Aust Polit Economy No 2* 1978

10  *Commission of Inquiry into Poverty, Poverty in Australia,* First main report (AGPS, Canberra, 1975)

11  F J Bromilow, "Productivity and the Affordable House" Session of Housing Industry Association's 12 National Conference (Canberra, April 1977)

12  *Royal Commission on Human Relationships, Final Report* Vol 1(v), p 19 (AGPS, Canberra, 1977)

13  S W Johnston, "Strengthening the Victorian Children's Court" in L Foreman *Children or Families?* Aust Govt Social Welfare Commission, 1975) p 50

14   Peter Boss, *On the Side of the Child* (Fontana/Collins, Melbourne, 1980) p 21

15   Judyanne Densen-Gerber, Monday Conference, televised Monday 14 March 1977 (Australian Broadcasting Commission)

16   Murray Straus, "Wife-Beating: How Common and Why?" in *Proceedings of Second International Conference on Family Law,* Montreal, Quebec, 1977 (Butterworths, Toronto, 1978) pp 34-9

17   J Carter, *Proceedings of Second Australasian Conference on Child Abuse* (Sept 20-25 Brisbane, 1981)

18   Royal Commission on Human Relationships, *Final Report* Vol 2 p 19 (AGPS, Canberra, 1977)

19   Jocelynne Scutt, "Violence in the Family: a Review of Legal, Social and Political Supports" *Living Together* (Centre for Continuing Education, ANU, Canberra, 1980) pp 223-39

20   V Johnson, "Children and Family Violence — Refuges" in J Scutt (ed) *Violence in the Family* (a collection of papers from a national conference hosted in November 1979 by the Aust Institute of Criminology) (Aust Institute Criminology Canberra, 1980) pp 195-203

21   C O'Donnell and H Saville, "Sex and Class Inequality and Domestic Violence" in *Violence in the Family* ibid, pp 79-94

22   Tess Rod, "Marital Murder" in *Violence in the Family* ibid, pp 95-105

23   Christina Gibbeson, *Research Report No 11* (see Royal Commission on Human Relationships, *Final Report* Vol 1(v) pp 144-5 (AGPS, Canberra, 1977)

24   Royal Commission on Human Relationships, *Final Report* "Family Violence" (AGPS, Canberra, 1977) pp 133-55

# Chapter 21

# Battered Professionals

Lyndsey Fletcher

Professionals who work with the problem of child abuse are at risk of becoming involved in an abusive cycle themselves, hence the title "Battered Professionals" that has been chosen for this chapter. The risk is of being caught in a system where the professional is psychologically and emotionally battered by his clients, by his colleagues, by the system and defensively may make inappropriate and sometimes destructive responses — battering. Despite the wealth of material written on child abuse, little attention has been paid to this emotional reaction of professionals.[1,2,3,4] Why is it so denied? Do professionals who work in this field find it too difficult to accept that there is the risk of abusive relationship patterns developing amongst them?

We are presently in a period of active interest in child abuse. There are great pressures to develop facilities for the management of abusive families. We are becoming more aware of the rights as well as the needs of these families. But what we have failed to recognize or have denied are the rights and the needs of the professionals who are being caught up in this process. For a child abuse team to function adequately the needs of the worker (paediatrician, psychiatrist, social worker, psychologist, nurse, welfare officer, parent aide) must be acknowledged and supported.

I have been involved in several different groups each working with various aspects of child abuse. I have been impressed by the consistency and intensity of certain emotional reactions that occurred in each instance. The all-pervasive feelings are those of anxiety, mistrust, competitiveness and anger. Professionals feel devalued, misunderstood and unsupported, all of which significantly inhibit their ability to function adequately.

Any worker left to cope with these reactions may deal with them by projection resulting in scapegoating. Put more bluntly they resort to colleague bashing. These feelings quickly alienate workers from one another. Collusion develops between some workers leading to the development of rival factions. Battles ensue over such issues as good or bad parent, defenceless or provocative child, parents' rights versus the child's rights, legal intervention or therapy. This results in rivalry between different professions, differing schools of thought and differing treatment modalities. Despite genuine caring intentions we end up acting out feelings quite analogous to those operating in the abusive families. In fact, what we may call the "professional family" shows strong relationship similarity to those of the abusive family.

As Leila Whiting has noted, "parents who abuse their children feel helpless, hopeless and overwhelmed and unsupported, isolated and inadequate and these feelings are often reflected in those professionals who work with them leading to distrust and suspicion".[5] What is it about child abuse that arouses such intensely disruptive feeling amongst professionals? What leads well-meaning workers to become so battered and battering and dysfunctional?

Understanding the phenomena of the battered professional will come by observing the parallel between the "professional family" and the abusive family. It then becomes possible to relate our understanding of the predisposing factors in the abusive family to the factors involved in predisposing the professional family to the risk of becoming abusive.

If we accept that abusive families can be helped, surely the same principles of prevention and management can be applied to the "professional family". There is some agreement that actual child abuse is precipitated by a crisis occurring in a family predisposed to abusing their child.[6] The predisposing factors include severe maternal deprivation, a sense of isolation with a lack of social supports and high, unrealistic expectations of the child. The crisis may emanate from the child's actual behaviour or what he represents for the parents, or it may arise from the very broad spectrum of environmental factors. A parallel sequence of predisposing and precipitating events may occur amongst the workers leading to mutual abuse.

## BATTERED PROFESSIONALS — PREDISPOSING FACTORS

### Deprivation

Deprivation may be intrapsychic and/or environmental for the professional as for the abusive family. Intrapsychic deprivation refers to the professionals' early childhood experiences which may or may not have been "good enough".[7] There is in each of us conflicts about early parental hurt which are activated when dealing with child abuse. Our emotional reactions may stem from unconscious issues related to our own childhood. It is therefore advisable for individual workers to firstly seek to understand what internal and external forces has lead them to choose to be involved in child abuse. Secondly, they ought to be prepared to question and explore their emotional reactions to facilitate taking responsibility for those related to their own inner conflicts. It is stressed that these personal conflicts belong to the individual and are not the responsibility of the professional group.

Environmental deprivation refers to the widespread lack of "good enough" knowledge and training of workers in this field. A common assumption is that professional training equals expertise in child abuse. In fact much of the specific knowledge required for work in this field is not part of any professional's basic training. Often it is not even provided at the commencement of work with abusive families.

The absence of a nurturing environment for the professional is comparable to the maternal deprivation suffered by the abusive parent.

My first contact with child abuse was as a clinical member of a hospital child abuse team. This team was set up without a preparatory training programme and without any commitment to ongoing education. We met regularly for case conferences which concentrated on gross management issues. The team's failure to avail itself of the current knowledge about child abuse was a significant factor in the group's lack of cohesion and its inability to develop a consensual approach to abusive families.

Rival factions developed within the group leading to hostility and devaluing of one another. This fragmented, warring team was seen by some of its members and by the hospital as failing in its task of helping abusive families.

It must be recognized that child abuse professionals, like children require a nurturing environment in which to develop and grow professionally. The provision of a preparatory training period followed by an ongoing in-service program is therefore essential for the development of a cohesive team. Such a team should be able to tolerate differences but able to develop a shared frame of reference for the assessment and management of these families. Such a group experience should also provide the opportunity for members to share their reactive anxieties, feelings and doubts about working in the field of child abuse.

## Unrealistic Expectations and Misconceptions

Initially professional workers coming into the field of child abuse are likely to have unrealistic expectations of what can be achieved. Like abusive parents who have unrealistic expectations of their children, the worker has similar unrealistic expectations of the abusive families, expecting improvement and responses far beyond their capacity. With the inevitable failure of some families to respond the worker feels exposed, inadequate and angry.

Professionals so deprived often develop an overinvolvement with this specialty and come to regard it as "their baby" through which they can achieve professional competence, recognition and satisfaction. They become very possessive, resisting involvement of others, exacerbating the feelings of rivalry and competitiveness.

Workers may often have gross misconceptions of the roles and areas of expertise of the various professional disciplines involved in child abuse, judging some as "all knowing" and others as "valueless", dependent on a worker's past experience and prejudices. This facilitates the development of rivalry, hostility and passive withdrawal.

A child abuse team or group often has unrealistic expectations of the team leader or consultant. Overwhelmed by their feelings of inadequacy and helplessness in the face of an abusive family, workers need to see the leader as omnipotent and feel enraged when he is unable to suggest the magic solution. Similarly, the general community often have highly unrealistic expectations of the child abuse teams, expecting dramatic cures or solutions from such experts. This phenomenon frequently exists between agencies. In this situation the agency is set up for failure with all the associated anger, mostly self-righteous and condemning.

Realistic expectations can only be achieved by the workers undergoing an intensive training program leading to an appreciation that there are no easy answers to child abuse. It is imperative that there be a shared acknowledgment of the limitations of current skills and knowledge regarding our ability to help extremely damaged abusive families. Through this process workers can gain a more realistic appreciation and respect for the specific contribution and areas of expertise of each professional discipline involved. Only then can workers, groups and agencies value and support one another and learn to work co-operatively rather than competitively.

### Isolation

Feelings of isolation and alienation readily develop amongst professionals working with child abuse similar to those so characteristic of abusive families.

Workers deprived of an adequate knowledge base, feeling misunderstood and prejudged, readily withdraw or act out to protect themselves from further exposure. The professionals can behave like abused children: some becoming overtly angry and provocative while others become compliant and withdrawn being very watchful and ever alert to meeting the needs of the group leader.

For such professionals any suggestion about management of a case can be felt as a hostile, devaluing attack. This can provoke a defensive counter attack. At some level this gives the worker a sense of being effective and of being noticed, but further alienates him from avenues of support. Too readily such workers hide behind a smoke-screen of being overworked; rationalizing that they are too busy to fully assess, follow up, record or co-ordinate their particular cases. Similarly, they are too busy to attend certain conferences or supervision for fear of such issues being exposed. Thus the feelings of isolation are further exacerbated making it even more difficult to offer them help and support.

Alternatively, workers protect themselves by selective withdrawal. Often seemingly compliant they are resistant to offering their opinion or asking for help for fear of being thought inadequate or a failure. In fact they often deny the specific clinical problems they are observing in their families. It is safer to concentrate on broader issues such as gross case management, communication problems between disciplines and between agencies. Such action on the part of the professional is similar to abusive families who have difficulty in asking for help and deny and withdraw to protect themselves, relying on splitting and projection to focus the problem away from themselves.

In order to relieve the problem of isolation any group of professionals working together in child abuse must work within a firm basic structure which has the mandate to hold and reach out to each worker. This structure should include a realistic procedure for the assessment, management and review of cases with the lines of accountability and responsibility defined. It should include the provision for regular case conferences and consultations as well as an ongoing in-service training programme.

Most importantly it should include the provision for each professional to have regular supervision from someone outside the group. It is now recognized that abusive parents with some ego-strengths need a mothering experience to improve their self-esteem as parents. Workers in this field also have a special need for a more "mothering" supervision to enhance their professional self-esteem. They need regular supervision which will give them the experience of feeling valued, and of being listened to and cared about.

This "holding" experience gives the workers an opportunity to recognize and contain their own anger. They are then in turn able to offer each other support rather than acting out their abusive feeling. Similarly, this experience helps them give the necessary support to their client families.

## Crisis

As with abusive families, professionals who are predisposed to abuse by deprivation, unrealistic expectations and isolation only require a crisis to precipitate an abusive event. One such crisis occurs when an abusive family is referred. Like the parents' expectations of the abused child, the family is expected to confirm the worker's competence both to himself and to his colleagues. A role reversal thus occurs as this need for professional reassurance takes precedence over the family's needs. When the family fails to meet the worker's expectations, the worker's feelings of inadequacy are increased, leaving the worker feeling as helpless and angry as the abusive parents. Workers, acting out their own needs and feeling abandoned and attacked by their colleagues are unable to work effectively. This can have very serious consequences when working in the field of child abuse.

A concern for the battered professional is not only for the resulting damage to the workers but also for the abusing families who come under their care. In such a professional family as described, internal conflicts become a major preoccupation. These conflicts can significantly inhibit the worker's ability to assess the extent of the psychopathology in each abusive family resulting in mismanagement.

The following clinical example emphasizes this point and illustrates the concept of the battered professional:

An abusive family was referred to a child abuse team following their baby's admission to hospital with a fractured leg. Within the team, the paediatrician in charge of the case, requested a psychiatric consultation for the family after he had had a disagreement with the social worker involved.

The psychiatrist, after a brief assessment offered to treat the parents. However he then also became involved in the battle between the paediatrician and the social worker and supported the social worker's wish to accede to the parents' request to take the baby home on a day pass.

Reassured by his good judgement when all went well on the day pass, the psychiatrist recommended the baby's discharge. Following discharge the parents attended for weekly therapy sessions and continued to do so right up to the time of the baby's readmission to hospital with a fatal head injury.

In retrospect and in the light of our understanding of the battered professional, some of the issues contributing to this tragic outcome are clear. This child abuse team was abusive and dysfunctional. It had been deprived of an adequate knowledge base upon which to assess and treat families. It was caught up in battles between rival factions as a result of the isolation and unrealistic expectation with the team. This team was then presented with an abusive family which was particularly difficult to assess and the conflict of professional opinions succeeded in splitting the team even further. The workers were so caught up in the abusive cycle within the team that their need to win internal wars overshadowed a realistic appraisal of the lethal war going on within the abusive family.[4]

## CONCLUSION

In conclusion I should like to stress that whenever a group of people become involved with the problem of child abuse such a group is at risk — at risk of developing an abusive cycle similar to the cycle of abuse which exists within abusive families.

If we can accept that such a potential does exist then it should be mandatory for some inbuilt structure for ongoing education, individual supervision and regular consultation to be an integral part of any facility developed to help abusive families. In fact it should be the basis of such a facility.

For the sake of the workers and the abusive families who come under their care we can no longer afford to deny the rights and the needs of the battered professional.

## Notes

1   J D Lipner, "Attitudes of Professionals in the Management and Treatment of Child Abuse" in N B Ebeling and D A Hill (eds) *Child Abuse: Intervention and Treatment* (Publishing Sciences Group, Massachusetts, 1975)

2   James S Elkind, Alma Berson and David Edwin, "Current Realities Haunting Advocates of Abused Children" (1977) *Social Casework* 58:527-31

3   Stuart Copans, H Kreil, H H Grundy, Janet Rogan and F Field, "The Stresses of Treating Child Abuse" (1979) *Children Today* 8(1):22-35

4   L Fletcher and R Adler, "The Prevention of Abuse by the Child Abuse Team — The Consultants' Responsibility?" (1980) *The Child in His Family* Vol 6

5   Leila Whiting, "Child Protection Team" (January/February, 1977) *Children Today* 6(1):10-12

6   C Pollock and B F Steele, "A Therapeutic Approach to the Parents" in C H Kempe and R E Helfer (eds) *Helping the Battered Child and His Family* (J B Lippincott, Philadelphia, 1972)

7   R W Winnicott, *Ego Distortion in Terms of True and False Self in the Maturational Processes and the Facilitating Environment* (Hogarth Press, London, 1972, first published 1960)

# Chapter 22

# Protecting the Child's Interests

Richard A H White

The last decade has seen a growing emphasis on consideration of children's rights. This chapter examines certain aspects of these developments commencing with a brief look at the concept of rights relating to children and relevant definitions of children. A number of areas in which children have specific interests are then discussed.

## THE CONCEPT OF CHILDREN'S RIGHTS

There is no satisfactory definition of children's rights nor established framework within which they can be exercised. There has been some discussion of parental rights usually linked with parental duties.[1] There have also been propositions for Bills of Rights for children and charters have been drafted.[2] The legal basis for the existence of such rights and how they might be enforced has received little attention.

This chapter is based on the fundamental premise that a child is a separate individual and has rights like any other person. Caution is necessary in the use of the term rights, since strictly it should be applied to interests which are legally enforceable against a person having a corresponding duty. Claims or freedoms may be equally important. A child may have a moral right to be treated like any other child or person, but this may be no more than an unenforceable claim. A child may have a right not to suffer corporal punishment, but this is more aptly described as a freedom from the imposition of punishment.

Generically all these concepts will be referred to as interests, and they are important because they provide the individual with a status within society. It should not be assumed, especially where children are involved, that they are necessarily enforceable. No analysis of these concepts is undertaken, but when considering proposals for furthering children's interests, it is helpful to ensure that terms are not used inappropriately.

## THE APPROACH TO CHILDREN'S RIGHTS

There is an essential division in children's interests, which has been described as the "nurturance orientation" and the "self-determination orientation".[3] Much has been written under the banner of children's rights about how children should be empowered to decide for themselves about issues in education, and where they live, to achieve financial independence and generally to decide what is good for them. No doubt there are some aspects of their lives in which children should have a greater say, but the more extreme proposals for self-determination are manifestly absurd.[4] There is clearly an age at which they are too immature to have the capacity to act for themselves. It would be unwise to generalize on the age at which self-determination should be given more weight than nurturance. Too many factors are involved like the mental capacity of the child and the reality of the self-determinating wish. This chapter seeks to avoid these insoluble disputes. It accepts the basic premise that, at a minimum, children are helpless at certain times and in respect of certain events in their life. At those times they need assistance from parents, supporters of parents or substitutes for parents to be adequately nurtured.

## PROTECTING THE CHILD'S INTERESTS

The nurturing approach focuses on the child who is helpless and unable to fend for himself, or unable to make or obtain from those around him an appropriate response in circumstances where his interests are being harmed. This leads to the need to protect the child's interests against harm, past, present or future. Our primary concern is with those children who suffer at the hands of the adults who look after them, and who are unable to take any action themselves to avoid such suffering.

For the young child there is an essential link between his welfare, his needs and his rights. His rights are to have his reasonable needs satisfied and his welfare assured. Since a child is incapable of protecting these interests it should be his fundamental right to have them protected on his behalf. How to give effect to the child's rights where he is abused or neglected, and what interests are deserving of protection is the concern of the rest of this chapter. The interests which will be considered relate to support for birth parents to enable them to care adequately for their own children, provision for the child separated from his birth parents, placement where long-term separation is necessary, and representation of the child.

### Support for Birth Parents

It is important to establish what good parenting will achieve for the child. For western society the following may provide a satisfactory aim: to produce a mature, responsible person capable of making and sustaining adult relationships. Such a person should be able to make a positive contribution to society, respond to the needs of his parents and his own children and fulfil his own needs.

There are variations in different civilizations, but natural law supports the view that a child should be nurtured by the parents to whom he was born, or within their family system. A child who is separated from his parents is therefore set apart and to some extent stigmatized. It follows that to give the best possible opportunity for achieving the aim above, every effort should be made to sustain the system of the birth family. This statement holds good whether viewed from the general interest of society, the rights of the parent or the child, or the future fulfilment of the individuals.

It is therefore in society's long-term interests to support the birth family. In western civilization most states have a system of financial support through social security benefits, though these are to some extent discretionary. In England discretionary payments and assistance in kind are available specifically to avoid children coming into care, but these are strictly controlled. In the United States the Adoption Assistance and Child Welfare Act 1980 introduced the mandatory provision of services to help children remain with their families, but states have to make available sufficient funding for service programmes to be adequately implemented.

Support for the birth family is more than a simple matter of money. It is also about the quality of service. At the present the ability to bring about change in an abusing or neglectful family seems limited. The tools to enable families to provide their children with a good nurturing system have either not been sufficiently developed or are not widely used. The experience in England, as indicated by reports of child abuse inquiries in the last decade, suggests that too often there is still a traditional social work approach of response to crisis and the occasional application of sticking plasters. To protect the child's interests it is necessary to develop and make widely available more positive methods of working with families.

It will be seen that discussion of children's rights is not just about how an individual child can enforce or should possess a particular interest. It is about how society is organized to further the interests of all its members, with children being considered as equal individuals and entitled to consideration in their own right. The first step will most frequently be to strengthen the child's first line of defence, his parents. (The extent to which parenting is adequate, a crucial question in this context, is considered in Chapter 23)

### Separation of Child from Birth Parents

Circumstances may arise when it is no longer in the interests of the child to live with his parents, because they are unable to provide adequate parenting. In cases of severe injury or danger to life or limb immediate separation of parents and child may be necessary. In other cases questions about the child's future in the short and long-term, and the future role of his birth parents, should be answered before separation.[5]

Once separation has occurred, a wedge may be driven between parent and child which can be difficult to loosen. If at the point of removal it is considered that the future of the child lies with the parents, then the implementation of such plans must be carried out forthwith. If action is not taken quickly both parents and child become accustomed to their new surroundings and there may be difficulties for all in adjusting sufficiently to enable the original family to be re-established.[6]

The interests of the child demand the establishment of a principle of minimum separation of parent and child if the family is to stay together. The financial, environmental or therapeutic resources to help the parent to become fit and adequate to care for the child must be made available to ensure that this principle is honoured.

Pending his return to birth parents the child should have a right to the provision of suitable substitutes for continuing his nurturance, though it is difficult to see how he can have an enforceable right to any specific substitute. In the short-term many options may be available and inevitably choice depends on individual assessment of the child's needs. There is currently a preference for fostering, where a child's needs for individual attention can be met, but this may depend on the supply of this particular resource.

During the period of separation the child should have a right of access to his parents, consistent with the intention to re-integrate the family. If parent and child are to live together, to be meaningful, access must prepare them for this. Unplanned or purposeless access does not satisfy the child's rights. If the state has taken over the care of the child because the parents have been deemed unfit to care, the child has at least a moral right to expect that the state will provide something better. Additionally the state should help to create the circumstances which will enable the parents to become fit, and seek to sustain the relationship during separation. If the state does not achieve these things, why should it be involved at all?

### Long-term Arrangements for the Child

It may not be possible for some parents to care for their child, either because they do not want to or because they are not fit to. The nurturing orientation requires that the welfare and needs of the child are considered. These are no longer necessarily connected with his birth parents. The concept of the "least detrimental alternative"[7] is then helpful for this is what must be sought for each child. What that solution may provide for the child will depend on resources, the attitudes and standards of society and interested professionals as well as the characteristics of the individual child. None of these considerations are absolute and may vary from time to time.

Children apart from their parents have been a forgotten group, though "foster care drift" is now a well recognized phenomenon. The failure to establish child care standards has served these children ill, but coping with drift still receives varied responses. One approach is to vest the child with "a right to permanent placement". This has been defined as a "placement which is intended to last and which is given the legal security to make this possible".[8] Effectively this means adoption since permanent legal relationship between a child and his new parents cannot be achieved in any other way. In England at least there is still concerted opposition to such a philosophy.[9] This is based on the importance to the child of his birth parents. It is felt that insufficient effort is made to ensure that parents stay involved in decisions and maintain contact with children for whom they do not care. Historically such a view has been associated with the importance of the blood-tie rather than with the bond established between the child and the person physically taking care of him.

The focus of recent legislation in England[10] establishing a comprehensive adoption service and adoption subsidies, though still unimplemented, suggests the balance is in favour of the former argument at the present time. The passing of the Adoption Assistance and Child Welfare Act 1980 suggests that a similar balance exists in the United States.

### Enforcement of the Child's Rights

Since a child is incapable of acting on his own behalf the enforcement of his rights to the provision of services presents problems. Normally it may be said that the duties of the parents are to enforce the rights of the child and act as his representative, but they have been deemed temporarily or permanently unfit, and are therefore not able to perform their duties. Having declared the parents unfit the state must take over the duties and perform them by enforcing the rights of the child and protecting his interests. If it does not the child's rights are no better protected than they were by the parent.

Yet the state may have conflicting roles. It has to act as a quasi-parent, but also to balance various competing interests of society. It has budgetary limitations on how it provides for children in its care. It must be impartial between them and cannot, as a normal parent does, be partial to one individual.

What solutions exist for such problems? The obvious answer is to appoint someone independent of the local authority to act as parent, and such a course underlies the proposal that a child should have a right to a permanent placement with individuals who will be partial to him. Until such a decision can be made other options all have drawbacks.

In theory the state can share the parenting role with the birth parents. This seems to be the traditional state prescription, but the reality may be rather difficult. The parent can have only occasional contact with the social worker who represents the caring agency, and the person with day to day care must have closer contact with the child than the parent. Important decisions about placement and access which affect the parent/child relationship may be discussed with the parent, but will ultimately be taken by the social worker or be decided by default. The decisions remaining with the parent to do with adoption, change of name or education will be insignificant if the relationship with the child has effectively ended.

A second option is for a separate appointment independent of the caring agency to represent the child's interests. While independence is attractive, it is likely to meet with opposition from caring agencies, who might reasonably question whether the skills that would be required for an independent voice would not be better used in improving primary care services.

A third option is for a court to be involved whenever a child is separated from a parent and to be responsible for all subsequent decisions. Courts are the usual agency for the enforcement of rights. If the caring agency fails to respect the child's rights, ultimately it will only be through the court that the child can achieve satisfaction.

Many separations currently made are voluntary, and sheer volume of cases may make court involvement difficult for every case where parent and child are apart. Since the child will not himself be able to activate proceedings, how should the court become involved? One solution is for the agency to be required to bring the case before the court specifying its plans for the child if he has been in the care of the state for more than say one year. The court can then scrutinize proposals for the child's future and review them from time to time if necessary. The experience of periodic court reviews suggests however that little time may be allowed for each case and that recommendations of the state agency are likely to be followed.[11] It is to be hoped that this is because appropriate recommendations are made, but separate representation for the child in proceedings about him is essential to be confident that his interests are fully protected.

## Right to Representation

Whatever role the court plays in decisions about the child, the question of representation arises. Traditionally the judicial system has reflected the usual approach to children; they are represented by their parents and proceedings are between parents and the state.[12] More recently there has been a move towards separate representation of the child. This is illustrated by the *Standards relating to abuse and neglect* in the United States:

"Appointment of counsel for child. Upon filing, the court should be required to appoint counsel at public expense to represent the child identified in the petition, as a party to the proceedings . . ."[13]

Goldstein, Freud and Solnit now partly disagree with this provision.[14] They consider that legal services for a child without parental consent should only be imposed "a) *after* an adjudication that establishes a ground for modifying or terminating a parent-child relationship or b) *before* such an adjudication, during an emergency placement when a child is temporarily placed under state care and outside parental control". This view is sufficient and in accordance with the proposals outlined above in the section "Enforcement of the child's rights", provided it is accepted that any separation of parent and child, voluntary or compulsory, modified their relationship within the Goldstein terms. It is also consistent with the views of Adcock and White who examined a sample of cases in court where the child had already been cared for by the state for periods ranging from four months to three years.[8] The proceedings were between parent and the state, and the child was not represented, but in their report the authors consider that separate representation would have been appropriate. This conclusion is based on the view that the proceedings are about the interests of the child and that as such he should be entitled to have an opportunity to put his own arguments through a representative. Dingwall, Eekelaar and Murray in a recent study of proceedings which authorized removal of the child from his parents, take the view that those proceedings should be between the parents and the state, acting to protect the rights of the child where the parents had failed to do so.[15] They consider that a child does not need to be party to the proceedings unless separation is intended to be long-term, in which case the court would have a discretion to appoint a guardian. The rationale for this view is that proceedings are about who has care and control of the child.

These views suggest that there are three questions to consider:
(a) What right has the child to representation?
(b) Who appoints a representative?
(c) At what stage should a legal representative be appointed for the child if his interests are separated from the parents?

There are arguments for the child not to be entitled to representation. It is said that to maintain the integrity of the family the parents must be allowed to represent the family, at least until it is shown that the child's interests are opposed to the parents.

Goldstein, Freud and Solnit say:
"To appoint counsel for a child without parental consent is to deny both parents and child due process. It deprives parents of their right to represent their child through their own counsel, counsel they choose for their child, or even without counsel. It is to presume on the basis of an unproven charge — an unestablished ground — that parents are incompetent to represent the interests of their family and consequently the interests of their child."[16]

The difficulty with this view is that once proceedings have begun, protection of the child's interests cannot be synonymous with those of the parents. Whether the case is proved must in part depend on how it is presented, so that if the child's interests are to be adequately represented they must be represented objectively. To regard a case merely as a presentation of facts to be proved or disproved underestimates the nature of the case.

It is equally impossible for the caring agency to be wholly objective in such proceedings, because although there are grounds to be proved, there are so many other considerations which will affect any decision about the case. The agency may itself be criticized for its failure to provide adequate services. The social worker may have a personal conflict with the parent. The agency may be influenced by resource implications. The inevitable conclusion is that for the child's interests to be fairly protected he must be entitled to separate representation. To maintain the independent position of the child it follows that the representative must be independently appointed, which can only be appointment by the court.

The timing of the appointment of a representative remains in question. If the appointment was made by the court it would be possible to have an initial judicial decision that there was prima facie evidence that the parents were failing to protect their child's interests.

CONCLUSION

It is sometimes said that a Bill of Rights for children would strengthen their position. As has been discussed, however, rights are only beneficial if the corresponding duties are respected, and if necessary enforced. The method of enforcement appears to present as many problems as defining the rights to which children should be entitled. Probably education about the interests and needs of children and the importance of their development will have a far more beneficial long-term effect for them and for society.

The right to representation in court, if the state fails to satisfy the child's interests, is, at least in theory, rather easier to establish. The court will enforce the right as a matter of course. The difficulty lies in creating a right which will balance the protection of the child's interests as an individual and the protection of the integrity of the family. Current experience suggests we need more discussion and research on this problem.

## Notes

1   See the Child Care Act 1980 (UK) in which the power to retain a child in care may be gained by the assumption of parental rights by a local authority. See also J Eekelaar, "What are Parental Rights?" 1973 89 *LQR* 210, and S Maidment, "The Fragmentation of Parental Rights and Children in Care" (1981) *J Social Welfare Law* 21

2   For example, *United Nations Declaration on Children's Rights*, 1959

3   Rogers and Wrightsman, (1978) *J Social Issues* 34(2)

4   See for example R Farson, *Birthrights* (Penguin, 1978)

5   See for example the principles set out in *Social Work in Child Care* (British Association of Social Workers, 1979): "Principle 3: Before a child is admitted to care, an assessment of his family and home environment should be undertaken which will include the preparation of the child and his family for the admission, and their participation in the plans that are made."

6   Many studies attest to the increasing difficulty of returning a child to his birth family the longer they are separated. See for example J Rowe and L Lambert, *Children Who Wait* (Association of British Adoption Agencies, London, 1973) and D Fanshel and E B Shinn, *Children in Foster Care: a Longitudinal Study* (Columbia University Press, New York, 1978)

7   J Goldstein, A Freud and A J Solnit, *Beyond the Best Interests of the Child* (The Free Press, McMillan, New York, 1973)

8   See eg N Adcock, "The Rights of a Child to Permanent Placement" in N Adcock, *Rights of Children* (British Agencies for Adoption and Fostering, 1981) p 19

9   See for example Holman "Inclusive Fostering" in J P Triseliotis (ed) *New Developments in Foster Care and Adoption* (Routledge and Kegan Paul, 1980)

10   Children Act 1975, Adoption Act 1976, Child Care Act 1980 (UK). Adoption subsidies will be available at the discretion of adoption agencies during 1982.

11   See Festinger, "The Impact of the New York Court Review of Children in Foster Care: A Follow up Report" (Child Welfare 1976) and M Wald, "State

Intervention on 'Behalf of Neglected Children' " (1975-1976) 28 *Stanford L R* 623. Note that the need to make a report to the court can still ensure that the state agency does actually plan for the child's future.

12   Care proceedings in England are unusual in that the child is the person brought before the court. This is because these proceedings are conducted as if the child was a delinquent facing criminal proceedings. One effect may be that the parents are unrepresented.

13   Institute of Judicial Administration, American Bar Association Joint Commission on Juvenile Justice Standards. Legislation in England has also empowered courts to appoint a guardian, though the powers are discretionary and in some cases unimplemented.

14   J Goldstein, A Freud and A J Solnit, *Beyond the Best Interests of the Child* (1973) p 111

15   R Dingwall, J Eekelaar and Murray J, *Care or Control?* SSRC, Oxford (in publication 1982)

16   J Goldstein, A Freud and A J Solnit, op cit (1973) p 114

# Chapter 23

# What Is Acceptable and Unacceptable Child-Rearing — A Cross-Cultural Consideration

Jill E Korbin

The survival and successful rearing of the next generation is the quintessential task of humanity. In this light, our conventional wisdom leads us to cherish the belief that human nature compels parents to rear their young with the best possible care and optimal concern. Over the past several decades, increasing public and professional awareness of the alarming number of children who come to harm through acts of commission or omission at the hands of their parents has forced the acknowledgment that child maltreatment is well within the repetoire of human behaviour. Conventional wisdom also leads us to believe that when unacceptable child-rearing behaviour occurs, it can be identified across cultural boundaries. Serious cases of child maltreatment do indeed bear a sad resemblance to one another the world over. As different nations begin to grapple with issues of child abuse and neglect, similar stories of children badly beaten, burned, and systematically starved are reported. Despite the similarity of these severe cases, anyone involved in child protection and child welfare endeavours, on an international basis or within the boundaries of multicultural societies, cannot help but be confronted with the issue of culture in defining and assessing abusive or neglectful parental behaviour.

Child maltreatment is universally known. It has been documented in the history of the western world[1,2,3] and is reflected in the myths, oral histories, and prescriptions and proscriptions for parental conduct found in every society. Child abuse and neglect, however, do appear to be rare in cultures that do not provide a context conducive to their occurrence.[4]

In the universal task of transforming the infant into the adult, the process by which, in Margaret Mead's words, "The little Manus becomes the big Manus, the little Indian the big Indian"[5], there is a remarkable range of variation throughout the world. This is all the more notable considering the commonality of tasks that must be accomplished in rearing the next generation:

... Child training the world over is in certain important respects identical ... in that it is found always to be concerned with universal problems of behaviour. Parents everywhere have similar problems to solve in bringing up their children. In all societies the helpless infant ... must be changed into a responsible adult obeying the rules of his society.

... even in these important respects, child training also differs from one society to another. Societies differ from each other in the precise character of the rules to which the child must be taught to conform ... societies differ, moreover, in the techniques that are used in enforcing conformity, in the age at which conformity is demanded to each rule of adult life ... and in countless other details of the socialization process.[6]

There is not a unitary and cross-culturally valid standard for either optimal child-rearing or for child maltreatment. What is acceptable or unacceptable becomes inextricably linked to ecological constraints and to the cultural context in which behaviour occurs. Current scientific and popular literature is replete with conflicting opinions as to how to "best" rear one's children. While in many traditional societies there exists a "folk wisdom" about how to rear children[7] most often there is no such consensus in the larger, urban, more heterogenous societies that are now most seriously grappling with issues of child maltreatment. A perusal of any bookstore yields a plethora of books on baby and child care, not all of them in significant agreement. One can also see the rapidly changing nature of advice on a variety of child-rearing topics: whether to feed on demand or on schedule; whether to pick up a baby immediately or let it cry for a few minutes; whether to toilet train or let the child take the initiative, and so on. Thus, in many industrial societies we have a circumstance where one generation bottle fed its infants because it was considered "best" for the child and the family while the next generation breast-feeds for precisely the same reasons.[7] Margaret Mead has noted that the greatest regularity of American child-rearing may be the commitment of one generation to do things differently than their own parents.[8]

The effort to reconcile cultural diversity with child protection involves simultaneous attention to two exquisitely sensitive subjects. The sensitive nature of child abuse and neglect has been repeatedly documented by professionals and community members dealing with the syndrome. Similarly, one's cultural affiliation is a matter of major consequence:

... human behaviour is highly patterned ... it reflects "culture" ... people everywhere not only follow cultural rules, but ... these rules often seem to be arbitrary, varying as they do so dramatically from one society to the next. Anthropologists have again and again reported the diverse and arbitrary nature of man's rules about dress, food, sex, religion, etiquette, marriage, politics, and the like. They have also reported that people cherish these seemingly arbitrary rules, live by them, and are sometimes willing to die for them ... however bizarre these rules might seem to outsiders.[9]

It is not a matter of surprise, then, that cultural practices related to child-rearing are adhered to so tenaciously. Traditional modes of child care and socialization are often maintained long after marked changes have occurred in other realms of culture such as religion, politics, and economics.

The high frequency of reports of child abuse and neglect among ethnically diverse populations in multicultural nations should alert one to the importance of culture. In the United States it is a matter of continuing debate whether ethnic minorities are over-represented in child abuse and neglect statistics because of closer scrutiny by social service agencies or because of an actual higher prevalence. The statistical picture is not entirely clear, and the evidence is often conflicting.[10,11,12,13,14] Further, culture and ethnicity are often so confounded with social class and poverty that the effects of cultural affiliation are difficult to untangle.[15] Since statistical breakdowns by ethnicity and social class have far-reaching implications for resource allocation and aetiological formulations, this issue demands further and more careful scrutiny.

The problem of disproportionate frequencies of ethnically diverse and low-income families reported for child maltreatment is not unique to the United States. For example, in New Zealand ". . . the reported incidence of abuse amongst Maori children was six times greater than amongst European children, (and) the incidence amongst Pacific Island children was nine times greater . . ."[16,17] While Maori children in 1972 comprised only 12 per cent of the population under 16 years of age, they nevertheless accounted for 51 per cent of the reports of a "detrimental environment", 41 per cent of reports of children "not under proper supervision", and 46 per cent of all children committed to the care of the state.[16,17] These facts are in contrast to an extensive review of the ethnographic literature for Polynesia, including New Zealand, which found child abuse and neglect to be extremely rare. This discrepancy results in part from cultural conflicts in assessments of practices such as sibling caretaking as neglectful and in part from changed circumstances that might in fact be conducive to an increasing incidence of child maltreatment.[17]

In clarifying the role of culture in child abuse and neglect, the first task is to sort out culturally appropriate definitions. It is helpful to distinguish three levels at which the cultural context comes into play in defining abuse and neglect: cultural differences in child-rearing practices and beliefs; idiosyncratic departure from acceptable cultural patterns; and societal abuse and neglect of children.[18]

The first level encompasses child-rearing practices that would be viewed as acceptable by one group, but as unacceptable, or even abusive and neglectful by another. As cultures come into contact with one another, differences in child-rearing practices and beliefs create a situation ripe for conflict in identifying both appropriate child care. Such conflicts can occur on an international level as well as among ethnically diverse groups in any one nation.

Members of western cultures, for example, consider the harsh initiation rites that occur elsewhere in the world to be abusive. During such rites, children undergo a range of hardships from genital operations to beatings and hazings to deprivation of food and sleep. Westerners also look askance at the harsh punishments to which children may be subjected in other cultures. Children may be beaten, have their hands cut or burned, or be ostracized for several days if they fail to adhere to their culture's rules.

At the same time, many of our accepted western child-rearing practices would be viewed as equally detrimental to children's welfare by members of these same cultures. Non-western peoples often conclude that the anthropologists, missionaries, and other Europeans with whom they come into contact at best do not know how to rear children and, at worst, simply do not love their offspring. Practices such as isolating children in rooms of their own at night, making infants wait a given number of hours to be fed, or allowing small children to "cry themselves out" would be at odds with the child-rearing philosophies of many cultures. While these practices might seem to us in comparison, benign and even enhancing of optimal development, to many other cultures such practices would be viewed as equally bizarre, exotic, and damaging to children as their behaviours seem to us. One might get better agreement on a world-wide basis of the acceptability of initiation rites than the acceptability of allowing infants to cry unattended (if they are not wet or hungry) or forcing them to spend the night in isolation from other family members.

Practitioners must be able to identify situations in which unacceptable child-rearing is attributed on the basis of cultural differences. These situations often come to light as anthropologists live in their field sites with their small children. For example, Emelie Olson, who took her twenty month-old daughter with her to Turkey, observed that the Turks she was studying dressed their young in thick wool caps and several layers of warm clothing even on the hottest of days. She worried that the babies, sweating profusely, were unduly uncomfortable and that this was bad for their health. The

Turks, however, believed that children become chilled easily, resulting in sickness, or even death. Thus, children should be dressed warmly at all times and should not be bathed too frequently. It should come as no surprise, then, that the Turks became alarmed when the anthropologist set out a tub of water for her daughter to play in on warm days. It was incomprehensible to them that she would jeopardize the health, and perhaps survival, of her only child.[19]

Cultural conflict in identifying acceptable and unacceptable behaviour towards children is not restricted to western versus non-western, industrialized versus developing, or large versus small scale societies. The 'Mbuti Pygmies of the Ituri Forest of Zaire and the nearby Bantu had a marked conflict over initiation rites. Among the Bantu, the transition from childhood to adulthood was marked by such rites, including circumcision and other physical hardships. Among the 'Mbuti, in contrast, the transition from childhood to adulthood was a more gradual process. The 'Mbuti considered the Bantu rites unnecessary and their harshness abusive. The Bantu, on the other hand, considered the 'Mbuti negligent in failing to provide their sons with the legitimate adult status that only came from successful participation in the rites. With increasing economic dependence on the Bantu for wage labor, the 'Mbuti agreed to have their sons initiated alongside the Bantu boys. Only through such a strategy could the 'Mbuti insure their youth adult status in the eyes of the Bantu. However, despite their mutual participation in the rites, the conflict persisted. Feeling that the Bantu were exceedingly harsh, the 'Mbuti men would break the rules of the initiation proceedings and intervene to protect their boys from beatings, to provide them with food when they were supposed to go without, to give them blankets when they were supposed to sleep in the cold, and to comfort them when they cried or were in pain. The Bantu felt that the 'Mbuti were overly indulgent and protective and that these actions harmed their sons by preventing them from truly passing into manhood.[20]

Examples such as these of cultural conflict concerning acceptable and unacceptable child-rearing, as happens with other domains of culture, abound.[4,18,21] If we fail to allow for a cultural perspective in defining child maltreatment, we will be hopelessly locked into an ethnocentric position in which one's own set of cultural beliefs and practices are viewed as superior to any other. At the same time, it would be irresponsible to suggest an extreme relativist view that any practice is acceptable as long as it is adhered to by a cultural group. Throughout history different cultures have sanctioned, or at least tolerated, an array of insults to the young. One may temper immediate condemnation of other cultures' practices with an awareness of the extremity of treatment accorded children in western society at various times. Descriptions of child labor in Europe during the Industrial Revolution present a bleak picture:

> Children from five years of age upward were worked sixteen hours at a time, sometimes with irons riveted around their ankles to keep them from running away. They were starved, beaten, and in many other ways maltreated. Many succumbed to occupational diseases and some committed suicide; few survived any length of time ... Sometimes they were dipped head first into cisterns of cold water to keep them awake.[22]

It is inescapable that some culturally-accepted practices are nevertheless painful and difficult for children. If change in such practices is to take place, however, it must make sense to the culture in question. The practice must be clearly demonstrated to be harmful, and accompanying changes in the cultural context must be taken into account. The eradication of footbinding in China is instructive in this regard[4], as are attempts to end excision and clitoridectomy in some African societies.[23]

Additionally, with rapid socio-economic change, some child-rearing patterns that were adaptive in the traditional setting may become problematical. For example, sibling caretaking was, and continues to be in many places, important, valued, and adapted to a Polynesian life-style. However, with the move to cities such as Honolulu and Auckland, dangers such as substandard housing that may catch on fire, busy streets, and an absence of nearby adult kin and other child caretakers contributes to an increased potential for harm to children engaging in this practice.[17]

Efforts to establish universally acceptable and unacceptable standards of child-rearing are fraught with issues of legitimate cultural differences. However, virtually all cultures, regardless of how harsh or indulgent their child care practices appear, have standards for acceptable child-rearing and individuals who deviate from those standards. Deviation from cultural norms, rather than the severity of the physical trauma, is the central issue in intra-cultural definitions of maltreatment. In Tikopia, for instance, the very act of hitting a child was regarded as an affront to the child's dignity as an individual. A permissible punishment was to pinch children lightly on the mouth. On one occasion a man pinched his grandson, left a barely visible scratch, and was soundly berated by his cultural peers for the abuse of the child.[24]

This brings the discussion to the second level of definitional concern, idiosyncratic departure from culturally accepted standards of child-rearing. It is in this domain that the question of acceptable or unacceptable child-rearing is most likely to be identified in a culturally-appropriate fashion.

The ability to distinguish culturally acceptable child-rearing practices from idiosyncratic maltreatment is a frequent concern of child protective workers. Problems in the identification of maltreatment are exacerbated by the nature of most service delivery systems. In general, service providers do not have exposure to community-wide criteria for acceptable and unacceptable care. Rather, service providers most often come face to face with individuals who have hurt their children and may adopt the plea that this is culturally acceptable. Practitioners tend to see the cases in which physical discipline results in buckle marks, excessive bruises, or welts and not the countless times that a threat of physical discipline is used or a child is hit, but not harmed, with a consensus by the parent, child, and community that the action is within acceptable bounds. The refrain "this is how we do things in our culture or community" deceptively resonates to the familiar refrain of abusive parents that "this is how we do things in our family". An understanding of the spectrum and meaning that physical discipline has within the entire cultural context is a necessity. The word of a Black American woman, concerned with the rise in juvenile delinquency, illustrates this:

> Children is not like they was. You never had no juvenile, nothin' like that. You never seed no police had nobody's child . . . And there's a law you can't whup your children, and if you can't whup your children, you look for all this to happen. *Everybody should know how to whup 'em without beatin' em and bruisin' em up.*[25]

Thus, is it the parents who maintain the right to physically discipline their children or the parents who beat and bruise them that are really of concern? If a parent claims that the injury he or she has inflicted is culturally acceptable, we need to know the rules concerning permissible physical punishment. It is likely that the act of discipline may be culturally sanctioned but the harm of injury will be disapproved. There is evidence in the United States that those cultural groups who have been labelled the most punitive and neglectful do not, on a community-wide basis rather than on the basis of reports of identified maltreating parents, view child abuse and neglect incidents as any less serious than do professionals in the field.[26] Regardless of one's own cultural beliefs about physical discipline, it has been shown to be extremely frequent in American society.[27,28]

The third level of definitional concern, societal abuse and neglect of children, is often confounded with cultural differences. Many nations and communities suffer from poverty, with concomitant food scarcity, and inadequate housing and health care. These conditions that are so detrimental to children are beyond the control of individual parents and are more appropriately viewed as institutional or societal abuse and neglect.

In summary, one must pay careful attention to the levels at which cultural considerations are relevant to the assessment of acceptable and unacceptable child-rearing. At the first level, a behaviour may be acceptable in one culture, but interpreted as abusive or neglectful by another. The cultural context of the behaviour must be viewed holistically. As Erikson has noted ". . . a system of child care can be said to be a factor making for trust, even when certain items of that tradition, taken singly, may seem unnecessarily cruel".[29] At the second level, culturally acceptable child care practices must be distinguished from idiosyncratic departure from these standards. And, at the third level, societal conditions beyond the control of individual parents must be distinguished from culture.

It is well to keep in mind the mandate of the United Nations' Declaration of the Rights of the Child that "Mankind owes to the child the best it has to give".[30] A cross-cultural perspective underlines the importance of carefully considering the cultural context in which behaviour, including optimal and detrimental child care occurs. If this "best" is to be achieved care must be taken to respect the dignity of diverse cultures while also protecting children from undue affronts to their well-being.

---

Many of the ideas in this chapter have been previously discussed by the author (see references 4, 18, 21, 31).

## Notes

1   S X Radbill, "A History of Child Abuse and Infanticide" in R E Helfer and C H Kempe (eds) *The Battered Child* (University of Chicago Press, Chicago, 1968) pp 3-17

2   T Solomon, "History and Demography of Child Abuse" (1973) *Pediatrics* **51(4)**:773-6

3   B F Steele, "Violence in our Society" (1970) *Pharos of Alpha Omega Alpha* **33(2)**:42-8

4   J E Korbin, *Child Abuse and Neglect, Cross-Cultural Perspectives* (University of California Press, Berkeley, 1981)

5   M Mead, *Growing up in New Guinea,* (Mentor Books, New York, 1930)

6   J W M Whiting and I Child, *Child Training and Personality* (Yale University Press, New Haven, 1953)

7   B Whiting, "Folk Wisdom and Child-Rearing". Paper presented at the Meetings of the American Association for the Advancement of Science (1971)

8    M Mead, "Theoretical Setting — 1954" in M Mead and M Wolfenstein (eds) *Childhood in Contemporary Cultures* (University of Chicago Press, Chicago, 1955)

9    R B Edgerton, *Deviance: a Cross-Cultural Perspective* (Cummings, Menlo Park, California, 1976)

10   W A Altmeier, P M Vietze, K B Sherrod, H W Sandler, S Falsey and S O'Connor "Prediction of Child Maltreatment during Pregnancy" (1979) *J Child Psychiat* **18(2)**:205-18

11   J A Ebbin, M H Gollub, A M Stein and M G Wilson "Battered Child Syndrome at Los Angeles General Hospital" (1969) *Am J Dis Child* 118:660

12   B Lauer, E TenBroeck and M Grossman "Battered Child Syndrome, Review of 130 Patients with Controls" (1974) *Pediatrics* **54(1)**:67-70

13   R J Light, "Abused and Neglected Children in America, A Study of Alternative Policies" (1973) *Harvard Educational Review* 43:556-98

14   L Pelton, "Child Abuse and Neglect, The Myth of Classlessness" (1978) *Am J Orthopsychiat* **48(4)**:608-17

15   J Garbarino and A Ebata, "Ethnic and Cultural Differences in Defining Child Abuse". Paper presented at the Second National Research Conference, National Committee for Prevention of Child Abuse (Wingspread, Racine, Wisconsin, 1981)

16   D M Fergusson, J Flemming and D P O'Neill, *Child Abuse in New Zealand* (Wellington Government Printer, 1972)

17   J Ritchie and J Ritchie, "Child Rearing and Child Abuse, The Polynesian Context" in J Korbin (ed) *Child Abuse and Neglect, Cross-Cultural Perspectives* (University of California Press, Berkeley, 1981) pp 186-204

18   J E Korbin, "The Cross-Cultural Context of Child Abuse and Neglect" in C H Kempe and R E Helfer (eds) *The Battered Child*, 3rd ed (University of Chicago Press, Chicago, 1980) pp 21-35

19   E Olson, "Socio-economic and Psychocultural Contexts of Child Abuse and Neglect in Turkey" in J Korbin (ed) *Child Abuse and Neglect, Cross-cultural Perspectives* (University of California Press, Berkeley, 1981) pp 96-119

20   C Turnbull, *The Forest People, A Study of the Pygmies of the Congo* (Simon and Schuster, New York, 1961)

21   J E Korbin, "Anthropological Contributions to the Study of Child Abuse" (1977) *Child Abuse and Neglect: The International J* **1(1)**:7-24

22   S X Radbill, "A History of Child Abuse and Infanticide" in R E Helfer and C H Kempe (eds) *The Battered Child* (University of Chicago Press, Chicago, 1968)

23   I Tévòedjre, "L'enfant et la Violence dans la Societe des Adultes". Paper presented at the Third International Congress on Child Abuse and Neglect (Amsterdam, The Netherlands, 1981)

24   R Firth, "Education in Tikopia" in John Middleton (ed) *From Child to Adult, Studies in the Anthropology of Education* (Natural History Press, Garden City, 1970) pp 75-90

25   L Snow, "Popular Medicine in a Black Neighbourhood" in E Spicer (ed) *Ethnic Medicine in the Southwest* (University of Arizona Press, Tucson, 1977) pp 19-95

26   J Giovannoni and R Becerra, *Defining Child Abuse* (Free Press, New York, 1979)

27   R J Gelles, "Violence Towards Children in the United States" *Am J Orthopsychiat* **48**:580-92

28   M Straus, R Gelles and S Steinmetz, *Behind Closed Doors, Violence in the American Family* (Anchor Press, Garden City, New York, 1980)

29   E H Erikson, *Childhood and Society,* 2nd ed (W W Norton, New York, 1963)

30   *Declaration of the Rights of the Child* (United Nations General Assembly Resolution 1386 (XIV), 1959)

31   J E Korbin, "A Cross-Cultural Perspective on the Role of the Community in Child Abuse and Neglect" (1979) *Child Abuse and Neglect: The International J* **3(1)**:9-18

# Chapter 24

# Crossing Cultural Barriers

The need and potential for international action on child maltreatment: the experience of Defence for Children

## Nigel Cantwell

This chapter deals with child maltreatment as the concern of a community that one might not generally associate with the problem — the "international community". This term has two basic interpretations: the world population as a whole and, more frequently, those organizations and bodies, both inter-governmental and non-governmental, working internationally. Both are relevant to activities in the child maltreatment sphere, but here we shall be talking mainly of the latter conception.

### INTERNATIONAL ACTION

Our preoccupation with *international action* on child maltreatment stems from the following considerations:

— there is substantial evidence to show that it is a necessary element in work to combat the phenomenon;

— there is equally substantial evidence to show that the need for it has largely been dismissed or overlooked;

— there is also evidence to show that, when it has been undertaken, the methods used have often been inappropriate, or the impact achieved has been inadequate;

— and there are many indications — at this stage, it would be presumptuous to describe them in any more unequivocal terms — that it could be both appropriate and significant.

### Who Needs It?

There are just two basic justifications for international work in any sphere:

(a) to do what cannot be done nationally, for whatever reason this may be; and

(b) to enable as much as possible to be done, or to be done better, at the national level.

Logically, the order in which they are presented should be reversed — enabling is surely a more valid and important objective than carrying out something oneself. But the order as it stands corresponds to the sequence in which awareness of the need for international action on child maltreatment dawned. It did so as follows.

In recent years in particular, international organizations have been receiving a constant flow of requests — from individuals and agencies alike — to take up or intervene in cases of alleged maltreatment of children or disregard of their fundamental rights. The situations involved covered a wide range, from murder, torture, rape and imprisonment, through arbitrary separation from parents, contested legal decisions, abduction and "disappearance", to problems of service delivery for the children of abusing parents, as well as special situations involving two or more countries.

Whatever the alleged acts, one feature common to all was clear: under existing circumstances, none could be successfully dealt with within the frontiers of the country concerned, and hence the recourse to international bodies.

In some instances, the latter were able to comply, wholly or partly, with the request for action. For this to be so, much depended on whether the allegation arrived directly at an international agency in a position to take the matter in hand itself. In the great majority of cases, however, it has been shown that no follow-up was possible internationally. As a result, such requests and allegations were quite simply filed — or thrown away. Indeed, we have no means of knowing just how many cases have been brought to international attention in the past ten years (and even less do we know how many more should have been), but the indications are that they would run to several thousands.

This situation was highlighted as a build-up to the International Year of the Child (IYC — 1979) progressed, with its special focus on the needs of the child. In April 1978, Ambassador Ole Ålgård, Norway's representative to the United Nations in New York, deplored the fact that "children have no special human rights organization to address". The Secretariats set up by the United Nations to deal with matters arising from IYC, based in New York and Geneva and operative well before the Year began, started receiving what was to become an average of two or three letters a day requesting their intervention in specific individual and group cases of alleged maltreatment. However, not only were the IYC Secretariats themselves unable to intervene — not being mandated as action bodies — but also, in the vast majority of cases, they could not identify an appropriate body to which referral for action might be made.

There are six basic reasons for contacting international bodies on alleged cases of child maltreatment:

(1) a national body has failed, or is unwilling, to ensure an appropriate solution to the case;

(2) no national body with the required mandate exists or is known to exist;

(3) government policy and/or national legislation actively provides for, allows, or promotes the alleged act;

(4) government policy and/or national legislation does not sanction the act;

(5) government agents are, legally or illegally, implicated as, or with, the perpetrators of the act; and

(6) the problem goes beyond national boundaries, for example a conflict or situation involving two countries.

The frequent occurrence of cases where one or more of these elements is present provides clear evidence of the need for the concern of the international community in resolving them. This pragmatic evidence is only supported by the theoretical consideration that no measure, provision or policy can be foolproof or all-embracing, and that there will always be individual cases that are not, or cannot be, catered for or that "slip through the net".

But if the need to respond to cases by taking them up is clear, it is also necessary to carry out a prevention-oriented programme, from two angles:

(1) preventing situations which foster, engender, involve or constitute, in themselves, child maltreatment; and

(2) preventing the need for bringing such situations or actual alleged cases to international attention by encouraging the establishment or development of appropriate bodies at the national level.

Both angles fall very much within the realm of international action, and together constitute the latter's second justification. Equally, however, both depend very much on degree of links with, and support from, national bodies and concerned persons within each country. As such, preventive action demonstrates very clearly the place and role of work at the international level: not at the peak of a hierarchical pyramid ranging "*down*" to the local community, but at the strategic centre of concentric circles and providing a service through regional and "*out*" to national and local enterprises, on a two-way basis.

As regards the first element — preventing high risk situations — the part played by an international body is that of helping to identify those cross-national realities that tend to bring about maltreatment, and then of creating a focal point for solidarity with those working towards the elimination of such situations, internationally and nationally. A most obvious and simple example is war, but within the phenomenon of armed conflict lie more closely defined events, such as indiscriminate killing of villagers, including children. What conditions in fact give rise to "unmotivated" massacre? At the other end of the spectrum, one might cite housing policies that place families in such circumstances (overcrowding, lack of privacy or levels of rent that effectively over-restrict expenditure on other necessities) as to increase greatly the risk of frustration-release violence within the home.

Over and above the creation of solidarity and dissemination of information on these issues, what the international bodies concerned will then actually do, or need to do, in terms of action on the basis of their findings will largely depend on the degree to which effective national efforts are under way or being stimulated in the framework of the second preventive thrust — that aimed at avoiding the need for international intervention whenever possible.

For international intervention alone *should* be avoided wherever possible: it is ungainly and lengthy, nearly always delicate because of questions such as national sovereignty and political interpretations and, possibly worst of all in the sphere of child protection, has no formal basis in the form of legal instruments. It should be used only as a last resort or in conjunction with national initiatives. But international action *is* required, in order precisely to facilitate and assist such national activities.

In summary, therefore, both the general justifications for international action are met to a high degree, with respect to the child maltreatment sphere. But the move from justification to implementation is not just a short step.

### Why the Needs Have Not Been Met

Virtually every human activity, interest and concern, whether economic or social, sooner or later finds its reflection in the constitution of one or more international bodies. The overall sphere of child welfare is no exception. Indeed, it is even well-represented as a cause. How is it, then, that Ambassador Ålgård's 1978 statement, quoted above, could be true?

Yet it was, for five principal reasons:

(1) there is no universal agreement on what constitutes child maltreatment: whether an act or an omission is defined or not as maltreatment differs over time and space;

(2) child maltreatment's usual connotation has been intrafamilial, and therefore a problem that requires international work only in a limited way (exchange of experiences and ideas, for example);

(3) there are no legal instruments or provisions on which international action can be based, except those relating to certain specific aspects such as child labour, save a very general and totally unenforceable Declaration of the Rights of the Child;

(4) the millions of children who lack the basic physical necessities of food, shelter, education and access to health services outweigh the numbers whose rights are severely violated (although, of course, the very fact that they do lack such essentials already constitutes an infringement of their basic rights and neglect of their interests); priority has therefore been given to enabling children simply to survive;

(5) defence of rights and representation of interests are viewed as a politically delicate undertaking that cannot be carried out in conjunction with programmes to fulfil needs since they could jeopardize the co-operative relationship necessary for the latters' success.

We shall turn later to those international efforts that are nonetheless contributing to the protection of actual or potential child victims of maltreatment. At this point, however, we need to look more closely at the whys and wherefores of these five aspects that form the overall picture of the present situation. Their analysis not only serves to explain the meagre results, for child protection, of the "international encounter", but also indicates the unreasonable premises on which the arguments of those who decline to improve these results are based.

### Is There a Cross-Culturally Accepted Conception of Child Maltreatment?

Discussion of what in fact might constitute child maltreatment, fundamental to this entire chapter, has deliberately been left until this point. Although debates on definitions are often considered as anything from necessary evils to purely peripheral embellishments, such a discussion is both constructive and, we believe, vital in terms of international action on child maltreatment.

There are two fundamental questions in the debate:

(1) on what criteria are acts or omissions to be labelled abusive, neglectful or exploitative (the three forms of behaviour towards children that we take to constitute maltreatment) from an international standpoint?

(2) is there a distinction to be made according to who is the perpetrator of such acts or omissions as concerns their being labelled by "child maltreatment" or another term?

## DIFFERENT CONCEPTIONS OVER TIME AND SPACE

Studies and works by historians and anthropologists have clearly demonstrated vast differences, from one period to another and from one culture to another, regarding acts considered to constitute child maltreatment. These findings have been confirmed in at least four ways:

(1) through opportunities given to persons, relatively recently, from a wide variety of cultures — particularly those of countries outside the "First" and "Second" Worlds — to express the standpoint and situation as they see it in their respective countries:

(2) because of reaction to certain "international" efforts that did *not* take account of cultural differences;

(3) because of the existence today of certain laws, or *lack* of laws, on child maltreatment that have their roots in conceptions of a bygone era and that do not correspond to present-day norms and values; and

(4) because of the realization that even relatively similar countries, like Great Britain and Sweden, have different notions of the term "maltreatment".

In practice, the identification of these differences, rather than inspiring attempts to take them into account, has more often constituted an argument to be used by those who do not favour international action and solidarity in this sphere. Consequently, the very real *differences* have largely been seen as *barriers*. This, in our view, is a false projection. To demonstrate this, the normal approach of looking at specific acts in terms of their exclusion from, or inclusion in, any definition of "maltreatment" has to be abandoned. Rather it is necessary to identify those acts which are already universally recognized forms of maltreatment and to analyze them in terms of the motivation of the perpetrator and the context of the act, in order to determine the factor(s) underlying the universal condemnation and, hence, the elements constituting a possible cross-cultural conception.

With such an approach, it immediately becomes clear that a given act is not perceived — by the perpetrator, the "victim" and/or the community — in the same way regardless of circumstance. A parent who kidnaps a child from the other parent who nonetheless has legal custody may have excellent reasons for doing so in terms of the wishes and interests of the child. Someone who violently pulls a child away from danger commits, perhaps, the same act as another who does so in a bout of anger, but could hardly be accused of "maltreatment". However evident this may seem, there is little doubt that too little emphasis has been placed on this aspect in the debate over "what is maltreatment".

There are four basic styles of behaviour towards children: to harm, to take advantage of, to socialize and to show affection or concern.

We find that virtually all commissions or omissions motivated solely by the desire to *cause harm* to the child are universally condemned. Such acts include most instances of murder, torture, kidnapping and rape. Equally reproved are the consequences for children of acts directed towards others: the removal of a baby from his mother, for example, because of her imprisonment, or the "disappearance" of the parents.

*Taking advantage* of a child's defenceless situation in order to release one's own stress, to force a child to carry out an act, to neglect, ignore or threaten him or to obtain something for oneself, by "making use of" or exploiting a child, is a form of behaviour that is proscribed sufficiently universally for it to be a fundamental element in any cross-cultural conception of child maltreatment. At the same time care must be taken in order to identify the prime perpetrator of the act and, in some cases, the circumstances which are its basic cause — for example, when a family sells its child to an illegal factory owner because it is unable to provide for the child.

We take these two elements as basic to the search for a cross-cultural conception.

The third group is constituted by those acts motivated by *socialization,* involving both the actual process of integration into society and the sanctions imposed, that is punishment, if, in the eyes of the perpetrator, that process is not respected. This category will therefore include a wide range of acts such as female circumcision and corporal punishment. The problem of definition and judgement as to whether or not a given act in this category constitutes maltreatment cannot be resolved without reference to certain other considerations dealt with later.

However, it can already be said that all socialization processes are, by definition, designed to prepare the child for an integrated life in the community and they do not, therefore, take place in a vaccuum or for no perceived good reason. With certain exceptions, the degree of objectively perceived harshness of the socialization process — and, indeed, the form it takes and the sphere it concerns — tends to mirror the degree, form and type of harshness that the child will have to face in adolescent or adult life.

In other words, it may not be seen as "causing *unnecessary* harm to the child" (one of the more common criteria used in determining what constitutes child maltreatment) even if it involves severe physical pain or the sometimes fatal stress of proceeding through an education system in an industrialized country.

In cases where there seems to be cause to believe that children are suffering unnecessarily from the socialization process, it would appear logical to adopt an approach designed to modify the surrounding reality as much as to alter the procedure in itself. The latter, more obvious, course on its own would leave the process divorced from reality and likely to readapt itself gradually to that same reality.

Abuse and neglect arising from *punishment* are equally difficult to distinguish clearly. Acceptable forms of punishment have always differed over time and space. What a given society will accept at any one time depends on whether it sees excesses purely in terms of the degree and lasting effects of the physical or psychological damage effected or whether it also bases its judgement on the desirability of bringing about a less violent society. It is clearly necessary, whatever the case, for any approach to take account of the cultural or societal norms pertaining at the time if one believes that acts of maltreatment constitute to some extent a form of deviant behaviour.

It is obvious that behaviour motivated by, or consisting of, the *expression of affection* incorporates acts that, in themselves and out of context, may be violent in nature and, as a consequence, a potential form of maltreatment. Whilst we may consider the "violence" to be misplaced, and whilst we need not condone its use, an act such as this must surely be approached differently from one of the same level of violence designed to hurt or punish.

Approached from a motivational angle, then, two major elements must be present, simultaneously or individually, when acts are universally condemned:

(i) a desire to cause harm to a child, and
(ii) a willingness to subordinate the interests of the child to those of the perpetrator, whether by commission or omission, that is taking advantage with impunity of the child's relative "weakness" or dependency.

As we shall see, this does not mean that *only* such acts can be the subject of international concern, but that the latter should be expressed differently where other acts are concerned.

It is worth emphasizing at this point a fact that is basic to our thesis and that should already be perceptible: *all of the acts considered thus far, however motivated, can be and are perpetrated both within and outside the family.* It is essential, therefore, that the misleading connotation of child maltreatment as a purely intrafamilial phenomenon be dispensed with. Whilst the form of response to a given act committed, say, by a parent and a government agency, must differ, the fact that the acts occur is indivisible: one is not child maltreatment and the other something else.

## The "Context Qualification"

The above considerations on motivation are subject to what we might call a "context qualification", that is the degree to which an act may be deemed as constituting maltreatment, from an international standpoint, is attenuated or exacerbated by the context in which it occurs, this context being determined by one or both of the following elements which are in constant interaction:

(1) The *formal* acceptability or reproval of the act, according to existing legislation, or by default of such legislation. A simple example here is the fact that corporal punishment is outlawed both in the school and in the family in Sweden, whereas it is permitted in both in the United Kingdom. This surely means that the same act perpetrated in Sweden and the UK must be interpreted differently because of the different legislative norms set in each country. At the same time, the legality of an act does not necessarily mean that it cannot be looked upon as maltreatment.

(2) The *informal* acceptability or reproval of the act, according to prevailing norms and traditions in the society concerned. It is quite clear that if societies alter their views on what constitutes child maltreatment, this is because their norms and values change, and in this respect child maltreatment can be seen as a form of deviant behaviour, the acts involved being explicitly or implicitly defined at a given time by a given society.

These formal and informal contexts must be taken into account in determining what response, if any, is to be made in a given case or situation.

## Attitudes Towards Children and Violence

Fundamental to the make-up of both contexts, are attitudes towards children and violence.

Certain quarters find it difficult or undesirable to envisage extending the concept of "child maltreatment" to cover extra-familial or structural abuse and neglect. These they feel to be more a question for child advocacy or children's rights than one of maltreatment as such. The problem is not only semantic, but also depends on the way child maltreatment is viewed as a phenomenon.

The debate basically revolves around whether or not intrafamilial — and possibly institutional — child abuse and neglect are seen in a vacuum, or whether they are seen as an intrinsic reflection of attitudes that prevail in society as a whole, and of actions that are perpetrated at all levels of that society.

Just as "people who are different" may be described, according to their situation, as either eccentric or mentally ill, and just as social drinking is perfectly acceptable in most countries whereas alcoholism is a "social ill", so certain acts of physical violence, such as corporal punishment, and neglect of a child's best interests may be committed — but only up to an undefined point which frequently varies according to who is the perpetrator.

Three basic attitudes are involved here:

(1) attitudes towards children;
(2) attitudes towards minorities in general; and
(3) attitudes towards violence as an appropriate way of resolving conflicts.

### Attitudes Towards Children

In the industrialized countries, there is every indication that children are perceived more and more as a burden and as obstacles to the achievement of material goals and values set by society. Some writers have gone as far as to speak of adult hatred towards children. Manifestations of this might be exemplified by the existence of apartment blocks and hotels where children like dogs, are not allowed. The "economics" of child-rearing, the hidden costs of "free" education, and the vastly restricted freedom encountered by those looking after children within a nuclear family all tend to promote the image of the burdensome child. In addition, the benefits of a professed "family policy" may be more than neutralized by policies in other fields: long working hours, need for both parents to work, etc. The attention paid to the needs of children is in fact often purely superficial, and may come down to being no more than an attempt to compensate for not fulfilling their needs in the most elementary and fundamental ways.

In the traditional societies of developing countries, attitudes vary considerably, sometimes according to the child's sex, "normality", etc. These considerations apart, however, children are still perceived as anything but a burden, and more a guarantee for survival.

### Attitudes Towards Minorities

Children probably constitute the ultimate form of the voiceless minority, and like any other minority they are a relatively underprivileged, exploited group. Adult traffic takes precedence over children's safety, for example, and children constitute a profitable consumer target-group.

As with all minorities, the societal response, when it is not overtly repressive — is to provide a certain last resort protection, grant a number of resources on an almost charitable basis, and marginalize the minorities through the ploy of refusing participation. Minorities in general are relatively weak, and therefore become the defenceless and easy victims of all forms of abuse and neglect.

## Attitudes Towards Violence

Underlying or overt attitudes towards violence as a means of resolving conflicts or attaining goals (sometimes within special approved confines, as a form of frustration-release) are at least ambiguous and frequently approbatory at the societal level. If these attitudes find their reflection in, for example, the visual media and certain sports, they also necessarily influence interpersonal relationships, including those between adults and children at all levels.

## The Total Picture

If we merge attitudes towards children, towards minorities, and towards violence, particularly from a societal or structural standpoint, we arrive at a somewhat disturbing picture of ambiguous norms reflecting considerable ambivalence about violence towards children.

Furthermore, the picture that emerges is one in which intrafamilial violence and neglect would seem to be very much related to values and acts that prevail in society. It is this fact that makes it extremely difficult to examine, and more especially respond to, intrafamilial child abuse and neglect as a phenomenon totally apart. Hence the problems involved in attempting to draw a line between what constitutes maltreatment and what comes under the heading of children's rights or child advocacy.

In the last resort, it would be hard to make any semantic differentiation between parental abuse and neglect of a child and the abuse or neglect of a child's interests brought about by a given decision on the part of societal, legal or political authorities. Yet the former is generally deemed to be a child maltreatment question, whereas the latter is said to be one of child advocacy or rights.

There may be many reasons behind this, but two at least are certain:

(1) in the same way as "cruelty to children" was seen as "isolated acts by unworthy parents" until it was demonstrated to be a social phenomenon, so extrafamilial maltreatment will have to be shown for the fully-fledged phenomenon that it is;

(2) it is less delicate to present a request or claim in the name of the child advocacy than as an allegation of child maltreatment. The considerable power that is held over parents enables an accusation of maltreatment to be levelled against them. The lack of power that

is held over institutions, agencies and organizations precludes this, and the request is generally couched in other terms.

But for the child, the physical and mental bruises remain the same . . .

Put another way, if we begin to tackle the problem of the severely abused child, it is because we judge there to be a right to protection from abuse, and we take up the child's cause as an advocate. Exactly the same analysis applies to every other situation where the interests of the child, however vaguely defined, are not being taken into account. It is therefore illogical to draw a dividing line between maltreatment and rights on any basis other than the specificity of the action envisaged. It is necessary at least to be aware of, and take into account, the overall context in which an alleged abusive or neglectful act has taken place.

This reality — the child's "voicelessness" and the "violence circle" — means that any basis for international action on child maltreatment must include unequivocal adherence to the twin aims of improving the representation of the interests of the child and of reducing the causes and incidence of violence. These goals constitute, in the last resort, the only possible basis or justification for attempts to ensure a legal basis for combating maltreatment at all levels; and modify socialization processes that involve physical and/or psychological harm.

### The Cross-Cultural Basis for International Work

At this point we should summarize our reasoning so far. Universally acceptable criteria are the *sine qua non* of universal action. If it seems undesirable to define given *acts* as constituting acceptable or unacceptable behaviour towards children, it is equally unwarranted, particularly from an international standpoint, to define given *persons* (eg family members, institution staff) as being the only potential perpetrators of maltreatment. This approach not only takes into account the different priorities that exist from one community or country to another in terms of the maltreatment forms to be combated, but also, and more importantly, stems from the logical view that there is no *fundamental* difference for the child whether he falls victim to a certain act perpetrated by an individual or agency, within or outside his family, even if the preventive and curative *response* will differ according to the identity of the perpetrator and circumstances.

In line with this and the preceding considerations, a feasible cross-cultural basis for action is as follows:

Child maltreatment is constituted by any situation, decision, act or omission if:

(i)  it is designed to harm a child, and/or

(ii) the perpetrator subordinates, actively or passively, the interests of the child to his own, and

(iii) it is formally or informally reproved by the community or society concerned.

The child is further entitled to effective representation in the event of any other situation, decision, act or omission that implicitly, explicitly, indirectly or directly, perpetuates violence, in any form towards him.

We believe, therefore, that the basis clearly exists for the concern of the international community to be aroused, expressed and activate. In doing so, we make no attempt to deny the existence of cultural differences. We do, however, refute the argument that these constitute *barriers* to work on the child maltreatment problem from an international standpoint.

### The Lack of a Formal, Legal Action Basis

For child welfare, the results of the international encounter have so far been relatively meagre in terms of formal provisions on which international action can be based. Such provisions exist in certain closely defined situations: conflict (the 1949 Geneva Conventions/Additional Protocols), child labour (the 1973 ILO Convention), and in various proclamations and conventions related to human rights in general or to certain country situations in particular. In global terms the basic document remains the 1959 Declaration of the Rights of the Child, which:

(i)  not being a convention, is not an international legal instrument;

(ii) has no specific or recognized monitoring body, either intergovernmental or non-governmental;

(iii) makes no reference whatsoever to what acts or otherwise might be interpreted as maltreatment, stating simply that (Principle 9): "The child shall be protected against all forms of neglect, cruelty and exploitation. He shall not be the subject of traffic, in any form," before going on to talk more especially about child labour.

Whatever the degree of implementation of the principles in the Declaration, and however little they are respected, the lack of definition of this particular fundamental right is symptomatic of the apparent problem faced when dealing with child maltreatment from a cross-cultural perspective. The question is still begging: "Who" says "what" constitutes "cruelty, neglect and exploitation"?

The Declaration is therefore inadequate as an international agreement on which action to combat maltreatment might be based.

It was for this reason that an initiative was launched just prior to the International Year of the Child to transform the Declaration into a Convention. Later, when it became clear that the terms of the Declaration were not appropriate as provisions of an international legal instrument like a Convention, a working group of the Sub-Commission of Human Rights was set up to draw up the principles of such a Convention in adequate form.

That a Convention on the Rights of the Child may exist is encouraging, but it must be remembered that:

— the degree to which it defines the rights and their violations determines the degree to which it can usefully be employed in work to combat child maltreatment;

— a Convention has to be ratified after adoption, whereas a Declaration is valid simply by adoption. Many examples exist of Conventions that have not come into force because they have not been ratified by a sufficient number of countries, or that such ratification has taken many years. Equally, any country that chooses *not* to ratify the Convention obviously can not be bound by it;

— a Convention has to be enforced, like any other legal instrument, and once again there is no shortage of eloquent examples that proper enforcement poses considerable problems.

The strongest potential of a Convention is that it provides a more or less clearly-defined legal basis on which action can be taken with, or vis-à-vis, the contracting parties. It neither presages any automatic improvement in the situation it governs, nor provides an automatic means for bringing about such an improvement.

In other words, neither the existing Declaration nor any future Convention does or will constitute an end, precluding the need for international action. On the contrary, they can provide, in some measure, a means to moving further towards an end, if they are used optimally. At the same time, the *lack* of such a means constitutes a considerable handicap to international efforts on the child maltreatment question.

### Priority to "Needs"

It is blatantly obvious that, in a world where a child under five years of age dies every two or three seconds because of malnutrition, out-of-reach health services, lack of shelter, etc, few could doubt the justification for the urgent and tremendous task of meeting these children's basic needs. In no way do we question this reasoning. What has occurred, however, in the international community is the emergence of a situation in which the task of meeting needs is perceived as being totally divorced from — and even generally incompatible with — that of ensuring prevention of, and protection from, maltreatment. The argument is that meeting needs is a politically neutral, humanitarian operation based on, and requiring, close co-operation with the authorities of the receiving country, whereas international advocacy and protection activities in favour of maltreated children are politically delicate, likely to be interpreted as interference, and therefore jeopardizing co-operation. Several aspects of this argument provoke comment, in particular:

— meeting needs is a political option, both in itself (not all ideologies advocate support for the destitute and underprivileged members of society) and in terms of the situation to which it constitutes a response (the intra- and international distribution of resources);

— many or most elements in child maltreatment work can be — and indeed, are best — carried out in a spirit of co-operation rather than conflict;

— lack of action on child maltreatment by international agencies is tantamount to saying that one can provide food and shelter to a child without taking any account of what his survival is to entail for him;

— the "megafigures" of children lacking basic necessities are themselves evidence of abuse, neglect and exploitation at the highest level, and therefore an area in which the defence of children's rights is both appropriate and necessary.

In adopting the attitude they do, such international agencies are in a way frequently limiting the scope and effectiveness of those efforts on child maltreatment undertaken by other bodies. Lack of solidarity at this level is often far more of a "barrier" to action than any cultural perception of what constitutes maltreatment.

## Fields of Current Concern

At the same time, several international bodies are concerned in some way with the question. One has to look to organizations not specially devoted to the child in order to find international action that goes beyond the exchange of information, experience and views: Amnesty International, from a human rights standpoint, as regards child victims of torture, imprisonment and murder; the Anti-Slavery Society as regards the exploitation of child labour, International Social Service in terms of the children of migrants and refugees; the International Committee of the Red Cross as concerns family reunion for unaccompanied minor refugees — and a limited number of others.

In general, inter-governmental organizations, such as UNICEF, are limited to the "fulfilment of needs" approach. Certain notable exceptions are: the International Labour Organization, which is working intensively on the child labour question; the World Health Organization, active on the questions of female circumcision, the health effects of child labour and the "Fourth World" environment, and the promotion of breast-feeding (in conjunction with UNICEF); and the United Nations Division of Human Rights, whose mandate is to establish country dossiers and reports on the basis of information received, and to request that the authorities of countries whose practices are questioned allow a commission of enquiry to investigate the situation. But as we have seen, there is no intergovernmental agency or body entrusted with identifying responses to child maltreatment.

## Inappropriate Responses

"Defence of children's rights" actions have been carried out internationally. Invariably these have been launched in the form of campaigns based on "western" standpoints but directed towards "non-western" societies. They are often conducted in a sensationalist manner and in a way that has failed to respect cultural differences, perhaps in part because the latter are seen as insurmountable obstacles and therefore ignored in the interests of the campaign.

It would be wrong to condemn such campaigns completely out of hand. They have managed to bring to international attention certain disturbing practices which undoubtedly have pernicious effects for the children concerned — indeed, sometimes going as far as death. The original denunciations have sparked off concern and action that, in all probability, would not have been aroused otherwise, or at least only at a very much later date. Exemplary here is the campaign against female circumcision. The existence of the phenomenon was first publicized by "western" organizations, whose *approach* was generally condemned by the societies concerned as being insensitive (sometimes thoroughly degrading) judgemental and "western-centred", since it initially took no account of the context of the act. The latter is not gratuitous cruelty but an inherent part of the socialization process. This does not mean that the act should be condoned, but that attempts to halt it have to find support within the societies concerned (involving attitude change and a widespread information campaign) rather than arousing their indignation.

The polemics over the female circumcision issue typified the perceived "cultural barriers" to international action — and solidarity — in the field of child abuse and neglect. Constructive work on this issue, based on concertation and acknowledgement of realities, only got under way after the creation of serious rifts, accusations of "neo-colonialism", and a form of reconciliation which narrowly avoided the serious jeopardization of international action.

## Overcoming the Problems: Defence for Children's Experience

In this descriptive analysis, we have demonstrated why, and in what ways, effective international action on the child maltreatment question is both justified and necessary, and have identified a series of shortcomings and problems that have militated against its successful implementation.

It was in an attempt to respond to the need and the difficulties that, during the International Year of the Child, the Defence for Children international movement was established in Geneva, Switzerland, by a committee of 13 child welfare/human rights specialists from 11 different countries, themselves convinced of the possibility of overcoming the three major problems.

### Problem 1: There is No International Children's Rights Organization

Defence for Children was set up as a focal point for all allegations of maltreatment that have not been resolved nationally, guaranteeing investigation and, if justified, action. Wherever possible, it works in co-operation with national or other international bodies, when these can help in reaching an appropriate solution. At the same time, it attempts to promote national bodies that are competent and able to deal with such allegations, thereby avoiding the need for international intervention, which must always be seen as a last resort.

### Problem 2: There is No Cross-Cultural Consensus on What Constitutes Child Maltreatment

With regard to certain acts, and their definition as "child maltreatment", this is true at the present time. This is why Defence for Children defines its field of action no more strictly than "situations in which children's interests are not taken into account", and is ready to respond to any allegation falling within that definition. It is also why it adopts a flexible approach in dealing with cases, differentiating between allegations of acts that can be described as universally condemned and those that are not intended to harm a child or to exploit his weakness. It acts on all cases, but in ways designed to reflect cross-cultural realities, believing that these in no way constitute insurmountable barriers to protecting the interests of the child. Defence for Children therefore places considerable emphasis on the importance of formulating a cross-cultural basis for international action and solidarity.

*Problem 3: The "International Community" as a Whole Cannot, or Will Not, Support Action on Child Maltreatment*

This is only true to the extent that no perceived "lead" agency existed in the field of children's rights at the international level, and that no attempt had been made to arouse the solidarity of other organizations, both non-governmental and intergovernmental taking account of the specific mandate of each.

It is here, too, that the concept of the "international community" as the world's population takes on special importance. The potential agreement with, and solidarity around, work to combat child maltreatment internationally, as conceived above, is immeasurable both numerically and in terms of impact. Realistically, the defence of children's interests, like those defended by any other lobby or pressure group, depends on little more than the active strength of its voice . . .

**Experience So Far**

Based on the above elements, Defence for Children's experience so far has confirmed the justification for and appropriateness of the type of "preventive" and "curative" action it proposes.

Of the dozens of cases so far submitted to it, concerning countries throughout the world, it has rejected just two as not constituting violation of the interests of the child and has never received a complaint that its action on the others was inappropriate or unjustified.

It has dealt with cases wherever possible with or through other agencies both international and national, and in some instances has aroused the co-operation of organizations that, in several decades of existence, had never previously put their name to, or worked on, child maltreatment action internationally.

It has proved that such action can be effective in certain cases, but that most require a far higher level of solidarity and concern of the international community if they are to be resolved appropriately.

It is worth looking at some of the concrete situations in which Defence for Children has been involved to date in order to demonstrate, by way of conclusion, the needs and potential for international action on child maltreatment evoked in this chapter's sub-title. This is perhaps best done, as regards responses to alleged cases, by considering the kinds of role the organization has played.

*Role 1: The Focal Point*

Many people, and indeed organizations, do not know to whom they should turn for help or advice on cases of child maltreatment, especially those of an extrafamilial nature. One of the first cases referred to Defence for Children concerned an expectant mother whose fiance lived in a country where he was unable to obtain a visa to rejoin and marry her. She had written to UNICEF which, not being a case-action agency, passed her request on to Defence for Children. The latter took it up on the grounds that the expected child had the right to the presence of his father. Defence for Children contacted the mother for more details, and on the basis of these requested the assistance of an agency with proven experience in this sphere. Within a few months, Defence for Children learned that the appropriate visa had been granted. Whilst its own active role had been limited, the organization had served as a focal point which had been able to set in motion the proper machinery for resolving the situation.

## Role 2: The Last Resort

A couple contacted Defence for Children expressing their conviction that their own daughter, for several years, had been severely neglecting and humiliating her eldest son, and alleging that the social service agency concerned was not taking the necessary steps to ensure the child's normal development. They explicitly asked Defence for Children to intervene "as a last resort". The organization has contacted the statutory service concerned, and is now working with it, placing particular emphasis on the need for a solution that takes into account the child's point of view, which seems so far to have been neglected. Interestingly, in this case from Western Europe, the couple had found no local or national organization to address on this issue.

## Role 3: The Pressure Group

Defence for Children was informed that a mother and 10-month-old child were being detained in deplorable conditions that were severely affecting the health of both. At the suggestion of the informant the organization contacted certain government officials in the country concerned. Less than two months later, it was learned that the child had been released into the care of his grandmother, but that the mother remained in prison, remanded without charge. Defence for Children, on the basis of the child's need of his mother, has therefore requested her release — and at the same time has taken up a similar case referred because of the apparent success of its initial intervention.

## Role 4: The Facilitator

A local social work agency in a West European country requested Defence for Children's help on a complicated and delicate case in which two adolescent sisters had allegedly been married against their will, and retained, in a Middle East country. The girls are nationals of both the countries concerned. The differences in legislative and cultural realities between the two countries are considerable. However, by basing its intervention on the sole interests of the children concerned, Defence for Children has negotiated with representatives of the country of marriage, and has obtained their co-operation in carrying out a thorough investigation and, if justified, in facilitating the girls' return home.

### Role 5: The Enabler
In keeping with its principle of intervening, as an international agency, only when absolutely necessary, Defence for Children has provided contacts, and in some cases financial assistance, to individuals and local/national organizations when this form of help was the major element lacking in their ability to resolve one or more cases. Instances are: family reunification, logistical needs and destitution of children because of politically-motivated killings.

### Role 6: The "Child Welfare Element"
In several instances, human rights and other organizations have requested Defence for Children's help on cases they are dealing with that involve children. In the subsequently joint, yet distinct, approaches taken on the cases in question, Defence for Children thus provides the "child welfare element" in what otherwise would risk being considered a partisan, wholly political intervention.

### Role 7: Arousal of Solidarity
In certain specific cases, Defence for Children has sought and received the active solidarity of other international organizations in approaches to agencies and individuals that are in a position to contribute to, or effect, the resolution of situations in which children's interests are neglected. In virtually all such cases, it was the first time that the organizations concerned had taken united stands on individual situations of maltreatment. Exemplary here is the precedent-setting support obtained from the International Association of Juvenile and Family Court Magistrates in an approach to all juvenile judges in a province of a South American country, urging them to review all adoption cases dealt with by their court in order to ensure that no cases involved children reported as "disappeared".

If these are the seven major roles of Defence for Children in its action on cases of maltreatment it should be noted that each of the more than 60 cases submitted to the organization in its two years of existence has demanded an individually-tailored response, such is the variety of situations which require international action that has so far been conspicuously lacking.

At the same time, the organization is most attentive to the preventive aspect which constitutes a vital element in its action. Modest to date, limited by availability of resources and priority given to responding to cases, preventive work is planned to expand rapidly in the near future, on the basis both of initial experience and of the lessons to be drawn from responding post facto to concrete situations such as those described above. The preventive "advocacy" role consists primarily of:

— taking up specific issues on a globel level, for example children in prison, sexual exploitation, inter-country problems, etc, on the basis of needs perceived whilst responding to individual cases;

— fostering and assisting local and national initiatives;

— ensuring the greatest possible diffusion of information on situations, needs and responses in the wide child maltreatment sphere.

Like the responses on a curative level, these preventive actions are necessary at the international level. Their success depends on active solidarity, and here we come back to our initial considerations concerning the "international community". For Defence for Children was set up deliberately, not as a committee or bureau or council, but as an *international movement*. Thus, whilst it depends on the forces it can activate within the international community of *organizations,* the very activation of these forces depends greatly on the support it receives from the international community of *people.*

For, in the final analysis, child maltreatment is a worldwide human problem, and as such it has to be dealt with, worldwide, by human beings.

A concern of the international community.

# Chapter 25

# Management — The Myth and the Reality

R Kim Oates

Although much has been written about child abuse management there remains much confusion and many misconceptions. The literature has served both to clarify and confuse the field. This is in some measure due to the fact that there are many different disciplines with different professional backgrounds working in the child abuse field. Their approaches to the management of child abuse problems reflect their own training, the teachings of their own discipline and their own personal experience. These varying approaches add to the confusion. It is not that this is necessarily wrong as a variety of different approaches may be beneficial depending on the case involved. What is most important of all in treatment, is that the approach needs to be tailored firstly to the specific needs of each individual child and secondly to that child's family. Management of the child and family should be combined if possible, providing that the plan for the child is not compromised in the process.

There are a number of myths about child abuse management. What follows is a list of some of these myths. It is by no means exhaustive and to some extent reflects the writer's own bias. As already stated, professional attitudes are conditioned by professional background and experience and the writer is not immune to this. However I believe that there is evidence available to dispel some of the current myths about child abuse management.

### "Medical Practitioners are Automatically Child Abuse Experts"

This is a myth which exists largely in hospitals and other areas working closely along the medical model. Professionals working outside these areas are only too aware of the limitations of the medical practitioner in child abuse. It can be argued that child abuse is not a medical problem at all although, by the very nature of the problem, medical practitioners are often the first people to see the child, particularly if the injury is severe. In addition, much of the pioneering child abuse work came from the medical profession.[1,2,3,4] However many medical practitioners are not suitable by inclination, training or experience to work in this area. Child abuse is becoming more of a speciality and requires a medical practitioner who is interested and experienced in this field, who has had some training in family problems and most importantly, one who can work comfortably and on equal terms with other professional groups involved in child abuse work. It is no longer reasonable to expect medical practitioners to automatically be interested, and competent in child abuse management. What is reasonable however, is to expect medical practitioners to be aware of the problem and to refer a suspected case on to a colleague or other agency as that practitioner would do with any other complicated problem which might be beyond his experience and expertise.

### "Professional Services Alone Will be Able to Solve the Problem"

The extent of child abuse is such that there will probably never be enough professionals to provide the services to help these families. This means that voluntary agencies and the use of trained volunteers have to be considered as additional resources. Examples of the success of these programmes have already been documented.[5,6,7,8] In addition to the use of volunteers, families need to be put in contact with community agencies so that they can be integrated into their local community support system. The problem with relying solely on one professional doing casework is that there is a high turnover of professionals in the child abuse area and once the social worker or therapist involved is transferred to a new job or leaves, the family is likly to become "lost in the system" or overlooked unless they have been integrated with community facilities which can continue to help them, often on a practical level and which can continue to support them until a new case worker is available.

With an increasing trend to early retirement and increased leisure in our society, consideration could also be given to enlisting the support of the retired age-group to assist in supporting families with parenting problems.

### "Child Abuse is Equally Distributed in all Social Classes"

There are some reasons for the perpetuation of this myth. It is accepted that child abuse occurs in all social classes and that professionals must be particularly alert to the temptation to avoid or to overlook making the diagnosis in the higher socio-economic groups. The danger of the concept that child abuse is equally distributed in all social classes is that child abuse then becomes seen as a psychodynamic problem in the medical model, that is, a disease to be diagnosed, treated and cured. This psychodynamic model is useful to some extent but it is important to realize that child abuse has a definite link with poverty. This has been shown by Gil in his nationwide study of violence against children in the United States[9] and by Smith and colleagues who showed that in a controlled study, the families of battered children had a higher incidence of adverse economic circumstances than control families.[10] Weston showed that of 24 children dying from child abuse, 80 per cent of the families were receiving some form of public support.[11] As well as the actual higher incidence of adverse economic circumstances, it has been shown that battering families perceive themselves as having a higher incidence of financial difficulties than that perceived by a control group.[12]

While accepting and emphasizing that child abuse can occur in all socio-economic groups there is good evidence that it occurrs disproportionately among the lower socio-economic groups and that it probably has a direct link with poverty.

### "All Families Can be Helped"

Most workers in this area now no longer naively believe that all families can be helped and that in a proportion of cases the child is far better off in another family. One also has to accept that some children may already be severely emotionally damaged by the time they present for treatment. However Rutter has shown that children are far more resilient than many believe and that surprisingly good results can often be obtained once the child is placed in a good environment.[13]

### "Intervention Always Helps"

We would *like* to believe this, but follow-up studies indicate that the problem persists in many families and suggest that in some cases earlier court action may have been more appropriate so that the child could be placed in a more suitable environment. In other cases experience has shown that intervention should be more intensive, more long-term and in particular should be child-related.[14,15,16]

### "All That's Needed is an Assessment"

There is no such thing as a simple assessment. Assessments take time and skill. It may be easy to determine whether the problem is one of sexual abuse, physical abuse or neglect. However, far more important than an assessment of the type of injury, is a careful assessment of the family's strengths and weaknesses. A relatively minor injury may be a far more serious problem in a family with very few strengths and no social supports than a more serious "one off" injury which occurs in a family where there is the potential for coping effectively.

While much attention in the past has been paid to the assessment of the family, in many instances inadequate attention has been paid to assessing the needs of the child. Assessment of the child should include an assessment of the child's developmental level, personality and emotional needs. Assessment of the siblings is also desirable. A single evaluation of the child can be misleading. Clinicians who work closely with abused children have observed that the residual effects of the abuse or neglect, especially a "hyper-monitoring" of adults may prevent the child from giving full attention to a test. This may result in the child being more concerned with the tester than the test — a situation which would depress intelligence scores.[17]

Any child abuse service which overlooks the treatment needs of the abused child is failing to do an adequate job. This is particularly relevant in view of the evidence showing that abused children do have long-term emotional and physical damage including a high risk of damage to the central nervous system and mal-development of ego function.[18,19,20]

There is a tendency to place abused children in day care. This has the advantage of allowing the child to mix and develop with other children as well as providing the parent with some relief from the constant strains of child rearing. However careful consideration should be given to deciding on *appropriate* day care. Just "rescuing" an abused child from further abuse may not be sufficient to break the cycle of child abuse which really represents a problem in relationships. In day care programmes the staff need to be shown how to pay special attention to the child's social relationships and development. Day care workers should know that the abused child may greet them with rejection and avoidance.[21] This must be responded to with steady affection, rather than the natural tendency to respond to this sort of behaviour with diminished interest in the child.

In developing treatment plans for children who remain with their family, one must be aware of the problems likely to occur if the child is changed by the treatment and stripped of some adaptive behaviours which are valuable in a dangerous environment. For example, exploration, questioning and initiative may not be encouraged in an abusive home. It follows that any treatment plan for the child must be offered in the context of a carefully devised treatment plan for the whole family.

In assessing the child, the links between the acute centre where the child presents and where the assessment is usually done and the community agencies which are usually involved in the long-term follow-up, should be remembered. It is important to remember to involve these community agencies in the initial assessment of the child and to consult them about treatment programmes. It is sometimes unreasonable to ask agencies to follow-up cases where they have not had any involvement in the initial assessment, or any input into the development of the treatment programme, particularly if they already know the family. Acute assessment centres are usually not burdened with the very difficult problem of long-term follow-up. Staff working in these centres need to have realistic expectations of the community services which become involved in the more arduous task of providing continuing care for these children and their families.

## "What is Needed is a Treatment Programme"

Certainly a carefully planned programme of treatment is essential. However we have to remember that many of these families are difficult to work with and as a result of this many treatment programmes break down. Typical problems are: failure of the parents to take children to pre-school programmes, failure to keep appointments and failure to be at home when the visiting worker calls. Some of these problems can be interpreted as the parents' difficulty in forming a trusting relationship so that workers in this field need to be both understanding and persistent. Parents sometimes become jealous of the amount of attention and care that their child is receiving in treatment programmes and this has to be anticipated and catered for. The message is that we cannot set up a treatment programme and assume that our responsibility ends there.

## "Removing the Child From the Family is the Answer"

Most workers in this area would agree that certain children are far better off removed from their families. However the question has to be asked: what sort of environment is available for the child following removal? Alternative care offered must not only be safer, it must also be therapeutic in that it should heal the emotional, social, intellectual and physical damage that the child has suffered. A poor placement may harm the child more than the original injury. Child abuse cases are notorious for being moved from one foster situation to the other, often with disastrous effects for the child. There is no guarantee that foster placement is better. As well as breaking down (evidence from US and UK studies consistently show that 15 per cent of long-term foster placements break down) there is evidence of disturbed behaviour in children in foster placements. Thorpe showed that 39 per cent of children in foster care were disturbed compared with 23 per cent of a socially similar population.[22] Bolton and colleagues in a study in Arizona, showed that 7 per cent of the child population in foster care had suffered from abuse and neglect compared with 2 per cent of the normal population of children living with their parents.[23] Obviously it cannot be assumed that foster care will automatically solve the problems, particularly when the child being placed is likely to be disturbed as a result of his experiences with his natural family.

It has long been known that some of the side effects of medical treatment given without proper care and planning may be more serious than the disease itself.[24] These problems also need to be kept in mind when planning foster care placements to ensure that foster families are carefully selected and given continuing support. Decisions about placing the child are often clouded by legal problems. In cases where parental rights are not severed, the courts sometimes make a decision which puts the child in a limbo situation. The child may be put in the custody of the State, or moved among several foster parents but never be available for adoption or for any meaningful commitment from foster parents who, despite their good intentions for the child, always have hanging over them the concern that if they become too attached to the child, the parting may be too difficult should the State deem that the child should be returned to his family.

When children lose their parents by natural means, such as following an accident, we are aware of the adverse psychological effects on the child and appropriate treatment and counselling is provided. In child abuse cases where we may be *recommending* the loss of a parent as part of the child's treatment, we should be even more concerned about providing ongoing support and treatment to a child who may already be disturbed.

Mia Pringle has described the needs of children as[25]:

> The need for love and security
> The need for new experiences
> The need for praise and recognition
> The need for responsibility

These are basic needs which need to be considered in any treatment programme or placement of abused children.

### "The Law is on the Side of the Child"

Unfortunately the legal system does not always recognize the rights of the child. In many situations children are not provided with court advocates. In cases where public solicitors are available to represent the needs of the child, they may have a poor understanding of the problems of child abuse. It is distressing to go to court only to find that on occasions the solicitor appointed by the court to represent the child is quite unprepared, has preconceived prejudices about child abuse and family problems and has little interest in this sort of case. It is important that all of those who work in the child abuse field should strive to improve child advocacy. The legal profession at all levels could be far better informed about child abuse. This could be achieved by having a degree of specialization so that certain judges, magistrates, solicitors and barristers do develop some expertise in understanding both the developmental needs of children and the psychodynamics of family situations which can lead to child abuse.

The passage of laws to deal with child abuse problems has made an important contribution, particularly reporting laws which have brought many cases which may not have been detected otherwise, out into the open. However it would be deceptive to believe that legislation in itself will provide a solution. Legislation must be closely linked with treatment programmes and perhaps legislation should go further than it has at present in stipulating the need for the provision and regular review of treatment programmes. Recognizing the problem is not enough. "Failure to provide treatment services for child abuse victims and their families falls into the same category as withholding steroids from children with nephrosis."[26]

## "Teaching Adolescents the Principles of Good Parenting at High School will Solve the Problem"

It would be nice to believe that this was so. However there is no evidence for this. It is a principle of education that people first need to be motivated to learn. Probably the most important time for providing practical advice about parenting as well as emotional support for some of the problems of parents is in the first few months after a child has been born. The widespread use of ante-natal classes is accepted. What is now required is a move to commence post-natal classes for problems encountered in child rearing.

Rather than give adolescents in high schools theoretical knowledge about child care, the approach that may be most effective would be to encourage adolescent females and males to have experience in the actual care of young children at pre-schools and child care centres. This would both enable them to understand some of the problems and stresses involved with caring for young children and would also give them practical experience and confidence in the management of such down-to-earth procedures as nappy changing, feeding and bathing.

## "Research is the Answer"

Recent years have seen a vast outpouring of literature and research studies into child abuse and much of this has provided valuable information. It is certainly important for there to be regular, critical evaluation of treatment programmes as well as the carefully planned development of new assessment procedures and treatment programmes. Because of the number of different disciplines involved in child abuse work there has been a wide exchange of ideas through research publications and conferences so that many disciplines have learnt from each other.

A danger is that because of the very real pressures on child abuse workers, there is a tendency on the part of many of us to want to get out of the front line. This can be done by giving supervision to the front line workers rather than working in the front line personally, by teaching and lecturing on child abuse and by doing research. The temptation is that there may be a tendency for needless research and information gathering. It is all too easy to be busy in child abuse work but not busy being helpful to families.

## "The Problem is too Big"

Gil is probably correct in his conclusion that child abuse cannot be eradicated without a radical restructuring of society:

"There simply is no way of escaping the conclusion that the complete elimination of child abuse on all levels of manifestation, requires a radical transformation of the prevailing unjust inegalitarian, irrational, competitive, alienating and hierarchical social order into a just, egalitarian, rational, co-operative, human and truly democratic decentralized one. Obviously this realization implies that primary prevention of child abuse is a political issue which cannot be resolved through professional and administrative measures."[27] However this does not mean that nothing can be done. Although, as Gil says professional and administrative measures will not eliminate the problem there is no doubt that on an individual level many children and families have been and will continue to be helped. Rather than wait for the revolution (which may never come and which even if it does will not guarantee an improvement) families can continue to be helped on an individual level while child abuse workers should also use what influence they have to modify the social structure so as to try to eliminate some of the causes of child abuse and to improve facilities for those being treated.

## CONCLUSION

Doubtless the reader could think of other myths and misconceptions about child abuse management. We should also be looking at innovative methods of treatment as well as improving current treatment programmes. Areas that need to be considered are an improvement in the court system with increased child advocacy; an increased use of volunteers, perhaps utilizing the leisure time of retired people; residential facilities where whole families can receive treatment[28]; family crisis centres where the whole family can attend for help at short notice, and crisis nurseries where parents who fear that they may damage their child can, at short notice, have the child temporarily cared for. The importance of promoting a positive parent-baby relationship has been described in Chapters 5 to 9 of this book and more attention is now being paid to looking at ways of predicting and preventing child abuse, before or soon after the child is born.

Helfer and Kempe have described a number of preventive measures aimed at parents and children at different stages of their lives which, taken together are thought to be likely to prevent many cases of child abuse.[29] These are:

(1) Perinatal coaching to provide new parents with the skills necessary to communicate with their new child.

(2) Home care assistance where parents are provided with visitors to help them with practical child care problems and to improve their communication skills with their infants.

(3) Expanded well-baby care.

(4) The development of interpersonal, cognitive problem-solving skills to teach pre-school and primary school children to solve everyday problems.

(5) The teaching of interpersonal skills for high school children with emphasis on teaching students how to get on with people of all ages and at all levels in society.

(6) A crash course in childhood for adults and some young adults who need a second chance to learn skills which should have been learnt during their childhood.

(7) A pre-parent refresher course for "soon to be" parents to revise previously taught concepts of appropriate ways to interact with their partners and children.

People working with children and their families must be optimistic and there is much to be optimistic about. Since child abuse was first brought to the notice of the public there has been an explosion of professional interest and knowledge and many successful treatment programmes have been developed. However optimism must be based in reality, a careful analysis of the available data and an ability not to become confused by some of the many myths and misconceptions which have been an understandable result of the great interest shown in this field.

# Notes

1   P V Woolley and W A Evans, "Significance of Skeletal Lesions in Infants
    Resembling Those of Traumatic Origin" (1955) *JAMA* **158**:539

2   H Bakwin, "Multiple Skeletal Lesions in Young Children due to Trauma" (1956)
    *J Paediatrics* **49**:7

3   H K Silver and C H Kempe, "Problems of Parental Criminal Neglect and
    Severe Physical Abuse of Children" (1959) *Am J Dis Child* **95**:528

4   C H Kempe, F N Silverman, B F Steele, W Droegemueller and H K Silver,
    "The Battered Child Syndrome" (1962) *JAMA* **181**:17

5   R K Oates, "The Use of Non-Professional Workers", *Proceedings of the First
    National Conference on the Battered Child* (Western Australian Dept of
    Community Welfare, 1975)

6   J Gray and B Kaplan, "The Lay Health Visitor Program, and Eighteen Month
    Experience" in C H Kempe and R E Helfer (eds) *The Battered Child* 3rd ed
    (University of Chicago Press, Chicago, 1980)

7   J Barbour, "Adopt a Family — Dial a Granny", *Proceedings of the Second
    Australasian Conference on Child Abuse* (Queensland Government Printer,
    1981)

8   J Hinson, "Parent Aides — Crisis Workers", *Proceedings of the Second
    Australasian Conference on Child Abuse* (Queensland Government Printer,
    1981)

9   D G Gil, *Violence Against Children* (Harvard University Press, Cambridge,
    Massachusetts, 1970)

10  S M Smith, R Hanson and S Noble, "Social Aspects of the Battered Baby
    Syndrome" (1974) *Br J Psychiat* **125**:568-82

11  J T Weston, "The Pathology of Child Abuse and Neglect" in C H Kempe and
    R E Helfer (eds) *The Battered Child* (University of Chicago Press, Chicago,
    1980)

12  R K Oates, A A Davis and M G Ryan, "Predictive Factors for Child Abuse"
    (1980) *Aust Paediat J* **16**:239

13  M Rutter "The Long-term Effects of Early Experience" (1980) *Devl Med Child
    Neurol* **22**:800

14  I W Hufton and R K Oates, "Non-organic Failure to Thrive, a Long-term
    Follow-up" (1977) *Paediatrics* **59**:73

15  E Elmer, "A Follow-up Study of Traumatized Children" (1977) *Paediatrics*
    **59**:273

16  H P Martin, *The Abused Child* (Ballinger, Cambridge, Massachusetts, 1976)

17  M Rodeheffer and H P Martin, "Special Problems in the Development and
    Assessment of Abused Children" in H P Martin (ed) *The Abused Child*
    (Ballinger, Cambridge, Massachusetts, 1977)

18  H P Martin, P Beezley, E S Conway and C H Kempe, "The Development of
    Abused Children, I — a Review of the Literature, II — Physical, Neurological
    and Intellectual Outcomes (1974) *Advances in Paediatrics* **21**:25

19  M Lynch, "The Prognosis of Child Abuse" (1975) *J Child Psychol Psychiat*
    **19**:175

20  C Jones, "The Fate of Abused Children" in A W Franklin (ed) *The Challenge
    of Child Abuse* (Academic Press, London, 1977)

21   C George and M Main, "Social Interactions of Young Abused Children, Approach, Avoidance, Aggression" in N Frude (ed) *Psychological Approaches to Child Abuse*" (Batsford Academic, London, 1979)

22   R Thorpe "The Experiences of Children and Parents Living Apart, Implication and Guidelines for Practice" in J Triseliotis (ed) *New Developments in Foster Care and Adoption* (Routledge and Kegan Paul, London, 1980)

23   F G Bolton, R H Laner and D S Gai, "For Better or Worse? Foster Parents and Foster Children in an Officially Reported Child Maltreatment Population" (1981) *Children and Youth Services Review* 3:37

24   I Illich, *Medical Nemesis, The Expropriation of Health* (Lothian, London, 1975)

25   M K Pringle, *The Needs of Children* (Hutchinson, London, 1975)

26   A B Bergman, "Abuse of the Child Abuse Law" (1978) *Paediatrics* 62:266

27   D G Gil, "Unraveling Child Abuse" (1975) *Am J Orthopsychiat* 45:346

28   C Ounsted, R Oppenheimer and J Lindsay, "Aspects of Bonding Failure, The Psychopathology and Psychotherapeutic Treatment of Families of Battered Children" (1974) *Devl Med Child Neurol* 16:447

29   R E Helfer and C H Kempe, "An Overview of Prevention" in C H Kempe and R E Helfer (eds) *The Battered Child*, 3rd ed (University of Chicago Press, Chicago, 1980)

# Chapter 26

# Where Are We Going? — A Review of the Past and Suggestions for the Future

Raymond L Castle and Sarah P Briggs

"I have come to see violence more and more in terms of a gigantic web in which countless generations of people are caught. A violent adolescent who has just kicked in someone's teeth is yet one more creature snared in the web, and probably it is already too late for him ever to free himself completely. Violence breeds Violence." (Jean Renvoise, *Web of Violence*, Pelican 1980).

Services to prevent the abuse of children began to emerge in the late nineteenth century, primarily in the United States of America and the United Kingdom. As these two nations were primarily responsible for much of the pioneering work in this field it seems appropriate to base a review of the past on the significant events in these countries that have led to greater international co-operation and understanding of this complex problem.

Although these two industrial nations had legislation to protect animals, there was none to protect children who were viewed very much as the possessions of their parents rather than in their own right as young human beings. Practices such as baby farming were rife and children worked long hours in terrible conditions in factories, as chimney cleaners and as cheap labour in mines.

In the home many children died as the direct result of being overlaid in bed by drunken parents. Others were the victims of a variety of inflicted injuries and were exposed to all kinds of physical and mental torture.

It was against this background that public awareness and indignation were aroused in the United States following a case involving a young child who had been seriously abused over a long period.[1,2] A volunteer missionary trying to get help for her finally turned in desperation to the Society for the Prevention of Cruelty to Animals in New York having been told "this is a very dangerous thing for you to undertake. You are not the guardian. The parents have a right to correct the child. You may be arrested if you interfere in such a case". On bringing the case before that Society the statute books were searched in vain for some law which would justify the rescue of the child. There was none — animals were protected but not children.

Finally it was decided with the help of Elbridge T Gerry, a great pioneer in humanitarian work and legal adviser to the animal society, that the child should be treated as a "little animal" of the human race. Officers of the society removed the child from her home, seized the scissors with which her head and body had been beaten and brought her before the Supreme Court. The public outcry following this case led to the setting up of the first society for the protection of children in New York and the first Bill of Children's Rights in the United States.

As the American movement developed, increased concern was being expressed in the United Kingdom that children were suffering needlessly and that the community could no longer remain blind to this fact.

An interesting illustration of the thinking at that time is that on suggesting to Lord Shaftsbury in 1881 that parliament should give children rights in their own homes, the Rev George Staite received the reply: "The evils you state are enormous and indisputable, but they are of so private, internal and domestic a character as to be beyond the reach of legislation, and the subject would not, I think be entertained in either House of Parliament."[1] He did, nevertheless, give the project his support.

In that same year[3] a Liverpool banker, T F Agnew, was visiting New York and came across the premises of the New York Society. He was so impressed by what he heard there that he visited similar societies which were then forming in other American cities, finally returning to Liverpool in 1882.

The first Society for the Prevention of Cruelty to Children in England was established in Liverpool in 1883 followed in 1884 by the formation of the London Society. After a visit to the shelter opened by the Liverpool society, Miss Hesba Stretton, a well-known authoress of children's stories, wrote of the plight of the 378 children that were helped during the first six months. In a letter to the Times[4], she wrote:

If this is the result of one half year's operation of the Liverpool Society, what is the sum of cruel oppression and of dumb misery amongst the countless children who fill our streets? I venture to say that there is scarcely a parish in England where some cases of cruel neglect would not be brought to light if there was a National Society for the Prevention of Cruelty to Children.

Within four years her wish was to come true for in 1889 all but one of the existing committees amalgamated as the National Society for the Prevention of Cruelty to Children (NSPCC) under the patronage of Queen Victoria.

Also in 1889, following five years of active campaigning to bring to the attention of both the general public and influential bodies, anomalies in the law with regard to children, Britain achieved its first Act of parliament for the prevention of cruelty. This became known as the Children's Charter. The following major changes were brought about by the Charter and by the Acts for the Prevention of Cruelty to Children of 1894 and 1904: The offences of neglect and ill-treatment were created as was the offence of injuring a child's mental health or failing to call a doctor if one was required. Children were enabled to give evidence without taking the oath and the innocent parent was allowed to give evidence against the guilty one. The courts were empowered to place a child with a new guardian. The police were empowered to arrest anyone whom they saw ill-treating a child and it was now possible, where reasonable suspicion existed that all was not well with a child, to obtain a warrant to enter the home and to arrange for a doctor to examine the child.

At the time of the Children's Charter a number of countries within the British Commonwealth including Australia and New Zealand, brought down similar legislation to the British Model.

Thus, the United States and England had laid the foundations for developments in the field of child abuse which were to have international implications in the twentieth century.

It is important to appreciate some of the attitudes prevalent at that time since they have a direct bearing on how services progressed. The most positive factor to emerge from the literature available[5] is the fact that right from the start it was clearly recognized that child abuse knows no social boundaries. One of the first cases brought before the courts was that of a doctor who beat his three-year-old daughter until she fainted, revived her with port wine and then beat her again until she collapsed because the child could not spell the word "fox".[6]

There was no attempts to try to understand the underlying problems of parents who abused their children. They were, according to the letters and editorials available, "criminals" and "ruffians" who deserved the most severe of punishments, including flogging.[7]

In the immediate years following the Acts there was considerable criticism of the sentences passed by courts implying that they were far too lenient. One has only to read some of the letters received by newspapers and helping agencies today to realize that some of these attitudes continue within the community.

Another important factor was the recognition that the children would need shelter, or places of safety, as they later became known. In those early days the Societies operated their own shelters because local authorities in the form of Poor Law Guardians could refuse to receive children in to the local poor houses (work houses) unless they were "destitute".

For many years to follow, children's legal rights and their protection were to be the focus of attention. In both America and England the early 1900's saw the establishment of Juvenile Courts. These courts initially dealt with children who had committed crimes but recognized that the child's welfare was of paramount importance and "that the most vital factors affecting any child were his home and family". (British Children's Act 1908.)

In 1904 NSPCC officers were empowered to remove children from their homes when there was evidence of cruelty or neglect, and to bring them before the courts as in need of care and protection (a Statute which is still in being in the 1980's).

It was after the second world war that real attention was first paid to the underlying motivation that led to child abuse and to actual quality of the family life of those families in which it occurred. Among many studies carried out was one by John Bowlby into mental health and maternal care.[8] He was able to illustrate the damaging effect that loss of a mother or removal from her could have on the emotional development of a child under the age of five. This study was to have a dramatic effect on thinking with regard to child abuse and the possible subsequent removal of children from homes.

Poor housing, poverty and unemployment were all identified as factors involved in child abuse as was the need for better medical care and supervision. A number of these needs were to be met in Britain by the introduction of the welfare state and its various benefits as a right of the individual.

While these developments were beginning to take place, a child, who had been removed from his own home and boarded out together with his brother, died because of prolonged neglect and cruelty at the hands of foster parents while under the supervision of the local authority.

Jean Heywood in her book *Children in Care*[9] writes:

The public disquiet was profound. That a child, removed from his own home because of its bad conditions and entrusted, for his greater good, to the public care, should yet experience even worse neglect and cruelty leading directly to his death, caused such concern that the government set

up a public and independent legal enquiry[10] into the circumstances leading
to the boarding out in this particular foster home and to the supervision
given there to the children's welfare.

The enquiry immediately threw into startling relief the lack of trained
and skilled social workers and the confusion and defects of the administrative machinery provided for the care of children removed from their
own homes and committed to the care of local authority.

This in turn led to an interdepartmental committee of enquiry to
enquire into the existing methods of providing for children who
from loss of parents or from any cause whatever are deprived of a
normal home life with their own parents or relatives; and to consider
what further measures should be taken to ensure that these children
are brought up under conditions best calculated to compensate them
for the lack of parental care.

This enquiry by the Curtis Committee[11], together with a similar
committee in Scotland were the first committees in Britain to
produce reports of an enquiry undertaken into the care of several
different groups of deprived children. They found a wide variety of
standards, particularly in residential and foster homes. Many homes
displayed a lack of personal interest in and affection for the
children. The children in these homes were not recognized as
individuals with their own needs, rights and possessions. They were
merely one of a large group.

The Curtis Report recommended that there should be a central
responsibility for deprived children vested in a single government
department. This eventually led to the setting up of Children's
Departments and to each area having a Children's Officer under the
Children's Act of 1948. It was also at this time that the National
Assistance Act came into being in the United Kingdom which ended
the old Poor Law and created the Welfare State.

During the next ten years much attention was paid to looking at
ways of preventing emotionally deprived children coming into care.
In 1952 the Children and Young Persons Amended Act made the
local authorities in Britain responsible for making enquiries into the
position of any child or young person about whom they might
receive information suggesting that the child was in need of care or
protection. The emphasis was very much on preventing the break-
up of family life and on the provision of professional social work
services. It was at this time that the emphasis was shifted from
protection to prevention with much research being carried out into
neglect and families with recurrent problems.

Britain had gone through a period of social change and it was at
that time that particularly skilled services were developed with
increased concentration on the actual needs of the family and the

children within it. It was not until some years later that the Seabohm Report recommended that there should be an amalgamation of all social services under one department and that the Children's Departments gave way to Social Service Departments which were expected to provide for all the welfare needs of the family.

During these years important developments were also taking place internationally. In 1923 the Save the Children International Union had promulgated the first Declaration of the Rights of the Child, also called the "Declaration of Geneva". In the aftermath of the Second World War the United Nations Organization adopted the Declaration of Geneva with a few modifications. In 1959 the United Nations General Assembly adopted the new ten point Declaration of the Rights of the Child which included the following point:

The child shall enjoy special protection and shall be given opportunities and facilities, by law and by other means, to enable him to develop physically, mentally, morally, spiritually and socially in a healthy and normal manner in conditions of freedom and dignity. In the enactment of laws for this purpose, the best interest of the child shall be the paramount consideration.[12]

By the 1960's many countries had laws and provision for deprived children. There were, however, still those who despite the United Nations' Charter did not implement the kind of services which brought real relief to abused and ill-treated children. For some countries, this remains the case in the 1980's.

It was during the 1950's that social workers and other professionals formulated the approach towards abused children and their families, and ways of helping to improve the lives of the families and children involved, which is the basis of many of the methods used when working in this area today. It deserves consideration that the following findings and suggestions were first made thirty years ago by the Association of Children's Officers[13] and in a study *The Neglected Child and His Family*.[14]

Both studies recognized the need for early diagnosis followed by a specialist service treating the family as a unit. The need for adequate assessment, treatment and advice that was readily available from experts was also recognized. The necessity of co-ordination and co-operation between the social work agencies involved was stressed as was the importance of helping the family within the setting of their own home. There are several references to the benefits of providing treatment for the whole family and the many factors involved in the decision to remove a child from his home, not least the expense of providing residential care for a child.

The factors resulting in child abuse and neglect were recognized as not being reliant on material surroundings alone. The personality of the mother and her capabilities were considered to be of far greater relevance than those of the father. The parents were found to be apathetic, to lack confidence and to be hostile towards the social worker.

It was recognized that there was a need for intensive family care work services to help these families overcome the whole range of their difficulties. Social workers were recommended to use intensive visiting, reassurance rather than criticism, friendliness and willingness to give practical help in order to be accepted by the family. It was recognized that these measures would be concerned with the children's material and physical well-being and also with their mental and spiritual development; the general approach being through the family and the understanding of their needs. There was concern expressed that there was little public awareness of emotional suffering. Despite this report of 30 years ago, it was only in 1980 that emotional abuse was included in the criteria for entry onto a child abuse register in Britain.

Research into non-accidental injury was initially influenced by the discipline of paediatric radiology. In 1946 Caffey first made observations regarding the common association of subdural haematoma and abnormal X-ray changes in the long bones.[15] In 1955 Woolley postulated that the trauma noted on the X-rays was in many cases wilfully inflicted.[16]

Since that time research has concentrated very much on the physical, non-accidental injury of children, primarily brought into focus by the work of Kempe, Steele and Helfer from the University of Colorado Medical Centre in the United States. It was Henry Kempe who in 1962 coined the phrase "the battered child syndrome" which he defined as being a child who had received serious physical injury, generally at the hands of his parents or guardians.[17] Kempe stressed the importance of reaching out into the homes in which child abuse occurs. This lesson had already been implemented by the NSPCC whom through years of experience, knew that problems frequently arose when "normal offices were closed", and that it was vital to provide a 24 hour on-call service for these families.

Prior to 1964 there were no effectual child abuse reporting laws in any country.[18] At a conference in 1962 held in the United States, and chaired by Professor C H Kempe, the model child abuse law that was to be adopted by every American state within five years was engendered.

In October 1968, having followed with great interest the work of Kempe and his team in the United States, the NSPCC in Britain decided to establish its own Battered Child Research Department, which in 1974, became the NSPCC National Advisory Centre on the Battered Child.

The studies carried out there were primarily social work orientated and community based. A consultant psychiatrist and psychologist were available to the team for consultation and assessment purposes. As part of its clinical treatment programme a 24-hour on-call service was provided to hospitals and communities of four London Boroughs. Facilities provided included a therapeutic day nursery, play therapy for the children and group therapy for the parents. The knowledge accumulated from the work carried out by the Centre resulted in the publication of several important research reports [19,20,21,22] and the findings concerning the pathology of the parents and children involved were supported in subsequent research studies in other countries.

It is worth recording the results of these studies because they have not been superseded and form the basis of our knowledge about the parents and children involved in child abuse as we enter the eighties. The greatest number of children coming to attention at the Centre were in the five months or younger category. It was apparent that the younger the child the more serious the injury was likely to be with trauma to the soft tissue of the face and mouth appearing in almost half of all the cases notified. It became clear that bruises and injuries of a seemingly minor nature could signify the beginnings of increasingly violent forms of injury. It was also realized that a high incidence of trauma to the face might, like bruising, be an aid to early diagnosis of a nurturing problem that, if modified, might avert serious injury to the child.

The research showed that in families where a first born child had been injured there was a 13:1 chance that a subsequent child would also be injured when adequate help was not ongoing. The ability to identify high risk families is of particular importance to all those who have the task of assessing the risks involved in supervised home care for the non-accidentally injured child as opposed to possibly removing the child from home.

American and British studies have both found similarities between the parents who are abusive towards their children. The largest study of child abuse carried out in Britain, encompassing 13 per cent of the child population of England and Wales, identified four major factors.[23] These were poor self-image, marital problems, unemployment and financial difficulties. Many abusive parents were themselves abused children and their childhood experiences frequently leave them with feelings of inadequacy, frustration and resentment. The study "At Risk" reported that parents who injured their children were relatively less able in their command of verbal concepts than in their practical abilities suggesting a rather concrete style of thinking consistent with relative difficulty in seeing the consequence of actions and controlling the impulse to act.[19] Although masked by hostility many of the parents showed signs of depression and anxiety. Personality problems of long-standing were found to be more common among abusive parents than the general population. However, the majority were neither mentally sub-normal nor frankly psychotic.

The model established by the Battered Child Research Department led to a project proposal being put forward by the Head of Department recommending the setting up of Units providing specialized services. This resulted in the NSPCC establishing a further ten Special Units. The 1976 Government Select Committee on Violence in the Family reported that "The NSPCC's method of giving support to the parents does seem to be successful in greatly reducing the danger of physical harm and re-injury". It should be noted that in those areas where the Special Units have operated the re-injury rate has dropped from 60 per cent to 14 per cent.

Although reporting laws were established in the United States during the 1960's, and despite the fact that British studies had shown that it was not uncommon for a child to be seen at several different hospitals with a variety of unaccountable injuries, but not to be monitored by any central body, there was considerable opposition to the establishment in Britain of laws similar to the American ones. However, there followed several public enquiries in the United Kingdom into cases where children at risk and known to the statutory agencies did, nevertheless, eventually die at the hands of their parents or guardians. The first of these enquiries concerned the case of Maria Colwell. It was shortly after this that Regional Registers of Child Abuse were established with the aim of ensuring that "at risk" children were regularly monitored and were assured of receiving priority services.

There was also the establishment in Britain of Area Review Committees which were responsible for the setting up and review of local procedure which were to be followed in the event of the notification of a child abuse case.

What was tragically clear was that despite the provision of statutory welfare services they often did not reach the families who were in need at an early enough stage, if at all. Consequently social work services were often not involved until after a child had been injured. One of the reasons for this appeared to be the reluctance of parents to seek help from professionals and this resulted in the setting up and rapid growth of parents' self help groups and anonymous telephone help lines. These enabled parents who felt that they might be getting into difficulties with coping with their children to speak in confidence and without shame to other parents who had experienced similar problems.

It has been increasingly recognized that child abuse is a phenomenon that knows no national or cultural barriers and that accordingly much can be gained by sharing experiences internationally. A group of concerned professionals from all over the world who had been in contact over a number of years realized this and, led by Henry Kempe, they met to discuss the international situation.

Following this the First International Congress on Child Abuse took place in Geneva during September 1976, bringing together professionals and lay people from many different countries. Thus the foundations were laid for the formation of the International Society for the Prevention of Child Abuse and Neglect which was to provide a forum for the exchange of information and ideas between countries through the International Journal on Child Abuse and Neglect. Since the first congress membership has grown rapidly and congress delegates include workers from developing countries.

In July 1979 the international movement "Defence for Children" was founded with the aim of acting as a focal point and stimulus for local and international efforts designed to protect and defend children exposed to acts of cruelty, neglect and exploitation.

So far we have identified some of the major developments that have occurred in the child abuse field during the twentieth century. In most developed countries there is an awareness by professionals of both the problem of child abuse and identification of some of the causes. As a result of this awareness there has been the formation of a variety of treatment programmes for children and their parents, the establishment of training programmes for workers and the growth of self-help groups within the community. In many countries child abuse is no longer shrouded in shame and denial. It is discussed both by International Congresses and by lay groups; it is written about in medical journals and the popular press. But the abuse of children continues. We do not even have evidence to show that, despite increased knowledge, child abuse is on the decline. This fact must pose the question: how successful have we really been, and what can be done to achieve success?

The remainder of this chapter makes suggestions about certain developments which, if implemented, might bring earlier and more effective relief to those children and parents who are under stress, remembering always that the aim has to be to prevent the occurrence of abuse, rather than attempting to restore stability after the event.

It is hoped that the international exchange of information and ideas which is already well established will continue to expand and strengthen and that through this network all countries will be able to benefit from shared knowledge and international co-operation. As the international organizations develop it is to be hoped that the children from countries that do not or will not acknowledge child abuse problems will begin to benefit from pressures exerted on their behalf. Everything possible must be done to encourage workers who are not being supported by their governments in their endeavours to establish services for abused children.

The role of the government is of equal importance in countries which already have established services. If effective provision is to be made for these families it is essential that governments recognize their needs and afford them appropriate political priority. One way of ensuring that a nation's children are adequately represented might be through the appointment of a children's minister or ombudsman. However successfully services are provided at local level, it is nationally that decisions concerning legislation and resource allocation are usually made.

It is particularly important that it is recognized that the majority of the children who are abused become the victims of abuse while they are very young. Accordingly many of these children have, by the time they reach school age, been emotionally damaged and are potentially the next generation of abusive parents. Consequently it is clearly essential that suitable provisions are made for children under five. A 1980 report by the Children's Committee in the United Kingdom concluded that young children do not have any high political priority and that their needs tend to be regarded as optional extras in the main programme.[24] The inadequacy of services for young children is bound to affect the kind of education and social provision which is made for them as they grow older and the use they ae able to make of the educational services available. The provision of day care is extremely important, particularly for abusive or potentially abusive families as the low points of tolerance of the parents involved may be greatly relieved by a period of separation during the day, ensuring a "breathing space" for both the parents and children. What should be remembered is that if the prime responsibility of the parents is to be maintained it is essential that the various forms of day care should welcome the parents' participation.

In recent years the community has become increasingly involved in providing support for parents. However there is still tremendous potential for the development of this invaluable resource and any such development may well result in a network of volunteers providing a key success in early intervention and prevention.

We know that parents are often reluctant to seek professional advice for their problems, partly because of their fear of the possible repercussions of involving "the authorities" and often because they find it easier to share their anxieties with other parents, who might have been in a similar situation. To have a source from which anonymous, uncritical help on child care problems can be obtained often leads to parents asking for assistance at an early stage when real improvement might be possible in the home situation. The variety of self-help advisory schemes already in operation have a number of characteristics in common. They seek to keep open the telephone line for 24 hours a day, the caller is assured of a sympathetic and non-judgemental response and is at liberty to remain anonymous. The volunteer will try to get the agreement of the caller to be put into contact with professional services where this is appropriate.

It is extremely important that professional workers are aware of the benefits that might be derived from these groups. There is a need for close liaison between volunteers and professionals. Professionals can do much to ensure adequate training and preparation for the volunteers who are likely to be the vital link between parents and professionals.

There is a tremendous need for workers to come out of their clinics and offices and to go into the homes of families, partly to gain a real understanding of the family situation and, most importantly, because it is in this setting that the advice and help they have to offer is likely to be most acceptable to the parents. We know that the pathology of the parents involved makes them wary of those they see in authority and reluctant to come forward to seek help. It must be taken to them in their homes.

Because of the time factor involved in travelling between clients' homes and the length of time for which families need support there may be many benefits in the professionals' visits being supplemented by visits from a volunteer. Either, volunteers may be used to carry out specific duties as a drop-in foster mother or mothering aid, or might befriend a family or parent thereby offering friendly support. The careful selection, training and supervision of all volunteers is of vital importance and active involvement in these areas by professionals is likely to prove a valuable investment.

Whoever it is that is working with a family the common aim is to encourage and develop the self confidence of the parents to the point where they are able to cope with their own problems and respond more appropriately to the needs of their children. Many parents no longer have the support given by an extended family. Such a loss could largely be substituted for by a caring and reponsive community aware of the problems that these families have and able and willing to provide friendship and encouragement to lonely and anxious parents.

One important method of taking knowledge about the problems that families experience into people's homes is by the further development of the use of the media. Items on television and radio and articles in the national press and in magazines can do much to further reduce the shame that a parent might feel at their inability to cope with their children. Phone-in radio programmes can provide a direct "life-line" for isolated parents offering help over the radio and giving information on whom to contact for ongoing assistance. Very often it is the parents who need help most that have the least knowledge about what help is available and how to go about getting it. Professional workers contributing to the media can do much to put into perspective reports of children dying from terrible injuries inflicted by their parents and provide a balance between this and the positive improvement that can be achieved with many families after a period of support and treatment.

The most vital area of all for future focus is the need to provide effective treatment for the emotional and psychological problems that are often suffered both by physically abused children and by those children who, although possibly unharmed physically, are the subjects of an emotional battering which, untreated, may adversely affect the rest of their lives. In past endeavours to treat the family it seems that quite often the particular treatment needs of the child have been responded to inadequately, or even completely missed.

During the work carried out at the National Advisory Centre in London it became apparent that although the techniques used there had dramatically reduced the rates of physical injury and re-injury, personality tests carried out on the children, after a period of casework for families and nursery care for the children, revealed a long-term distortion in the child's relationship with the mother that was less amenable to change.[19]

In recommending future provision it was realized that whether the child had to be removed from home or remains with the family, it is likely that specific and intensive therapeutic intervention will be required if there is to be any chance of ending this distortion. The goal of the worker must not only be to prevent the abuse from re-occurring in the immediate situation, but also to prevent the continuation in this and the next generation of the whole abusive style of parenting.

Abused children have problems in their own right. They may be unable to relate to their peers, have difficulty learning in school and may exhibit anti-social behaviour out of school.[25] This presents the problem of not only educating parents to function as the parents of well-adjusted children, but at the parents of children who may be severely emotionally disturbed. This task may be seemingly impossible as the pathology of the parents often results in their being deprived, depressed and egocentric with no emotional space for the child. Without doubt there are some children who are so disturbed that without intervention it can be confidently predicted that they will suffer from major psychiatric illnesses as they grow up. It is therefore apparent that if we are to prevent parents from abusing their children, it is in childhood that these adults first need support and treatment, and we should now be developing our ability to provide individually tailored treatment programmes for the child victims of abuse.

A particular need is for play therapists to grain others in the community in order to ensure better communication with children and to teach them the importance of play with children. Experience suggests that social workers are frequently unable to communicate with children or to interpret their actions.

Ideally treatment for abused children should begin before they reach school age, but provision for the older abused child is no less important. If a child has been the subject of abuse for a number of years, and this situation continues unabated, then, by the time intervention begins these children are likely to be very disturbed as the result of their past experiences. Delinquency, lack of self confidence and respect, distorted relationships and aggressive behaviour are some of the manifestations that may be the result of prolonged abusive treatment. These children require particular support and counselling. Schools in particular should be alert to the problem. It is vital that these children are encouraged to communicate their feelings freely and without embarrassment with the worker. In addition, a suitably chosen volunteer might be invaluable in the role of befriender.

Undoubtedly one of the main areas of concern over recent years has been the sexual abuse of children. There has been some research carried out into this form of abuse in the United States but internationally there is only recent acknowledgement of what is possibly one of the most complex problems in the field of child abuse. There are undoubtedly many gaps in our understanding about what Kempe has described as "the last taboo" and there is a need for further research and the development of treatment programmes for the perpetrators and, even more importantly, for the children.

It is well-known that one of the difficulties of combating the level of child abuse in society is its self perpetuating nature. Abusive parents model the upbringing of their children on the only one they know — their own. We know that appropriate parenting is not instinctive. There is therefore a strong case for preparation for parenthood classes being included as part of the school curriculum, giving pupils the opportunity of fully discussing the implications of being responsible for a child and the inherent difficulties of bringing up a family, as well as the fulfilment that parenthood can bring.

Whatever is done to provide help for abusive parents and their children, there will always be cases where therapy for the parents is either unrealistic or, if helpful for them, is insufficient to protect their children from further abuse. Children at times are left in the care of their parents despite clear indications that they should be removed to a safer environment. It must be recognized that there are some situations where it is vital that the child is speedily removed from the source of danger. Ongoing treatment plans need assessment and re-assessment, with careful monitoring of the child's progress. The authors also feel that in cases where serious child abuse has occurred there should be an obligation on the whole family to be psychiatrically and psychologically assessed as part of the overall consideration.

A clearer focus on the childs' specific treatment needs, will, we hope, help that child break out of the pattern of parenting that has led to his own abused childhood.

Much as been learned, and whilst we can never hope to eradicate completely the suffering that may be inflicted on children by their parents or guardians, the numbers of children seriously injured and re-injured are dropping as the result of improvements in provision and flexibility of approach.

We believe the position can be further improved by the increased co-operation between professionals and volunteers within the community, thus ensuring a much wider and comprehensive network of preventative, supportive and treatment options.

## Notes

1   A Morton, "Early Days" *Occasional Papers* XXIII (NSPCC, London, updated)

2   Y J Fontana, "The Maltreated Child" in *The Maltreatment Syndrome in Children* (Charles C Thomas, Springfield, Illinois, 1964)

3   A Allen and A Morton, *This is Your Child* (Routledge and Kegan Paul, London, 1961)

4   H Stretton, Letter to *The Times* Newspaper 26 May 1884

5   B Waugh, *The Child's Guardian* Vols 1 and 2 NSPCC London (1887-1892)

6   B Waugh, *The Child's Guardian* Vol 1 No 2 NSPCC London (1887) p 9

7   B Waugh, *The Child's Guardian* Vol 1 "The Flogging of Adult Criminals" (NSPCC London, 1887) p 96

8   J Bowlby, *Maternal Care and Maternal Health* (World Health Organization, Geneva, 1951)

9   J Heywood *Children in Care* (Routledge and Kegan Paul, London, 1979)

10  W Monkton, HMSO CMD 6636 (London, May 1945)

11  Warrant of Appointment of the Care of Children Committee (Curtis Committee) HMSO CMD 6922 (London, September 1946)

12  *Declaration of the Rights of the Child* (United Nations General Assembly Resolution 1386 (XIV), 1959)

13  Association of Children's Officers, *Cruelty to Children* (London, March 1953)

14  The Women's Group on Public Welfare and the National Council of Social Services, *The Neglected Child and his Family* (Oxford University Press, London, 1946)

15  H Kempe and R Helfer, *The Battered Child* (The University of Chicago Press, Chicago, 1968)

16  P V Woolley and W A Evans, "Significance of Skeletal Lesions in Infants Resembling those of Traumatic Origin" (1955) *JAMA* **158**:539

17  C H Kempe, F N Silverman, B F Steele, W Droegemueller and H K Silver, "The Battered Child Syndrome" (1962) *JAMA* **181**:17

18  H Kempe and R E Helfer, *The Battered Child,* 3rd ed (University of Chicago Press, Chicago, 1980)

19  NSPCC Battered Child Research Department, *At Risk* (Routledge and Kegan Paul, London, 1976)

20  R Castle and A Kerr, *A Study of Suspected Child Abuse* (NSPCC, London, 1972)

21  A E Skinner and R L Castle, *Seventy-Eight Battered Children: A Retrospective Study* (NSPCC, London, 1969)

22  R L Castle, *Case Conferences: A Cause for Concern?* (NSPCC, London, 1976)

23  S J Creighton, *"Child Victims of Physical Abuse, 1976"* The Third Report on the findings of NSPCC Special Units Registrar. (NSPCC, London, 1980)

24  Children's Committee, Mary Ward House, *The Needs of the Under Fives in the Family* (UK, December 1980)

25  J Trowell and R Castle, *Treating Abused Children* (Presented at International Congress, Amsterdam, 1981)

# Glossary

AFFECT ... The feeling experienced in connection with an emotion.

AETIOLOGY ... The cause of a disease.

APNOEA ... The cessation of breathing.

BRADYCARDIA ... A slow heart rate.

COGNITIVE ... The mental process of awareness, including all aspects of perceiving, thinking and remembering.

CONGENITAL ... Present and existing from the time of birth.

CYTOMEGALOVIRUS ... A virus which can affect the unborn child and may result in the child being mentally retarded.

DOUBLE-BLIND ... A study of the effects of a particular treatment in which neither the person giving the treatment, nor the person receiving it, knows whether the form of treatment being studied, or another form of treatment is being given.

EGO ... The conscious sense of the self.

EPIDURAL ANAESTHESIA ... An anaesthetic injection given into the spinal canal which produces anaesthesia in the body below the level of the injection.

GESTATION ... The period of time of development of an infant from fertilization to birth.

HYPERPHENYLALANINAEMIA ... An excessive amount of phenylalanine in the blood. Excessive levels of phenylalanine in the blood of a pregnant woman will damage the brain of the foetus, causing mental retardation.

INTRA-UTERINE AND IN UTERO ... Within the uterus.

LESION ... An injury.

MECONIUM ASPIRATION ... The inhalation by the baby during birth of some of the intra-uterine fluid mixed with material which has been passed from the intestine of the foetus (meconium). When this mixture is inhaled it is likely to cause respiratory difficulty in the baby.

MICROCEPHALY ... An abnormally small brain and head.

MORBIDITY ... A condition of being unhealthy or diseased.

MULTIPAROUS ... Having had two or more complete pregnancies.

NEONATAL ... The period of the baby's first 28 days after birth.

OESTROGEN ... The major female sex hormone.

ORIFICE ... The entrance or outlet of any body cavity.

OXYTOCIN ... A hormone which stimulates contraction of the uterus and ejection of milk.

PERINATAL ... The time from the onset of labour to the end of the first week of life.

PETHIDINE ... A drug which relieves pain and in larger doses induces a state of stupor.

PHENYLKETONURIA ... An inherited, metabolic disorder causing mental retardation if not detected and treated within the first few months of life.

POLYPHAGIA ... Excessive eating.

POSTNATAL ... Occurring after birth, referring to the child.

POSTPARTUM ... Occurring after childbirth, referring to the mother.

PREMORBID ... Occurring before the development of disease or injury.

PRIMIPAROUS ... Having had one pregnancy resulting in a live-born child.

PRIMIGRAVIDOUS ... Pregnant for the first time.

PUERPERIUM ... The period after childbirth.

RAD ... A unit of measurement of the dose of radiation which is absorbed.

RETINOPATHY ... Disease of the innermost layer of the eyeball.

TERATOGEN ... Something which causes physical defects in the developing embryo.

TOXOPLASMOSIS ... An infection which may infect the foetus and may result in damage to the brain.

TRIMESTER ... A period of three months. The course of a pregnancy is often described as consisting of three trimesters, each of three months.

SKELETAL SURVEY ... An X-ray of the entire skeleton to look for evidence of injury to bones.

# Index

## DATE DUE

| MAY 2 0 1999 | | | |
|---|---|---|---|
| DEC 0 7 1999 | | | |
| 12/4/01 | | | |
| NO 08 06 | | | |
| | | | |
| | | | |
| | | | |
| | | | |
| | | | |
| | | | |
| | | | |
| | | | |
| | | | |
| | | | |
| | | | |
| | | | |
| | | | |
| | | | |
| GAYLORD | | | PRINTED IN U.S.A |